our
chemical
environment

our chemical environment

edited by

J. Calvin Giddings
Manus B. Monroe
The University of Utah

Canfield Press ⏀ San Francisco

a department of harper & row, publishers, inc.
new york • evanston • london

This book is printed on recycled paper.

OUR CHEMICAL ENVIRONMENT

International Standard Book Number: 0-06-382791-3

Library of Congress Catalog Card Number: 70-186645

72 73 74 10 9 8 7 6 5 4 3 2 1

To mother Earth and the Earth children:
Steve and Gary and Mike and another Mike

contents

preface

Chemical substances surround us. They are the fundamental ingredients of earth, air, and the oceans. Oxygen and water, both essential to life, are chemical substances. So, too, are the pollutants and pesticides of modern civilization. All that we eat, breathe, and drink is chemical, and, in fact, we ourselves are composed of chemicals, both simple and intricate.

Since our environment is chemical, it acts and reacts according to chemical principles. To have a basic understanding of our environment, therefore, we must understand these principles. There are a number of excellent courses that teach chemical principles, but frequently they do not forge a bridge between chemistry and the environment, and the student is left feeling that these are two unconnected aspects of his existence.

The purpose of this collection of articles is to build these bridges between chemistry and the environment. We do this by emphasizing chemical topics and the chemical substances that make these topics relevant. We learn about the substances that pollute our water, contaminate our air, and that are added to our foods. More specifically, we establish the environmental impact of chemical substances such as sulfur dioxide, carbon monoxide, DDT, mercury, lead, phosphorus, and other compounds and elements about which there is presently much talk but little public understanding. All along we keep in view the basic chemical nature of these substances, their place in the periodic table, and their underlying atomic and molecular heritage.

The chemical environment of man has changed a great deal in this century. Throughout this book we are concerned with the nature, magnitude, and repercussions of this change. We have focused specifically on the polluting chemical substances that now make our world less productive and less beautiful. We have sought to present answers and options where serious problems appear to exist.

We have also made a point of examining the sources of environmental change—among them, population growth, which, though it may not seem very chemical, is in fact very much so in its relationship to resources, fuels, food, pollution, and recycling.

The book is organized into ten sections, though this does not mean, of course, that the earth's chemical environment is found in ten separate compartments. In fact, the interrelationships are overwhelming: air, water, metals, foods, pesticides, energy, man's future, population, solid wastes, nuclear power—all are linked together in an environmental web of awesome intricacy.

We have tried to offer a wide diversity of articles to suit a wide range of purposes. Lengths vary from two-page summaries to long and detailed expositions of selected environmental subjects. The broad scope of each section is usually stated in the first one or two articles of the section, and then specific subjects and environmental concerns are examined in depth. None of the articles is technically difficult. Some require some first-year chemistry background; others require none at all.

Spaceship earth is the only home we will ever have, a home worth being concerned and educated about. The issues involved here transcend political differences, racial barriers, and cultural gaps, for without such a home and its life-support systems, all mankind will perish.

j.c.g.
m.b.m.

acknowledgments

Many people have been indispensable to the fruition of this work. The authors and their publishers have been most kind in permitting us to reprint articles. Wayne Oler and Brian Williams of Canfield Press have been instrumental in the creation and execution of the book. Our talented secretary, Dorothy Martin, has kept us organized. Assistance in pointing out some appropriate selections was kindly offered by William Brown and Steven Giddings. Helpful suggestions regarding organization were made by William Epstein. This book is an outgrowth of a nonmajors course in environmental chemistry inspired in large part by our department chairman, David M. Grant.

our
chemical
environment

environment, man, and the future

This section seeks to establish a perspective for the human environment, exploring two topics of sweeping importance to everyone: man's hopeful and sometimes fearful links to the future, and man's chemical links with the environment. These topics are not unrelated, since our prospects for a decent future hinge ultimately on our recognizing the integral relationship between man and nature.

The first three articles in this section probe the prospects and problems of man's future into the 21st century. Although the three agree that our present resource base is changing and that population growth is a problem of utmost concern, there the consensus ends, no doubt because nothing is so unclear as the future. Still, this lack of clarity should not deter us from careful study of tomorrow's world—it is, after all, *our* future, a future that promises radical change and altogether too many brushes with cataclysm. If we can gain any inkling at all of tomorrow's options, our time will be well spent.

Each of these first three articles represents an important

school of thought on man's future. The first, "Scientists Forecast Changes Due by 2000," gives us a glimpse of technological-environmental changes we can expect if things go well. The second, "An End to All This," tells us that, on our present course, things will not go well, that we are courting disaster in not looking broadly enough at the population-pollution-resource problem. Though clothed in scientific trappings, this view is not too different from the warnings long issued by the Sierra Club and like-minded organizations about the folly of our present direction and its emphasis on endless growth. In the third article, John Platt admits to these problems and others, particularly nuclear escalation. But his emphasis, as the title states, is on "what we must do" in this age of rapid transformation. More than that, it is a call to action, a call deserving both attention and implementation.

Article 4, "The Actions of Poisons," is of a different nature. It reminds us that human existence is a chemical phenomenon, and that *our* chemistry is intricately entwined with the chemistry of our environment. The wrong chemical at the wrong concentration in the environment can disrupt the intricate chemical machinery of life. Author Ryan Huxtable shows us how this occurs in fascinating detail. He discusses the toxic actions of a broad range of environmental chemicals, including mercury and other heavy metals, DDT, and the widely used predator control poison, sodium fluoroacetate, or 1080 poison. His concern with the "indiscriminate pollution of our environment with poorly understood chemicals" is central both to our present environmental crisis and to the future of man. It is a concern that will crop up again and again throughout this book.

one:

scientists forecast changes due by 2000

staff of chemical & engineering news

Nuclear breeder reactors, carbohydrates, and genetic engineering may be central to 21st century technology.

Man can look forward to a very different 21st century, if he can overcome the threats of atomic war, genetic mutation, pollution, and other dangers to his continued existence. A fascinating look into that century was ventured by more than 100 eminent humanists and scientists, gathered in New York City [in 1970] for a joint conference of the American Geographical Society and the American division of the World Academy of Art and Science.

Among the forecasts presented at the conference:

• The chemical process industry may turn from petroleum to carbohydrate fermentation as a source of raw materials, suggests organic chemist Ernst D. Bergmann of the Hebrew University, Jerusalem, Israel.

• The "green revolution"—introduction of new high-yield varieties of wheat and rice—may buy time to meet the food needs of a world population grown to more than 6 billion, says Dr. Lester R. Brown, senior fellow of the Overseas Development Council.

• Therapeutic strategies based on gene correction may eradicate cancer, liver diseases, and other maladies, predicts biologist Hudson Hoaglund, Worcester Foundation for Experimental Biology, Shrewsbury, Mass.

• Nuclear breeder reactors could become the principal source of heat and electricity in the next century, proposes Dr. Francis Perrin, French High Commissioner of Atomic Energy.

energy

Dr. Perrin estimates that the earth's fossil fuels will be exhausted in another 100 to 200 years, depletion of oil causing problems in supply of energy and chemicals. He believes that the energy problem can be solved by use of breeder reactors. Present nuclear power reactor operation is based

Reprinted from *Chemical & Engineering News,* Vol. 48, May 11, 1970, pp. 68–70. Copyright 1970 by the American Chemical Society. Reprinted by permission of the copyright owner.

5

on ^{235}U, which makes up only about 1% of naturally occurring uranium. The rich ores relied on at present for uranium will be exhausted by 2000.

However, Dr. Perrin suggests that by using plutonium produced in reactors of the present first generation as nuclear fuel for fast neutron reactors, operating without moderator, more plutonium would be produced by conversion of ^{238}U than would be consumed by fission to generate energy. Even the few parts per million of uranium in granite could be recovered, providing fuel for man's needs for 10 million years.

Dr. Perrin thinks total world consumption of energy will triple by 1990, with electrical energy quadrupled in 1990, and multiplied by six to eight in 2000. He believes that breeder reactors could meet this need with no increase in cost, and avoid pollution problems.

chemicals

With oil wells running dry, the second problem to solve will be chemicals. Dr. Bergmann asserts that a former link in man's carbon cycle is broken—plants are no longer converted to fossil fuels by geological processes. He proposes to restore the chemical side of the cycle by a shunt from plant carbohydrates to basic chemicals through fermentation. By appropriate modifications, carbohydrates can produce ethanol, isopropanol, *n*-butanol, acetone, and 2,3-butanediol. These oxygen compounds can be converted to ethylene, propylene, butylenes, and butadiene—all basic intermediates in the chemical industry.

To use fermentation instead of petroleum cracking, further basic research and development is needed in fermentation chemistry and agriculture. Dr. Bergmann thinks that genetic engineering plus desalting technology for sea water will be necessary to "invent" plants that can thrive in arid environments and to water arid wastes.

In shifting the chemical industry from oil to plants, Dr. Bergmann says, "the implications of such a change of view are obvious. They may be of particular importance to the planning of the developing countries, which are located in the tropical and subtropical areas of the world and are therefore capable of producing large amounts of carbohydrates in their various forms." In his view, great powers might arise in Africa, Asia, and South America, deriving industrial muscle from harvesting of rain forests, while resources decline in North America, Europe, and the Middle East. Mining of the ocean floor may be the next century's route to inorganic raw materials, Dr. Bergamnn adds.

green revolution

With an early 21st century population between 6 and 7 billion, the world will obviously depend heavily on agriculture for food as well as for industrial raw materials. High-yield varieties of wheat and rice, recently introduced into Mexico, the Philippines, Indonesia, Pakistan, India, and Turkey, have temporarily removed some of the pressure from the population problem, says Dr. Brown. "This phenomenon, popularly referred to as the green revolution, is buying additional time in which to stabilize population growth."

Dr. Hoagland, on the other hand, emphasizes the stopgap nature of this food growing advance. "At best it can fend off the day of reckoning by only about a decade."

A supranational organization is Dr. Brown's answer to food difficulties. He has in mind not only cultivation of the tropics and desalting of sea water, but also a massive, systematic study of the earth's climatic conditions for the purpose of altering them. He envisions a kind of "International Monetary Fund" of rainfall.

Pesticide usage will also increase, especially in newly cultivated tropical lands. Fertilizer consumption will quadruple 1970 levels in the next century.

protein

A more subtle problem than sheer amount of food will arise in developing countries, Dr. Brown thinks. Diets in developed countries have high protein content, whereas those in developing countries have high starch content. As incomes rise in developing countries, he says, meat, milk, and eggs—relatively inefficient forms of crop utilization in terms of grazing cattle and feeding poultry—will be in greater demand.

Dr. Brown believes that vegetable proteins will come into increasing use—artificial bacon derived recently from soybeans, for example. However, protein derived from vegetable sources tends to be less useful nutritionally than animal proteins, says Dr. Bergmann. The amino acid content is different, and the materials tend to be less well digested. Vegetable protein hydrolyzates coupled with a liberal lacing of missing amino acids could solve this problem of nutritional utility. Dr. Bergmann points to the fermentative production of glutamic acid and lysine from carbohydrate/ammonia starting materials and says that "In general it can be foreseen that biotechnology will become a major constituent of the chemical industry."

Since chlorinated hydrocarbons will probably be in disfavor in the 21st century, new pesticides will be needed. Pheromones and sterilizing agents will very likely provide the answer, the Israeli scientist indicates. Pheromones—insect sex attractants—could be used to lure specific insect pests to a site for radiative or chemical sterilization.

health

With the eradication of infectious diseases in developed countries, most of the maladies remaining are related to defective metabolism or old age. Dr. Hoagland cites the apparent relationship of cancer to DNA imperfections, noting that incidence of cancer may be built into life processes. Gene correction may eliminate this scourge altogether, and progress is being made in the isolation of viruses that cause cancer. In a decade, he believes, there will be vaccinations against at least some human cancer viruses. Dr. E. L. Tatum, 1958 Nobel Laureate, has even proposed treatment of liver diseases by genetic modification of liver tissue cultures outside the patient's body, followed by reimplantation.

More careful aim in chemotherapy will come through better understanding of the biochemistry of disease, Dr. Bergmann adds. He cites the example of acetylcholine esterase, the enzyme that hydrolyzes the nerve transmitter substance acetylcholine. Poison-antidote experiments, with Paraoxon blocking and PAM freeing the enzyme active site, have led to an understanding of the anion-transesterification mechanism of the enzyme plus the possibility of disease control through precisely predictable enzyme control.

two:

an end to all this

richard m. koff

If the poor of all nations were to move up to the standard of living now enjoyed by a majority of Americans, we would have a pollution load on the environment ten times today's level.

With the careful disregard of their respective governments, two dozen eminent men were gathered last June [1970] in one of the great old *grande luxe* Swiss hotels. They strode familiarly down wide, carpeted halls—an Italian industrialist, a Belgian banker, two university presidents, a professor at MIT, the director of a major Swiss research institute, a Japanese nuclear physicist, a science advisor to an international economics organization, several economists whose pessimism, if quoted in the press, could cause a stock-market crash.

They moved purposefully toward a conference room. They did not drift, though side conversations delayed several members of the executive committee. Their one common characteristic was a certain firmness about the lips and jaw indicating an intention to get things done. They were activists in the most responsible meaning of the term. Each had been invited to join the group, called the Club of Rome, by its founder, Aurelio Peccei, himself a member of the management committee of Fiat, vice-president of Olivetti and managing director of Italconsult. Each served quietly, without compensation nor even paid expenses, as a full-fledged member.

They represented the best analytical minds of the world, with considerable influence to make funds available if a promising approach could be found to stop the suicidal roller coaster man now rides. Their concern during the two days in Bern was formidably titled A Project on the Predicament of Mankind. The predicament is simply stated: World population is growing by 70,000,000 people every year. This is the fastest growth in man's history, and the rate is still accelerating. We will number four billion in 1975 and, if current trends continue, we can expect to reach eight billion well before the year 2000. This population is making more and more demands on its environment. We are taking fresh water out of the ground roughly twice as fast as natural processes replace it. The demand for electric power in the U.S. is doubling every ten years, and most power comes from the heavily polluting combustion of coal. We are building 10,000,000 cars a year—twice as many as we made only 17 years ago, and cars burn gasoline, grind rubber tires to dust, wear asbestos brakes into an acrid powder.

Until 1970, these figures were considered proud evidence of progress. After all, it was reasoned, if power demands, automobile production and water consumption are increasing even faster than population, then the standard of living of each individual must be improving; and for the advanced countries, this is certainly true. Edward C. Banfield, professor of urban government at Harvard, wrote a few years ago: "The plain fact is that the overwhelming majority of city dwellers live more comfortably and more conveniently than ever before. They have more and better housing, more and better schools, more and better transportation, and so on. By any conceivable measure of material welfare, the present generation of urban Americans is, on the whole, better off than any other large group of people has ever been anywhere."

It's not surprising, then, that the industrialized nations consider progress synonymous with economic growth and that the underdeveloped nations share that article of faith. The world wants and expects more people, more and faster jet planes, more television sets, more dishwashers. If one car in the garage is good, two must be better.

But consider the price of this plenty: Death due to lung cancer and bronchitis is doubling every ten years. The U.S. incident of emphysema has doubled in the past five years. Crime in large cities has also doubled in the past five years.

Population biologist Paul Ehrlich describes an experiment in which a pair of fruit flies is put into a milk bottle with a small amount of food. In a matter of days, the population of fruit flies has multiplied to the point where the bottle is black with them. Then the limited food and their own effluvia raise the death rate, and the population drops suddenly down to zero. After 10,000 years of uninhibited propagation, mankind is beginning to sense the confines of its bottle. Man is beginning to realize that he's going to have to stop multiplying his numbers and gobbling up his world—and do it soon—because if the decision isn't made by him, it will be made *for* him by the laws of mathematics and nature.

The trouble is that man has never been very successful in controlling the destruction of community property. We have laws that keep a man from raping his neighbor's daughter, but we have few that keep him from despoiling his air. We have tried governmental action to remedy social ills before, but, as Banfield writes, "Insofar as they have any effect on the serious problems, it is, on the whole, to aggravate them."

This was the "predicament" facing the Club of Rome that June day. MIT professor Jay W. Forrester was a relatively new member of the club. He was lean, graying and spoke with the dry, didactic factuality of the trained lecturer. His theory was startling in its directness—that governmental inadequacy is an example of predictable and consistently self-defeating human behavior. His studies had suggested that the human mind is not adapted to interpreting the behavior of social systems, that human judgment and intuition were created, trained and naturally selected to look only in the immediate past for the cause of a problem. The hot stove burns the finger, not the curiosity that made one reach out to touch it.

All human solutions tend to be that simplistic. We see thousands of people in rat-infested, leaky-roofed tenements. Our traditional answer has been to tear down the tenements and put up large, low-income housing projects. The Pruitt-Igoe project in St. Louis was built to solve this problem and now 26 11-story glass-and-concrete apartment buildings are being boarded up a scant 15 years after they were built—and long before they were paid for. Vandalism, physical deterioration and an impossible job of maintaining essential services made the project a social, architectural and financial disaster. Elevators stalled, windows were broken faster than they could be replaced, residents were assaulted in the halls, apartments were broken into and doors never repaired. The poorest of the poor refused to live there and vacancies climbed even as surrounding housing became more scarce. The buildings now stand vacant as monuments to governmental waste.

Our streets and highways are bumper to bumper with cars, so our answer has been wider and longer highways. But more highways attract more traffic, until the density is the same as—if not worse than—before. No highway system has ever caught up with the traffic it carries. When a rapid-transit system is in financial trouble, fares are raised to produce more income. But this only persuades more people to use cars, which clog the roads even more and provide less net income to the transit system. And it takes longer to drive through a modern city in a 300-horsepower automobile than it did in a one-horsepower buggy 100 years ago.

Forrester had his first hint of social nearsightedness while analyzing corporate problems. "Time after time, we have gone into a corporation which is having severe and well-known difficulties—such as a falling market share, low profitability or instability of employment," he says. "We find that people perceive correctly what they are trying to accomplish. People can give rational reasons for their actions. They are usually trying in good conscience to solve the major difficulties. Policies are being followed on the presumption that they will alleviate the difficulties. In many instances, it then emerges that the known policies describe a system which actually *causes* the troubles. The known and intended practices of the organization are fully sufficient to create the difficulty, regardless of what happens outside the company. A downward spiral develops in which the presumed solution makes the difficulty worse and thereby causes redoubling of the presumed solution."

The same destructive behavior appeared when Forrester studied the solutions to urban problems. Actions taken to improve conditions in a city actually make matters worse. The construction of low-cost housing such as the Pruitt-Igoe project eventually produces more depressed areas and tenements, because it permits higher population densities and accommodates more low-income population than can find jobs. A social trap is created in which excess low-cost housing attracts low-income people to places where even their low incomes cannot be maintained. "If we were malicious and wanted to create urban slums, trap low-income people in ghetto areas and increase the number of people on welfare, we could do

11

little better than follow the present policies," says Forrester. And, further, "The belief that more money will solve urban problems has taken attention away from correcting the underlying causes and has instead allowed the problems to grow to the limit of the available money, whatever that amount might be."

Forrester's approach differs from that of ecologists, economists or demographers, because he does not narrow his attention to a single, specific cause-and-effect relationship. In his study, he was trying to make an all-encompassing, quantitative measure of the city as a social and biological system. It is a macrocosmic view that weaves the statistics of birth and death with the economics of mass production, variations in the job market with the realities of real-estate-investment returns. It is a complex, highly interrelated system of analysis that recognizes that you cannot break a city down into its component parts without distortion so extreme as to make the effort useless.

He had never tried to analyze the entire world, but his studies of the dynamics of corporations and of cities showed why programs begun in good faith worked out as badly as they often did. Why shouldn't the method be expanded to deal with the dynamics of the whole world system?

When men of action agree, obstacles disappear. A European foundation was happy to make a sizable grant to support the project. Two months later, under the direction of Professor Dennis Meadows, a team of nine researchers at MIT was being recruited to examine Forrester's theories in detail, expand the analysis and see what mankind could do to avoid the seemingly inevitable. As this article is written, almost a year into the project, it is confirming everything Forrester predicted.

Starting with cause-and-effect relationships he was sure of, Meadows went to the specialists for evaluations of exact, quantitative influences. We know that the death rate is directly affected by food availability, pollution levels and crowding. Experts can even reach consensus on how the material standard of living—meaning health services and housing, as well as the other fruits of technology—sharply reduces the death rate as it climbs above some minimum level necessary to sustain life. But further improvement in the standard of living doesn't do much to reduce the death rate, no matter how high it goes. Similarly, deaths caused by 1970 pollution levels are almost negligible when compared with the effects of the other factors. But if pollution levels climb ten or a hundred times higher than they have reached already—and pollution *will* reach such levels if current trends continue—we can anticipate a death rate high enough to make the worst plagues in history seem like mild outbreaks of flu.

Crowding also has its effect on the death rate. In the extreme case, people will kill one another for room to stand, but long before that limit is reached, the psychological effects and social stresses of crime, war and disease will do their damage. Garrett Hardin of the University of California writes of a more subtle effect of crowding. The cyclone that struck East Pakistan in November 1970 was reported to have killed 500,000 people. The newspapers said it was the cyclone that killed them. Hardin says crowding was the cause. "The Gangetic delta is barely above sea level," he says. "Every year, several thousand people are killed in quite ordinary storms. If Pakistan were not overcrowded, no sane man would bring his family to such a place.

. . . A delta belongs to the river and the sea; man obtrudes there at his peril."

Birth rate is calculated in a similar way. Food production, pollution levels, crowding and material standard of living have their separate and predictable influences on the rate of growth. The difference between births and deaths establishes net population gain; and, given the current figures for standards of living, food availability, pollution and crowding, the total population can be recalculated at annual intervals as far into the future as you like.

It isn't necessary to go into all the details of Forrester's method: The analysis includes all the effects mentioned here, plus such factors as natural-resource usage (dependent on population and capital investment) and capital investment (dependent on population, material standard of living, and discard or wear-out time of capital equipment). Forrester also calculates something he calls quality of life. This goes up when there are adequate food, medical service, housing and consumer goods, and low levels of crowding and pollution.

The amount of calculation necessary overloads the human brain. It would take 1000 men at 1000 calculators to work out the numbers year by year, following the labyrinthine relationships of the system. But it takes only a few seconds to run the projection on a computer. With the relationships agreed to up front by agricultural and industrial experts, census takers and financial and economic advisors, Forrester pushes the start button and lets the computer plot out curves that start with the year 1900 and go to 2100. The results offer some object lessons in how close man is to committing suicide.

The first thing we learn is that the enemy is our love of growth. Enormous pressures are now appearing on all sides that will act to suppress growth. Natural resources are being depleted; pollution levels, crowding and inadequate food supplies, either separately or in concert, are going to arrest and reverse population growth forcibly and disastrously. Exactly which will deliver the *coup de grâce* is unclear, but the curves show the possible alternatives. It is for man to decide which he prefers.

In this first projection [Figure 1-1], Forrester showed mankind running out of natural resources. He assumed that irreplaceable coal, oil, gas and metal ores will require more and more effort to tear out of the earth and that technology will not find quick substitutes for them. Compared with some of the others, these curves look almost tolerable. This projection shows population rising steadily until about 2020, when natural resources start falling sharply. The world is already running out of easily mined ores and fuel for power that drives mass-production machinery and raises agricultural yields. But a growing population needs more resources—at first just for the amenities of life, later for survival. The industrialized nations are growing rapidly and are placing ever-increasing demands on the resources that often come from underdeveloped countries. What will happen when the resource-supply nations start to hold back because they see the day when their own demands will require available supplies?

In this projection, the material standard of living (not graphed) will climb until about the year 2000; capital investment per person will continue to increase until then—before the depletion of natural resources has had a chance to make itself felt. Then, in about 2050, industrialization will turn

13

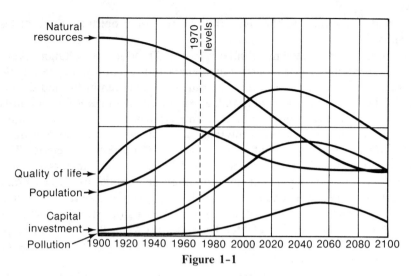

Figure 1-1

down as resource shortages become grave. Pollution will rise to approximately six times 1970 levels, but this won't be high enough to create a runaway pollution catastrophe. There will, however, be widespread dissatisfaction because the quality of life will drop slowly as pollution grows and as crowding adds its irritations.

For his second projection, Forrester assumed we wouldn't be so lucky as to run out of natural resources. Suppose science finds plastic or glass substitutes for metals, and new power sources make it possible for us to reduce demands on coal, gas and oil reserves. He went back to the computer with the natural-resources-depletion rate after 1970 reduced to 25 percent of its former value [Figure 1-2].

In this case, capital investment and population grow until pollution levels get so high that death rate, birth rate and food production are drastically and dangerously affected. Population goes to almost six billion by 2030 and then, in a scant 30 years, drops to one billion. This is a world-wide catastrophe of mind-boggling proportions. War, pestilence, starvation and infant mortality turn the world into a morgue. The highly industrialized countries probably suffer most, because they are least able to survive the disruption to the environment and to the food supply.

Some writers have suggested that before we experience a catastrophe of this magnitude, mankind will stop the pollution-generating process by legislation or even revolution; but this is not very likely. The most important generator of pollutants is industrialization, which is also the major contributor to a higher standard of living. It is difficult to imagine underdeveloped nations agreeing to a curtailment of their industrial growth. The rich nations cannot say to the poor ones, "OK, we've gone as far as we can go. Let's hold still right here." It is just as impossible to say to the poor of our own country, "We've really got to stop. Sorry, you can't have shoes for the children, an indoor toilet, a gas stove, a hearing aid for grandma." Yet, if the poor of all nations were to move up to the standard of living now enjoyed by a majority of Americans, we would have a pollution load on the environment ten times today's level.

The conclusion is inescapable. If the world is to achieve equilibrium

14

at a material standard of living at or close to the level now enjoyed by the developed nations, world population and industrialization must be considerably lower than the current averages. And that is political dynamite.

This projection demonstrates a vitally important characteristic of the world system: It is going to reach equilibrium one way or another. We are entering a turbulent time, a time when the dedication to growth in the advanced nations will have to give way. It is impossible for every citizen of the world alive today to enjoy the standard of living that has been taken for granted in the West. The goals of our civilization will have to change, and when goals change, traditions no longer serve. We can predict a period of great unrest and uncertainty, with a frighteningly greater possibility of world war, unless enough people see that the true enemy is the system, not one another.

A second discouraging characteristic of the system is that major scientific achievement in the form of reduced depletion of natural resources has the effect only of postponing the date of catastrophe. It permits greater overshoot of industrialization and population and will actually magnify the catastrophe when it finally comes.

With this firmly in mind, it is relatively easy to predict what will happen if the next solution is attempted. Suppose we agree with the underdeveloped nations that their material needs should be met, and they agree to join us in trying to curb population growth. That means we increase capital investment (to give them a better standard of living) but apply extreme moral and economic pressure to hold down the birth rate. In this projection [Figure 1-3], Forrester assumed we cut the birth rate in half in 1970 and increase capital investment by 20 per cent. For the first few years, things look good. Food per person increases, material standard of living rises and crowding is held close to present levels. But the more affluent world population ends up using natural resources too fast. Capital investment zooms and the pollution load on the environment reaches the critical level even earlier than it did in the previous run.

The reduction in birth rate temporarily slows population growth, but lower death rate, greater food production and eased crowding conditions

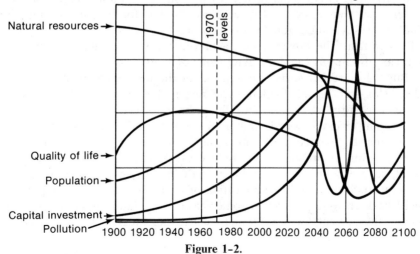

Figure 1-2.

15

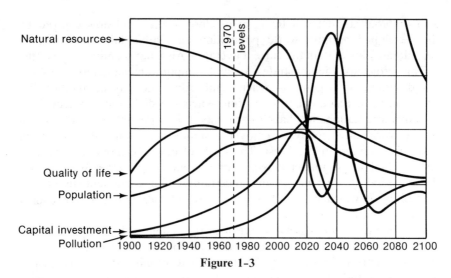

Figure 1-3

soon encourage the population to start up again, and it is now a richer and more polluting population. This shows the curious interrelationships of what systems analysts call negative feedback. By starting a promising birth-control program, we simultaneously release other natural pressures that help defeat the program. Here is the core of the nature of systems. When one pressure or combination of pressures is lightened, the result is likely to be the substitution of a new problem for the old. Often the new problem is more difficult to solve or less tolerable to live with than the old one. Advanced societies have come to expect technology to solve their problems. Technology works well when there are unlimited natural resources and geographical space to expand into; but in the real world, we reach limits. Ehrlich's milk bottle is close around us.

The projections also demonstrate the trade-off between short-term and long-term consequences of a decision. The developed nations all achieved their higher material standard of living by devoting a generation or two to building up a store of capital equipment. They used the productive capacity of labor to make machines and factories rather than food and other consumable goods. Robber barons did it for England during the Industrial Revolution and for the U.S. during the early expansion phase of its growth. The Soviet Union achieved the same result by arbitrarily denying its citizens the immediate fruits of their labor.

But there are few social mechanisms in the underdeveloped nations to defer short-run benefit for long-term return. The scarcity of such mechanisms may turn out to be a good thing, because it has the desirable effect of keeping average world capital investment under control. If we can simultaneously reduce capital investment, agree to hold the material standard of living at present levels, reduce the birth rate to half its current level, reduce pollution generation to half its current level (by a cutback in industrialization and by application of science to the problem), perhaps hold back on food production somewhat (if population is stabilized at or below the current level, we won't be needing much more food than is

16

now produced), then, for the first time, we see the possibility of reaching equilibrium without catastrophic overshoot and population decline [Figure 1-4].

On the surface, it seems anti-humanitarian to reduce capital investment and stop the effort to raise food production. Such drastic measures couldn't possibly be accepted without years of study and discussion. But the alternatives are dire and inescapable. The population explosion and pollution are direct descendants of old gods—industrialization and science. Without drastically changing its priorities, world population will collapse in less than a century from the effects of pollution, food shortage, disease and war.

Forrester emphasizes that his analyses are not intended as literal year-by-year predictions; but he does insist that man's viewpoint must become world-wide and centuries deep if the species is to survive. Dennis Meadows and nine clean-cut young researchers, meanwhile, study dull books of statistics, scribble numbers on lined pads and occasionally push a few buttons on a computer console in what surely must be the least dramatic attempt ever made to save the world.

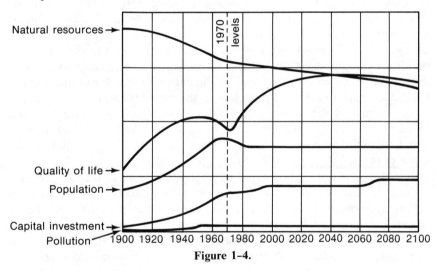

Figure 1-4.

three:

what we must do

john platt

A large-scale mobilization of scientists may be the only way to solve our crisis problems.

There is only one crisis in the world. It is the crisis of transformation. The trouble is that it is now coming upon us as a storm of crisis problems from every direction. But if we look quantitatively at the course of our changes in this century, we can see immediately why the problems are building up so rapidly at this time, and we will see that it has now become urgent for us to mobilize all our intelligence to solve these problems if we are to keep from killing ourselves in the next few years.

The essence of the matter is that the human race is on a steeply rising "S-curve" of change. We are undergoing a great historical transition to new levels of technological power all over the world. We all know about these changes, but we do not often stop to realize how large they are in orders of magnitude, or how rapid and enormous compared to all previous changes in history. In the last century, we have increased our speeds of communication by a factor of 10^7; our speeds of travel by 10^2; our speeds of data handling by 10^6; our energy resources by 10^3; our power of weapons by 10^6; our ability to control diseases by something like 10^2; and our rate of population growth to 10^3 times what it was a few thousand years ago.

Could anyone suppose that human relations around the world would not be affected to their very roots by such changes? Within the last 25 years, the Western world has moved into an age of jet planes, missiles and satellites, nuclear power and nuclear terror. We have acquired computers and automation, a service and leisure economy, superhighways, superagriculture, supermedicine, mass higher education, universal TV, oral contraceptives, environmental pollution, and urban crises. The rest of the world is also moving rapidly and may catch up with all these powers and problems within a very short time. It is hardly surprising that young people under 30, who have grown up familiar with these things from childhood, have developed very different expectations and concerns from the older generation that grew up in another world.

Reprinted from *Science,* Vol. 166, pp. 1115–1121, 28 November 1969. Copyright 1969 by the American Association for the Advancement of Science. The author is a research biophysicist and associate director of the Mental Health Research Institute at the University of Michigan, Ann Arbor, Michigan 48104.

What many people do not realize is that many of these technological changes are now approaching certain natural limits. The "S-curve" is beginning to level off. We may never have faster communications or more TV or larger weapons or a higher level of danger that we have now. This means that if we could learn how to manage these new powers and problems in the next few years without killing ourselves by our obsolete structures and behavior, we might be able to create new and more effective social structures that would last for many generations. We might be able to move into that new world of abundance and diversity and well-being for all mankind which technology has now made possible.

The trouble is that we may not survive these next few years. The human race today is like a rocket on a launching pad. We have been building up to this moment of takeoff for a long time, and if we can get safely through the takeoff period, we may fly on a new and exciting course for a long time to come. But at this moment, as the powerful new engines are fired, their thrust and roar shakes and stresses every part of the ship and may cause the whole thing to blow up before we can steer it on its way. Our problem today is to harness and direct these tremendous new forces through this dangerous transition period to the new world instead of to destruction. But unless we can do this, the rapidly increasing strains and crises of the next decade may kill us all. They will make the last 20 years look like a peaceful interlude.

the next 10 years

Several types of crisis may reach the point of explosion in the next 10 years: nuclear escalation, famine, participatory crises, racial crises, and what have been called the crises of administrative legitimacy. It is worth singling out two or three of these to see how imminent and dangerous they are, so that we can fully realize how very little time we have for preventing or controlling them.

Take the problem of nuclear war, for example. A few years ago, Leo Szilard estimated the "half-life" of the human race with respect to nuclear escalation as being between 10 and 20 years. His reasoning then is still valid now. As long as we continue to have no adequate stabilizing peace-keeping structures for the world, we continue to live under the daily threat not only of local wars but of nuclear escalation with overkill and megatonnage enough to destroy all life on earth. Every year or two there is a confrontation between nuclear powers—Korea, Laos, Berlin, Suez, Quemoy, Cuba, Vietnam, and the rest. MacArthur wanted to use nuclear weapons in Korea; and in the Cuban missile crisis, John Kennedy is said to have estimated the probability of a nuclear exchange as about 25 percent.

The danger is not so much that of the unexpected, such as a radar error or even a new nuclear dictator, as it is that our present systems will work exactly as planned!—from border testing, strategic gambles, threat and counterthreat, all the way up to that "second-strike capability" that is already aimed, armed, and triggered to wipe out hundreds of millions of people in a 3-hour duel!

What is the probability of this in the average incident? 10 percent? 5 percent? There is no average incident. But it is easy to see that five or ten more such confrontations in this game of "nuclear roulette" might indeed give us only a 50-50 chance of living until 1980 or 1990. This is a shorter life expectancy than people have ever had in the world before. All our medical increases in length of life are meaningless, as long as our nuclear lifetime is so short.

Many agricultural experts also think that within this next decade the great famines will begin, with deaths that may reach 100 million people in densely populated countries like India and China. Some contradict this, claiming that the remarkable new grains and new agricultural methods introduced in the last 3 years in Southeast Asia may now be able to keep the food supply ahead of population growth. But others think that the reeducation of farmers and consumers to use the new grains cannot proceed fast enough to make a difference.

But if famine does come, it is clear that it will be catastrophic. Besides the direct human suffering, it will further increase our international instabilities, with food riots, troops called out, governments falling, and international interventions that will change the whole political map of the world. It could make Vietnam look like a popgun.

In addition, the next decade is likely to see continued crises of legitimacy of all our overloaded administrations, from universities and unions to cities and national governments. Everywhere there is protest and refusal to accept the solutions handed down by some central elite. The student revolutions circle the globe. Suburbs protest as well as ghettoes, Right as well as Left. There are many new sources of collision and protest, but it is clear that the general problem is in large part structural rather than political. Our traditional methods of election and management no longer give administrations the skill and capacity they need to handle their complex new burdens and decisions. They become swollen, unresponsive—and repudiated. Every day now some distinguished administrator is pressured out of office by protesting constituents.

In spite of the violence of some of these confrontations, this may seem like a trivial problem compared to war or famine—until we realize the dangerous effects of these instabilities on the stability of the whole system. In a nuclear crisis or in any of our other crises today, administrators or negotiators may often work out some basis of agreement between conflicting groups or nations, only to find themselves rejected by their people on one or both sides, who are then left with no mechanism except to escalate their battles further.

the crisis of crises

What finally makes all of our crises still more dangerous is that they are now coming on top of each other. Most administrations are able to endure or even enjoy an occasional crisis, with everyone working late together and getting a new sense of importance and unity. What they are not prepared to deal with are multiple crises, a crisis of crises all at one time. This is what happened in New York City in 1968 when the Ocean Hill–Brownsville teacher and race strike was combined with a police strike,

20

on top of a garbage strike, on top of a longshoremen's strike, all within a few days of each other.

When something like this happens, the staffs get jumpy with smoke and coffee and alcohol, the mediators become exhausted, and the administrators find themselves running two crises behind. Every problem may escalate because those involved no longer have time to think straight. What would have happened in the Cuban missile crisis if the East Coast power blackout had occurred by accident that same day? Or if the "hot line" between Washington and Moscow had gone dead? There might have been hours of misinterpretation, and some fatally different decisions.

I think this multiplication of domestic and international crises today will shorten that short half-life. In the continued absence of better ways of heading off these multiple crises, our half-life may no longer be 10 or 20 years, but more like 5 to 10 years, or less. We may have even less than a 50-50 chance of living until 1980.

This statement may seem uncertain and excessively dramatic. But is there any scientist who would make a much more optimistic estimate after considering all the different sources of danger and how they are increasing? The shortness of the time is due to the exponential and multiplying character of our problems and not to what particular numbers or guesses we put in. Anyone who feels more hopeful about getting past the nightmares of the 1970's has only to look beyond them to the monsters of pollution and population rising up in the 1980's and 1990's. Whether we have 10 years or more like 20 or 30, unless we systematically find new large-scale solutions, we are in the gravest danger of destroying our society, our world, and ourselves in any of a number of different ways well before the end of this century. Many futurologists who have predicted what the world will be like in the year 2000 have neglected to tell us that.

Nevertheless the real reason for trying to make rational estimates of these deadlines is not because of their shock value but because they give us at least a rough idea of how much time we may have for finding and mounting some large-scale solutions. The time is short but, as we shall see, it is not too short to give us a chance that something can be done, if we begin immediately.

From this point, there is no place to go but up. Human predictions are always conditional. The future always depends on what we do and can be made worse or better by stupid or intelligent action. To change our earlier analogy, today we are like men coming out of a coal mine who suddenly begin to hear the rock rumbling, but who have also begun to see a little square of light at the end of the tunnel. Against this background, I am an optimist—in that I want to insist that there is a square of light and that it is worth trying to get to. I think what we must do is to start running as fast as possible toward that light, working to increase the probability of our survival through the next decade by some measurable amount.

For the light at the end of the tunnel is very bright indeed. If we can only devise new mechanisms to help us survive this round of terrible crises, we have a chance of moving into a new world of incredible potentialities for all mankind. But if we cannot get through this next decade, we may never reach it.

task forces for social research and development

What can we do? I think that nothing less than the application of the full intelligence of our society is likely to be adequate. These problems will require the humane and constructive efforts of everyone involved. But I think they will also require something very similar to the mobilization of scientists for solving crisis problems in wartime. I believe we are going to need large numbers of scientists forming something like research teams or task forces for social research and development. We need full-time interdisciplinary teams combining men of different specialties, natural scientists, social scientists, doctors, engineers, teachers, lawyers, and many other trained and inventive minds, who can put together our stores of knowledge and powerful new ideas into improved technical methods, organizational designs, or "social inventions" that have a chance of being adopted soon enough and widely enough to be effective. Even a great mobilization of scientists may not be enough. There is no guarantee that these problems can be solved, or solved in time, no matter what we do. But for problems of this scale and urgency, this kind of focusing of our brains and knowledge may be the only chance we have.

Scientists, of course, are not the only ones who can make contributions. Millions of citizens, business and labor leaders, city and government officials, and workers in existing agencies, are already doing all they can to solve these problems. No scientific innovation will be effective without extensive advice and help from all these groups.

But it is the new science and technology that have made our problems so immense and intractable. Technology did not create human conflicts and inequities, but it has made them unendurable. And where science and technology have expanded the problems in this way, it may be only more scientific understanding and better technology that can carry us past them. The cure for the pollution of the rivers by detergents is the use of nonpolluting detergents. The cure for bad management designs is better management designs.

Also, in many of these areas, there are few people outside the research community who have the basic knowledge necessary for radically new solutions. In our great biological problems, it is the new ideas from cell biology and ecology that may be crucial. In our social-organizational problems, it may be the new theories of organization and management and behavior theory and game theory that offer the only hope. Scientific research and development groups of some kind may be the only effective mechanism by which many of these new ideas can be converted into practical invention and action.

The time scale on which such task forces would have to operate is very different from what is usual in science. In the past, most scientists have tended to work on something like a 30-year time scale, hoping that their careful studies would fit into some great intellectual synthesis that might be years away. Of course when they become politically concerned, they begin to work on something more like a 3-month time scale, collecting signatures or trying to persuade the government to start or stop some program.

But 30 years is too long, and 3 months is too short, to cope with the major crises that might destroy us in the next 10 years. Our urgent problems now are more like wartime problems, where we need to work as rapidly as is consistent with large-scale effectiveness. We need to think rather in terms of a 3-year time scale—or more broadly, a 1- to 5-year time scale. In World War II, the ten thousand scientists who were mobilized for war research knew they did not have 30 years, or even 10 years, to come up with answers. But they did have time for the new research, design, and construction that brought sonar and radar and atomic energy to operational effectiveness within 1 to 4 years. Today we need the same large-scale mobilization for innovation and action and the same sense of constructive ugency.

priorities: a crisis intensity chart

In any such enterprise, it is most important to be clear about which problems are the real priority problems. To get this straight, it is valuable to try to separate the different problem areas according to some measures of their magnitude and urgency. A possible classification of this kind is shown in Tables 1-1 and 1-2. In these tables, I have tried to rank a number of present or potential problems or crises, vertically, according to an estimate of their order of intensity or "seriousness," and horizontally, by a rough estimate of their time to reach climactic importance. Table 1-1 is such a classification for the United States for the next 1 to 5 years, the next 5 to 20 years, and the next 20 to 50 years. Table 1-2 is a similar classification for world problems and crises.

The successive rows indicate something like order-of-magnitude differences in the intensity of the crises, as estimated by a rough product of the size of population that might be hurt or affected, multiplied by some estimated average effect in the disruption of their lives. Thus the first row corresponds to total or near-total annihilation; the second row, to great destruction or change affecting everybody; the third row, to a lower tension affecting a smaller part of the population or a smaller part of everyone's life, and so on.

Informed men might easily disagree about one row up or down in intensity, or one column left or right in the time scales, but these order-of-magnitude differences are already so great that it would be surprising to find much larger disagreements. Clearly, an important initial step in any serious problem study would be to refine such estimates.

In both tables, the one crisis that must be ranked at the top in total danger and imminence is, of course, the danger of large-scale or total annihilation by nuclear escalation or by radiological-chemical-biological-warfare (RCBW). This kind of crisis will continue through both the 1- to 5-year time period and the 5- to 20-year period as Crisis Number 1, unless and until we get a safer peace-keeping arrangement. But in the 20- to 50-year column, following the reasoning already given, I think we must simply put a big " × " at this level, on the grounds that the peace-keeping stabilization problem will either be solved by that time or we will probably be dead.

At the second level, the 1- to 5-year period may not be a period of great destruction (except nuclear) in either the United States or the world.

Table 1-1. Classification of Problems and Crises by Estimated Time and Intensity (United States).

GRADE	ESTIMATED CRISES INTENSITY (NUMBER AFFECTED × DEGREE OF EFFECT)		ESTIMATED TIME TO CRISIS*		
			1 TO 5 YEARS	5 TO 20 YEARS	20 TO 50 YEARS
1.		Total annihilation	Nuclear or RCBW escalation	Nuclear or RCBW escalation	× (Solved or dead)
2.	10^8	Great destruction or change (physical, biological, or political)	(Too soon)	Participatory democracy Ecological balance	Political theory and economic structure Population planning Patterns of living Education Communications Integrative philosophy
3.	10^7	Widespread almost unbearable tension	Administrative management Slums Participatory democracy Racial conflict	Pollution Poverty Law and justice	?
4.	10^6	Large-scale distress	Transportation Neighborhood ugliness Crime	Communications gap	?
5.	10^5	Tension producing responsive change	Cancer and heart Smoking and drugs Artificial organs Accidents Sonic boom Water supply Marine resources Privacy on computers	Educational inadequacy	?
6.		Other problems— important, but	Military R & D New educational	Military R & D	
7.		Exaggerated dangers and hopes	Mind control Heart transplants Definition of death	Sperm banks Freezing bodies Unemployment from automation	Eugenics
8.		Noncrisis problems being "overstudied"	Man in space Most basic science		

*If no major effort is made at anticipatory solution.

But the problems at this level are building up, and within the 5- to 20-year period, many scientists fear the destruction of our whole biological and ecological balance in the United States by mismanagement or pollution. Others fear political catastrophe within this period, as a result of participatory confrontations or backlash or even dictatorship, if our divisive social and structural problems are not solved before that time.

On a world scale in this period, famine and ecological catastrophe head the list of destructive problems. We will come back later to the items in the 20- to 50-year column.

The third level of crisis problems in the United States includes those

Table 1-2. Classification of Problems and Crises by Estimated Time and Intensity (World).

GRADE	ESTIMATED CRISES INTENSITY (NUMBER AFFECTED × DEGREE OF EFFECT)		ESTIMATED TIME TO CRISIS*		
			1 TO 5 YEARS	5 TO 20 YEARS	20 TO 50 YEARS
1.	10^{10}	Total annihilation	Nuclear or RCBW escalation	Nuclear or RCBW escalation	× (Solved or dead)
2.	10^9	Great destruction or change (physical), biological, or political)	(Too soon)	Famines Ecological balance Development failures Local wars Rich-poor gap	Economic structure and political theory Population and ecological balance Patterns of living Universal education Communications-integration Management of world Integrative philosophy
3.	10^8 tension	Widespread almost unbearable participation	Administrative management Need for Political Group and racial conflict Poverty—rising expectations Environmental degradation	Poverty Pollution Racial wars rigidity Strong dictatorships	?
4.	10^7	Large-scale distress	Transportation Diseases Loss of old cultures	Housing Education Independence of big powers Communications gap	?
5.	10^6	Tension producing responsive change	Regional organization Water supplies	?	?
6.		Other problems—important, but adequately researched	Technical development design Intelligent monetary design		
7.		Exaggerated dangers and hopes			Eugenics Melting of ice caps
8.		Noncrisis problems being "overstudied"	Man in space Most basic science		

*If no major effort is made at anticipatory solution.

that are already upon us: administrative management of communities and cities, slums, participatory democracy, and racial conflict. In the 5- to 20-year period, the problems of pollution and poverty or major failures of law and justice could escalate to this level of tension if they are not solved.

The last column is left blank because secondary events and second-order effects will interfere seriously with any attempt to make longer-range predictions at these lower levels.

The items in the lower part of the tables are not intended to be exhaustive. Some are common headline problems which are included simply to show how they might rank quantitatively in this kind of comparison. Anyone concerned with any of them will find it a useful exercise to estimate for himself their order of seriousness, in terms of the number of people they actually affect and the average distress they cause. Transportation problems and neighborhood ugliness, for example, are listed as grade 4 problems in the United States because they depress the lives of tens of millions for 1 or 2 hours every day. Violent crime may affect a corresponding number every year or two. These evils are not negligible, and they are worth the efforts of enormous numbers of people to cure them and to keep them cured—but on the other hand, they will not destroy our society.

The grade 5 crises are those where the hue and cry has been raised and where responsive changes of some kind are already under way. Cancer goes here, along with problems like auto safety and an adequate water supply. This is not to say that we have solved the problem of cancer, but rather that good people are working on it and are making as much progress as we could expect from anyone. (At this level of social intensity, it should be kept in mind that there are also positive opportunities for research, such as the automation of clinical biochemistry or the invention of new channels of personal communication, which might affect the 20-year future as greatly as the new drugs and solid state devices of 20 years ago have begun to affect the present.)

where the scientists are

Below grade 5, three less quantitative categories are listed, where the scientists begin to outnumber the problems. Grade 6 consists of problems that many people believe to be important but that are adequately researched at the present time. Military R & D belongs in this category. Our huge military establishment creates many social problems, both of national priority and international stability, but even in its own terms, war research, which engrosses hundreds of thousands of scientists and engineers, is being taken care of generously. Likewise, fusion power is being studied at the $100-million level, though even if we had it tomorrow, it would scarcely change our rates of application of nuclear energy in generating more electric power for the world.

Grade 7 contains the exaggerated problems which are being talked about or worked on out of all proportion to their true importance, such as heart transplants, which can never affect more than a few thousands of people out of the billions in the world. It is sad to note that the symposia on "social implications of science" at many national scientific meetings are often on the problems of grade 7.

In the last category, grade 8, are two subjects which I am sorry to say I must call "overstudied," at least with respect to the real crisis problems today. The Man in Space flights to the moon and back are the most beautiful technical achievements of man, but they are not urgent except for national display, and they absorb tens of thousands of our most ingenious technical brains.

And in the "overstudied" list I have begun to think we must now put most of our basic science. This is a hard conclusion, because all of science is so important in the long run and because it is still so small compared, say, to advertising or the tobacco industry. But basic scientific thinking is a scarce resource. In a national emergency, we would suddenly find that a host of our scientific problems could be postponed for several years in favor of more urgent research. Should not our total human emergency make the same claims? Long-range science is useless unless we survive to use it. Tens of thousands of our best trained minds may now be needed for something more important than "science as usual."

The arrows at level 2 in the tables are intended to indicate that problems may escalate to a higher level of crisis in the next time period if they are not solved. The arrows toward level 2 in the last columns of both tables show the escalation of all our problems upward to some general reconstruction in the 20- to 50-year time period, if we survive. Probably no human institution will continue unchanged for another 50 years, because they will all be changed by the crises if they are not changed in advance to prevent them. There will surely be widespread rearrangements in all our ways of life everywhere, from our patterns of society to our whole philosophy of man. Will they be more humane, or less? Will the world come to resemble a diverse and open humanist democracy? Or Orwell's *1984*? Or a postnuclear desert with its scientists hanged? It is our acts of commitment and leadership in the next few months and years that will decide.

mobilizing scientists

It is a unique experience for us to have peacetime problems, or technical problems which are not industrial problems, on such a scale. We do not know quite where to start, and there is no mechanism yet for generating ideas systematically or paying teams to turn them into successful solutions.

But the comparison with wartime research and development may not be inappropriate. Perhaps the antisubmarine warfare work or the atomic energy project of the 1940's provide the closest parallels to what we must do in terms of the novelty, scale, and urgency of the problems, the initiative needed, and the kind of large success that has to be achieved. In the antisubmarine campaign, Blackett assembled a few scientists and other ingenious minds in his "back room," and within a few months they had worked out the "operations analysis" that made an order-of-magnitude difference in the success of the campaign. In the atomic energy work, scientists started off with extracurricular research, formed a central committee to channel their secret communications, and then studied the possible solutions for some time before they went to the government for large-scale support for the great development laboratories and production plants.

Fortunately, work on our crisis problems today would not require secrecy. Our great problems today are all beginning to be world problems, and scientists from many countries would have important insights to contribute.

Probably the first step in crisis studies now should be the organization of intense technical discussion and education groups in every laboratory. Promising lines of interest could then lead to the setting up of part-time or full-time studies and teams and coordinating committees. Administrators and boards of directors might find active crisis research important to their own organizations in many cases. Several foundations and federal agencies already have in-house research and make outside grants in many of these crisis areas, and they would be important initial sources of support.

But the step that will probably be required in a short time is the creation of whole new centers, perhaps comparable to Los Alamos or the RAND Corporation, where interdisciplinary groups can be assembled to work full-time on solutions to these crisis problems. Many different kinds of centers will eventually be necessary, including research centers, development centers, training centers, and even production centers for new sociotechnical inventions. The problems of our time—the $100-billion food problem or the $100-billion arms control problem—are no smaller than World War II in scale and importance, and it would be absurd to think that a few academic research teams or a few agency laboratories could do the job.

social inventions

The thing that discourages many scientists—even social scientists—from thinking in these research-and-development terms is their failure to realize that there are such things as social inventions and that they can have large-scale effects in a surprisingly short time. A recent study with Karl Deutsch has examined some 40 of the great achievements in social science in this century, to see where they were made and by whom and how long they took to become effective. They include developments such as the following:

Keynesian economics
Opinion polls and statistical sampling
Input-output economics
Operations analysis
Information theory and feedback theory
Theory of games and economic behavior
Operant conditioning and programmed learning
Planned programming and budgeting (PPB)
Non–zero–sum game theory

Many of these have made remarkable differences within just a few years in our ability to handle social problems or management problems. The opinion poll became a national necessity within a single election period. The theory of games, published in 1946, had become an important component of American strategic thinking by RAND and the Defense Department by 1953, in spite of the limitation of the theory at that time to zero-sum games, with their dangerous bluffing and "brinksmanship." Today, within less than a decade, the PPB management technique is sweeping through every large organization.

This list is particularly interesting because it shows how much can be done outside official government agencies when inventive men put their brains together. Most of the achievements were the work of teams of two or more men, almost all of them located in intellectual centers such as Princeton or the two Cambridges.

The list might be extended by adding commercial social inventions with rapid and widespread effects, like credit cards. And sociotechnical inventions, like computers and automation or like oral contraceptives, which were in widespread use within 10 years after they were developed. In addition, there are political innovations like the New Deal, which made great changes in our economic life within 4 years, and the pay-as-you-go income tax, which transformed federal taxing power within 2 years.

On the international scene, the Peace Corps, the "hot line," the Test-Ban Treaty, and Antarctic Treaty, and the Nonproliferation Treaty were all implemented within 2 to 10 years after their initial proposal. These are only small contributions, a tiny patchwork part of the basic international stablization system that is needed, but they show that the time to adopt new structural designs may be surprisingly short. Our clichés about "social lag" are very misleading. Over half of the major social innovations since 1940 were adopted or had widespread social effects within less than 12 years—a time as short as, or shorter than, the average time for adoption of technological innovations.

areas for task forces

Is it possible to create more of these social inventions systematically to deal with our present crisis problems? I think it is. It may be worth listing a few specific areas where new task forces might start.

1) *Peace-keeping mechanisms and feedback stabilization.* Our various nuclear treaties are a beginning. But how about a technical group that sits down and thinks about the whole range of possible and impossible stabilization and peace-keeping mechanisms? Stabilization feedback-design might be a complex modern counterpart of the "checks and balances" used in designing the constitutional structure of the United States 200 years ago. With our new knowledge today about feedbacks, group behavior, and game theory, it ought to be possible to design more complex and even more successful structures.

Some peace-keeping mechanisms that might be hard to adopt today could still be worked out and tested and publicized, awaiting a more favorable moment. Sometimes the very existence of new possibilities can change the atmosphere. Sometimes, in a crisis, men may finally be willing to try out new ways and may find some previously prepared plan of enormous help.

2) *Biotechnology.* Humanity must feed and care for the children who are already in the world, even while we try to level off the further population explosion that makes this so difficult. Some novel proposals, such as food from coal, or genetic copying of champion animals, or still simpler contraceptive methods, could possibly have large-scale effects on human welfare within 10 to 15 years. New chemical, statistical, and management methods

29

for measuring and maintaining the ecological balance could be of very great importance.

3) *Game theory.* As we have seen, zero-sum game theory has not been too academic to be used for national strategy and policy analysis. Unfortunately, in zero-sum games, what I win, you lose, and what you win, I lose. This may be the way poker works, but it is not the way the world works. We are collectively in a non–zero-sum game in which we will all lose together in nuclear holocaust or race conflict or economic nationalism, or all win together in survival and prosperity. Some of the many variations of non–zero-sum game theory, applied to group conflict and cooperation, might show us profitable new approaches to replace our sterile and dangerous confrontation strategies.

4) *Psychological and social theories.* Many teams are needed to explore in detail and in practice how the powerful new ideas of behavior theory and the new ideas of responsive living might be used to improve family life or community and management structures. New ideas of information handling and management theory need to be turned into practical recipes for reducing the daily frustrations of small businesses, schools, hospitals, churches, and town meetings. New economic inventions are needed, such as urban development corporations. A deeper systems analysis is urgently needed to see if there is not some practical way to separate full employment from inflation. Inflation pinches the poor, increases labor-management disputes, and multiplies all our domestic conflicts and our sense of despair.

5) *Social indicators.* We need new social indicators, like the cost-of-living index, for measuring a thousand social goods and evils. Good indicators can have great "multiplier effects" in helping to maximize our welfare and minimize our ills. Engineers and physical scientists working with social scientists might come up with ingenious new methods of measuring many of these important but elusive parameters.

6) *Channels of effectiveness.* Detailed case studies of the reasons for success or failure of various social inventions could also have a large multiplier effect. Handbooks showing what channels or methods are now most effective for different small-scale and large-scale social problems would be of immense value.

The list could go on and on. In fact, each study group will have its own pet projects. Why not? Society is at least as complex as, say, an automobile with its several thousand parts. It will probably require as many research-and-development teams as the auto industry in order to explore all the inventions it needs to solve its problems. But it is clear that there are many areas of great potential crying out for brilliant minds and brilliant teams to get to work on them.

future satisfactions and present solutions

This is an enormous program. But there is nothing impossible about mounting and financing it, if we, as concerned men, go into it with commitment and leadership. Yes, there will be a need for money and power to overcome organizational difficulties and vested interests. But it is worth remembering that the only real source of power in the world is the gap between what is and what might be. Why else do men work and save and plan? If there is some future increase in human satisfaction that we can point to and realistically anticipate, men will be willing to pay something for it and invest in it in the hope of that return. In economics, they pay with money; in politics, with their votes and time and sometimes with their jail sentences and their lives.

Social change, peaceful or turbulent, is powered by "what might be." This means that for peaceful change, to get over some impossible barrier of unresponsiveness or complexity or group conflict, what is needed is an inventive man or group—a "social entrepreneur"—who can connect the pieces and show how to turn the advantage of "what might be" into some present advantage for every participating party. To get toll roads, when highways were hopeless, a legislative-corporation mechanism was invented that turned the future need into present profits for construction workers and bondholders and continuing profitability for the state and all the drivers.

This principle of broad-payoff anticipatory design has guided many successful social plans. Regular task forces using systems analysis to find payoffs over the barriers might give us such successful solutions much more often. The new world that could lie ahead, with its blocks and malfunctions removed, would be fantastically wealthy. It seems almost certain that there must be many systematic ways for intelligence to convert that large payoff into the profitable solution of our present problems.

The only possible conclusion is a call to action. Who will commit himself to this kind of search for more ingenious and fundamental solutions? Who will begin to assemble the research teams and the funds? Who will begin to create those full-time interdisciplinary centers that will be necessary for testing detailed designs and turning them into effective applications?

The task is clear. The task is huge. The time is horribly short. In the past, we have had science for intellectual pleasure, and science for the control of nature. We have had science for war. But today, the whole human experiment may hang on the question of how fast we now press the development of science for survival.

four:

the actions of poisons

ryan huxtable

What are the problems caused by indiscriminate pollution of our environment with poorly understood chemicals?

Recently, much concern has been expressed about toxic substances which are deliberately put into the environment. These substances include sodium fluoroacetate, also known as 1080 poison, used for predator control and as a rodenticide; chlorinated hydrocarbons such as aldrin, dieldrin, or DDT, used as insecticides; heavy metals placed in the biosphere for a variety of reasons, the malathion and parathion organophosphates; and a whole host of other chemicals. The public mind is much confused about the relative dangers of these substances, and indeed there is much misunderstanding about the whole concept of toxicity, as used technically. When it comes to publicly stating the case for greater restraints on the use of certain chemical agents, knowledge is strength, and he who argues from a basis of fact rather than emotionalism or overstatement will have a much more receptive audience. With this in mind, therefore, there follows a discussion of some of the concepts involved in an understanding of the nature of poisons and a description of the mode of action of some of them.

Substances are often thought of as being poisons or nonpoisons. This is entirely incorrect. Toxicity is not an intrinsic property of a substance as such, but is a manifestation of its interaction with a living system. This is the basis of selective toxicity, where a substance is poisonous to a plant, germ, insect, or animal level but not at the same dose considered undesirable to humans, stock, or crops exposed simultaneously. However, no substance fails to produce toxic symptoms when used in large enough amounts, and all substances are harmless when used in low enough amounts. "Good," "bad," and "neutral" are anthropomorphic categories which have no application to the chemicals themselves but apply only to the social situation in which they are used or to the attitude surrounding their use. Morphine is a useful ("good") substance when given by a nurse to a wounded man but the apotheosis of the devil incarnate when used on the street corner. Chemicals are by their essence amoral, and only the uses to which they are put are good or bad. This has not stopped man from ascribing the whole gamut of characteristics to chemicals, ranging from "the devil's brimstone" (sulfur) to the Aztec plant gods of teonanacatl, ololiuqui and peyotl. These were, respectively, a mushroom *(Psilocybe mexicana)*; a type of morning glory *(Ipomoea rubrocuerulea)*; and a cactus *(Lophophora williamsii)*, containing the hallucinogenic chemicals psilocybin, an ergot derivative (similar to LSD); and mescaline. Following the Spanish invasion, the Jesuit priests obligingly demonstrated the impermanence of divinity by renaming the last-mentioned plant the "devil's root" and sending to the stake those they caught worshipping it. An Arab sect used to revere hashish (or marijuana) under the influence of which they believed they went to heaven, and for whose sake they murdered unsuspecting passersby. Hence our word assassin. Do we still give marijuana divine status? The noxious and foul stench complained of by King James is still to many a smooth relaxer of the mind, opening visions of Marlboro country and lightening the burdens of life. Or at least postponing them as the skin yellows and the lungs clog. Even morphine is named for the Greek god of dreams, Morpheus. And alcohol. Every age has produced gifted poets to raise a paean to the purple grape. A few have produced Cary Nations. For the sake of western culture one can be only grateful that the Romans never discovered the art of distillation. Considering what they did with wine one can only surmise what they would have done with whiskey—a word which is a corruption of the Gaelic *uisge beatha* or "water of life."

And so it goes on. Man cannot help ascribing human and superhuman characteristics to chemicals. No age can survive without some chemical pabulum to replace mother's milk. Even we, sophisticated as we like to think we are, are possibly the most drug-conscious nation ever. Who of us gets through the day without our morning vitamin pill, lunchtime martini, afternoon aspirin, evening tranquilizer or pep pill, nighttime sleeping tablet, or contraceptive pill? That is the inside story. There is also the outside one, where we spray on our bacteriocidal antiperspirants, gargle mouthwash, and spray chemicals into every secret recess of our bodies. The answer that many of these substances are not drugs is only an indication of to what extent we accept such a way of life.

We live in a world of drugs and each day we are exposed to literally hundreds of chemical substances, many of them in trace amounts. The line by which we intuitively divide poisons from nonpoisons is a tenuous one, and any one substance may stray back and forth across the line depending on the viewpoint. The belladonna plant, for example, has been used for centuries by women to beautify themselves, as the plant, eaten in small amounts, causes enlargement of the pupils—hence the name belladonna, or beautiful lady. In excess the plant causes a horrible death, so the northern Europeans named it "deadly nightshade." The ambiguity of attitude is even expressed in the scientific name for the plant—*Atropa belladonna.* Atropos was the Greek Fate who cut the thread of life. Yet the pure extract of the plant, the drug atropine, is used widely today in medicine to aid examination of the eye. Useful pharmacological agents are often powerful poisons in a new guise. Curare is a potent toxin, but has medicinal use. Ergot is a terrible substance, responsible for the medieval epidemics of the dreaded St. Anthony's fire, but is widely used as a smooth muscle relaxant for childbirth. There are many examples of a dire poison being used in a controlled manner for beneficial purposes. The converse

33

of an apparently innocuous substance manifesting toxic action when abused is also well documented. The reason for the high incidence of heart trouble in the southern highlands is the excessive consumption of salt, in salted pork for instance—plain, common salt. Too much rhubarb is poisonous, and if you are overly fond of almonds you may suffer cyanide poisoning. Milk and cheese elicit a toxic reaction to anybody taking MAO inhibitor drugs (used for treating depression). Saddest of all, excess apples or cider are slow poisons because of their content of malonic acid. Yes, apple pie can be bad for you.

Why are so many of these substances toxic to us? The body is a complex machine, and the addition of poisons is like putting sand in the works. To cause real damage there must be interference with some important mechanism. If the radio antenna on your car is broken, it is a nuisance, but the car still runs. If sugar is put into the tank, though, it is quite a different situation. It is the same with bodies; something important has to be damaged for a poison to be really dangerous. To function, energy is needed—and the equivalent of gasoline in the tank is, of course, food. This is digested in the stomach and transported into the body where it is burnt to provide energy. A piece of food will provide the same amount of energy whether it is put on a fire and consumed quickly, producing much heat, or whether it is burnt more slowly in the body. On a fire most of the energy is released as heat and a little bit as light. In the body, some energy is given out as heat, which is why we are hotter than our surroundings, but most is coupled to fulfill the energy requirements of the body needed for new protein and cell synthesis and mechanical work, such as the heart beating. The coupling process involves taking the energy released as food is burnt and storing it by making high-energy compounds, such as adenosine triphosphate, or ATP for short. These compounds are in turn coupled to the energy utilizing systems of the body, whether for protein synthesis, mechanical work, or electrical work. If ATP is added to an extract of fireflies, for instance, a flash of light will be seen. So substances like ATP can be considered gears coupling the processes of breakdown and synthesis.

Energy is released by the breakdown of foodstuffs, such as glucose, in two steps. The first is a breakdown in the absence of oxygen, and this releases one-third of the energy. The other two-thirds if provided by breakdown in the presence of oxygen by a continuous process known as the citric acid cycle.

The products from the first step in glucose breakdown react with one of the intermediates in the cycle and are carried around the cycle in a complex set of interconversions. The net effect of this process is the completion of the breakdown of glucose to carbon dioxide and water along with the production of energy. The cycle then repeats itself, picking up another molecule from the first stage of breakdown. (See Figure 1-5.)

That is a brief account of how the body produces energy, and a large number of poisons act on this mechanism. Malonic acid, which is contained in small amounts in apples (its name derives from the Latin word for apple, *malum*) is somewhat toxic because of its similarity to succinic acid, one of the intermediates in the citric acid cycle (see drawings). It resembles it enough to climb onto the enzyme catalyzing the next step in the cycle

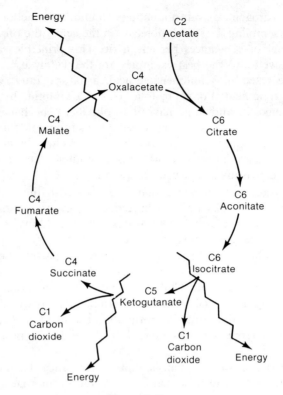

Energy

C2
Acetate

C4
Oxalacetate

C4
Malate

C6
Citrate

C4
Fumarate

C6
Aconitate

C4
Succinate

C6
Isocitrate

C5
Ketogutanate

C1
Carbon
dioxide

C1
Carbon
dioxide

Energy

Energy

Figure 1-5.

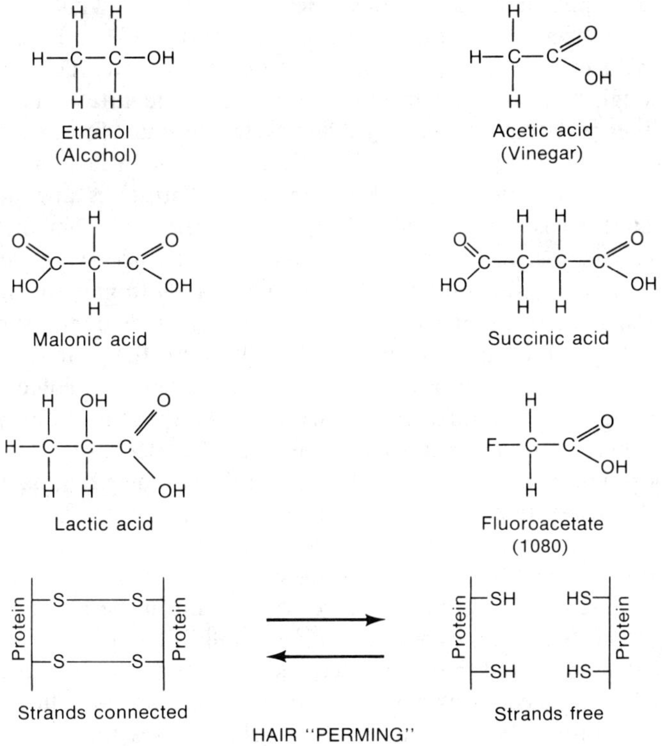

Ethanol
(Alcohol)

Acetic acid
(Vinegar)

Malonic acid

Succinic acid

Lactic acid

Fluoroacetate
(1080)

Protein — S —— S — Protein
Protein — S —— S — Protein
Strands connected

Protein — SH   HS — Protein
Protein — SH   HS — Protein
Strands free

HAIR "PERMING"

Figure 1-6.

35

(succinic dehydrogenase), but not enough to undergo reaction, so it blocks the cycle. Resembling a natural molecule in the cell is the process whereby a vast number of substances become toxic. This principle can be put to good use as well and the best examples are the widely used sulfonamide drugs. These resemble aminobenzoic acid, a natural intermediate in the synthesis of folic acid. For man, folic acid is a vitamin. In other words, we cannot make it, and must have it in our diet. The bacteria infecting us and causing illness, make their own, and the sulfonamide drugs interfere with this process and hence kill the bacteria. As we do not make folic acid, these drugs are harmless to us. This is another example showing how closely related poisons and drugs are. (See Figure 1-5.)

Cyanide is another substance that interferes with the production and use of energy. This breaks the link connecting energy production with energy use by its effect on the cytochrome oxidase enzyme. Many fruits and their seeds have cyanide-containing substances in them, among them peaches, apricots, and almonds. The smell of almonds is partly due to cyanide. Cyanide is usually described as smelling like bitter almonds, but in reality it is the other way around. Children have died from cyanide poisoning after overeating almonds, or apricot kernels. This is not to imply that one should not eat these fruits. As normally consumed they pose no danger, but if eaten in large amounts there is a definite risk, particularly with almonds.

Fluoroacetate, or 1080 poison, is another substance that interferes with the citric acid cycle. The toxic action is not due to fluoroacetate itself but to a metabolic conversion product. Given fluoroacetate, the body manufactures its own poison by a so-called "lethal synthesis." This is chemical suicide. Fluoroacetate resembles acetate sufficiently well enough to enter the citric acid cycle, where it is converted to fluorocitrate. This resembles citrate enough to fit the enzyme for the next step, aconitase enzyme, but it can neither react, nor break loose. The cycle continues for a short while, piling up citrate behind aconitase until the cycle stops for lack of materials. In bodies poisoned by 1080 a large amount of citrate is always found. One reason 1080 is such an effective poison is that an atom of fluorine is the same size as an atom of hydrogen, so when acetate is converted to fluoroacetate by substituting a fluorine for a hydrogen the molecule retains the same shape, so it can deceive enzymes which recognize substances partly by shape. But the fluorine completely alters the reactivity of the molecule, and thus disaster. For the cell, fluoroacetate is a biological Trojan horse, eluding the body's natural defenses and accepted hospitably within the cell, whereupon it discloses its true identity. Because fluoroacetate poisoning produces convulsions many people think it acts by attacking the central nervous system. This is incorrect. Convulsions are a nonspecific response to anoxia and energy deprivation. The action of 1080, as described above, explains the confusion regarding its stability. The carbon-fluorine bond is a stable one, and the substance will remain in the ground without decomposition. Being highly water soluble it will follow ground water. On ingestion, it is not stored, but converted very rapidly to fluorocitrate. When the animal dies, it contains a mixture of fluoroacetate and fluorocitrate, and it is the unmetabolized fluoroacetate which poses the greater threat to a carrion eater. So fluoroacetate is highly stable in the environment, but very reactive once ingested.

Plants also contain the citric acid cycle, and so fluoroacetate is poisonous to them. A South African range plant, gibflaar, or *Dichapetalum cymosum*, makes fluoroacetate naturally, and is lethal to grazing animals. It is an unexplained mystery as to how it protects itself against its own poison.

There are several other fluorine-containing poisons which have found use, or misuse, such as fluoroacetamide and fluorobutyric acid. These work by being first converted to fluoroacetate.

There has been increasing concern over heavy metal pollution, particularly lead, mercury, and in Japan, cadmium. There is a slight difference in the way heavy metals distribute themselves and the length of time they remain in the body, but their modes of action in expressing toxic effects are very similar, and thus an understanding of one metal leads to a general comprehension of heavy metal poisoning, including arsenic and thallium (used for predator control). Applied locally, heavy metal salts have an irritating action on mucous membrane, due to their precipitating effect on protein. This explains the ashen color of the mouth when calomel is ingested. This behavior with protein is the basis of their use as antiseptics, because of the similar effect on bacterial or spirochetal protein. Hence the putting of silver nitrate into the eyes of newborn babies. The basis for this reaction with protein is the high affinity heavy metals have for the sulfur present in protein. The major cause of heavy metal toxicity is their reaction with body sulfur.

The great attraction heavy metals have for sulfur is the reason so many of them are found in nature as sulfides and are mined as such. Iron, lead, and mercury, for example, commonly occur as sulfides. If eggs are eaten with a silver spoon, the spoon turns black because the silver has reacted with the sulfur in the egg (responsible for the smell of bad eggs) to form black silver sulfide. One reason why old paintings look so dark is that white lead sulfate, used as such or mixed with other colors, has changed through the ages to black lead sulfide. The solution in this case is for an expert to carefully treat the painting with hydrogen peroxide, to oxidize the lead sulfide back to sulfate. When milady wishes to "permanent wave" her hair she first treats it with a chemical agent to break the sulfur-sulfur bonds holding the protein strands fixed in a mutual relationship (see Figure 1-5) and after rearranging the hair to her pleasure, she then treats it with an oxidizing agent to reform the bridges and to "freeze" her hair into its new shape. As *la donna e mobile* the "perm" sometimes turns out to be not quite so permanent as the husband (who has to pay for the chemistry) would wish.

Because of the large amount of sulfur in the hair, heavy metals, particularly arsenic, are readily trapped there. Within a few days of poisoning, the arsenic level in the hair is a very good medico-legal indicator of the amount ingested—which is one very good reason why the sophisticated murderer has turned to other poisons, to the disappointment of whodunit fans. Following analysis of Napoleon's hair it was claimed he had been poisoned by arsenic. Closer investigation showed the soil in which he was buried contained high levels of arsenic which could account for the amount in the hair. If hair is suspended in arsenic solution it will absorb a large amount from the solution over the course of a day or two.

Unlike fluoroacetate, metals are slowly accumulated in the body, due to very slow excretion. Therefore a low exposure over a long time can result in highly toxic levels being built up. One of the worst manifestations of this is lead poisoning in children. This happens over a long period of time and usually goes unnoticed until irreversible damage has been done. One of the main sources of the lead is the eating of small pieces of lead-containing paints. House paints containing lead are now banned, but many houses, particularly older ones in decaying neighborhoods, still have such paint on the wall. This affliction is, therefore, a socioeconomic one, affecting poor people in particular. It is not a minor problem, but affects many thousands of children throughout the country. If death does not result, the children often face life-long hemiplegia or mental retardation. In an adult, lead poisoning, although still bad, less often causes irreversible damage if treated in time. Moonshine liquor is a prime cause of adult poisoning in the southern states, as such liquor is often prepared in old car radiators.

The recent fuss over mercury is an indication of how incompetent the bureaucratic agencies meant to protect us can be. For thousands of years mercury has been a known poison. It was the cause of the "Mad Hatter's disease" in the London hatters of the eighteenth century, immortalized by Lewis Carroll. The slaves in the Spanish mercury mines digging up the bright red cinnabar, or mercuric sulfide, had good reason to know the effects of mercury poisoning on the nervous system. In more recent times, over 40 people died in Japan between 1953 and 1960 in the Minamata Bay area from mercury poisoning after eating contaminated fish. Twenty-two children were born with severe mental retardation. A similar crisis occurred later at Niigata, Japan. The Swedes have done an extensive amount of research on mercury pollution and toxicity, following alarming discoveries of the effect of mercury pollution on wildlife in the early sixties. All this information was passed on to the U.S. government. An international conference was held in Sweden in 1966 to discuss the problem. Five official U.S. delegates attended. At that time American agriculture was using 400 tons of mercury pesticides per year, compared with Sweden's two tons. Yet following the conference, no action was taken by U.S. officials.

In December 1969, a New Mexico family was accidentally poisoned by a mercurial fungicide, "panogen," used to protect seeds from fungi. The family, including an unborn boy, developed the classical symptoms of heavy neurological mercury poisoning, including blindness, loss of muscle control, deafness, and delirium. After admittance of the first child to the hospital, it was about five weeks before a correct diagnosis of mercury poisoning was made and the proper therapy instituted.

Despite the large body of knowledge on mercury poisoning, it took a tragedy like this before the government concerned itself about restrictions on the use of mercury and its compounds. Even worse than occasional examples of acute poisoning like the New Mexico case, which involved a direct human error in that seeds labeled as poisonous had been fed to pigs from which the family obtained the poisoned pork, is the possibility of slow chronic poisoning of whole communities by contamination of foodstuffs with mercury. Tuna and other large seafish were found to be dangerously contaminated, and portions of the Great Lakes have been closed for fishing for the same reason. The origin of most of the mercury in the biosphere is industrial dumping. This is ingested in small amounts by animals and fish at the bottom of the food chain. Because of the very slow rate of excretion of mercury from the body, concentrations of it slowly rise. As the animal is eaten by those farther up the food chain, so the mercury is further concentrated. The longer an animal lives and the bigger it grows, so the higher the concentration of mercury it has. For this reason, the bigger fishes like tuna contain dangerous levels, whereas the small fishes do not.

Because of the varying sizes of animals, effects of giving poisons to different animals cannot be compared directly. One aspirin is obviously going to have a much more powerful effect on the family cat than on an adult. Doses, therefore, are usually compared on a per weight basis—in everyday units, ounces of poison per pound of body weight. The scientific units used are milligram poison per kilogram body weight, or mg/kg for short. This also happens to be the same as parts per million, or ppm. So if you read that some birds have 15 ppm DDT in their body fat, this also means 15 mg/kg DDT. A kilogram is approximately 2.2 pounds, and a milligram roughly 1/28,000th of an ounce. To give some idea of what body levels of pollutants you may read about in the newspapers mean, below is a table giving the dose of a representative number of ethical drugs:

Table 1–3

DRUG	MG/KG	
Barbiturates—Amytal (sedative)	0.3–0.7	4 x daily
Amytal (hypnotic)	1.4–2.9	1 x daily
Phenobarbital	0.2–0.4	4 x daily
Chlorpromazine (psychoactive)	0.3–1.4	1 x daily
Dilantin (anticonvulsant)	4.3	per day
Morphine (pain killer)	0.1	per day
Aspirin	2.1–8.4	per day
INH (anti T.B.)	4.0–5.0	per day
Sulfadiazine (antibacterial)	1.0	per day

It goes without saying that this table is for illustration only, and it should not be used as a guide to self-medication!

Because there is so much individual difference in response to the same dose of a substance, toxicities are expressed in terms of the dose needed to kill half of a tested population of, say, rabbits or mice. This is called, in short, the L.D.$_{50}$ (L.D. meaning lethal dose). Because toxicity depends on the route of administration, this also must be stated. For example, lindane is a widely used insecticide (unfortunately) and its toxicity to the housefly is expressed as: L.D.$_{50}$ 2 mg/kg (spray). In other words, if lindane is sprayed onto flies at a concentration of 2 mg per kg of flies, half of the flies will die.

So just how toxic are some of the substances put deliberately or accidentally into the biosphere? A list is given in the table below. [Table 1-4]. Bear in mind that these figures refer to *acute toxicity*—in other words, a single dose. The biggest concern with many of these substances, such as

DDT, is not their acute effect, but their chronic effect. The results of prolonged exposure to small amounts of them is the real concern. Lethal dose expressed as L.D.$_{50}$ is a very crude measure of the toxicity of a substance. DDT causes profound drops in reproductive success of certain birds at levels one hundredth to one thousandth of the L.D.$_{50}$. As far as toxicity to humans goes, one is more concerned about levels at which cancers are caused, or intelligence is interfered with, or at which neurological involvement becomes obvious, rather than levels at which death occurs. Heavy metals have deleterious effects on humans way below the L.D.$_{50}$ concentration, and these effects may not even be traced back to the metal. Ghetto children traditionally have lower intelligence quotients than other children. How much of this is due to undiscovered lead poisoning? (Please see Table 1-4.)

Table 1-4.   Toxicities (L.D.$_{50}$) in mg/kg or p.p.m.

SPECIES

AGENT	MOUSE	RAT	RABBIT	DOG	GUINEA PIG	BEE	COCK-ROACH	FLY	MOS-QUITO	MAN
DDT (o)	150	400	300		800	17				500
(ip)		150	2100	50		31	7			
(t)		3000	300–2820		1000	114	10	8–21	5.5	
Chlordane	430 (o)	700 (o)	100–300 (o)			2 (o)	26–52 (i)	16 (t)		85–850 (o)
Heptachlor	68 (o)	90 (o)	90 (o)		116 (o)		1 (t)	1.7 (t)		
Aldrin		46–67 (o)	150 (t)	80 (o)						
Dieldrin		65 (o)	90–150 (t)	65–95 (o)		1 (o)	1 (i)	6.3 (o)		
Endrin		11–17 (o)	7–10 (o)		16–30 (o)					
Nicotine	0.8 (i)	1 (i)	9 (i)	5 (i)	5 (i)	315 (t)	650 (t)			1 (o)
Pyrethrins	40 (i)	820 (o)		8 (i)	1500 (o)		3–8 (t)	57 (t)	1 (t)	1000 (o)
Fluoroacetate	18 (i)	5 (i)	0.5 (i)	0.1 (i)	0.35 (i)		43 (i)	21 (i)		2–10 (o)
Sodium fluoride	80 (o)	200 (o)	80 (i)	75 (o)	250 (o)	12 (o)	350 (o)			70 (o)
Lindane	86 (o)	125 (o)	200 (o)	100 (o)	127 (o)	0.3 (o)	5 (t)	2 (t)	3 (t)	
Lead arsenate		100 (o)	125 (o)	500 (o)		4.3 (o)	150 (o)			100 (o)
Lead		1000 (i)			250 (i)					
Mercury	23 (i)	37000 (o)	100 (t)							14–56
Arsenic		20 (o)	20 (o)	85 (o)		0.8 (o)	500 (t)			3–4 (o)
Parathion	5.5 (i)	4 (i)	40 (t)	12–20 (i)	32 (o)	0.8 (o)	0.9 (t)	0.5 (o)		4 (o)
Phenobarbital	325 (o)	660 (o)	185 (i)							70 (o)
Cyanide	5 (i)		0.3 (i)	3 (i)	0.1 (i)					7–10 (o)
Thallium	0.5 (i)	16 (o)	14 (i)	45 (o)						14 (o)

Abbreviations: (o) Oral, (i) Injection, (t) Topical.

Another example of this is the recent fuss over the acute toxicity of DDT. We have seen the head of a California extermination company heroically swallowing a capsule of DDT each day to the cheers of the press. This is a red herring, for DDT has rather a low acute toxicity to humans. The real concern of the substance is what it does to other animals and birds, and the extraordinary stability of it in the biosphere. It is not without dangerous effects for humans, however. Being highly fat-soluble, it is readily stored and concentrated in the body, and only excreted very slowly. Because of its fat-solubility it is absorbed with great ease through the skin. No one knows what long-term effects this storage has on the body. In a severe wasting illness, however, because the fat is then mobilized and used by the body, DDT can be released from its relatively safe storage in the fat in sudden large amounts to cause convulsions and neuritis at a time when the sick body is least able to bear it. Another potentially dangerous effect of DDT is that it can interfere with the effects of drugs given medicinally. Depending on the particular drug, DDT can neither intensify the action of the drug nor lessen it. Both situations are extremely dangerous, especially as the effect is insidious and a doctor would fail to realize what had happened. His patient shows a highly toxic reaction to a normally innocuous drug, and the doctor records in his notes that the patient was allergic or sensitive to it, and leaves it at that. It is impossible to judge how many examples of this occur each year. It is a problem with international ramifications. The people of the United States contain higher levels of DDT in their bodies than the peoples of most other nations. A drug which has been tested on an American population may have different effects on a foreign population, because of the differing DDT levels.

This effect, known as induction, is due to the action of DDT on the enzymes in the liver which metabolize drugs. Small amounts of DDT affect the liver in such a way that the amounts of these enzymes are much increased. These same enzymes metabolize many other foreign chemicals apart from DDT, and so the behavior of many drugs may be altered.

The study of the interaction of chemicals with biological systems is complex, but fascinating. We have but briefly skimmed the surface. Apart from the interest, it is a study of great practical importance to many aspects of our daily lives. Here we have been mainly concerned with the problems caused by indiscriminate pollution of our environment with poorly understood chemicals. Politics is intimately bound up in economics, and we will succeed in protecting ourselves and our country from the ravages of indiscriminate chemical pollution only by cogent economic arguments based on factual statement. We may wish to control pollution of the environment and decimation of extinction of animal species for any number of personal reasons: esthetic, the recognition that the extinction of any species makes our life that much poorer; humility, a feeling that we are the stewards and not the owners of the good earth; responsibility, concern for the next generation. But none of these reasons carry political weight. What will carry weight is the knowledge that pouring mercury into waters causes a heavier economic loss than disposing of it other ways—in the social disruption caused by mercury poisoning and the economic loss engendered by closing down the tuna-fishing industry and closing recreational waters. Pity for the coyote and the unbalancing of a delicate ecosystem caused by unrestrained poisoning campaigns have no political weight. The demonstration that the taxpayer is paying $100,000 in exterminating animals to save a few ranchers $5,000 in stock losses does. Demonstrations such as these require facts, not emotional letters to your congressman. Conservationists need to be as politically oriented and as hard-nosed as the interests they are lobbying against.

air pollution

The atmosphere is a thin cloak of air wrapped around the earth. Although it contains only one atom for every 200,000 atoms in the earth's interior, it is still far more important to life than is the great interior mass of our planet. The atmosphere supplies oxygen (O_2) to breathe, carbon dioxide (CO_2) for photosynthesis, an ozone (O_3) screen against deadly ultraviolet light, rain to water the continents, and insulation from the cold of space.

The chief atoms of the atomosphere are: nitrogen (N), oxygen (O), hydrogen (H), carbon (C), and argon (Ar). These are nonmetallic elements, and in the periodic table (see a chemistry textbook) are found predominantly in the upper right-hand region. This is the gas-forming region, and among the many atmospheric gases and vapors to which this region gives birth are the five major constituents of clean air. The constituents and their percentages of the atmosphere are as follows:

diatomic nitrogen (N_2)	78%	
diatomic oxygen (O_2)	21	Fixed percentage
monatomic argon (Ar)	0.93	of dry air
carbon dioxide (CO_2)	0.032	
water (H_2O)	1–3	

Natural air also contains variable amounts of small dust particles and trace amounts (mostly under one part per million) of the gases methane (CH_4), diatomic hydrogen (H_2), carbon monoxide (CO), ozone (O_3), ammonia (NH_3), nitrogen dioxide (NO_2), sulfur dioxide (SO_2), and hydrogen sulfide (H_2S).

So far, man's activities have had little effect on the three abundant gases—nitrogen, oxygen, and argon. But nearly every other chemical constituent has increased in local areas, and some throughout the world.

Enough carbon dioxide has been pumped into the air by fossil fuel combustion to raise its content in the atomosphere *10 percent* in only one century—a trend that threatens worldwide changes in climate. The presence of particles in the air has also increased throughout the world, and could have similar repercussions. Worse, the atmosphere above many urban areas is now laden with toxic substances like carbon monoxide, sulfur dioxide, and ozone. These exist in amounts up to hundreds of times greater than are found in fresh air. In addition, exotic chemical substances that our ancestors never encountered are now common above cities.

Clearly, we cannot afford to ignore these changes in the chemical environment of our atmosphere, for each day we inhale—and thereby bathe our sensitive lung tissue in—about 20,000 quarts of air. There is no other part of our chemical environment with which we are in such intimate and continuous contact.

The following selections describe the details of our altered air. The first one, Article 5, introduces us to the broad scope of air pollution. Article 6 explores one of the most crucial but still unanswered questions to man's future: "Is Man Changing the Earth's Climate?" Articles 7 through 10 explore, in turn, the four major components of air pollution: carbon monoxide, photochemical smog, particulate matter, and sulfur dioxide. The section ends with Article 11, "Citizen Role in Implementation of Clean Air Standards," which describes the U.S.'s present legal offensive against air pollution and the citizen's part in implementing it. Without citizen involvement, of course, none of the problems outlined in these articles have much chance for solution.

five:

air pollution

dermot a. o'sullivan

"Looking down the ecological road 10 years hence, let us keep in mind what our astronauts have let us verify for ourselves: We really do live on a relatively small spacecraft whirling through space. We always knew that our astronauts would perish in space if they exhausted their life-support systems, but we did not evidently heretofore fully comprehend that we are all in space and that if we exhaust the life-support systems of our planet spacecraft, we will all perish."—Los Angeles Mayor Samuel Yorty, San Francisco, April 3, 1970

Next week [in June 1970] some 3000 conventioneers will meet in St. Louis, Mo. It won't matter too much if the graceful Gateway to the West arch that towers 630 feet above the banks of the Mississippi is half hidden by a blanket of smog. If such happens to be the case, it will lend an extra degree of forcefulness to the event. For the occasion will mark the 63rd annual meeting of the Air Pollution Control Association.

The program includes 150 lectures that cover the whole gamut of air pollution topics from metering and forecasting to controlling stack emissions, to meteorology, and to the socio-economic effects of pollutants.

Some share Konrad T. Semrau's viewpoint that air pollution is more of an economical and political problem than a technical one. The senior chemical engineer at Stanford Research Institute in Menlo Park, Calif., who has 20 years experience to his credit studying air pollutants from stationary sources says, "Most people think that air pollution control presents a tremendously complicated technical problem. But in most cases the barrier to effective control is not technology, but economics. We know how to do it, at least in a general way; the real question is, at what cost?"

Unquestionably, the cost of cleaning up the air and rectifying the pollution sources will be staggering. In the report entitled "The Cost of Clean Air," that the U.S. Health, Education, and Welfare Department compiled last year, the number of dollars estimated to be spent at all levels of soci-

Excerpted from *Chemical & Engineering News,* Vol. 48, June 8, 1970, pp. 38–58. Copyright 1970 by The American Chemical Society and reprinted by permission of the copyright owner. The author is bureau head of *Chemical & Engineering News* in San Francisco.

45

ety—government, industry, and the private sector—will likely approach $7.5 billion during the period 1970 to 1974.

Often without realizing it, the polluted air they now must endure is costing people money. Garments must go to the cleaners more frequently to rid them of the grime they pick up. Auto tires and other rubber products crack and fail. Buildings need painting and cleaning.

Most critical, of course, are the ill effects that air pollutants can have on people's health and well-being. Aside from the cost in physical misery, the monetary cost of respiratory illnesses that are exaggerated, if not actually caused by air pollution, may be well over $2 billion annually.

what is it?

People have varying reactions to air pollution depending on where they happen to be because it varies from place to place. "It's icky" is how Nancy Pitts, a pert California housewife, describes the eye-searing, photochemical haze that shrouds her lovely home and neighborhood in suburban Riverside during most of the year. "It's depressing when you can barely discern the end of the garden let alone the mountains in the distance."

"It makes me sick," is the blunt way Bernie Hynes of Phoenix, Ariz., refers to the waste gases coming from the copper smelters he must drive by.

Even areas once considered remote are coming in for their share of air pollution. In Laramie, Wyo., 7500 feet above sea level at the foot of the Snowy Range Mountains where one would expect to find the air very clear and crisp, "Clean air is a thing of the past," says resident Jeff Reetz. "One cement plant a mile out of town spews gases, soot, and dust particles over much of the area. Houses and cars, livestock, and pets have a dull slate grey appearance due to the clouds of wastes settling on them." Comments a resident of mile-high Denver: "People come here to enjoy the view of the mountains. But our worsening smog problem is seriously affecting visibility."

There's nothing unusual about air pollution. In fact it's part of the natural life cycle. For example, the shimmering blue haze from which Virginia's Blue Ridge Mountains derive their name is caused by submicroscopic aerosol particles that refract the sun's rays. Dr. Frits Went of the University of Nevada's Desert Research Institute near Reno, who studied the phenomenon, theorizes that terpenes and other natural products escaping from the trees undergo a photochemical reaction that gives rise to the aerosol particles. Each year, up to 1×10^{12} tons of emissions enter the global atmosphere from both natural and man-made sources, points out Dr. Robert D. Englert, executive director of Stanford Research Institute's Irvine, Calif., laboratories.

In contrast, about 5×10^8 tons per year of the emissions arise from the activities and inventions of modern man, he adds. That's a mere 0.05% of the total, but that amount causes the problems of reduced visibility, irritated eyes and throat, damaged property, and various health hazards.

The bothersome pollutants range from asbestos to zinc. They come from a variety of sources: from industrial processes such as smelters, iron and steel mills, paper and pulp operations, petroleum refineries and chemical plants; from community operations such as garbage dumping, trash incineration, and agricultural burning; from power generating facilities and space heaters; and from automobiles, trucks, and jet aircraft.

The National Air Pollution Control Administration, an arm of the Department of Health, Education, and Welfare, is drawing a bead on some 30 of the pollutants that it considers most necessary to abate from the standpoint of their relative abundance and toxicity.

Litton Industries' Environmental Systems division in Camarillo, Calif., last year [1969] completed a study for NAPCA in which it investigated 27 classes of pollutants, how they get into the air, their effects on health, methods of monitoring and controlling them, and so forth. The list extends from aeroallergens to zinc and its compounds. The findings are being used by NAPCA toward setting priorities for the development of criteria and control technique documents.

simple and complex

The chemicals that find their way into the air are fairly simple in themselves, but the reactions and interactions that they undergo when subjected to the physical conditions of the atmospheric environment can be very complex. There's probably no better example of this than the photochemical events that lead to the pollution that hangs as a pall over Los Angeles and many of the larger metropolitan areas during most of the year. Commonly referred to as smog, it is formed through a series of sunlight-initiated chemical reactions.

The first definitive study into the chemistry of photochemical smog stemmed from a chance observation that biochemist Arie J. Haagen-Smit made during an attempt to isolate the odor principles of pineapple in his Caltech lab. His technique consisted of drawing air through a preparation of the fruit and then through a trap cooled with liquid nitrogen. "One day when the smog level happened to be exceptionally high, I noticed a distinct odor of ozone from the condensate," he recalls. "So I decided to see what would happen if I repeated the operation without the pineapple."

After he had pumped some 350 cubic feet of smog-laden Pasadena air through his apparatus, Dr. Haagen-Smit had collected in the cold trap a sizable quantity of murky liquid that had a very disagreeable odor. Analysis of this condensate by gas chromatography showed the presence of a variety of aldehydes and organic acids, nitrates, sulfates, and other compounds.

Precise details of the chemical reactions that lead to formation of photochemical smog aren't understood completely. Basically, three factors play a predominant role. One is a mixture of nitrogen oxides, chiefly NO and NO_2 and usually referred to as NO_x. Much of the NO that gets into the air is formed by nitrogen fixation in the intensely hot environment of automobile cylinders during the combustion of gasoline and air mixtures. When the NO is emitted into the atmosphere, it rapidly undergoes photochemical oxidation to NO_2 in the presence of hydrocarbon pollutants.

Hydrocarbons make up the second key factor in photochemical smog formation. Some of these hydrocarbons come from automobiles either as unburned or partly burned fuel or by evaporation, some come from a variety of industrial sources. The most critical of these hydrocarbons from the standpoint of being potential photochemical pollutants are those with reactive sites such as olefinic double bonds, substituted aromatic hydrocarbons, aldehydes, and ketones. The third essential factor is sunlight with a wavelength between 3000 and 4200 A.

The initial step in the chain of events that leads to photochemical smog probably involves the splitting of nitrogen dioxide molecules into nitric oxide and atomic oxygen under the influence of uv light. This is followed by the interaction of the atomic oxygen with molecular oxygen to form ozone or with hydrocarbons to form complex oxidation products. A number of investigators have proposed different schemes to explain what may occur beyond this stage. In general, it seems that the ozone reacts with the nitric oxide to provide a fresh supply of nitrogen dioxide, whereas the atomic oxygen and reactive hydrocarbons in the air form free radicals. These in turn react very readily with oxygen, nitric oxide, nitrogen dioxide, and with other hydrocarbons.

singlet oxygen

One of the most perplexing aspects of the photooxidation reaction is the very rapid oxidation to NO_2 that NO undergoes as it emerges from automobiles, notes Dr. James N. Pitts, Jr., chemistry professor at the Riverside campus of the University of California. "Thermal oxidation wouldn't be expected to occur sufficiently rapidly at the low concentration (about 0.5 ppm) of NO in the air," he observes.

Dr. Pitts is convinced that singlet oxygen, an electronically excited species of molecular oxygen with a greater-than-normal share of inherent energy, is an important oxidizing species produced in photochemical smog. He and his colleagues, Dr. Ashan Khan, now at Florida State University, and Dr. Brian Smith and Dr. Richard Wayne of England's Oxford University, have suggested that singlet oxygen may play a significant role in the rapid and complex oxidation of NO to NO_2.

In contrast to CO, NO, SO_2, and other primary pollutants, singlet oxygen is a secondary pollutant, since it is one of the products of the photochemical reactions, Dr. Pitts notes. So, too, are the peroxyacyl nitrates, a homologous series of chemicals the most abundant of which is peroxyacetyl nitrate.

PAN's, as they are called, are formed when sunlight acts on air that is polluted with trace concentrations of organic compounds and nitrogen oxides, notes Dr. Edgar R. Stephens of the University of California Statewide Air Pollution Research Center at Riverside, Calif., who has done much of the pioneering research on these chemicals. PAN's have a high degree of biological activity. They are suspected of being the principal cause of photochemical smog's eye-searing effect, and they can bring about visible damage to crops even when present in the parts-per-hundred-million concentration range. In fact, Dr. John T. Middleton, who is a plant pathologist by training and who headed the U.C. Statewide Air Pollution Research Center before he was appointed Commissioner of the National Air Pollution Control Administration, pegs the loss of agricultural crops wrought by PAN's at millions of dollars. The characteristic damage symptoms these chemicals induce in plants now are widespread throughout the U.S. and elsewhere.

Dr. Pitts points out that peroxyacetyl nitrate, the simplest member of the PAN's, also is remarkable in another sense. He and his associates, Dr. Ronald Steer, of the University of Saskatchewan, and Dr. Karen Darnell, recently have shown that it undergoes hydrolysis to form singlet molecular oxygen by way of a highly exothermic, "dark" reaction. This air pollutant thus provides one pathway for singlet oxygen to be formed in intimate contact with biological tissue, a fact that has immense biological implications, Dr. Pitts avers. Deep within a person's lungs, for instance, the high-energy oxygen could react right at the site of formation.

Research in the field of atmospheric photochemistry is made difficult by the variety and array of components in the air that occur in ever-changing concentrations and in a medium that can undergo sharp fluctuations of physical condition. It's one thing to trace photochemical changes as they take place in the carefully controlled environment of a laboratory reaction vessel; it's quite another matter to try to interpret the events in metropolitan air, points out Dr. Sheldon Friedlander, professor of chemical engineering at Caltech. He and his associate, Dr. John Seinfeld, are working on the design of chemical reactor models for urban basins.

climate and location

The chemical makeup of the atmosphere determines the degree to which it is polluted. However, weather conditions that prevail at any particular time, as well as the topography of an area, have a marked influence on the effects of the pollution.

Denver provides a good example of this. Though a mile above sea level, air pollution there, which is steadily getting worse, is aggravated further by a high frequency of temperature inversions in the area, especially during the winter months. What happens, explains Leonard Dobler, an engineer with the City and County of Denver Air Pollution Control Section, is that during the nights an air mass dribbles down the sides of the nearby mountains and into the river valley where Denver lies. In so doing, it pushes up the warmer air, but the warm air expands adiabatically, maintaining its total heat content. The result is a so-called inversion layer, a blanket of warm air that extends over colder air and prevents the cold air from rising as it otherwise would when the morning sun warmed it. Sometimes, this inversion layer can be as low as 100 feet above ground level, Mr. Dobler notes.

As the morning traffic rush gets under way, the amount of hydrocarbons, carbon monoxide, and oxides of nitrogen from the automobile exhausts builds up. The gases can't dissipate, however, since they are held in place by the layer of warm air that acts as a lid over the region. "Thus it is," comments Mr. Dobler, "that carbon monoxide readings can rise from about 4 ppm in the early morning hours to about 16 ppm or so by 8 A.M."

There's another factor that helps compound the situation, Mr. Dobler continues. Because of Denver's height above sea level, auto engines must be adjusted to operate on the more rarified air. The engines use a slightly richer fuel-to-air mixture so that they may run smoothly. Consequently, there's less efficient combustion and a greater amount of carbon monoxide and unburned, or partially burned, hydrocarbons emitted.

One bright spot in an otherwise gloomy picture is that automobiles in the Denver area put out a smaller amount of nitrogen oxides than they would at sea level. This is because engine combustion temperatures are somewhat lower leading to a lower degree of fixation of atmospheric nitrogen within the cylinders.

Climate, topography, and local atmospheric conditions also combine to aggravate the disagreeable photochemical air pollution in the Los Angeles basin. Chemists frequently liken the area to a giant reactor since it is bordered on its north, east, and south sides by mountains and on the west by the Pacific Ocean. Breezes blowing in from the sea hold the air mass within the confines of the basin that stretches some 170 miles along the ocean and some 50 miles deep. Compounding the situation are atmospheric inversions that cap the area. During prolonged periods of the year, the pollutants are trapped. Their concentration builds up while they are held to stew in the hot southern California sunshine.

Regional climatic conditions are coming under greater scrutiny by engineers who are charged with the responsibility of curbing air pollution from industrial sources or guarding against such pollution. For instance, Portland General Electric Co. has erected a 500-foot tower adjacent to the site of its proposed 1.1 GW Trojan nuclear power generating plant that's under construction 40 miles northwest of Portland. Electronic meteorological instruments at the 200-, 350-, and 500-foot levels automatically monitor wind directions, wind speeds, air temperatures, and the like. Such information is critical for the proper design and subsequent operation of the nuclear power plant to ensure that the level of radioactivity that might escape into the atmosphere doesn't exceed safety limits set by the Atomic Energy Commission.

Prediction of the movement of contaminants in the air is becoming an increasingly important branch of environmental engineering. Central to such predictions is the design of mathematical models that take into account wind variables, temperature fluctuations, rainfall, the topographical characteristics of an area, the heights of buildings, locations of freeways, traffic density, and the like.

A NAPCA-sponsored study being carried out by Battelle-Northwest is aimed at evaluating how rain and snow remove SO_2 from the smoke that issues from a coal-fired power generating station. The study points up the increasing attention being given to the interplay between climate conditions and air pollution. "Such removal could be a major factor in cleaning or scrubbing the atmosphere," comments Michael A. Wolf, who is directing the project. "However," he adds, "self-cleansing of the atmosphere in this way might lead to potential health hazards or other detrimental effects at the earth's surface."

Site of the study is Pennsylvania Electric Co.'s Keystone generating station where Battelle-Northwest scientists already have collected information during the five-month period between October 1969 and February of this year [1970]. The study augments another NAPCA project aimed at determining the characteristics of smoke plumes that come out of the two 800-foot-tall stacks at the Keystone station and the effects of the power plant emissions on agriculture in the adjacent area.

Most serious, of course, are the catastrophic effects on people's health that can follow exposure to pollutants during unusual meteorological conditions. The first of what has since become a growing list of such tragic episodes that have attracted worldwide concern occurred in Belgium's Meuse River Valley in December 1930. There, some 60 people died and 6000 others became seriously ill from breathing abnormally high levels of particulates and gaseous pollutants in the air. Other calamities took place in the mill town of Donora, near Pittsburgh, Pa., in 1948, and in London, England, in 1952 and again in 1962.

All these episodes that led to chronic respiratory ailments and death took place during the winter months, a time when power generating plants as well as home fires and domestic heating units usually are going full blast. In each case, a high pressure system had created a temporary inversion layer over the entire region, trapping cold, dense air beneath a layer of warmer air. Moreover, winds had dropped, and a calm prevailed for several days, further reducing dispersion of the pollutants.

It's likely, too, that there were small water droplets present, theorizes Dr. John R. Goldsmith, who heads the environmental epidemiology unit at the California State Department of Public Health in Berkeley, Calif. If such were the case, both aerosols and gaseous pollutants were involved, a combination that presents a much greater health hazard than gaseous pollutants alone.

A host of airborne pollutants are coming under increased scrutiny as to their effects on the health and well-being of man and his possessions. The list of materials is a long one. It includes carbon monoxide, sulfur dioxide, nitrogen oxides and ozone, polynuclear hydrocarbons, such as benzo[a]pyrene, members of the peroxyacyl nitrate family of compounds, fly ash, lead, vanadium, and a variety of trace metals.

There is emerging, too, evidence linking the level of air pollution to higher death rates from coronary heart disease and strokes. Epidemiologists Warren Winkelstein, Jr., and Michael L. Gay at the University of California's School of Public Health in Berkeley have correlated death statistics for Buffalo, N.Y., over a preselected time span with data on that city's level of suspended particulate air pollution during the same period. They studied people in two age groups—50- to 69-year-olds and those 70 years and older. People of modest financial means, they note, who make their homes in the areas of the city with the highest pollution level, suffer death from cardiovascular disease by a significantly higher margin than do their counterparts who live where the air is cleaner. The two doctors' findings also point to a statistical relationship between air pollution levels and death from chronic respiratory disease and cancer of the stomach.

In New York's Albert Einstein College of Medicine, Dr. Leonard Greenburg, a pioneer in the study of the ill effects of air pollution on health, and statistician Marvin Glasser conducted a study into the possible link between the number of deaths in New York City and the level of sulfur dioxide in the air. The data the two workers reviewed covered the period between 1960 and 1964. There were 10 to 20 more deaths per day when the mean SO_2 readings were 0.4 ppm or more compared to days when these readings were 0.2 ppm or less, they found. "For the first time we are satisfied that we have some definite correlations between sulfur dioxide in the air and excess deaths," Dr. Greenburg comments. Airborne asbestos particles are now entering the limelight of public concern. These may lead to lung cancer, mesothelioma, and cancer of the peritoneum or the pleura, notes Dr. Robert Rickles, recently appointed Air Resources Commissioner for the City of New York.

Apart from being a potential health hazard by themselves, minute particles of asbestos adsorb molecules of gases such as sulfur dioxide on their surface. When inhaled, the particles, with the adsorbed gas, can lodge deep in the air passages of the lungs where they may cause severe irritation.

Sparking the concern is the rapidly growing practice by office construction teams of using asbestos spray-on techniques for insulating buildings. Last April [1970], Dr. Rickles issued a 10-point order that spells out precautions to be taken and operating procedures that must be followed to minimize the danger of getting too much of the asbestos dust into the air.

The adverse effects of air pollutants on crops and plant life can be more readily assessed than they can be for humans. In one of a series of carefully controlled field experiments, for instance, Dr. O. Clifton Taylor, acting director of the University of California Statewide Air Pollution Research Center in Riverside, with Dr. C. Ray Thompson and coworkers, have been studying the effects that oxidants—mainly ozone, nitrogen oxides and PAN's—that occur in photochemical smog have on the growth and fruit yield of citrus trees. Around some trees in the citrus grove they erected specially constructed greenhouses fitted with filters to purify the air before it reaches the trees. In the case of the trees exposed to the ambient polluted air, the California scientists observe a sharp reduction in the rate of water uptake and photosynthesis. In addition, there is a greater tendency of fruit to drop from these trees. The yield of fruit has been reduced by half in some cases.

In a related series of experiments, Dr. Thompson discovered that photochemical smog cuts the average grape yield by as much as 60%, a fact of key importance to the economy of California where the bulk of U.S. wines are produced. Working with Zinfandel grape vines, he finds that the average vine produces a mere 6.9 pounds of grapes when it grows in an ambient (smoggy) environment compared to 17.8 pounds when the vines get clean air. In addition, smog stunts the growth of the vines and results in grapes that are smaller and less sweet, Dr. Thompson observes.

Meanwhile, Dr. J. Brian Mudd, professor of biochemistry at the neighboring Riverside campus of the University of California, is exploring the interaction of photochemical oxidants with cell constituents at the molecular level. He finds that enzymes that depend on free sulfhydryl groups for their biological activity lose their effectiveness.

When he exposes the enzymes to peroxyacetyl nitrate, there is conversion of sulfhydryl groups both to disulfides and to S-acetyl compounds. The effect of ozone is somewhat more complex because of its greater oxidizing capability, he notes.

Dr. Mudd points to an interesting correlation between his findings and the characteristic eye-watering effect that photochemical smog induces. "It ties in with the fact that many lachrymatory gases also appear to interact with sulfhydryl groups," he says.

On the other hand, experiments have led to some seemingly conflicting results. For instance, in a study undertaken at Hazleton Laboratories, Inc., in Falls Church, Va., and sponsored by the Edison Electric Institute, American Public Power Association, Tennessee Valley Authority, and Bituminous Coal Research, Inc., guinea pigs breathing 5 ppm sulfur dioxide had a higher survival rate and a lower incidence of lung disease than animals breathing a smaller amount of the gas.

Similarly, Dr. Charles Hine, clinical professor of environmental and occupational medicine and toxicology at the University of California, San Francisco, finds that artificially produced air pollution in the laboratory at concentrations higher than those ordinarily encountered doesn't adversely affect the healing of injured eyes. Moreover, he finds, repeated exposure of rats to high levels, on the order of 10 ppm of nitrogen oxides, during the three-month period didn't produce any evidence of lasting damage in the animals. "I'm not convinced that general air pollution in the western U.S. presents the alarming dangers to health claimed by some," he says. "It depresses people, it causes emotional problems. But I also think that what some public health people have classed as smog's effect on health needs careful re-evaluation."

cleanup

"Technology is responsible in large measure for pollution, so let's use technology to clean it up," is the stand that many environmentalists take. They also frequently cite the fact that if we can land men on the moon and bring them safely back to earth again, we should be able to apply a like degree of American ingenuity and engineering skills to overcome the pollution problem.

There's no denying a certain degree of logic to these arguments. On the other hand, there is the very real question as to whether it will be possible, or indeed feasible, to mobilize the same degree of national effort to clean up the environment that it took to translate into reality President John F. Kennedy's vow to put man on the moon before the end of the '60's.

Nevertheless, efforts to reduce the emission of pollutants from various sources are rapidly gaining momentum. The results of such efforts may not be as dramatic as a space shot nor the results immediately evident, but at least a start has been made.

emotional issue

Probably the most controversial and emotion-packed issue that the auto exhaust cleanup drive has given rise to so far centers on the question of whether or not to remove lead tetraalkyl antiknock compounds from gasoline. Proponents of the "get lead out" camp cite some impressive arguments in support of their stance. They note that lead poisons the catalysts that convert noxious carbon monoxide and nitrogen oxides in the exhaust to harmless carbon dioxide and nitrogen; that lead expelled into the atmosphere is unhealthy; that lead aerosols contribute to the buildup of particulate concentration in city air; that the halogen-containing chemicals accompanying lead antiknock compounds in gasoline formulations cause corrosion of mufflers and tail pipes and more rapid deterioration of engine parts, spark plugs, and engine oil.

On the other hand, those who champion the cause of lead point to the development of exhaust control devices such as the ones that Du Pont and Ethyl Corp. have designed; devices, they claim, that will effectively control carbon monoxide, nitrogen oxides, and unburned hydrocarbons before these gases escape into the atmosphere. What's more, these people say, lead aerosols have yet to be proved a health hazard, and lead antiknock compounds lead to better performance, at greater economy, of the high-powered cars that the American public demands. Ethyl Corp. chairman Floyd D. Gottwald, Jr., makes the added point that the higher content of aromatics and aldehydes in unleaded gasoline will increase the emission of these chemicals into the air, raising the likelihood, he thinks, of an even greater amount of photochemical smog being formed by using the unleaded fuel.

The outcome of the issue goes deeper than the ultimate fate of the $400 million annual market for lead tetraalkyl antiknock compounds that Ethyl Corp., Du Pont, Nalco Chemical, and PPG Industries' Houston Chemical now share. If lead is banned from gasoline, then petroleum refining operations will need to be modified to produce more of the costlier high-octane compounds for blending into unleaded, "clear" gasoline. These compounds would raise the fuel's octane rating to 91, the minimum needed to ensure adequate performance of engines designed for regular-grade gasoline.

Such a modification won't come cheaply. Ethyl Corp. engineers who updated the cost estimates that Bonner & Moore Associates arrived at several years ago in a study that firm undertook for the American Petroleum Institute say that the conversion would call for a capital investment of a staggering $6 billion, and would add about 4 cents to the price of a gallon of "regular" grade gas. Yet another point that has been raised is that the additional quantities of platinum catalysts called for by the modified refining operations would outstrip supplies of the precious metal.

Not everyone agrees with Bonner & Moore's original assumptions, however, nor with Ethyl's updating of them. Universal Oil Products engineers argue that the study doesn't take into account improvements in catalyst technology that should, they think, more than offset the added catalytic requirements. John O. Logan, UOP's president, believes that conversion to production of lead-free gasoline would result in an added cost of only a cent per gallon or less at the refinery.

The climate of opinion generally favors removal of lead antiknock additives, however. Henry Ford, II, and GM president Edward N. Cole have urged petroleum refiners to make unleaded gasoline. Moreover, when 1971-model cars come out, the engines will be built to function on unleaded fuel. The California Air Resources Board hopes that California will adopt its recommendation to ban lead antiknock compounds from gasoline sold there after Jan. 1, 1977.

Taking the cue, a number of the major oil refiners plan to have a grade of fuel on the market soon that contains 0.5 gram of lead per gallon in place of the usual 4 grams or so. Ultimately, the idea is to phase lead out of regular gas entirely.

Catalytic systems have been devised that, their inventors claim, will greatly reduce the level of undesirable exhaust components. Invariably, though, lead poisons these catalysts thus shortening their life. UOP's single-catalyst converter will reduce hydrocarbons, carbon monoxide, and nitrogen oxides by up to 90% if the car is running on lead-free gasoline, the company claims.

Meanwhile, several companies are coming out with devices that can be retrofitted on pre-1966 model cars to reduce the amount of emitted pollutants. Each of the Big Three auto makers are touting their individual units, which sell for about $50 apiece. GM, for instance, claims that its invention cuts emission of hydrocarbons by 52%, of carbon monoxide by 37%, and of nitrogen oxides by 31%. At Esso Research and Engineering, Dr. W. Glass and coworkers have devised what they call a "synchrothermal" emission control system. This, they say, results in an overall 92% reduction of hydrocarbons, carbon monoxide, and nitrogen oxides.

Azure Blue Corp. engineers have come up with a specially designed spark plug that causes mass ignition of the fuel-air mixture throughout the entire cylinder chamber instead of igniting the mixture at a point source. As a result, engine "knock" is eliminated. And because combustion is complete, the fuel is converted almost entirely to carbon dioxide and water, claims Alvin W. Evans, president of the El Dorado, Calif., company. Also, combustion rate is so rapid that oxides of nitrogen haven't time to form to the extent that they normally do in today's engines, he says. And coming as an added bonus, the ignitors, as Mr. Evans calls them, allow a car to operate on unleaded "raw" casing head fuel that has an octane rating of about 54.

other fuels

Fuels other than gasoline are being eyed because of the lower level of pollutants that they give rise to. Compressed natural gas will be used to power a number of vehicles in the General Services Administration's motor pool. Indeed, GSA officials are reportedly so enthusiastic with the outcome of trial tests conducted in and around Los Angeles that some 1000 GSA vehicles will be running on compressed natural gas by the end of the [1970] year. The cars will use a dual fuel system developed by Los Angeles-based Pacific Lighting Co. The system permits a vehicle to be operated either on natural gas or on gasoline at the flip of a switch.

Pacific Lighting itself will have 1100 of its customer service vehicles rigged out with the dual fuel system before year-end. Some 20 private utilities companies around the country are also testing the idea.

San Diego Gas and Electric Co., on the other hand, favors liquefied natural gas. The University of California's San Diego campus is opting for bottled propane to power its fleet of cars.

Search for a clean automobile isn't stopping with a look for alternate fuels. There are some who hold that the internal combustion engine should go. Steam, electricity, and gas turbines are among the many alternate power sources that are being actively investigated. The consensus is, though, that the IC engine will be around for a while longer.

Billowing smoke from stacks, generally regarded as the symbol of a nation's industrial might, now is taking the brunt of the attack by environmentalists. Power generating companies, particularly, are being caught in the middle of the squeeze between the surging demand for more electricity in the years ahead and the call for cleaner air.

Power plants and industrial operations are the major source of particulates and sulfur dioxide that get into the air. Attempts to control the level of emission of these pollutants are being made on two fronts. One way is to trap the particulates and the SO_2 before they leave the stack. The other way is to burn low-sulfur fuel, which at least will correct one of the offending situations.

The particulate that's collected from power plant smoke is a greyish, very fine powder called fly ash. Its recovery from smoke creates something of a solid waste disposal problem. There are a number of studies in this country and elsewhere that seek to put fly ash to practical use—to make building blocks or a filler for rubber, for example. Commercialization of any of the projects is considered to be some time away.

The sulfur content of much of the coal being burned by power generating plants in the nation varies from 1.5 to 3.5%. This is too high for the liking of air quality control people. New York officials are demanding that the maximum allowable level be lowered to 1% or less by next year [1971]. The move will add to the cost of operating the power plants because low-sulfur coal is more expensive to buy. Although there's no shortage of it in total tonnage of reserves, the way it is dispersed in the ground makes it more difficult to mine.

Yet another complicating factor associated with the burning of low-sulfur coal is that electrostatic precipitators don't work so well because the fly ash particles from low-sulfur coal are more resistant to electric charge. This is one of the problems that Power Service Co. of Colorado is facing at its plants in the Denver area and elsewhere. The company uses coal mined in Wyoming and other western states. By some strange quirk of nature, this coal is low in sulfur, which is fortunate in many respects, but it places a heavy burden on engineers who seek to remove particulates from the flue gases. No satisfactory and economical solution has yet been devised to overcome the problem.

Control of the SO_2 in stack gases has been the focal point of a concerted attack by NAPCA and others. A $3.3 million, NAPCA-funded study is now under way at TVA's Shawnee steam plant near Paducah, Ky. There, a dry limestone injection process that TVA engineers have developed will be tested. The limestone absorbs the SO_2, then electrostatic precipitators remove the limestone.

The TVA process is but one of many SO_2 removal schemes that 11 companies, as well as the Bureau of Mines and TVA, have under development. Enviro-Chem Systems, Inc.'s Cat-Ox system is the only one of the various approaches tried that has reached commercialization. Since it appeared on the commercial scene in 1968 it has been operating "virtually free of major problems" in one of Metropolitan Edison Co.'s generating

56

stations at Portland, Pa., notes Jack L. Leech, v.p. and general manager of the environmental systems division of Enviro-Chem, Monsanto's recently formed subsidiary.

The Cat-Ox system uses a vanadium pentoxide catalyst to convert the SO_2 to 78% sulfuric acid. On average, 90% of the SO_2 in the flue gases is recovered, Enviro-Chem claims. What's more, income from the sale of the sulfuric acid, which Enviro-Chem pledges to help move, offsets some of the cost.

During the past few months, techniques have evolved that are touted by their developers to be able to efficiently remove sulfur from gas, oil, and coal as well as from flue gases. The product of these processes is elemental sulfur or sulfuric acid.

costs

Between now [June 1970] and 1974, all levels of government will spend upward of $1.6 billion on programs aimed at cleaning the air. During that same period, the tab for the fuel combustion companies might be as high as $2.75 billion, while the major industrial processors likely will spend more than $0.5 billion. Meanwhile, motorists will have spent some $2.64 billion for motor vehicle emission control systems. All that adds up to nearly $7.46 billion in expenditures in the next four years according to HEW estimates.

is man changing the earth's climate?

staff of chemical & engineering news

More needs to be known, scientists conclude, to predict consequences of man-made changes to the atmosphere.

Man's injection into the atmosphere of carbon dioxide can, through the "greenhouse effect," cause a temperature rise around the world, perhaps enough to melt polar ice caps. This thaw of land-based ice could raise ocean levels by about 7 meters, thus submerging at least some of the world's urban centers. But the initial temperature rise could also lead to more evaporation of the oceans, therefore to more clouds and cooling of the atmosphere because of greater reflection of the sun's rays. Each process could cancel the other, with very little net change to the atmosphere. So what's the problem?

Basically, the problem is that the example is hypothetical, and not enough basic information is available to allow scientists reasonably to predict consequences of man-made changes to the atmosphere. However, some of the world's leading experts on climate are concerned enough to recommend a program with an initial cost of about $25 million to gather fundamental data on atmosphere and climate. The scientists recently [in 1971] concluded a three-week study at Stockholm, Sweden, on man's impact on climate. The study, sponsored by MIT, was under the direction of MIT's Carroll L. Wilson.

levers

Man's impact on climate works through several levers, according to Dr. William W. Kellogg, National Center for Atmospheric Research, Boulder, Colo.:

- Carbon dioxide production from fuel combustion.
- Particle and trace gas emissions.
- Energy production and heat release.

- Manipulation of surface and underground water.
- Transportation's effects on land surfaces and the upper atmosphere.
- Change and destruction of vegetation.
- Changes to arctic ice pack.

All of these levers influence the atmosphere by affecting removal, absorption, or transfer of heat, Dr. Kellogg notes. But man is competing with large natural forces in affecting the climate. No one is certain what contribution if any man has made to the change in average temperature of the world. Between 1880 and 1940 the global temperature rose by 0.5° C., but has since fallen by about 0.3° C. The variation may be natural or may be partly due to man-made changes, Dr. Kellogg suggests.

Scientists are more certain about levels of emission of man-made particles and gases, even if they are not yet certain of their ultimate effects. For example, Dr. Christian Junge, of Max-Planck Institute für Chemie, Mainz, West Germany, estimates that man-made particles account for 10 to 50% of the atmosphere's total particles. Natural injection of particles into the atmosphere totals 773 million to 2.2 billion metric tons annually. Man-made emissions total 185 million to 415 million metric tons per year, he says. All but 10 million to 90 million metric tons of the man-made annual total comes from chemical precursors, such as sulfur dioxide from combustion of fuels and nitrogen oxides from industrial emissions.

Gaseous oxides convert in the atmosphere to sulfate and nitrate particles, Dr. Junge says. Man-made sulfate particles attain about the same level as natural species (130 million to 200 million metric tons annually) and are the largest single man-made contribution of particles. Dust and smoke emission account for 10 million to 90 million metric tons of the man-made annual total, nitrate for 30 to 35 million metric tons, and hydrocarbons for 15 to 20 million metric tons, Dr. Junge estimates.

sulfate

Meanwhile, natural sources of sulfur yield 130 to 200 million metric tons annually of sulfate particles, ammonia and nitrogen oxides give 140 to 700 million metric tons of nitrate, and hydrocarbons form 75 to 200 million metric tons annually of particles in the atmosphere. Sea salt, soil, volcanic ash, and forest fires account for the remaining 438 million to 1.1 billion metric tons annually of natural particles, Dr. Junge notes.

A 50% increase in the particle load from man-made sources could lead directly to a 0.5° to 1.0° C. reduction in the earth's surface temperature. A further reduction of the same size could be induced by related cloud formation and greater reflection of solar energy. The number of water droplets in the atmosphere is directly related to the number of particles, Dr. Junge points out. He is almost certain the amount of cloud related to man-made particles is increasing, but notes that there are no data on global cloud levels. Emission of particles by man has increased by about 50% since the start of industrialization in the mid-1800's, he says.

Levels of atmospheric carbon dioxide are also on the increase, according to Dr. Hans-Walter Georgii of the University of Frankfurt, West Germany. Concentration of the gas is now about 322 p.p.m., compared with 292 p.p.m.

in 1860 and 310 p.p.m. in 1950, he says. By the end of this century, the level will reach 375 p.p.m.

A rise to this level from about 290 p.p.m. in theory will induce a global temperature rise of about 0.5° C., Dr. Georgii says. However, a 1% increase in cloud density would decrease temperature proportionately, so the net result is difficult to predict. Meanwhile, carbon dioxide evolution from burning of fossil fuels is growing at about 4% annually.

unknown

With few exceptions, global trends for other gases are not known, he points out. And in any case their effects may be local and indirect. Sulfur dioxide and ammonia each yields particles. Nitrogen oxides and hydrocarbons, although forming particles, may exert only local effects, such as the Los Angeles smog. Carbon monoxide levels may be rising from the global average of 0.1 p.p.m. (compared to 5 to 50 p.p.m. in urban areas), but will have only local effects. Methane and oxygen concentrations in the atmosphere are constant, and have no global influence, Dr. Georgii says.

Turning their attention to the stratosphere (above 15 kilometers altitude) and the troposphere (up to 15 kilometers), scientists say that small changes could have relatively large effects on conditions at the earth's surface. For example, a 1% drop in the stratospheric ozone concentration could induce an 8% increase in radiation intensity of ultraviolet light at the surface, notes Dr. Lester Machta, National Oceanic and Atmospheric Administration, Silver Spring, Md. Incidence of skin cancer increases toward the earth's equator because of higher radiation intensities, he adds. Dr. Machta considers that a 0.1% change in ozone concentration (which totals about 10^{-8} moles per liter in the stratosphere) would be significant in terms of skin cancer.

ozone

Scientists are not sure of the climatic impact of changes in ozone concentration in the stratosphere. Ozone concentration has increased in the past decade by 2.5 to 10%. Also, little is known about chemical reactions at very low concentrations between ozone and man-made contaminants, such as nitrogen oxides, several of the scientists tell *Chemical & Engineering News*. Reactions probably involve such short-lived species as the $HO_2\cdot$ free radical, which are difficult to study at very low pressures in the laboratory, they add.

Water vapor trails from supersonic aircraft in the upper troposphere and lower stratosphere could increase the amount of cirrus cloud. Measurements of high cloud over the U.S. have shown an increase since 1965, Dr. Georgii says. Current effects are small, but such clouds could alter climate by changing the radiation balance and by precipitating ice crystals, which could fall and seed lower clouds into rainfall.

carbon monoxide

philip c. wolf

It's invisible but can be more dangerous than photochemical smog. That's why knowing the level of carbon monoxide in densely populated areas is becoming more important as auto population continues to soar.

People no longer take air for granted. Since concern over air pollution is widespread today, more accurate information on the amount, distribution, and toxic effects of pollutants is vitally needed. Carbon monoxide, a product of almost all combustion processes and one of the most widespread and toxic pollutants, cannot be detected (unfortunately) by sight or smell.

The internal-combustion engine is the largest single source of carbon monoxide in ambient air. As a result, the highest concentrations are found in urban areas having dense automobile traffic. The greatest potential hazard exists, therefore, where the greatest number of people may be affected.

CO effects

Carbon monoxide (CO) reduces the ability of the bloodstream to carry oxygen to body tissues by displacing oxygen from hemoglobin (Hb) to form carboxyhemoglobin (COHb). The most important factor involving carbon monoxide effects on humans is the COHb level in the blood, which is directly related to the CO concentration in the ambient air.

For any given carbon monoxide concentration, the COHb level reaches equilibrium after a time period and retains this level without further increase. The effect can be reversible, however; COHb levels decrease as the concentration of CO in the ambient air decreases.

Acute effects of relatively high concentrations of CO and levels of COHb depend on exposure time and physical activity. The length of time required for the COHb level to reach equilibrium is a function of the level of physical activity of the exposed person—i.e., the more strenuous the activity, the more rapidly equilibrium is attained.

Excerpted from *Environmental Science & Technology*, Vol. 5, March 1971, pp. 212–214. Copyright 1971 by the American Chemical Society and reprinted by permission of the copyright owner. The author is affiliated with Intertech Corp., Princeton, New Jersey.

Until recently, most studies of the toxic effects of carbon monoxide dealt with acute effects of exposure to relatively high concentrations. Today, because of the widespread distribution of CO in the ambient atmosphere by the automobile, attention has turned to the chronic effects of long-term exposure to lower concentrations. The National Academy of Science (NAS) and the U.S. Department of Health, Education and Welfare (HEW) indicate that definite mental and physical impairment results from much lower levels of COHb than previously indicated. In fact, NAS states: "There is no level of CO in ambient air that is known to be without effect." (See Figure 2-1.)

As COHb Levels or Duration of Exposure Increase, Health Effects Become More Serious

COHb LEVEL, PERCENT	DEMONSTRATED EFFECTS
Less than 1.0	No apparent effect.
1.0 to 2.0	Some evidence of effect on behavioral performance.
2.0 to 5.0	Central nervous system effects. Impairment of time interval discrimination, visual acuity, brightness discrimination, and certain other psychomotor functions.
Greater than 5.0	Cardiac and pulmonary functional changes.
10.0 to 80.0	Headaches, fatigue, drowsiness, coma, respiratory failure, death.

Source: National Academy of Science and National Academy of Engineering

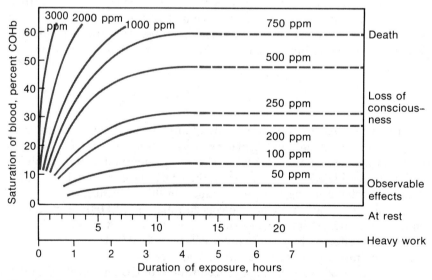

Figure 2-1. Acute effects. COHb levels in the blood depend upon the amount of CO in the atmosphere, duration of exposure, and type of physical activity.

Continuous exposure to ambient air containing 10 ppm carbon monoxide will produce a COHb equilibrium level greater than 2.0%, the point at which effects upon the nervous system become apparent. Similar exposure to concentrations of 30 ppm produces COHb levels greater than 5.0%.

CO levels of 50 to 100 ppm are not uncommon in crowded center-city

62

streets during the evening rush hour. Fortunately, at the present time, these levels are generally not of long duration. Levels of carbon monoxide in parking garages and tunnels are usually much higher and more persistent. These conditions show that carbon monoxide pollution of the atmosphere obviously presents a serious potential health hazard.

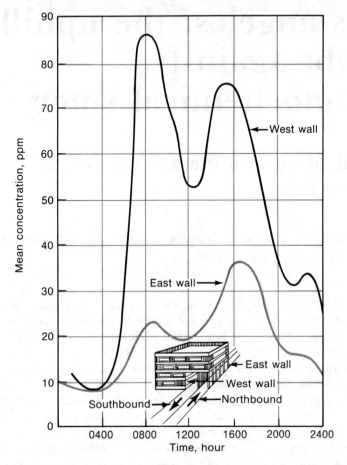

Figure 2-2. CO concentrations peak at rush hours. CO concentrations, taken at three different levels, 75 feet inside the FDR Drive at 54th St. in New York City show the differences in carbon monoxide buildup in completely enclosed areas versus partially open areas.

los angeles: the uphill fight against photochemical smog

staff of environmental science & technology

The nation's toughest emission controls do not seem enough to ensure clean air by 1980.

"When Los Angeles is clear, no other city has to worry any more about photochemical smog." The speaker is Arie Haagen-Smit, chairman of the California Air Resources Board; the place, the recent [1971] American Chemical Society meeting in Los Angeles. Haagen-Smit speaks with some authority: not only is his board responsible for air quality in the nation's most populous state, he personally is one of the men who first demonstrated that the type of smog experienced in Los Angeles is fundamentally different from that which still plagues cities such as Pittsburgh, Pa., and London, England. (London smog is a mixture of smoke and fog, whereas L.A. smog is produced by atmospheric chemical reactions between pollutants.)

Haagen-Smit is quick to add, however, that getting rid of smog in Los Angeles is anything but a simple task. Considering that Los Angeles has been actively working on air pollution abatement for over 20 years and is still subject to frequent smogs, progress must be regarded as somewhat discouraging.

first control attempts

Los Angeles County, an extensively urbanized area in Southern California, is located in a natural air trap. There are thermal inversions on 300 days of the year and the prevailing gentle westerly winds confine the air against a chain of hills to the east of this populated area. The county has a current population of about 7 million people; they possess—and seemingly are forever driving—4 million motor vehicles.

Reprinted from *Environmental Science & Technology,* Vol. 5, May 1971, pp. 394–395. Copyright 1971 by the American Chemical Society. Reprinted by permission of the copyright owner.

The big growth in the population of the county came during and after the Second World War. Eye irritation, now regarded as one of the qualitative indicators of smog, seems to have been noticed as early as 1942, although it was at that time assumed to be caused by industrial emissions. In fact, a butadiene plant which was shut down at the end of the war was a prime suspect.

The county board of supervisors in 1945 created an office of air pollution control, and this office promulgated some smoke emission ordinances. But recognizing the fact that such an office can have little real effect in a county that consisted of over 40 semiautonomous cities (there are now 77), the State of California in 1946 passed an act empowering each county to have jurisdiction over air pollution control within its boundaries. Thus the Los Angeles County Air Pollution Control District (LACAPCD) came into being. Similar districts in the neighboring counties of Orange, Riverside, and San Bernardino have since been set up.

Louis McCabe, first air pollution control officer of LACAPCD, initiated in 1947 a series of measures which resulted in a sharp decline in smoke and sulfur dioxide emissions from industrial plants. Equally important, McCabe also organized a research program that, by 1950, had established that Los Angeles-type smog was due to atmospheric reactions taking place between hydrocarbons and nitrogen oxides (nitric oxide, NO and nitrogen dioxide, NO_2, commonly expressed together as NO_x) in the presence of sunlight. . . .

Measures in the early fifties succeeded in markedly reducing hydrocarbon emissions from refineries in the county. By 1956, reports Haagen-Smit, emissions of hydrocarbons from these sources were reduced from 800 to 110 tons per day. Reducing emissions from automobiles, the major source of hydrocarbons and NO_x, turned out, however, to be a vastly more difficult job.

state steps in

In 1959, California passed a law giving the state control over motor vehicle emissions, thus preempting the power which had previously been wielded by the counties. LACAPCD is not entirely happy with what the state has done with that power, but it certainly gave California a bigger stick with which to berate the automakers in Detroit, who subsequently became the main target of pollution control efforts. California auto exhaust control regulations have in fact consistently preceded those of the federal government.

Los Angeles County, shorn of its jurisdiction over moving sources of pollution, went to work on stationary sources with a vengeance, using a series of rules and regulations that by almost everybody's admission lead the country in stringency. (Air pollution agencies in other parts of the country have often been forced to follow suit once "it has been done in L.A.") It is incredibly difficult today to spot in Los Angeles the types of visible emissions that are everywhere to be seen in midwestern and eastern cities. Sulfur dioxide (SO_2) emissions have been dramatically slashed: no coal is burned in the county and the common fuels are natural gas from Texas and low-sulfur (typically 0.2%S) fuel oil from Alaska or Indonesia.

65

The SO_2 emissions curve has flattened out after a steep decline. but promises to dip again when some new rules to control industrial emissions are put into effect.

alerts

Nonetheless, Los Angeles still experiences smog which, according to the accounts of residents, seems to be getting worse, not better. Official LA-CAPCD figures back up residents' impressions. There is severe eye irritation on approximately 70% of August and September days in the San Gabriel and Pomona Walnut valleys, and these locations in the northeast part of the county regularly experience ozone concentrations up to 0.50 parts per million (ppm) during the same periods. There have been 80 first alerts due to ozone called since 1955, nine of them during 1970. (A first alert is called when the instantaneous concentration of a pollutant closely approaches the maximum allowable concentration for the population at large; the value for an ozone first alert is 0.5 ppm.)

In fact, 1970 was "the worst year since 1956," according to Robert Chass, the current air pollution control officer for LACAPCD. There have even been three first alerts for carbon monoxide (CO) in 1971, each called when the instantaneous concentration at one of LACAPCD's 12 air monitoring stations reached 50 ppm.

Chass is an outspoken critic of the state and federal roles in air pollution control of motor vehicles. By his reckoning there will not be acceptable air quality in Los Angeles until at least 1982. The nub of his criticism is aimed at control of nitrogen oxides emissions, which, unlike the declining emissions of hydrocarbons, CO, and SO_2, are on the increase in the county. "By 1980, NO_x emissions from autos will be back to where they were in 1960. This is no progress at all," Chass claims. His feelings are understandable; he is responsible for air quality in a county where only 10% of the emissions—those from stationary sources—is under his jurisdiction. "We are nipping away at the 10%, while the state and federal people let the other 90% go unmolested," says the LACAPCD chief.

Of course, it is not quite true to say that California and U.S. authorities are letting the auto industry get off scot free, but progress is slow, to be sure. Crankcase vent controls were required on 1963 model year autos sold in California and exhaust control systems to reduce hydrocarbon and CO emissions were installed on 1966 models sold in the state. (Similar federal controls have since been instituted.) Unfortunately, the measures taken to reduce hydrocarbons and CO also had the effect of increasing NO_x emissions. NO_x control [was] required starting with 1971 automobiles, but it will take until 1980 to get NO_x emissions from the total vehicle population back to where they were in 1960, according to Chass.

headway

Progress on minimizing emissions from the internal-combustion engine is slow, and some people (not including Chass) doubt whether control sufficient to make L.A. photochemical smog disappear once and for all is ever possible in practice. However, extensive work in Detroit and by

66

government and nonprofit groups has shown that by suitable tuning of the engine (use of lean fuel–air mixtures and retarding of spark timing, for instance) and by installation of some form of catalytic or thermal reactor, the emissions goals in terms of CO, hydrocarbons, and NO_x can all be met.

At the same time, thoughtful people are asking whether emission control by itself can ever be more than just a temporary remedy. As Haagen-Smit suggests in his covering letter to California Governor Ronald Reagan which accompanies the 1970 report of the Air Resources Board, "Those who look beyond the 1980's know that a new and revolutionary course must be followed. This course will require a broader look at measures other than emission control. It will involve intelligent long-range planning and may require drastic changes in our way of living."

Whether Angelenos, already plagued by earthquakes and mud slides, will have the patience to wait for as long as it takes to start planning is another matter.

invisible particles in air

staff of chemistry

Four villains are the invisible particles of asbestos, lead, carbon, and silica.

To the naked eye, solid particles polluting the atmosphere can be either visible or invisible. Visible particles, being heavier, usually settle quite rapidly, but they are a nuisance and in some areas they are hazardous.

The real villains are the invisible particles, 10 microns or less in diameter, according to Gary B. Paulson, Louisiana State University in Baton Rouge. These particles, said Paulson, can ride indefinitely on wind currents and also carry still smaller, more dangerous particles which adhere through electrical charge. He points to four types of invisible particles: asbestos, lead, carbon, and silica.

Asbestos enters the atmosphere from sources such as brake linings, household ironing boards, and building insulation. For example, because of building projects, the asbestos content of the atmosphere in New York City has increased tremendously during the last 10 years. The particles are dart-shaped and can actually stick into walls of the lungs.

Carbon and lead enter the atmosphere from automobile exhaust. Lead has long been recognized as a health hazard, but little is known about the chemistry and physiological effects of lead complexes emitted by internal combustion engines.

Silica stems from foundries, mining operations, and natural erosion. In the lungs, it collects moisture, forming a gel which can gradually fill the lungs.

Using an electron microscope, Paulson plans to examine particles collected from the atmosphere in the vicinity of Baton Rouge. Also, he hopes to devise chemical techniques for analyzing very small quantities of materials having a health significance.

ten:

so$_2$ pollution: the next 30 years

f. a. rohrman, b. j. steigerwald, and j. h. ludwig

Will sulfur dioxide emission increase in the years to come? To what extent can we expect to control it? What's the range of possibilities? Here's a report of a study that probes these questions and turns up some surprising predictions.

Using today's control methods, projections based on Public Health Service studies indicate that sulfur dioxide emission levels in the United States will more than double within the next 20 years. Our studies conclude that this pollution will come primarily from the combustion of coal and oil in power plants. A secondary contributor will be the combined effect of all other sources of sulfur dioxide emission. The rate of increase should decline after 1970 as a result of nuclear plants replacing obsolete plants, and absorbing many new load requirements. An actual decrease in emission levels is anticipated after 1990.

These predictions and calculations are based on the degree of control now applied. However, some degree of increased control should take place over the next few decades. Increased public concern for the hazards of air pollution will certainly promote increased research into emission control techniques. Los Angeles County and the cities of New York and St. Louis have already enacted legislation restricting the use of fuels with excess sulfur. The Secretary of the Department of Health, Education, and Welfare has forbidden the use of high sulfur fuels in New York, Chicago and Philadelphia federal facilities. He's recommended the use of low sulfur fuels in the N.Y.–N.J. interstate area.

The extent to which emission-control technology is advanced and implemented will determine the extent to which the projected pollution levels

Reprinted with permission of *Power Magazine*, copyright May 1967, pp. 82–83. The authors are affiliated with the National Center for Air Pollution Control, Public Health Service.

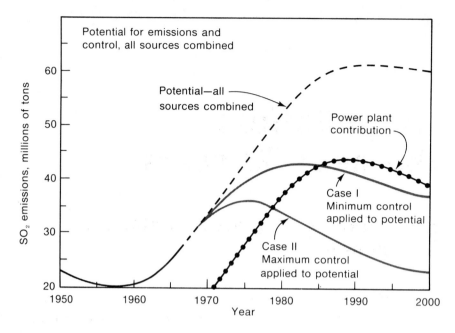

Figure 2-3. Several sources contribute to total SO₂ emission levels. The combustion of coal and oil in power plants is a major source of sulfur dioxide emissions in the United States. Other sources add significantly to the total emission levels. These additional sources include coal and oil combustion for processes other than power plant operations, ore smelting operations, and petroleum refining operations. The potential for increased emissions of sulfur dioxide in the future is tremendous. To what extent we can hope to reduce the potential depends on the degree of control we apply. It may be to only a minimally reasonable degree (Case I curve), or to a degree corresponding to our maximum technological capability (Case II curve).

will be decreased. However, it is much more difficult to predict the extent of future control than it is to project future emission levels. Control technology is not firmly established for power plants; fuel desulfurization methods are under scrutiny and the potential exists for rapid changes; the economics of bulk energy fuels is very changeable; a great deal of new research is underway to determine the levels of sulfur dioxide that can be tolerated in urban atmospheres. These factors greatly influence the speed with which control techniques will be improved and the degree of control which ultimately will be achieved.

In order to indicate a range of possibilities, two control schedules were considered. These schedules were applied to the present-control projections, and the above-curves calculated. They suggest a range in the degree of control which we should be able to attain. The schedules are based on assumptions believed adequate for the purpose of indicating such a range of future emission levels.

The term "control" used in these two cases is meant to include all technological methods by which sulfur dioxide emission is reduced. One hundred percent control would mean that a plant emitted no sulfur dioxide to the atmosphere.

case i

The assumptions are severe but realistic: i.e., that there will be no early developments, and no widespread use of highly effective gas cleaning methods; also that there will be no rapid application of available methods of fuel desulfurization.

Beginning in 1970, 1% control would be applied to existing power plants; this would increase 1% each year. Starting in 1975, 5% control would be applied yearly to new power plants and would increase to a maximum of 80% control for new plants put on steam in 1990. After the initial year, control for these new plants, as for existing plants, would increase 1% each year. This scheme assumes some increase in the use of fuel desulfurization, selection of fuels with lower sulfur content, uses of fuel additives, improved design of plants, and eventual perfection of processes to remove sulfur dioxide from plant stacks.

For all sources of emission other than power plants, 1% control will begin immediately, increasing 1% each year to an ultimate 35%.

case ii

The control assumptions are very severe and probably represent the maximum that can be achieved technically. They would require an immediate and vigorous program of research and pilot plant efforts on methods of gas cleaning and fuel desulfurization. Application of control methods as they become available would be mandatory.

As a result, for new power plants put into operation in 1975 (including replacements or expansion of existing plants), 75% control of sulfur dioxide emission would be expected. This 75% control would be increased 1% each year after 1975, to a maximum of 90% in 1990. Since there is a minimum 5-year lag between initial power plant design and the time when the unit is put on steam, the initiation of control by 1975 requires that proven designs be available by 1970. Extensive developments in the next few years are required in order to achieve this goal.

Beginning in 1970, a control level of 2% is assumed in all coal and oil combustion processes. This would increase 2% each year to a maximum of 50% control in 1994. (New power plants built after 1975 are excluded here, being covered by the standards already discussed.) This assumption requires increased use of available techniques for fuel desulfurization; selection of fuels with lower sulfur content; and the utilization of miscellaneous schemes for control of sulfur dioxide, such as the use of fuel additives.

further off

Even a casual study of the predicted sulfur dioxide emission levels indicates the seriousness of the situation. As a result of our study we foresee a continued increase of coal and oil combustion in power plants until nuclear fuels become dominant. These predictions are shown in Table 2–1. The prob-

71

Table 2-1. Anticipated Power Plant Coal and Oil Consumption

YEAR	COAL-TONS x10⁶	OIL-BARRELS x10⁶
1966*	267	142
1970	375	175
1975	550	225
1980	750	240
1990	875	250
2000	800	230

*Federal Power Commission data

lem is even more acute when you remember that power plants are traditionally constructed near the demand—heavily populated urban areas. Therefore, the levels of sulfur dioxide emissions in selected areas of the country will be even greater than the national average figures represented in our prediction.

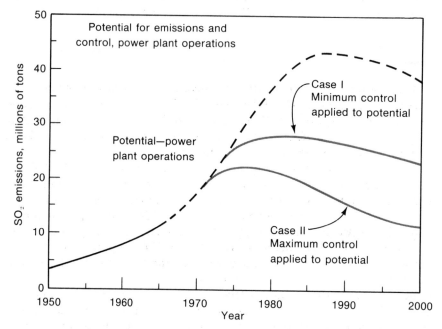

Figure 2-4. Greatest control opportunities are in power plant operations. Our study was concerned with figures representing a national average. On such a scale, more emissions result from power plant operations than from any other source. The absolute amount of power plant emissions can not help but increase in the years to come. This is where the greatest opportunities for control exist. Again we have a choice. Will we reduce emissions by applying only a technologically attainable degree of control? Or will we push our technology to its limit and apply the maximum degree of control possible? Once more we're presented with a range of possibilities, and an indication of what we can look forward to in the remainder of this century.

If today's control techniques are not expanded in quality and extent of implementation, sulfur dioxide emission levels will be more than doubled by 1990. Even with advanced control techniques, to the maximum extent technologically possible, future emission levels will increase by nearly 25% before 1975. Even with the application of realistic, though still severe control methods, we can expect to see a 75% increase over today's levels.

The two cases are not meant as arguments for what should be done, but do present a picture of the extent to which improved control techniques can affect the future. The day when we can expect to eliminate sulfur dioxide emissions completely is still many years away. Until that day arrives, however, we do have the opportunity and capability of doing a great deal to minimize these emissions.

citizen role in implementation of clean air standards

u.s. environmental protection agency

What are the national air quality standards for hazardous pollutants as established by the Environmental Protection Agency?

the national air quality standards

Under the Clean Air Act of 1970, the Administrator of the Environmental Protection Agency is required to establish national air quality standards for hazardous pollutants. National primary standards, to protect health, and secondary standards, to protect public welfare, have been promulgated for six pollutants. . . .

To achieve these clean-air objectives, the States must set and enforce limits on emissions of these pollutants from existing sources. The Administrator of EPA has the responsibility to set limits on emissions from new stationary sources and new sources of hazardous pollutants, but the primary responsibility for enforcing these limits also lies with the States. EPA enforces its own limits on emissions from new motor vehicles.

The law requires each State to submit to EPA by January 31, 1972, its plan for regulating the six pollutants in order to achieve the national standards. EPA must review this plan by May 31, 1972, and will approve and adopt those plans that show clear promise of cleaning the air enough by 1975 to comply with national standards. If, however, a State fails to submit an acceptable plan within the prescribed period, or fails to revise a plan EPA finds unacceptable, then EPA must design and promulgate an implementation plan that will do the job.

compliance schedules

One of the most critical steps in the implementation of a plan is the development of the compliance schedule. Within 6 months after EPA ap-

Edited from an October 1971 report by the U.S. Environmental Protection Agency, Washington, D. C. 20460.

proves a State implementation plan, the State must submit such a schedule showing when individual industries in a region will reduce their emissions to meet the national air quality standards in the time allowed by law. A schedule that allows unnecessary time for compliance will needlessly delay the achievement of the region's clean-air objectives—a schedule that is more rigid than necessary may be needlessly burdensome to an industry.

State implementation plans may, if the citizens wish, provide for public hearing of these compliance schedules and review of any variances that may be sought by specific industries to delay their achievement of emission limits.

how much reduction of pollutants will meet the national standards?

After an agency has defined the existing air quality and identified the source of pollution in a region, a determination can begin as to how much to reduce existing emissions to reach the national air quality standards.

A simple mathematical calculation permits a general estimate of the percentage of reduction necessary throughout the region. Three facts must be known: (1) the existing concentration of a pollutant; (2) the air quality standard for that pollutant; and (3) the background level of that pollutant in the region. This is the "rollback" technique:

$$Percentage\ of\ Emission\ Reduction\ =\ \frac{(A\text{-}C)-(B\text{-}C)}{(A\text{-}C)}$$

$$A = existing\ concentration$$
$$B = air\ quality\ standard$$
$$C = background\ concentration$$

Once the percentage of rollback has been determined, the emission control strategy may be devised. This strategy is expressed in regulations and timetables for the prevention, abatement, and control of a pollutant.

The primary impact of control regulations, especially emission limits, will be on the readily identifiable sources of pollution. If it is necessary to effect a major reduction in total emissions of a given pollutant, and if small improvement would result from the state control of existing transportation sources, small home heating and commercial sources, then the larger and more significant individual sources must accept relatively more stringent control of their emissions.

techniques of emission control

Techniques available for control of a pollutant may include: (1) fuel substitution; (2) changes in processes; (3) installation of gas cleaning equipment; (4) process relocation and use of tall stacks; (5) source shutdowns; (6) changed transportation policies; and (7) new land use policies.

Fuel substitution commonly involves the replacement of fuels having a high sulphur content with fuels having less sulfur. The availability of fuels with sulfur contents of 1% or less may be dependent upon the market peculiarities of the fuel industry. The cost of fuel substitution is usually calculated on a differential basis, that is: the control cost is the difference between present fuel costs and the cost of the alternative low-sulfur fuel. Another form of fuel substitution might call for a change from energy production, which requires burning, to an energy source that does not involve burning, such as nuclear or hydro-electric power. The environmental aspects of such a substitution should be clearly understood and given full consideration.

Process changes may require increased maintenance or the purchase of more modern equipment and facilities. Costs are difficult to isolate since new equipment may replace obsolete or worn equipment. Process changes can sometime be instituted at minimal or no cost, or in some cases result in actual savings.

The effectiveness of *gas cleaning* or other equipment to collect pollutants may be successful in some cases, but not in others, if the resulting emissions contain small, fine particles that may cause problems of health and visibility.

Process relocation and the use of tall stacks do not reduce emissions, but may reduce ground-level concentrations of pollutants in a region. There is a possibility that the pollutant may be transported by air currents to another region where it may add to the burden of pollution of that area.

Source shutdown is an alternative to air pollution control. Its social costs and benefits should be carefully weighed in any consideration of its use. Worn out, obsolete plants may elect to close rather than undertake necessary control measures to protect the health of a community. If such a plant produces a socially valuable product, and is located elsewhere, a source shutdown is, in effect, a source relocation.

Transportation policies may be developed or improved to reduce the impact of pollution from moving sources. Construction of urban highways and freeways may take second place to the development of rapid and mass transit systems. Patterns of motor vehicle use may be changed, and inspection programs may be initiated to assure that vehicular emissions are not excessive.

Land-use policies may be viewed as a tool to reduce future pollution in some areas. An environmentally sound land-use policy would ensure that sources of pollution would be located, designed, constructed, equipped, and operated so as to produce the least adverse effect on its environment, and would not interfere with the maintenance of applicable air quality standards.

national air quality standards

SULFUR OXIDES

Sulfur oxides come primarily from the combustion of sulfur-containing fossil fuels. Their presence has been associated with the increased incidence of respiratory diseases, increased death rates, and property damage.
Primary standard
• 80 micrograms per cubic meter (0.03 ppm) annual arithmetic mean.
• 365 micrograms per cubic meter (0.14 ppm) as a maximum 24-hour concentration not to be exceeded more than once a year.

• 60 micrograms per cubic meter (0.02 ppm) annual arithmetic mean.
• 260 micrograms per cubic meter (0.1 ppm) maximum 24-hour concentration not to be exceeded more than once a year.
• 1,300 micrograms per cubic meter (0.5 ppm) as a maximum three-hour concentration not to be exceeded more than once a year.

PARTICULATE MATTER

Particulate matter, either solid or liquid, may originate in nature or as a result of industrial processes and other human activities. By itself or in association with other pollutants, particulate matter may injure the lungs or cause adverse effects elsewhere in the body. Particulates also reduce visibility and contribute to property damage and soiling.
Primary standard
• 75 micrograms per cubic meter annual geometric mean.
• 260 micrograms per cubic meter as a maximum 24-hour concentration not to be exceeded more than once a year.
Secondary standard
• 60 micrograms per cubic meter annual geometric mean.
• 150 micrograms per cubic meter as a maximum 24-hour concentration not to be exceeded more than once a year.

CARBON MONOXIDE

Carbon monoxide is a by-product of the incomplete burning of carbon-containing fuels and of some industrial processes. It decreases the oxygen-carrying ability of the blood and, at levels often found in city air, may impair mental processes.
Primary and secondary standards
• 10 milligrams per cubic meter (9 ppm) as a maximum eight-hour concentration not to be exceeded more than once a year.
• 40 milligrams per cubic meter (35 ppm) as a maximum one-hour concentration not to be exceeded more than once a year.
Both the one-hour limit and the eight-hour standard afford protection against the occurrence of carboxy-hemoglobin levels in the blood of 2 per cent. Carboxy-hemoglobin levels above 5 per cent have been associated with physiological stress in patients with heart disease. Blood carboxy-hemoglobin levels approaching 2 per cent have been associated by some researchers with impaired psychomotor responses.

PHOTOCHEMICAL OXIDANTS

Photochemical oxidants are produced in the atmosphere when reactive organic substances, chiefly hydrocarbons, and nitrogen oxides are exposed to sunlight. Photochemical oxidants irritate mucous membranes, reduce resistance to respiratory infection, damage plants, and contribute to the deterioration of materials.

Primary and secondary standards
• 160 micrograms per cubic meter (0.08 ppm) as a maximum one-hour concentration not to be exceeded more than once a year.

HYDROCARBONS

Hydrocarbons in the air come mainly from the processing, marketing and use of petroleum products. Some of the hydrocarbons combine with nitrogen oxides in the air to form photochemical oxidants. The hydrocarbons standards, therefore, are for use as a guide in devising implementation plans to achieve the oxidant standards.
Primary and secondary standards
• 160 micrograms per cubic meter (0.24 ppm) as a maximum three-hour concentration (6 to 9 a.m.) not to be exceeded more than once a year.

NITROGEN OXIDES

Nitrogen oxides usually originate in high-temperature combustion processes. The presence of nitrogen dioxide in the air has been associated with a variety of respiratory diseases. Nitrogen dioxide is essential in the natural production of photochemical oxidant.
Primary and secondary standards
• 100 micrograms per cubic meter (0.05 ppm) annual arithmetic mean.
The Environmental Protection Agency is examining other pollutants to determine whether any may be covered by future air quality standards.

the
abuse
of
water

No chemical substance is more integral to life on earth than water (H_2O). Life began in the water of ancient seas, and even today those creatures that have since evolved to desert climates survive by virtue of strict water conservation.

Also, no chemical substance is more integral to our earth's physical environment than water. As a vapor it absorbs radiation to influence the heat balance and temperature of our environment, and it brings moisture to the continents. As a liquid it erodes and shapes our land, creates soil, transports minerals, and moderates climate. More recently it has served the workhorse role of carrying millions of tons of man's wastes out of sight. In so doing, it has become polluted.

Even polluted water serves our physical environment, but it spells disaster to our biological environment. Poisonous substances, organisms of disease, and sun-inhibiting silt which blocks photosynthesis are all destructive to life. Still, nothing so universally degrades water as the pollutants that rob it of free oxygen, the oxygen critical to most aquatic life and necessary for water's remarkable self-purification.

Oxygen from the atmosphere dissolves poorly in water, rarely reaching a level higher than 10 parts per million. Yet on this remarkably small content of dissolved oxygen falls the burden of maintaining a water environment viable for life. Because of the normal paucity of oxygen, this water environment is the most delicate of all and is easily upset by any unusual demand, chemical or biological, for oxygen. Organic chemicals, garbage, and animal and human wastes all contain carbon and hydrogen, which deplete free oxygen through chemical combinations that turn it to carbon dioxide and water.

Nutrients like phosphorus (P), a major constituent of most laundry detergents, have a more subtle influence on oxygen. With other nutrients, phosphorus stimulates the growth of algae. Offensive enough in their great floating mats, the algae eventually die and sink, there to gobble up the scarce supply of oxygen. In this way, clean water becomes putrid, and phosphorus-containing detergents are indelibly stamped on the growing list of ecological no-no's.

On analysis, today's water problems stem almost exclusively from man's *short-term* exploitation and misuse of water. The articles that follow substantiate this conclusion over a wide range of water resource topics. Article 12, "The Aswan Disaster," shows how our errors can be monumental if we do not consider water as part of the total environment. Article 13 shows how the same is true when we use the ocean as a major dumping ground, and Article 14, when we are careless about marine oil spills. Article 15, "Waste-Water Treatment: The Tide Is Turning," shows that at least a start has been made in waste-water treatment, a start impelled by the spread of disease that accompanied waste water in the past. But it is only a start, barely good enough to get by.

As the last three articles show, the effects of phosphorus on water exemplify man's thoughtless disregard for broad consequences. One consideration alone brought phosphorus into detergents: better cleaning power. Questions about water quality in every corner of our complex, life-giving environment were brushed aside while we focused on the narrow environment of the washing machine. Only in the past few years have the wide consequences of this myopia become apparent. These consequences, and some options for their cure, are described in the final three articles on eutrophication, phosphate replacements, and soap.

twelve:

the aswan disaster

claire sterling

After harnessing the world's mightiest river by building the most extravagantly ambitious dam ever conceived by man, the Egyptians have less water than they had before.

Of all the dams built by rich nations for poor nations hoping to grow richer that way, the one built by Soviet Russia for Egypt is in a class of its own. The High Dam at Aswan is the biggest and most expensive in the world. The late President Nasser spent over a billion dollars on it and changed the course of history to get it: broke with the West, nationalized the Suez Canal, brought on the Suez War and so invited Soviet penetration of Egypt, the Middle East, and the Mediterranean. It made his political fortunes, but spread such ecological havoc that his country may never get over it.

This isn't just Nasser's fault. The blame must be shared by the West German engineers who designed the High Dam, the World Bank which approved it, the American State Department which agreed to finance it and backed out only for political reasons, the Russians who finally let Nasser have it—in short, an entire generation distracted by politics and bemused by technology.

There was no excuse for all the eminent international experts who did not see what was coming, since at least one did. A few weeks before ground was broken for the High Dam in 1960, the distinguished Egyptian hydrologist, Dr. Abdel Aziz Ahmed, warned the Institution of Civil Engineers in London that the dam's conception was "foreign to Egypt and a complete reversal of time-honored Nile irrigation policy." To build it, he said, would be "unwise and indeed extremely hazardous." He was fired as soon as he got back to Cairo—which took care of Dr. Ahmed but not, unfortunately, of what he had warned about. These were some of the things he rightly predicted would go wrong:

• The dam, built without sluices, would trap an annual 134 million tons of Nile sediment "containing volcanic materials which produce the most fertile soil on the face of the earth." Since practically all cultivated soil

This August 1971 article is taken from *National Parks and Conservation Magazine* and was adapted from a series that first appeared in the *Washington Post,* copyright © The Washington Post Company. Reprinted by permission of the Washington Post Company and *National Parks and Conservation Magazine.* The author is a free-lance journalist living in Rome.

in Egypt was formed and nourished by the sediment, for which no adequate man-made substitute has yet been devised, the lack of it would strike at the heart of Egyptian agriculture.

• The silt-free water would scour the riverbed downstream, eroding the Nile's banks and undermining every barrier-dam and bridge on its 600-mile course from Aswan to the sea.

• Evaporation, seepage, and changes in underground water movements would cause such colossal losses in the lake forming behind the High Dam that Egypt *would almost certainly end up with less water than it had before.*

Dr. Ahmed couldn't think of everything. He failed for instance to anticipate the decimation of marine life in the eastern Mediterranean, erosion of the Delta coastline by sea currents, a rise in soil salinity threatening to put millions of acres irreversibly out of cultivation, an unnerving increase in the exhausting water-borne disease called bilharzia, a potential invasion from the Sudan of a killer-mosquito carrying the deadliest kind of malaria. What he did predict, though, has come true with a vengeance.

If the Egyptian fellah has been freed of ancestral fears that the annual Nile flood would bring too much water, or too little, he knows with chilling certainty now that the miraculous muddy brown floodwaters will never come again. One need only look down upon the limpid Nile and see through to its sandy bottom, as I did from a balcony of Cairo's Semiramis Hotel, to sense the enormity of this change. "Terrifying, isn't it?" an Egyptian friend murmured, clutching my arm as he pointed. It is.

Without the Nile sediment, much of Egypt's six million cultivated acres need chemical fertilizer already, as all farmland will in the next few years. A team of Egyptian soil experts has found that potassium, phosphorus, nitrogen, calcium, and magnesium must also be added to the Delta's once inexhaustible soil within four or five years, and copper, zinc, molybdenum, borum, and manganese in fifteen or twenty. Apart from these micro- and macro-nutrients, Egyptian agriculture is absorbing 2,350,000 tons of artificial fertilizer so far. Two-thirds of it, according to Egyptian and World Bank calculations, is the amount needed to make up for lost fertility and mineral content once supplied by the silt. The cost of just this much comes to upwards of a hundred million dollars a year, cutting about a fifth of the average income from the yield per acre—quite a cut for a farmer earning perhaps $75 a year. This is a recurrent, annual expense, for eternity.

Furthermore, without the flood to flush the earth of soil salts, salinity is reaching alarming levels not only in the heavily waterlogged Delta where it has been a problem for years, but throughout Middle and Upper Egypt. The situation could become "dramatic" in barely a decade, soil scientists say, with yields steadily declining until millions of acres are lost to cultivation entirely. There is a remedy: closed underground drains can do wonders to counteract salinity and raise yields, and the World Bank is already helping Egypt to install them on a million acres of Delta land. But this alone—the most ambitious tile drainage scheme in the world—will cost $147 million, of which the World Bank will put up less than a tenth, as a loan. To install tile drains and the pumps to go with them in the rest of Egypt would cost well over a billion dollars: a quarter of Egypt's national income, as much again as the High Dam itself.

Meanwhile, reclamation of desert land with the Dam's stored waters

85

has been sharply disappointing. Although Nasser had hoped to reclaim 1,300,000 acres, still the government's figure, he knew from soil studies done in 1964 that there wasn't half that much suitable land to be reclaimed in all Egypt at less than astronomical expense. It is impossible to be certain of how much has actually been reclaimed, the official answer depending on which official is asked. Nevertheless, the known reclamation projects under Egyptian and foreign auspices add up to less than 300,000 acres. At an average $1,200 an acre, even this comes to over a third of a billion dollars—yet another third of the High Dam's cost.

A good part of this stunning figure can be traced to the same lost silt. The silt was so invaluable to build up badly degraded desert soil that some reclamation companies dug tons of it out of the Delta and trucked it to the new lands. That alone cost $240 an acre. The alternative, though, was four to five years of laborious build-up before the soil could be used at all.

On the other side of the ledger is a clear and substantial gain: the conversion of 700,000 acres from flood to canal irrigation. With double-cropping, that has added half again to the yearly production of these lands. Yet here, too, the Nile has found a way to strike back. The fellaheen working on these converted lands were not afflicted with bilharzia before. They are now.

There has always been bilharzia in Egypt: parasites' eggs have been found in mummified viscera from Tutankh-Amen's tomb. But it did not become the plague it is until men made it so by introducing extensive irrigation at the start of this century. Even then the number of carrier-snails was kept down by the annual Nile floods washing them out to sea, until the High Dam was sealed at Aswan in 1964, ending the floods forever.

The snail-carrier of bilharzia (known in medical circles as schistomiasis) cannot survive for long in fast-flowing rivers. It is most at home in placid waters, where it may be carried by migrating birds or the wind. Once settled, the snails can multiply at a rate which will increase their numbers 50,000-fold in four months. Lake Nasser, forming behind the High Dam, is thickly infested with these snails along its entire 300-mile shoreline. That is not yet the calamity it might be only because hardly anybody lives there. Infestation is much the same in the canals dug since the High Dam was built, as in all the others lacing the country.

The snail does not attack human beings. It simply plays host to the prickly-spined blood flukes which do. The fluke's larvae need only be deposited in the water by an infected person's urinating, defecating, or merely bathing, whereupon it homes in on the snail to lie in wait for the next human being to come in contact with the infested water.

A man can die of bilharzia, but is more often condemned to live in growing pain and exhaustion. The chronic sufferer becomes steadily weaker from stomach cramps and damage to the heart, lungs, liver. He may contract cirrhosis, bladder and kidney infections, cancer; and even if not, he is rarely able to put in more than three hours' work a day. There is no lasting cure for bilharzia, since anybody who shakes it off in the morning can pick it up again before nightfall.

For all the efforts made by Egyptian and UN agencies, therefore, endemic bilharzia persists. Even before the High Dam was built, 14 million of Egypt's then 40 million people had it; one out of every ten deaths was caused by it; and the cost to the state in lost working time alone ran to half a billion dollars yearly. No official figures have been released on the number of additional victims since new canals came into being after the High Dam was sealed. But in some areas, such as Kom Ombo just below Aswan, the rate is known to have jumped from zero to 80 per cent. Consultants of the World Health Organization think the national total of fresh cases is somewhere around 2,650,000—an increase of roughly 20 per cent, at an added yearly cost to Egypt of $80 million.

This is not the only health menace created by the High Dam. Less known but potentially more sinister is the threat of killer-malaria from the *Anopheles gambia* mosquito, the deadliest carrier in Africa. *A. gambia* has a high biting frequency, prefers a human blood meal to any other, feeds on humans a hundred times more than other mosquitoes do, has a higher life expectancy, and can breed with perfect equanimity in anything from a pond or pool to a muddy hoofprint or puddle in an old rubber tire. It is found, all too often, in areas of the Sudan barely fifty miles from the southern shores of Lake Nasser.

A fifty-mile hop is nothing to *A. gambia,* which has wandered much deeper into Egypt on occasion, with memorable results. In 1942 it got far enough to infect a million Egyptians, killing 100,000 of them: the World Health Organization calls that epidemic "one of the saddest events in the history of tropical medicine." In reminding Egypt of this experience when Lake Nasser began to form, UN experts have rendered an invaluable service. For if it was hard enough to catch up with *Anopheles gambia* in 1942, it would be all but impossible should this murderous insect get a foothold now in the vast expanse of Lake Nasser's impounded waters, with all those idyllic inlets and swamps, and an endlessly twisting shallow shoreline.

So far, it has failed to show. Vigilance, of a sort, is kept at several malaria stations run jointly by the Sudan and Egypt, at Abu Simbel, Kom Ombo, Edfu, and the High Dam itself. Travelers coming from the Sudan are sprayed with insecticides, though the right kind are not always handy: one UN official checking on the checkpoint recently was sprayed with Flit. Since some strains of *Anopheles gambia* have already developed immunity even to DDT, these malaria stations are going to have to do better than that. The situation might improve under steady if discreet UN pressure. As things stand now, though, one vicious little mosquito nestling in the tweed pocket of a tireless tourist could put a curse on all Egypt.

It is chastening to reflect upon the fact that after harnessing the world's mightiest river by building the most extravagantly ambitious dam ever conceived by man, the Egyptians have less water than they had before. Whether this happened because experts didn't know enough or politicians simply didn't care to listen is not altogether clear. Whoever made the mistakes, though, the High Aswan Dam is unmistakably losing the water it ought to be saving.

This is particularly hard on the Egyptians, whose existence depends wholly on the Nile's waters. Rain almost never falls in most of their country, though a light shower did fall once on Thebes during the reign of Psammenitus: "an unparalleled event," Herodotus tells us. The instinct to hoard every drop of Nile water has therefore been strong since civilization began on the river's banks; and it is a lot stronger now that Egypt's 13,510 square miles of habitable land must support 33 million people, doomed to become 60 million in just three decades.

The whole idea of the High Dam was to store enough of the Nile's yearly floodwaters to irrigate existing lands, reclaim more from the desert, and guarantee eternally against drought and famine. Nilologists thought the minimum needed would be 163 billion cubic meters. Lake Nasser was supposed to hold that much, and should have filled up by 1970. But it is not yet [as of mid-1971] half full and, according to Egypt's foremost limnologist, Prof. Abdel Fattah Gohar, is unlikely to get much fuller for at least two centuries.

One reason is a presumably elementary error in arithmetic. Any engineer will tell you that calculating probable evaporation losses in a large body of water is child's play—even if the body is as large as Lake Nasser, in the hottest and driest corner of the globe. Yet where the High Dam's planners had allowed for a colossal evaporation loss of 10 billion cubic meters a year, the figure turns out to be 15 billion. What the planners overlooked, it seems, was the much higher wind velocity over such a vast expanse of water, adding greatly to evaporation losses.

As a string of smaller and cheaper dams closer to Cairo would have avoided this, it seems a shocking waste. But it is nothing compared to other losses entailed by tampering so casually with a river whose watershed spans nearly the entire breadth of the African continent.

Three-quarters of a century ago, an eminent hydrologist named John Ball demonstrated that, for some 300 miles between Wadi Halfa and Aswan, the Nile cut across an immense underground bed of water, part of an aquifer of porous Nubian sandstone a million kilometers square, underlying the Libyan Desert from Egypt and the Sudan to Chad and Senegal. Incalculable quantities of water were feeding into the river, he said, from the permeable bed beneath it and the sandstone lining its Western banks.

Then, in 1902, the first Aswan Dam was built. In a remarkably short time, the millenial movement of this groundwater was reversed. Under counter-pressure from that first Aswan reservoir, the water began to move elsewhere through countless fissures in the sandstone; and a tremendous quantity also began to seep out through the porous rock from the reservoir itself. From 1902 to 1964, when the new High Dam was sealed, the Aswan reservoir stored some 5 billion cubic meters of water a year for seasonal use. By building it, however, the Egyptians lost 12 billion cubic meters a year from the Nile through seepage and reversed underground flows.

So far, nobody knows how much more than that is escaping from Lake Nasser. But one might guess at the calamitous figure by a simple comparison: the new lake is meant to store thirty times more water than the old Aswan reservoir; and seepage tends to be greater in deep reservoirs with long shore lines and large depths of permeable material along the banks.

This doesn't necessarily mean that the Egyptians are condemned to drought and famine. They could be, with Lake Nasser less than half full, if the floods should run low for several summers on end. But even if not, they must make do now with 2 billiion cubic meters of water less than the 55.5 billion that are their "established right" under the Nile Waters Agreement with the Sudan—and 10 billion less than the famous nilologist, Dr. H. E. Hurst, has said they must have for irrigation, river transport, and the High Dam's turbines.

There is always the chance of working out some other plan to increase the flow into Lake Nasser. The biggest scheme, talked of for years, is the projected Jonglei Canal to drain the Sudan's great Sudd swamps, where 14 billion cubic meters of the White Nile's waters are lost in evaporation each year. Recently, however, surveys have revealed that nearly a million semi-nomads live amongst these swamps: nobody, apparently, had the smallest idea of this. Even if it were practical to resettle so many people, at a cost of around a billion dollars, the water thus gained might well be lost in Lake Nasser as so much of the rest.

Things might get better in time, as the fine clay suspended in Lake Nasser's waters starts to seal the porous banks. But if the fissures are large in these endless banks of sandstone, and the escaping water finds an outlet to the sea, or another lake, or a land depression, it could flow downhill forever.

It was in the same month of the same year—May 1964—that two of the world's biggest man-made lakes began to form: Volta Lake behind the Akosombo Dam in Ghana, and Lake Nasser.

Lake Volta is about full now, and teeming with fish. The Ashantis native to the area believe the water is lying in wait to pull them in, and so will not go near it. But the fish had no sooner appeared, incredible in size and numbers, than the fishermen to catch them turned up from nowhere. Today there are 60,000 Tongas, Adas, Gas, and Fantis who came to the lake on their own initiative. The annual catch has now reached 60,000 tons.

On the other hand, Lake Nasser is not yet half full; and though it should supposedly be choked with fish—it is a much better fed lake than Volta, since 134 million tons of marvelously rich Nile sediment sink to its bottom each year—the annual fish-catch is not yet a tenth of Lake Volta's, running to only 4,500 tons a year. This is all the sadder for the Egyptians for their having lost 18,000 tons of sardines in the Mediterranean just because the Nile silt is sinking to Lake Nasser's bottom instead of flowing out to sea as it had always done. Without it, the whole continental shelf running along Egypt's Mediterranean coast has only a third of the nutrient plankton and organic carbons it used to have: not only sardines, but mackerel, lobster, and shrimp have therefore disappeared.

It is possible that Lake Nasser has a lot more fish, but simply hasn't the people to pull them out. So far only 3,000 fishermen have wandered into this hostile wilderness, living in conditions too wretched to attract more.

There is not much chance of conditions improving soon, because Lake Nasser is not filling up as it was supposed to. Until the lake's final shoreline is certain, there can be no permanent settlements around it, still less the water to grow food enough to sustain settlers. As things stand now, every drop of water in this new reservoir is needed downstream of the dam.

The danger in these circumstances is that Lake Nasser will be too long underfished: unless the fish population is cropped sufficiently it may not even reach the level UN experts count on for 1980, when it should by paper-reckoning yield a yearly catch of 16,600 tons.

The spawning, eating, fattening, sporting, traveling, and dying habits of fish in these enormous new tracts of water are still largely a mystery to the experts, as experience in the lake behind Zambia's great Kariba Dam has shown. Formed five years earlier than Lakes Volta and Nasser, the one at Kariba started out with an explosion of fish to dazzle the mind. Predictions were that the catch would reach 20,000 tons a year in no time. But by 1963 the catch had dropped to 4,000 tons, by the next year to 2,100 tons, and by 1967 to so little that a corps of 2,000 fishermen dwindled to 500.

Nobody is quite sure why this came about. But among the reasons already known are at least two of appreciable interest: an aquatic fern called *Salvinia auriculata* suddenly grew up in the lake, quickly forming a mat too thick for boats to penetrate, so that fishermen could not do the necessary cropping; and, after being initially dispersed by changed ecological conditions in the river, predator fish began to multiply at a terrifying rate.

It could happen anywhere, and may in fact be happening in Lake Volta already, where, after going up like a rocket, the fish population is starting to go down.

The one thing we may be sure of, therefore, is that we cannot be sure of very much where fish in new super-lakes are concerned. Even for those of us who don't care much for fish, the story is worth noting, if only as a cautionary tale.

ocean dumping poses growing problem

staff of chemical & engineering news

Dillingham study surveys extent, nature, effects of marine disposal, recommends remedial action.

Public concern about environmental pollution is zeroing in on a new target: an increase in ocean dumping of waste materials. Three months ago [August 1970] the media focused on the case of *S.S. LeBaron Russell Briggs,* which the Army sank with tons of nerve gas aboard. The outrage aroused by the incident caused the U.S. to assure the world it would never again dump chemical warfare weapons into the sea.

Last month, [October 1970], President Nixon received a report by the Council on Environmental Quality (CEQ) on current marine waste disposal activities. The President said he would implement the report's recommendations by proposing legislation in the next Congress to regulate all dumping, and ban or strictly limit dumping of harmful materials. Moreover, the chairman of the Senate Subcommittee on Air and Water Pollution, Sen. Edmund S. Muskie (D.-Me.), is already introducing a bill with the same objectives in the final weeks of this Congress.

major resource

Information on the extent, nature, and effects of ocean dumping activities has been hard to come by. A major resource in future action on ocean dumping will therefore be a 220-page systematic study of oceanic disposal by barge of liquid and solid wastes from U.S. coastal cities, prepared by Dr. David D. Smith and Robert P. Brown, Dillingham Environmental Co., La Jolla, Calif., for the Bureau of Solid Waste Management (BSWM). This study's findings played a key part in CEQ's report to the President. Now awaiting publication and release to the public by the Government Printing Office, a copy of the Dillingham report was made available to *Chemical & Engineering News* by BSWM.

Reprinted from *Chemical & Engineering News,* Vol. 48, Nov. 30, 1970, pp. 40–41. Copyright 1970 by the American Chemical Society. Reprinted by permission of the copyright owner.

Table 3-1. Dredging Spoils Constitute Bulk of Wastes Dumped at Sea

TYPE OF WASTE	PACIFIC COAST[a] ANNUAL TONNAGE	ATLANTIC COAST[a] ANNUAL TONNAGE	GULF COAST[a] ANNUAL TONNAGE	TOTAL TONNAGE	ESTIMATED COST
Dredging spoils	7,320,000	15,808,000	15,300,000	38,428,000 (80%)	$15,583,000
Industrial wastes[b]	981,300	3,013,200	696,000	4,690,500 (10%)	8,193,000
Sewage sludge[c]	0	4,477,000	0	4,477,000 (9%)	4,433,000
Construction and demolition debris	0	574,000	0	574,000 (<1%)	430,000
Refuse and garbage	26,000	0	0	26,000 (<1%)	392,000
Explosives	0	15,200	0	15,200 (<1%)	235,000
Total	8,327,300	23,887,400	15,996,000	48,210,700	$29,266,000

[a]Figures for 1968 for 20 coastal cities.
[b]Includes chemicals, acids, caustics, cleaners, sludges, waste liquors, and oily wastes.
[c]Tonnage on wet basis.

Source: Dillingham Corp.

Between June 1968 and October 1969 Dr. Smith and Mr. Brown surveyed ocean dumping from 20 U.S. cities: Seattle, Portland (Ore.), San Francisco, Los Angeles, San Diego; Galveston, Texas City, Houston, Port Arthur, and Beaumont, Tex.; New Orleans, Pascagoula, Miss., Mobile, Ala., St. Petersburg, Fla., Charleston, S.C., Norfolk, Va., Baltimore, Philadelphia, New York, and Boston.

The Dillingham duo find that in 1968 48.2 million tons of wastes were dumped at sea, with disposal costs of $29.3 million. About 80% of the tonnage was dredging spoils from harbor deepening operations, carried out mainly by the U.S. Army Corps of Engineers. Some of these spoils include appreciable amounts of pollutants from municipal and industrial discharges.

Tonnage and costs of industrial waste ranked second—with 4.7 million tons discharged at a cost of $8.2 million. In third place was sewage sludge—a slurry of solid material remaining after municipal waste water treatment, residual human wastes, and other organic and inorganic wastes. Other categories of wastes listed by the report include construction and demolition debris, refuse and garbage (chiefly paper, food wastes, garden wastes, and steel and glass containers), and outdated military explosives and chemical warfare agents.

discontinued

According to the report, sea disposal of U.S. radioactive wastes—from nuclear reactors and medical and research activities—was discontinued by the Atomic Energy Commission in 1967. The report says that some European nations still dump radioactive materials in the ocean, however.

The La Jolla investigators find that total tonnage of industrial wastes, sewage sludge, construction and demolition debris, and refuse and garbage dumped into the ocean increased more than fourfold in the 20 years between 1949 and 1968—from an average of 1.7 million tons per year in 1949-53 to an average of 7.4 million tons per year in 1964-68. Moreover, the Dillingham pair predicts that disposal of wastes at sea will increase considerably in the next 10 years.

The eventual solution to growing waste disposal problems will undoubtedly lie in a high degree of recycling—to conserve both scarce resources and the environment, they say. In the meantime, however, increasingly stringent water and air pollution laws, loss of land areas now used for sanitary landfill or ponding of liquid wastes, and growth in population and industry in U.S. coastal cities are already causing cities like San Francisco, New York, and Philadelphia to investigate sea disposal of municipal refuse and garbage.

doubled

According to the report, the largest factor leading to increased dumping in recent years is the increase in sea disposal of industrial wastes and sewage sludge. Industrial waste dumping more than doubled between 1959 and 1968.

Origin of the industrial wastes includes petroleum refining, steel and paper production, pigment processing, insecticide-herbicide-fungicide production, chemical production, oil well drilling, and metal finishing, cleaning, and plating. In 1968, barges dumped into the ocean 2.7 million tons of waste acid, 560,000 tons of refinery wastes, 330,000 tons of pesticide wastes, 140,000 tons of paper mill wastes, and 940 tons of other materials.

The Dillingham report identifies 126 present disposal areas, 42 in the Pacific, 51 in the Atlantic, and 33 in the Gulf of Mexico. Atlantic Coast discharge tonnages far exceed those elsewhere, especially for industrial wastes and sewage sludge.

Bulk industrial wastes are normally discharged from tank barges in motion, but containerized methods are also used. Unit costs of disposal range from 40 cents per ton for dredge spoils to $24 per ton for containerized industrial wastes. Industrial wastes in bulk shipments cost an average of about $1.70 per ton.

environment

Despite increasing dumping, Dr. Smith and Mr. Brown find that the environmental consequences are still largely unknown. A few studies have looked at short-term effects of industrial discharges on marine ecology, but little is yet known.

One area under study is the New York Bight, off Sandy Hook, N.J., which has received 11 million cubic yards of dredge spoil and sewage sludge in the past four years. Some studies in the Bight area have shown that sewage sludge in large concentrations destroys the marine habitat in its vicinity.

The report also notes that on several occasions the Army has disposed of potentially hazardous chemical warfare weapons in the ocean without determining if there would be harmful effects on the environment.

As with ocean oil pollution, . . . little is known about the long-term environmental effects of dumped wastes on the marine environment and on marine organisms. Dr. Smith and Mr. Brown note that the minute body of information they can list on long- and short-term environmental effects is totally disproportionate to the large amounts of wastes being dumped and the potential damage these wastes can do.

Major research is needed in this area, they conclude, both on effects on organisms and to develop reliable sampling and standard bioassay techniques. They recommend additional work not only on acute toxicity, but also on long-term chronic or sublethal toxicity—particularly for industrial wastes.

fish habitats

The California team points out that certain inert waste materials may be used to advantage in the sea. In particular, discarded auto bodies and tires, and other solid waste materials, have been used successfully to make 104 experimental artificial reefs for fish shelter, feeding, and spawning along U.S. coasts.

The Bureau of Sport Fisheries and Wildlife, in cooperation with BSWM, is investigating the building of such artificial fish habitats from discarded rubber tires and baled refuse. The baled refuse might also provide food for the fish. It has also been proposed that other structural uses of solid wastes be investigated—including artificial islands, breakwaters, and offshore bars (to create breakers for surfing).

regulation

One of the major conclusions of the Dillingham report is that present regulation and monitoring of marine disposal is completely inadequate. It notes that under the existing legislation regulating waste disposal activities in U.S. territorial waters, the U.S. Army Corps of Engineers "provides such guidance as exists." Inspection of disposal operations to ensure compliance with regulations is virtually nonexistent, the report finds. Additionally, since the corps is also the chief dumper of dredging spoils, there exists a potential conflict of interest.

Clear-cut regulatory responsibility, substantial increases in funding, and more personnel are needed for effective enforcement. New Federal legislation is recommended in the study to achieve this. Furthermore, there is a near regulatory vacuum in international waters, and international cooperation will be necessary to remedy the situation.

The report concludes by observing that under prevailing conditions there will be growing pressures to dispose of municipal and industrial wastes in the sea. With decreasing availability of waste disposal sites on land, the economics of sea disposal become increasingly attractive. On the other hand, increased public environmental concern will bring stricter laws and enforcement procedures, backed by sizable penalties for noncompliance.

The White House, in commenting on the CEQ report on ocean dumping, stated that unlike some other pollution situations, it may still be possible to take preventive and corrective action before environmental problems caused by ocean dumping become acute.

Dr. Smith tells *Chemical & Engineering News* that he believes the enormous volume and buffering capacity of the ocean should enable carefully controlled disposal of some wastes in suitable areas without damage. Or as put by Wesley Marx in his book *The Frail Ocean,* the ocean can continue to be a beneficial resource; however, if abused, it will deteriorate as a base for both marine life and man.

oil pollution

eugene coan

"If seven maids with seven mops
Swept it for half a year,
Do you suppose," the Walrus said,
"That they could get it clear?"
"I doubt it," said the carpenter,
and shed a bitter tear.

Over the past fifty years, there has been a dramatic increase in the importance of oil as a source of power. We are starting to "pay our dues" for our dependence on oil, sometimes in ways we could not have anticipated fifty years ago. Now we must reverse the damage that has occurred and prevent future damage while at the same time conserving this valuable resource for generations beyond our limited vision.

The world's production of oil is something on the order of 600 billion gallons per year. About sixty per cent of this amount is moved at sea, or about 360 billion gallons. (1) In addition, oil constitutes about sixty per cent of all goods transported at sea. (2) All of this 360 billion gallons is loaded and unloaded, and nearly all of it passes through restricted shipping lanes at least once.

A minimum estimate of the amount of oil lost at sea can be calculated from the extent of single large accidents and from what little information is available about the operating records of particular oil ports. Dr. Max Blumer of the Woods Hole Oceanographic Institution estimates that 0.1% of all oil moved at sea is spilled, or about 360 million gallons. The actual influx of oil into the sea is much higher because his calculations do not include accidents in the extraction of oil from the sea floor, as at Santa Barbara, the sloppy use of fuel oil by ships at sea, or the oil introduced into the ocean by sewage wastes.

Oil and oil products are very complex mixtures of chemicals. Low-boiling saturated hydrocarbons produce anaesthesia and narcosis at low concentrations and cause cell damage and death at higher concentrations. The higher-boiling saturated hydrocarbons occur naturally in marine life and may not be toxic to them, but Blumer(1) speculates that they might interfere with chemical communication. Many of the biological processes in marine organisms, such as finding food, escaping from predators, homing, habitat selection, and sex attraction, are mediated by extremely low concentrations of chemical messengers. In some cases, the amounts involved are less than one part per million. Pollution by organic compounds could easily interfere with these processes, either by blocking the organisms' chemoreceptors, or by mimicking natural stimuli. In this way, one chemical could upset a balance among several species.

The Oregon Standard (cause of San Francisco Bay disaster):
523 ft., 16,419 deadweight tons

Aromatic hydrocarbons are abundant in petroleum and its products, and they are its most dangerous part. The low-boiling aromatics are acute poisons, while the high-boiling aromatics are long-term poisons. For instance, among the latter are 3,4-benzo-pyrene and a wide array of similar 4- and 5-ring aromatics which are known to be carcinogenic.(1,21)

After its release, oil begins to *weather,* a term which describes the sum of a number of physical and biological processes. The lower-boiling components evaporate most quickly. Other sets of compounds dissolve in the surface layers of seawater. Neither chemical oxidation nor bacterial degradation takes place quickly, though after a substantial amount of time they help rid the sea of oil.(1,3)

Our knowledge about the immediate consequences of major oil spills comes from a limited number of experiences on which detailed studies have been done. (Extensive bibliographies on the biological consequences of oil spills are available.(4,5)) These major incidents are the wreck of the *Tampico Maru* in northern Baja California in 1957, the wreck of the *Torrey Canyon* on the south coast of England in 1967, the Santa Barbara blow-out in 1969, and the wreck of the barge *Florida* in Massachusetts in 1969.

Inevitably, no matter what kind of oil is spilled, thousands of marine birds are killed, especially species which live in close association with the sea surface,(6–8) rather than birds which fly much of their time or those which wade along the shore. These surface-dwelling birds are totally exposed, especially when they dive for food. Their feathers become coated with oil and their insulation breaks down. They become wet and cold and then lose a great deal of energy trying to keep warm. They attempt to clean themselves by preening, ingesting toxic substances from the oil in the process. If and when they arrive on shore they are nearly immobile, cold, wet, starving, and sick. Very little can be done to save them.

In the case of oil spilled well to sea, such as in the *Torrey Canyon* incident, or in the case of chronic pollution of the sea lanes by oil, the birds suffering the most are the auks (Alcidae), which are a surface-dwelling species found mostly on the open sea. These birds, among the most specialized for a marine environment, are unfortunately most susceptible to oil damage. They dive for food and have dense plumage which is easily ruined by oil. They congregate to feed and breed, so that populations from a large area may

97

become involved in a localized spill. And, most importantly, they have a low replacement rate. They breed late in life and are long-lived. They have few eggs per season. (Oil contamination may also reduce the viability of eggs, and oil toxins can directly reduce the reproductive ability of birds.)

A combination of the effects of chronic oil pollution of the sea lanes in the northern Atlantic, plus the long-term effects of the *Torrey Canyon* disaster, are probably responsible for the fact that half of the guillemots and a quarter of the razorbills failed to arrive at the breeding colonies in the Irish Sea in 1970.(9) In the English Channel the auks have been reduced from 100,000 in 1908 to 200 in 1967. On the Sept-Iles the puffins went from 14,000 in 1950 to 600 in 1967.

Other bird populations along the Atlantic sea lanes may also be in trouble, for instance penguins in South Africa and diving ducks in the North Atlantic.

Other immediate effects of oil on marine life after a major spill depend on the type of oil, where it is spilled, how quickly it reaches the shore, and what kind of shore it encounters. The experiences with each major spill have been different.

The Torrey Canyon (cause of famous spill of England, 1967): 974 ft., 117,000 deadweight tons.

In the case of the *Tampico Maru*, which was wrecked on shore, the release of its cargo of diesel fuel oil caused mass mortality of coastal marine life. There was a complete disappearance of all but a few species of animals on the nearby coast. Initial recolonization occurred fairly quickly, algae growing most rapidly in the absence of herbivores. Later, the algae-herbivore balance was restored. Some elements of the pre-accident fauna and flora had not returned after ten years, while others were present after ten years which had not been there before the accident.(10,11)

The crude oil from the *Torrey Canyon* was spilled well to sea,(12) and it had considerable time to weather before it reached the coast. In addition, the situation was considerably complicated by the fact that the British treated the oil extensively with various detergents, both at sea and on the coast. Most of the harm to coastal marine life can be traced to the toxic solvents in which the detergents were diluted, the detergents themselves, and the fact that the detergents remobilized and further dispersed the oil.

The effect of the *Torrey Canyon* oil alone was chiefly physical rather than chemical, smothering marine life, although some snails became sick and could be pried off rocks easily. Where large amounts of oil were incorporated into sand or among rocks, an anaerobic condition developed which, in turn, was responsible for the death of some marine life.

The blow-out at Santa Barbara was similar to the *Torrey Canyon* incident in that the spill was of crude oil, well offshore; dissimilar in that detergents were not used.(13,15) Aside from the characteristic bird mortality, there was little damage to shore marine life other than to surf grass, barnacles, and mussels. In the spring, some high-tidal marine life was killed by exposure when their shells absorbed sunlight to a greater degree than usual because of their newly acquired black coat.(16)

98

The various studies have reported no abnormalities in planktonic marine life, and fisheries appear to be unaffected. There was considerable controversy about the effect on marine mammals. No significant kills of mammals were observed, and coated sea lions appeared normal otherwise.

There are natural oil seeps in the Santa Barbara area, such as the one at Coal Point. On the shore near these seeps, it has long been noticed that tar deposits coat the rocks near the high-tide line. There was continued seepage around Platform A for some time after the blow-out. It is probable that continued chronic seepage in the Santa Barbara area or elsewhere could significantly reduce the availability of habitat in the high-tidal area.

A word should be said here about the effect of oil on commercial shell-fisheries.(4,17,18) It appears that shellfish tend to pick up the taste of oil easily ("tainting"), and thereby lose their commercial value. This can also occur when the pollution is in the form of persistent low-level contamination. After a spill in Yaquina Bay, Oregon, crabs and oysters became contaminated by oil, and fisheries had to be temporarily halted.

Unfortunately, biologists are beginning to discover that the problems caused by oil spills on the sea are not limited to the immediate kill of marine birds, the immediate toxicity of shallow-water marine life, the smothering of intertidal animals, or the tainting of shellfish. Work being carried out at the Woods Hole Oceanographic Institution demonstrates that, even eight months after a near-shore spill of fuel oil in Massachusetts, oil constituents, including the high-boiling aromatic compounds, were still present in bottom sediments, both inshore and offshore. They are still present in marine organisms, including commercially important clams. (1,19-22)

Japanese tankers now under construction: 1,280 ft., 500,000 deadweight tons.

These results were obtained with the use of gas chromatography, similar to that used in recent work on DDT. There was an initial massive kill of fish, shellfish, worms, crabs, and other invertebrates. Trawls in ten feet of water showed a ninety-five per cent mortality. Repopulation had not occurred in nine months. In fact, the contamination had spread beyond the area originally affected. The kill of shallow-water plants and animals reduced the stability of the marshland and sea bottom, and increased erosion occurring as a result may in turn be responsible for the spread of pollution along the sea bottom.

Sensitive benthic ampeliscid amphipod crustaceans, a major food source for many bottom-feeding fishes, continued to be killed for at least eight months. Bacterial degradation was found to attack the least toxic hydrocarbons, but, in general, to play an insignificant role in breaking down the rest of the oil.

Shellfish that survived the accident were found to take up oil. The 1970 crop was as heavily contaminated as the 1969 crop. Oysters transplanted to unpolluted water for as long as six months retained the oil contaminants

99

without change in either composition or concentration! Closure to the taking of shellfish had to be extended into 1970 and to more distant areas than in 1969. Mussels that survived the spill as juveniles have developed almost no eggs or sperm.

These workers have demonstrated that the presence or absence of an oily taste or smell in shellfish is no clue to the presence of oil pollution. Only a small fraction of petroleum has a pronounced odor, and this fraction is lost while the more harmful, long-term poisons are retained. Cooking may remove the odor, but will not eliminate the toxicity.(21)

The sensitive techniques used in this study were not available for use in other spills. If they had been, then we might now have an entirely different picture of long-term contamination.

With the frightening results of this study in mind, we should ask how extensive pollution of the marine environment has become. This spill in Massachusetts was of about 180,000 gallons.(20) In a modern port, Milford Haven, in England, approximately .01 per cent of the oil handled was spilled in that local area in one year.(1) This is equivalent to about 840,000 gallons. What about the long-term contaminations by that oil? What about the not-so-modern ports?

Half of the world's catch of fish comes from .1 per cent of the ocean surface. Large oil spills and smaller daily spills in coastal waters could contaminate these highly productive regions.(22)

In addition, the extent of pollution of the open seas causes considerable concern. Dr. Blumer writes: ". . . during a recent cruise of the Woods Hole Oceanographic Institution to the southern Sargasso Sea, many surface 'Neuston' net hauls were made to collect surface marine organisms . . . Inevitably, during each tow, quantities of oil-tar lumps, up to three inches in diameter, were caught in the nets . . . On the evening of 5 December 1968, the nets were so fouled with oil and tar material that towing had to be discontinued."

Thor Heyerdahl, on his trip across the Atlantic Ocean during the summer of 1970, also reported this ocean-wide pollution.(23) "Clots of oil are polluting the midstream current of the Atlantic Ocean from horizon to horizon . . . During the 27 days of sailing so far, oil lumps in varying quantities have been observed uninterruptedly every day . . . It is entirely possible that the pollution area spans the entire ocean, from the coast of Africa to the coast of tropical America."

Environmentally hazardous substances are those which persist in the environment because they are not easily broken down by natural biological or chemical processes, and/or which become widespread because of their physical or chemical properties, and which present a danger to living organisms either by their direct toxicity or by affecting the health or reproductive ability of organisms, including man. Often environmentally hazardous substances tend to become more concentrated in living organisms than in the surrounding environment and may tend to become still more concentrated as they move along food chains, phenomena known as "biological concentration" and "biological magnification."

Examples of dangers presented by environmentally hazardous substances are the effect of DDT on marine life and the potential dangers of mercury and lead to man as a result of their accumulation in marine animals. If

Proposed ship now on English drawing boards: 1,600 ft., 1,000,000 deadweight tons.

we begin to suspect that a widespread material is an environmentally hazardous substance, we should immediately stop all contamination by that material until we are certain that no danger exists. This is the "Guilty Until Proven Innocent Principle of Environmental Contamination." This is similar to the principle we use with regard to drugs; we first have to be certain that no unanticipated dangers exist before introducing a new drug into the market.

The studies reviewed here demonstrate that oil is introduced into the sea in large quantities in a variety of ways and constitutes a widespread contaminant on the surface of the sea. Oil contains toxic, cancer-producing substances and can be a long-lived environmental contaminant where it is spilled. Large spills and chronic pollution of the sea lanes present a threat to certain species of oceanic birds. The immediate kill of shallow-water marine life may be extensive and recovery slow, particularly that of preexisting balances. It is very possible that oil contaminants will be found to interfere with chemo-communication among marine organisms, thereby upsetting entire food chains. Chronic pollution of coasts can coat the high-tidal zone, and thereby reduce the intertidal habitat.

In light of these dangers, oil should be added to the growing list of environmentally hazardous substances. Public policy should prevent continued contamination of the sea by oil, whether in drilling, transport, sewage disposal, or in use as a fuel.

literature cited

1. Blumer, Max 1969. *Oil pollution of the ocean.* pp. 5–13. David P. Hoult, *"Oil on the sea."* Proceedings of symposium sponsored by the Massachusetts Institute of Technology and the Woods Hole Oceanographic Institution and held at Cambridge, Massachusetts. May 16, 1969. New York & London (Plenum).
2. *Introduction to International Conference on Oil Pollution of the Sea,* 7–9 October 1968 at Rome, Report of Proceedings. Winchester (Wykeham 414 pp.)
3. Dean, R. A. 1968 *The chemistry of crude oils in relation to their spillage on the sea.* pp. 1–6 in J. D. Carthy & Don R. Arthur, *"The biological effects of oil pollution on littoral communities."* Field Studies 2 (Supplement).
4. Battelle Memorial Institute, Richland, Washington 1967. *Oil spillage study literature search and critical evaluation for selection of promising techniques to control and prevent damage.* For the United States Coast Guard, Department of Transportation. See especially Chapter 6, *"Biological and ecological effects."* 92 pp.
5. Radcliffe, Donna & Thomas A. Murphy 1969. *Biological effects of oil pollution—bibliography.* A collection of references concerning the effects

of oil on biological systems. For the Federal Water Pollution Control Administration, Department of the Interior. 46 pp.

6. Bourne. W. R. P. 1968. *Oil pollution and bird populations.* pp. 99–121, in Carthy & Arthur (1968), see under footnote 3.

7. Bourne, W. R. P. 1970. *Oil pollution and bird conservation.* Biological Conservation 2 (4): 300–302.

8. Clark, R. B. 1968. *Oil pollution and the conservation of seabirds.* pp. 74–112, in *"International Conference . . . ,"* see under footnote 2.

9. Note in Marine Pollution Bulletin 1 (ns), No. 8.

10. North, Wheeler J.; Michael Neushul; & Kenneth A. Clendenning 1964. *Successive changes observed in a marine cove exposed to a large spillage of mineral oil.* pp. 335–354, in Comm. Intl. Explor. Sci. Mer Medit., Symp. Pollut. Mar. par Microorgan. Prod. Petrol., Monaco.

11. North, Wheeler H. 1967. *Tampico: a study of destruction and restoration.* Sea Frontiers 13 (4): 212–217.

12. Smith, J. E. 1968. *'Torrey Canyon': pollution and marine life.* A report by the Plymouth Laboratory of the Marine Biological Association of the United Kingdom. Cambridge (University Press) 196 pp.

13. Battelle Memorial Institute, Richland, Washington 1969. *Review of the Santa Barbara Channel oil pollution incident to the Department of Interior.* Federal Water Pollution Control Administration, and Department of Transportation, United States Coast Guard. See especially Chapter 12, *"Biological and ecological survey and findings."* 27 pp.

14. Neushul, Michael 1969. *Santa Barbara oil pollution; final report dealing with the early stages of the Santa Barbara oil spill.* For the Federal Water Pollution Control Administration, Department of the Interior. 49 pp.

15. Allan Hancock Foundation, University of Southern California 1971. *Biological and oceanography survey of the Santa Barbara Channel oil spill, 1969–1970.* Sea Grant Publication No. 2. Volume 1, *Biology and bacteriology,* compiled by Dale Straughan, 426 pp. Volume 2, *Physical, chemical and geological studies,* under the general editorship of Ronald L. Kolpack, 477 pp.

16. Mitchell, Charles T.; Einer K. Anderson; Laurence G. Jones; & Wheeler J. North 1970. *What oil does to ecology.* Journ. Water Pollution Control Federation, May 1970: 812–818.

17. Simpson, A.C. 1968. *The Torrey Canyon disaster and fisheries.* Fisheries Laboratory. Burnham on Crouch, Essex. Leaflet (ns) 18. 43 pp.

18. Simpson, A. C. 1968. *Oil, emulsifiers and commercial fisheries.* pp. 91–98, in Carthy & Arthur (1968), see under footnote 3.

19. Blumer, Max; G. Souza; and J. Sass 1970. *Hydrocarbon pollution of edible shellfish by an oil spill.* Marine Biology 5 (3): 195–202.

20. Blumer, Max; J. Sass; G. Souza; H. Sanders; F. Grassle; & G. Hampson 1970. *The West Falmouth oil spill: persistence of the pollution eight months after the accident.* Woods Hole Oceanographic Institution, Technical Report, Unpublished Manuscript. 32 pp.

21. Blumer, Max 1970. *Testimony before the Conservation and Natural Resources Subcommittee.* House Committee on Government Operations, July 22, 1970. See also testimony of Howard Sanders.

22. Blumer, Max 1970. *Testimony before the Subcommittee on Air and Water Pollution.* Senate Committee on Public Works, June 1970.

23. *United Press International story.* San Francisco Chronicle, June 14, 1970.

waste-water treatment: the tide is turning

robert w. holcomb

There have been significant advances in research and development for sewage treatment.

In this age of pollution one of the more encouraging developments is the work that is being done in sewage treatment. Although no massive reductions in water pollution have occurred, there have been a few cases of successful pollution abatement—parts of the Framington River in Connecticut, the Willamette in Oregon, and Lake Washington in Seattle, for example. The construction of new sewage treatment plants, while not spectacular, has been gaining on the population. From about 1940 until 1962, the number of new facilities just kept abreast with or fell slightly behind population increases. From 1962 to 1968, however, the population served by sewers increased from 60 to 68 percent.

But perhaps the most significant advances have been made in research and development for sewage treatment. Since 1960 the government has put more than $25 million into waste-water treatment studies. A recent article cites 85 processes being studied at more than 150 locations (1). Of special interest are three pilot plants operated by the Federal Water Quality Administration (FWQA) and a 7.5 million gallon per day (mgd) advanced treatment plant operated in California by the South Tahoe Public Utility District.

treatment

About 1.8×10^{11} gallons of water are used in the United States each year to carry wastes from industries, businesses, and homes. After use this vast quantity of sewage is still more than 99.9 percent pure water, but the contaminants cause deterioration in water quality of receiving rivers and lakes.

For treatment purposes, the contaminants generally are considered as groups such as suspended solids, dissolved organics, and dissolved inorganics. Nitrogen and phosphorus are considered separately because of their role in eutrophication. A property of sewage that particularly degrades natural

Reprinted from *Science,* Vol. 169, pp. 457–459, 31 July 1970. Copyright 1970 by the American Association for the Advancement of Science. The author is affiliated with *Science.*

waters is its ability to consume oxygen. A somewhat arbitrary but useful measure of this property is known as biological oxygen demand (BOD).

The sewage from a little less than a quarter of the population of the United States receives only primary treatment. (About a third of the nation's population lives in areas where there are no sewers, and the sewage from about 5 percent of the population receives no treatment.) Primary treatment consists simply of allowing the sewage to settle and separating the water from the sludge at the bottom and the scum on the top. Such treatment removes about a third of the BOD and suspended solids and a few percent of the refactory organic compounds and plant nutrients.

Sewage from about 40 percent of the population gets secondary treatment. The most widely used methods now in operation are the trickling filter and activated sludge processes. In the first process, effluent from primary treatment is allowed to trickle through a deep bed of rocks containing various microorganisms that utilize organic and nutrient materials in the sewage. In the second process, the microorganisms use up primary effluent materials in tanks through which air is passed. Well-operated activated sludge tanks can remove up to 90 percent of the suspended solids and BOD, and good trickling filters remove 80 to 85 percent. In practice, figures closer to 75 percent are more common.

The use of pure oxygen in the activated sludge process has been called the most significant recent advance in sewage treatment. The major capital cost of an activated sludge plant is the buying of land for the tanks, and the major operating expense is forcing compressed air through the waste water (which has a head of 10 to 15 feet). For about 20 years engineers have known that with pure oxygen, more bacteria could be supported in a smaller space and that less pumping would be required; but an economically competitive system in which pure oxygen is used has emerged only within the past 2 years.

The Linde Division of Union Carbide has developed a system in which oxygen is circulated in closed tanks. The system achieves 90 percent utilization of oxygen—as opposed to 5 to 10 percent in conventional systems—and can support more bacteria than the air system.

Last year [1969] the process was compared with conventional activated sludge treatment at the 2.5 mgd pilot plant in Batavia, New York. On the basis of this study, Union Carbide says that capital investment savings of 16 to 20 percent and operating savings of up to 50 percent should be possible.

One of the 20 mgd activated sludge tanks in a Brooklyn plant is to be converted to a pure oxygen system and should be in operation by the spring of 1971. If the system fulfills its potential, the Brooklyn plant will be the first of many.

Many sanitary engineers think that in the future physical-chemical methods of secondary treatment will begin to replace the conventional biological methods. In one method being tested on a relatively large scale, lime is added to raw waste water to precipitate phosphates and to hydrolyze the organic compounds. At the FWQA Blue Plains pilot plant (near Washington, D.C.) the method is being tested in a sequence that involves lime precipitation, carbon adsorption columns, and nitrogen removal. The main problems (apart from nitrogen removal) have been lime handling and biological growths on the carbon filtering columns.

The system is being compared directly with a conventional biological treatment scheme, and, during the few months of trial, the physical-chemical process has removed less of the BOD. In spite of the operational difficulties and lower BOD removal, some engineers think that the system is ready for full-scale operation in situations where its advantages—smaller size, better reliability, and efficient phosphorus removal—are needed.

advanced waste treatment

Until a few years ago when it was necessary to reduce the concentration of substances not eliminated in the secondary step, some additional treatment process—generally chemical precipitation or filteration—was tacked on and the process was called tertiary treatment. In the last 10 years, a wide variety of additional treatment steps have been considered, and they can often be introduced at earlier stages of the treatment sequence. An integrated system that includes such steps is called advanced waste treatment (AWT).

Most of the procedures used in AWT have been adapted from other industrial uses. For example, there are dozens of chemicals that can be used for precipitation and flocculation and as filter aids. Filters are also widely used in industry, and about 20 multimedia filters are being considered for use in waste-water treatment. Microscreens—metal screens with mesh on the order of a few tens of microns or less—are also being tested. Direct comparison of microscreens and filters by the Metropolitan Sanitary District of Chicago has shown that the multimedia filters (sand and coal) remove more carbon. However, there are several advantages of microscreens that make their development desirable. They cost less, are easier to clean by back-washing, and require almost no head (hence reduced pumping costs). They can remove about 50 percent of the BOD and suspended solids, and this kind of performance is adequate in some cases.

For refractory organic compounds, adsorption is required. Most adsorption is now done on granular carbon, but powdered carbon that is in flowing beds or that is added to the effluent can also be used. Powdered carbon requires much less contact time, but it is harder to handle. Both types remove 70 to 80 percent of the dissolved organic compounds.

The feasibility of using columns of granular carbon to completely replace secondary treatment has been demonstrated at the FWQA pilot plant at Pomona, California, and this technique will be used at a 10 mgd plant to be constructed at Rocky River, Ohio. The sequence will be chemical treatment of the raw sewage for settling and phosphorus precipitation, and then passage of the effluent directly to carbon adsorption columns (which in this case will also act as filters).

Granular carbon can be regenerated in multiple hearth furnaces with about 5 percent loss. The best method demonstrated for regeneration of powdered carbon is a sand-bed burner. The 15 percent loss of carbon might be partially due to the small scale of the pilot test. A larger unit is being installed in Salt Lake City.

105

nutrients

The role of nitrogen and phosphorus in the eutrophication of lakes and rivers has led to some legislation limiting effluent concentrations of these substances and will undoubtedly lead to more. Secondary biological treatment seldom lowers concentrations sufficiently to meet these standards, so some advanced treatment is necessary.

Scaling from phosphates is an old industrial problem, and the technology for removing it by lime precipitation has long been known. Likewise, regeneration of the lime—especially in the paper industry—has been practiced for many years. Both techniques have been applied more or less successfully to waste-water treatment.

The possibility of phosphate removal by biological methods remains open and is being studied. Activated sludge treatment typically removes about 30 percent of the phosphates in sewage, but in some cases—most notably at a plant in Baltimore—removal of up to 90 percent has been observed. The reason for this is not known. Both biological and chemical explanations have been proposed, and a test of the biological hypothesis is underway at a pilot plant in Manassas, Virginia. An understanding of the fundamental process could lead to a technique for phosphate removal during secondary treatment. This would be very useful in that phosphate removal is often the only advanced treatment needed for many pollution situations.

The methods now being used for nitrogen removal are not very satisfactory. In the ammonia stripping process, ammonia ions are converted to ammonia by raising the pH (usually by addition of lime), and the ammonia is driven from solution by vigorous agitation with air. Removal of 90 percent of the ammonia has been reported at Lake Tahoe and at Blue Plains, but in both places there have been problems. Precautions must be taken to prevent scaling, and temperature variations greatly alter the effectiveness of the process.

Methods of removing nitrogen biologically are also being tested at several places. Ammonia in the effluent can be converted to nitrates by biological oxidization. Another type of bacteria converts nitrates to free nitrogen. In this last step it is necessary to provide a source of carbon to the bacteria. Methanol is now used, and the cost of this chemical is the limiting factor in the process.

There are dozens, if not hundreds, of ion-exchange resins available for a variety of uses. Fairly successful removal of ammonia has been achieved with resins at the Blue Plains pilot plant, but the cost of resins is high.

One recent development with much promise is the discovery of a natural mineral ziolite, clinoptilolite, which adsorbs both phosphates and ammonium ions. More research on the reliability of different sources of the mineral, its durability, and methods of regenerating it is needed before it can be known whether this mineral will be suitable for general use.

demineralization

In some cases it is desirable to reduce the total mineral content of waste water rather than only that of nitrogen and phosphorus compounds. This can be done with ion-exchange resins, by reverse osmosis, or by electrodi-

106

alysis. All three techniques for water recovery are used in industry, and the last two have been tested for several years as a means of desalting seawater.

In ion exchange positive ions are exchanged with hydrogen ions, and the negative ions are exchanged with hydroxyl ions; the exchanged ions then combine to form water. The resins must be periodically recharged with acids and bases. As was mentioned in connection with nitrogen removal, the cost of ion-exchange resins and of regeneration is high by wastewater treatment standards.

In electrodialysis, an electric current is passed through the solution and the ions collect at the anode and cathode after passing through selective membranes (which are actually ion-exchange resins in sheet form). Brackish water collects in cells at the anode and the cathode, and partially purified water is taken out of the center cell. Organic molecules cannot be removed by this process, and they tend to collect on the membranes and reduce their effectiveness.

In reverse osmosis, water is simply forced through a membrane. One of the main difficulties is supporting large surfaces of the relatively weak membrane so it can withstand the necessary pressure. During the past decade four support schemes have been developed and are being tested. Organic molecules tend to foul these membranes also, but the problem is not so serious as with electrodialysis. Since it is the water, not the ions, that pass through the membrane, reverse osmosis reduces both organic and mineral content of the water.

At the Pomona pilot plant all three methods are used to demineralize the effluent from the same activated sludge-carbon absorption treatment. Typical results for reverse osmosis are 90 percent reduction of total dissolved solids and 75 percent recovery of water; results for ion exchange are also 90 percent reduction but 85 percent recovery; and results for a one-stage electrodialysis unit are about 35 percent reduction and 92 percent recovery. A process with about 35 percent reduction of total dissolved solids is useful, because this is about equal to the amount of solids added to water as the result of human use.

Electrodialysis and reverse osmosis produce large volumes of brackish waste water, and these processes may be practical only in areas where ocean disposal is possible. Sludge handling is by far the most difficult problem in sewage treatment. The cost of dewatering the sludge and disposing of the solids accounts for 25 to 50 percent of the total cost of treatment, with the higher figure being more common.

After all other treatment is done the plant is left with a mixture of 5 percent hydrophilic colloidal solids suspended in 95 percent water. A wide variety of techniques have been tried to separate this mixture. Chemicals to precipitate, flocculate, hydrolyze, and oxidize have been used; and it has been suggested that an attempt be made to isolate a flocculating agent produced by bacteria that are naturally present in the sludge.

Anaerobic digestion is commonly used. Cooking the sludge under pressure, freezing, radiation, and ultrasound have been tried—with the cooking process showing some promise. Mechanical separation devices include the development of a solid bowl centrifuge, which is now being used, and the design of vibrating screens.

107

Disposal of the solids by landfill, sale as fertilizer or soil conditioner, and settling of the sludge in lagoons have all been used but will probably decrease as disposal by incineration increases.

Again, a fundamental knowledge of the process might lead to a major new method of treatment. Some chemical or physical system capable of breaking up the colloidal system that so tenaciously holds the water would be the most significant single advance in waste-water treatment possible.

So long as no simple solution to the sludge problem is found, treatment processes that produce little sludge, or sludges that are easy to handle, will gain favor. The biological processes are especially troublesome because the cellular material produced by the microorganisms strongly hold several times their weight in water. This is why physical-chemical systems, although not yet widely used, are so attractive. Ideally, chemicals that produce no precipitates or precipitates from which the original chemicals can easily be extracted (as in the lime process) would be used. This chemical treatment would be combined with steps (such as screening, filtering, and absorption) in which solids rather than sludges are collected.

the battle has not been won

Although much progress has been made recently in waste-water treatment, many difficulties remain. The major one, of course, is getting the money to put the knowledge gained in the pilot plant studies into operational systems. The FWQA estimates that it will cost $10 billion to get domestic wastes up to recommended standards and $3.3 billion for industrial wastes.

On the scientific front, there is the necessity for understanding some of the fundamental processes of sewage treatment, such as phosphate precipitation and water retention by sludge. There is also the need for better survey and analytical work. For example, general characteristics like BOD and suspended solids are useful for plant management work and evaluation, but knowledge of exact chemical composition and particle size is needed for research.

Comprehensive surveys have been made of domestic sewage, but little is known of industrial wastes. The FWQA estimates that the volume of industrial waste water is about 2.6 times that of domestic. They also estimate that about half the volume of sewage treated in domestic facilities comes from industrial sources. This means that a volume of industrial sewage about three-fourths that treated in domestic facilities is unaccounted for. Disposal volumes for a number of specific industries have been estimated, but the overall industrial picture is not clear. The FWQA says: "The lack of reliable information on industrial water pollution control activities might be considered to be intolerable, if the nation had not become quite habituated to it. The guessing process has gone on for so long that it is considered quite normal; and every effort to initiate an industrial waste inventory has been frustrated without noticeable public comment" (2).

Another difficult but important survey that is required is to determine the composition of water that runs directly from land to natural waterways. In some cases—the Potomac River, for example—eroded soil is the major contaminant. Much waste from the agricultural industry also is direct runoff, and it has been estimated that perhaps half of the phosphates in natural water come from this source.

Finally, the problem of trace contaminants and health is not well studied. The recent series of discoveries of mercury contamination illustrate a process that has now been repeated several times. Routine water analyses are made only for major indicators of water pollution, so that measurable amounts of unusual substances can be present for long periods of time without being detected. Once a systematic search is made, some of the substances are found to be rather common. This happened with DDT, detergents, phosphates, and now it has been repeated with mercury. What other poisons have we not looked for?

The Waste Water Reclamation Committee of the American Water Works Association at their July [1970] meeting in Washington, D.C., cited the possible presence of the following substances as one reason for not utilizing reclaimed water if other sources were available: "chemical and biological toxins, trace elements, pesticides, carcinogens, antibiotics, hormones, viruses, and materials not yet studied."

Thus, although a broad-based research and development program in waste-water treatment is being pursued, much work remains—monies must be made available, fundamental research problems should be solved, and a major health catastrophe must be avoided by carefully monitoring our waters for small amounts of dangerous substances (3).

references

1. D. G. Stephan and R. B. Schaffer, *J. Water Pollut. Contr. Fed.* 42, 399 (1970).
2. Federal Water Pollution Control Administration, *The Economics of Clean Water* (U.S. Department of Interior, Washington, D.C., March 1970), vol. 1, p. 18; see also V. Reinemer, *Science* 169, 36 (1970).
3. For a thorough summary of water treatment and a bibliography, see Subcommittee on Environmental Improvement, Committee on Chemistry and Public Affairs, *Cleaning Our Environment: The Chemical Basis for Action* (American Chemical Society, Washington, D.C., 1969), pp. 93–162.

eutrophication: the case against phosphorus

committee on government operations

Phosphorus, a building block of life, can also cause death. When present in lakes and streams in more than the most minute quantities, it nourishes excessive annual crops of algae and other aquatic plants. As they die and decay, they use up the oxygen in the water, cause fish to suffocate, and finally much of their phosphorus content is redissolved to start the growth cycle anew. Eventually decayed vegetation fills in the body of water and ends its existence. This process is called eutrophication.

The element phosphorus is a building block of all living things. No plant or animal, from an amoeba to a human being, can exist without it. But the same property which gives phosphorus its greatest value as a resource—the ability to sustain life—is what makes it a pollutant when too much gets into waterways. Phosphorus is a fertilizer. Applied to cropland, it makes food and fiber grow. Dissolved in water, it stimulates the growth of aquatic plants. These plants—the suspended algae (phytoplankton) in open water and the rooted plants and attached algae on the bottom in shallow areas—directly or indirectly are the source of food for the entire community of animal life in the lake. In moderate amounts they support valuable sport and commercial fishes and the useful animal life upon which fish feed.

Overstimulated, the waterplants grow to excess. Seasonally they die off and rot, either in place or after washing up on beaches, where they may pile up in thick mats. In the process of decay they exhaust the dissolved oxygen of the water and produce the rotten-egg stench of hydrogen sulfide. Simultaneously they release their phosphorus content, to start the growth cycle anew. The game fish die of oxygen deficiency and are replaced, for a time, by rough varieties. Intake filters for potable water become clogged, and boat propellers fouled, with algae. The lake loses its value as a water

<hr>

Excerpted from the Twenty-third Report of the Committee on Government Operations, April 14, 1970, entitled *Phosphates in Detergents and the Eutrophication of America's Waters.*

supply, as an esthetic and recreational asset, and as an avenue of commerce. Finally, the water itself is displaced by the accumulated masses of living and dead vegetation and their decay products, and the lake becomes a bog, and, eventually, dry land.

Such destruction of a lake by plant growth is called eutrophication. It is similar to the natural process by which a lake matures, ages, and dies. But the natural process is so slow that it can be measured only on a geological time scale. Most lakes, for example, in north temperate regions were created by glacial action about 12,000 years ago—yet many of them are still in pristine condition. The extent of eutrophication which has occurred in the past few decades under the onslaught of 20th century man's pollution would require thousands of years under natural conditions. It has been estimated, for example, that man has aged Lake Erie 15,000 years in the last 50. Indeed, such excessive enrichment might never be possible naturally.

Just as increasing the amount of dissolved phosphorus in a lake can stimulate algal growth, so decreasing it can retard that growth.

Prof. P. H. Jones, associate director of the Great Lakes Institute at the University of Toronto, testified as follows at the committee hearing:

> *How do we associate algae with phosphorus? If we examine the nutrients required in significant proportions to promote the growth of algae we find that carbon, hydrogen, oxygen, nitrogen and phosphorus are required in biologically available forms.*
>
> *Carbon dioxide and water are, of course, universally available and cannot be controlled; sunlight energy is similarly not controllable. Thus we are left with two further nutrients [phosphorus and nitrogen] which must prove limiting; otherwise all fresh water bodies would be overgorwn with weeds and algae.*

Only one nutrient at a time, Professor Jones explained, can be limiting for plant growth. Plants require a "balanced diet"; that is, they must have their nutrients in fairly definite proportions. Thus, for one unit of growth a plant may require 33 units of carbon* to five units of nitrogen and one unit of phosphorus. If there are 66 units of carbon and 10 units of nitrogen available, but only one unit of phosphorus, the plant will still attain only one unit of growth. For a second unit of growth, it would need a second unit of phosphorus, which is lacking. In this example, therefore, phosphorus is the limiting nutrient.

Nitrogen, as Professor Jones pointed out, constitutes about 80 percent of the atmosphere. Some species of algae are capable of taking nitrogen for their nutrition directly out of the air. These are the blue-greens, which from the esthetic point of view are probably the most disgusting of algae. When blue-greens die, they release their nitrogen into the water, making it available to nourish the non-nitrogen-fixing species. Nitrogen, therefore, usually cannot be the nutrient in short supply which limits algae growth.

---

*The principle referred to by Professor Jones is known as Liebig's law of the minimum. The proportions, 33 to 5 to 1, were used by Dr. Jones only for purposes of illustration. The nitrogen-phosphorus ratios for various species of algae actually range between 18 to 1 and 30 to 1.

Thus, Professor Jones stated:

We are left with phosphorus, which is a material which is not widespread and generally available in nature.

Actual measurements of dissolved phosphorus in the western basin of Lake Erie show a rise from 14 micrograms per liter in 1942 to 30 micrograms per liter in 1958, 36 micrograms per liter in 1959, and 40 micrograms per liter in 1967–68. At the same time, planktonic (free floating) algae were increasing tremendously in numbers and becoming dominated by the blue-green varieties. The common attached algae, *Cladophora*, now grow in ever-widening mats in shallow waters all along the shores of the lake. At the same time, desirable fish, such as whitefish, blue pike, and walleye, have declined drastically or disappeared. Similar dramatic increases in phosphorus have been observed during the same period in other lakes in various parts of the world, accompanied by excessive growth of algae and many of the same catastrophic phenomena observed in Lake Erie.

Although phosphorus is not the only nutrient necessary for the growth of water plants, it is the one most susceptible to control. Dr. A. F. Bartsch, Director of the Pacific Northwest Water Laboratory of the Federal Water Pollution Control Administration, explained the situation to the committee as follows:

Now the plants that are produced in water are essentially in their physiology not much different from crop plants that are produced on the land. Like them, they require the same kinds of chemical elements in the form of fertilizer, if you will; and there are some 10 major elements and some six or seven minor ones. If we look at the history related to lakes throughout the world, it appears that when the growth of aquatic plants progresses, eventually it comes to a stop because the plants have run out of some critical element. Most commonly this element turns out to be nitrogen or phosphorus. This also means if we had the capability of limiting or eliminating entirely any one of these 10 major elements or seven minor elements we could curtail and finally stop the production of plants.

When we look at the possibilities related to this, it turns out that our technology is strongest in the area of removing phosphorus. We also find if we look at the experience throughout the world that more commonly than otherwise phosphorus is the critical nutrient.

Since phosphorus is indispensable to life, the growth of any plant can be stopped by taking it away.

The phosphorus in our waters comes from both natural and cultural sources. In the cases of Lake Erie and Lake Ontario, much more than half of the phosphorus input is from municipal and industrial wastes, and 50 to 70 percent of the phosphorus content of these wastes comes from detergents. In the Potomac estuary 90 percent of the phosphorus input is from waste water, and 60 to 70 percent of this is contributed by detergents. Thus, well over half of the phosphorus pollution of the "Nation's River" is caused by detergents.

112

seventeen:

phosphate replacements: problems with the washday miracle

allen l. hammond

Despite industry claims that nonphosphate detergents are "nonpolluting," they may have some possibly detrimental environmental effects—as well as leave unanswered questions about their safety and washing effectiveness.

Detergents containing phosphates have been under indictment for some time as a significant cause of the eutrophication of lakes and other waterways. Phosphates are believed to contribute to the unwanted growth of algae that often choke bodies of water and that, in their decay, can exhaust the oxygen supply in the bottom waters, so that the lake becomes uninhabitable for cold water fish and less attractive for recreational use. Although many scientists are convinced that phosphates should be controlled, there is evidence that under certain circumstances the availability of other nutrients such as nitrogen or carbon limits algal growth; in these waters, phosphates may be present in such amounts that their removal from detergents would make little difference in water quality. But detergents are marketed nationally, rather than regionally, and the federal government seems to be committed to removing phosphates as soon as suitable replacements can be found. In Canada and in some local areas of the United States laws have been passed restricting the phosphate content of detergents. The detergent industry is reluctantly getting ready to shift to phosphate replacements; and within the past year products containing both new materials, such as nitrilotriacetate (NTA), and new formulations of standard ingredients, notably carbonates and silicates, have appeared on the market. Some of these products have been accompanied by advertised claims that these detergents are "nonpolluting." However, the nonphosphate products available today are far from perfect; in addition to some possibly detrimental environmental effects, there are unanswered questions about their safety and washing effectiveness.

Reprinted from *Science,* Vol. 172, pp. 361–363, 23 April 1971. Copyright 1971 by the American Association for the Advancement of Science. The author is affiliated with *Science.*

113

detergents in the ecosystem

Most of the laundry detergents available today contain between 35 and 50 percent sodium tripolyphosphate, and sales of these products by the three largest detergent manufacturers, Procter & Gamble, Lever Brothers, and Colgate-Palmolive, account for about 80 percent of the total U.S. market. Almost 2.5 million metric tons of detergents are used in the United States annually, resulting in the release of about 1 million metric tons of phosphates into waste water, and hence into the environment, every year (1). Domestic waste water—in which detergents predominate, but which also contains phosphates from human wastes and industrial processes—is the largest single source of phosphates in most waterways. The relative contributions from waste water, urban storm sewer runoff, and agricultural runoff from fertilized fields and livestock feed-lots vary widely from place to place and, particularly in the case of agricultural runoff, show large seasonal variations as well. It is generally agreed, however, that detergents account for about 50 percent of the phosphates in waste water and for some lower fraction of the total amount entering waterways. Near large metropolitan areas where there is little dilution of waste water, some estimates of the relative contribution from detergents run as high as 70 percent.

Algae blooms are no longer a rare occurrence in many parts of the United States. In some instances it appears that phosphorus has clearly been the limiting nutrient, implying that a reduced supply of phosphates would have reduced the amount of algal growth; in other incidents, it is simply not known what the limiting nutrient was or how much of the algal growth could have been controlled by lower concentrations of phosphates. Research into the water chemistry of nutrient cycles is intensifying, but the complexity and variability of aquatic systems tend to obscure the details of how nutrients are taken up by algae and other primary producers, then released as the algae die and are decomposed by bacteria. Comprehensive field studies have so far been carried out in relatively few bodies of water.

The relative importance of phosphorus in contributing to excess algal growth and hence to the accelerated decay of a lake seems to depend on the trophic state of the lake. Phosphorus may be limiting to algal growth in nutrient-poor or oligotrophic lakes, but it may be present in excess in nutrient-rich waters. In the Great Lakes, for example, it is estimated by Fred Lee of the University of Wisconsin—in a talk given at the recent [1971] American Chemical Society (ACS) meeting in Los Angeles—that phosphorus is the limiting nutrient in the open waters of Lakes Superior, Huron, and Michigan; he believes that in more eutrophic waters, such as Erie and Ontario, phosphorus may be no longer limiting, but could be made so by removing phosphates from waste water. But in some shallow, near-shore sections of the lakes the total input of phosphates from other sources is such, Lee believes, that the removal of phosphates from detergents or even the removal of 80 percent of the phosphates from waste water in treatment plants—as is now planned for much of the Great Lakes region—would not improve water quality substantially. In order to make phosphorus limiting in these sections, Lee thinks it will be necessary to reduce urban and rural runoff as well.

Much less is known about nitrogen inputs to waterways, although both

114

natural and manmade sources of this nutrient appear to be abundant. The input from ammonia found in rainfall is apparently high in many areas, and fertilizers and sewage wastes contain large amounts. Some types of algae and bacteria can fix nitrogen, and although this process appears to be an insignificant source of nitrogen for lakes, it may give the nitrogen-fixing blue-green algae that usually are commonly found in blooms an advantage over other forms. Nitrogen sources are hard to control because of their diffuse nature, in contrast to many sources of phosphorus. At the ACS meeting, A. T. Prince of the Department of Energy, Mines, and Resources in Ottawa, Canada, estimated that 70 percent of the phosphates entering Lake Erie are from point sources that are potentially controllable, compared to only 40 percent of the nitrogen.

It is generally agreed, however, that nitrogen is a limiting nutrient in some lakes and in many or perhaps even most estuarine and coastal waters. John Ryther and William Dunstan of the Woods Hole Oceanographic Institute point out in a recent report that coastal waters receive the sewage of roughly half of the population of the United States, and their measurements in the New York City region indicate that nitrogen is the limiting nutrient in such waters (2). Hence they question the value of replacing phosphates in detergents in these regions.

Under some circumstances carbon may be the limiting nutrient, especially in extremely eutrophic, soft-water lakes, according to Pat Kerr of the Environmental Protection Agency (EPA) laboratory in Athens, Georgia. In her talk at the ACS meeting, Kerr emphasized the interdependence of algae and decomposing bacteria, which often compete for the same nutrients; typically they are linked in a daily cycle in which carbon dioxide is removed by algal growth by late afternoon and regenerated during the night by the bacteria. Because of this linkage, Kerr believes that the control of carbon may be important.

However, the circumstances in which carbon is really a limiting nutrient may be fairly restricted. For example, although Lake Erie is a highly eutrophic system, the carbon reservoir provided by dissolved bicarbonate in the lake appears to be much larger than all human inputs of carbon. Prince estimates the biological oxygen demand in the lake at about 200,000 tons per year, which is equivalent to about 75,000 tons of annual carbon input from sewage. The carbon content of the biomass in the lake is estimated to be about 1.8 million tons, clearly larger than could be supplied from the sewage source, but small compared to the 10 to 12 million tons of bicarbonate in the lake. Hence Prince believes that carbon in sewage waste is not an important nutrient in this lake. Many scientists also believe that where carbon does become limiting, further algal growth would lead to relatively little additional deterioration in water quality.

options in detergent formulation

A typical household laundry detergent is made up of a builder, a surfactant, and miscellaneous ingredients such as brighteners, perfumes, antiredeposition agents, and, in some products enzymes. The builder's primary role in a detergent is as a sequestering agent which ties up calcium and magnesium ions that are present in hard water and that would otherwise interfere with the surfactant. Builders also provide in the washing solution a source of alkalinity which is necessary for effective soil removal. The surfactant acts as a wetting agent, which helps to float off dirt from fabrics. The detergent action of most current surfactants, such as the widely used linear alkylate sulfonate (LAS), is poisoned by unsequestered hardness ions. Antiredeposition agents help to keep dirt—once it is removed from the fabrics—in suspension.

Phosphates are excellent builders for detergents, except for their detrimental effects on the environment. Phosphate detergents perform well in soil removal and have a good safety record as far as the phosphate content itself, although some questions have been raised about adverse health effects from enzyme additives. Continued low level exposure to the enzymes used in detergents may cause an allergic sensitization reaction in some persons, although there is considerable disagreement at present as to the exposure level at which this reaction might occur and the frequency of its occurrence.

The search for phosphate replacements has not as yet turned up any widely accepted substitutes, despite research efforts in the detergent industry and in some independent laboratories under contract to EPA. So far replacement efforts seem to be following one of two directions. The approach favored by the large detergent manufacturers is to look for a new builder that has properties similar to phosphates. The favorite candidate for at least partial replacement of phosphates was NTA, which was increasingly used in some products last year [1970] as large quantities began to be available from suppliers.

As of 18 December [1970], however, the industry agreed at the request of the Surgeon General to "voluntarily" suspend use of NTA pending further tests. The request was based on a report from the National Institute of Environmental Health Science (NIEHS) that NTA may have a teratogenic effect in combination with a heavy metal, such as cadmium and mercury, by increasing the transmission of these metals across the placental barrier to the fetus, thus increasing the likelihood of birth defects. NTA is normally degraded in waste treatment systems and in the environment and thereby loses its ability to combine with the metals. But NTA does not degrade in anaerobic systems such as may be found in some septic tanks. Since mercury and other heavy metals occur widely in many waterways, . . . there is apparently some basis for concern.

These preliminary findings were a major setback to industry plans. Procter & Gamble, for example, estimates that it has already spent many millions of dollars in the development and testing of NTA detergents, and since December the entire industry has been examining the NIEHS experimental data and conducting its own tests. The major companies might be expected, on the basis of substantial investments, to be reluctant to move on to other phosphate replacements while there is still hope for NTA, and in fact both the large detergent manufacturers and their suppliers continue to believe that NTA is a safe material at concentrations that would occur in the environment. They expect eventually to go ahead with NTA as, at least, a partial phosphate replacement. Apart from its possible role in the mobilization of heavy metals, NTA appears to be a nontoxic material that performs well as a detergent builder. Total dependence on NTA is unlikely, however, because the material is hygroscopic and would tend to absorb moisture from the air, causing the detergent to cake.

Another potential class of new builders is the polyelectrolytes, principally derivatives of polycarboxylic acids, which appear to have good sequestering properties and good washing characteristics and are available at reasonable cost. The trouble with these compounds is that those tested so far have poor biodegradability, an essential property in the quantities that would eventually be used in detergents. Other compounds including various proteins have been suggested as builders, but their safety has not yet been determined.

A second approach toward finding a nonphosphate detergent—and the approach which seems to be advancing most rapidly at the present—involves the development of surfactants that will work without a sequestering agent. Many of the nonphosphate products on the market are of this type. Small companies—some of them entering the detergent business for the first time—produce essentially all of these products. The surfactants are combined with a builder to provide alkalinity and to improve washing performance. The nonphosphate detergents on the market have largely used precipitating builders—carbonates and silicates—so called because they usually combine with calcium ions in hard water and precipitate as an insoluble residue. The buildup of this residue on cloth and in washing machines is apparently one of the major potential disadvantages with detergents which do not use sequestering builders. Nonphosphate detergents of the type now available have also been criticized for poor cleaning performance, although presumably the individual housewife will be the ultimate judge of washing performance, and so far many of the new no-phosphate products seem to be selling well. The large variety of possible combinations of soils, fabrics, and water hardness make most laboratory washing tests—and hence most claims about washing performance—unreliable.

If small companies have the advantage of a lesser commitment to existing methods and materials so that they can be more innovative in detergent formulation, they can also be more irresponsible, and the products on the market now include instances of both. The use of precipitating builders results in more alkaline detergents. Most phosphate detergents at normal use levels—about 0.15 percent solution—have a pH between 9 and 10.5, whereas the nonphosphate detergents based on silicates and carbonates typically have a pH between 10.5 and 11. A few products have been marketed with high concentrations of metasilicates—which are highly alkaline in contrast to the more widely used liquid silicate formulations—and products based on metasilicates have been reported to have pH higher than 11. Above pH 11, alkaline substances can apparently cause gel formation in protein tissue, making it difficult to flush out any of the material that comes in contact with the eyes or is accidently swallowed. The Food and Drug Administration (FDA) is beginning to screen new detergent products for skin corrosion, eye irritation, and ingested toxicity in tests on animals. Under the Hazardous Substances Act, the FDA requires all products alkaline enough to cause tissue damage to carry a warning label identifying the caustic substance, although with such a label even very alkaline substances can be sold. It was for violation of this labeling requirement that two detergents with high metasilicate content, Ecolo-G and Bohack, were seized last month [March 1971].

Many industrial detergents are highly alkaline, but the major manufacturers have avoided such products for home use on the basis that, even with warning labels, children would inevitably come into contact with the material. Some 2000 to 3000 cases of children swallowing detergents and other cleaning products are commonly reported each year, so that the trade off between the safety hazards of highly alkaline detergents and washing efficiency, which generally improves at higher alkalinities, is substantial. By no means all the nonphosphate detergents contain metasilicates, however, even though many of them carry warning labels.

social options

Essentially everyone agrees that the best long-range method for controlling nutrients in waste water lies with advanced sewage-treatment systems. Phosphates are easily precipitated by the addition of metal ions such as aluminum or iron, and methods for the removal of other nutrients are under rapid development. But because of the time lag in getting public financing for comprehensive treatment systems, many scientists believe that detergent reformulation to remove or reduce phosphates is necessary in the short run. It has been argued, for example by the large detergent manufacturers, that since the elimination of phosphates from detergents would only cut the input of this nutrient in sewage by about half, there would be little to no improvement in water quality. Critics of phosphates in detergents, while admitting that this estimate is probably correct in some areas, point out that such a reduction would at least help to reduce the rate of eutrophication in the future, and more importantly, would help to keep those lakes that are now relatively free of excess algae from becoming like the western basin of Lake Erie, which is largely choked with algae every summer.

If phosphates ought to be removed from detergents, then should laws banning phosphate-containing products by a specific date be passed? The industry has argued that antiphosphate legislation will not help them come up with replacements, and it is true that replacement chemicals need careful testing, as the questions about NTA make clear. On the other hand the large companies—which would be primarily affected by such laws—have not taken the lead in developing and test marketing no-phosphate products based on new surfactants, presumably in part because of their large investments in NTA and in current processing methods. National no-phosphate laws would probably restrict the available technological options too severely, since there are probably some regions of the country where phosphate nutrients are not a critical problem, but it appears likely that more regional and local legislation will be passed.

The replacement of phosphates in detergents with other formulations does appear to involve some trade offs among environmental quality, safety, washing performance and cost. This last factor is a significant constraint, because detergents based on surfactants alone, for example, would apparently be possible if about ten times more product—at a comparable increase in cost to the consumer—were to be used per wash.

118

Although there is some concern over the nutrient input from replacement products containing nitrogen or carbon, it appears that the amounts of these elements that would be released into waste water from detergents would augment the input from other sources at most only slightly—about 5 percent for nitrogen, in most estimates—as compared to the 50 percent relative contribution of detergent phosphates. More alkaline detergents, in the case of products based on precipitating builders, do pose greater safety problems for home use. According to the makers of phosphate detergents, the phosphate replacements now available are inferior in washing performance, and it is not yet clear whether they will satisfy most users—is whiter than white necessary, or will simply clean do? Although there seems to be no perfect answer, it might well be that regional marketing of products tailored to a given watershed–an idea that appears to horrify the industry because of the complexities involved and the greater expenses that the lack of a national market entails—would help to minimize environmental impact of detergents until adequate waste treatment systems are available while retaining maximum flexibility for the consumer.

references

1. Hearings on phosphates in detergents before a subcommittee of the Committee on Government Operations of the House of Representatives, 15 and 16 December 1969 (U.S. Government Printing Office, Washington, D.C., 1969).
2. J. Ryther and W. Dunstan, *Science* 171, 1008 (1971).

soap: some companies' answer to phosphate-containing detergents

staff of chemical & engineering news

Despite the rise of synthetic detergents, soap is still big business.

Johnny Standley's old song about Grandma's lye soap (allowing how it was good for everything in the home and how that its secret was in the scrubbing, for it didn't lather or foam) admittedly overstates the case. Soap, under proper circumstances, is an excellent cleansing agent. What's more, it's readily biodegradable, relatively nontoxic, and needs no added antideposition agents. Despite the ascendancy of synthetic detergents, soap is still big business: more than 800 million pounds per year, worth more than $300 million. Soap still accounts for about 15% by weight of the total soap/synthetic detergent market, almost 25% in terms of money.

In one major product line, bath and toilet bars, soap has so far resisted major incursions by the synthetics. Even if soap leaves a ring around the bathtub, most people still seem to prefer the "feel" of toilet soap to that of the syndet bars.

Soap's virtues notwithstanding, there are elements of truth in the song. Grandma probably had hard water. In hard water, soap doesn't foam until enough has been added to soften the water by precipitating the calcium, magnesium, and other "hardness" ions. The precipitate is a gummy curd of insoluble soap. Only a minor nuisance in the bathtub, this curd is a major problem in the laundry. It forms a dulling film on clothing and can clog the washing machine.

There are ways to get around this difficulty; it is technologically possible to get excellent results doing the laundry with soap. As a practical matter, environmental considerations aside, it is much easier to get equally good results with synthetic detergents. That's probably the main reason why syndets, with less than 10% of the market in 1948, overtook soap in 1953 and why they have been increasing their lead ever since.

Of course, it's no longer possible to set environmental considerations aside. Makers and users of phosphate-based detergents are accused of crimes against nature, and many voices are calling for the elimination of phosphates from cleaning products. Some people are seriously advocating a return to soap as the solution to the "phosphate problem." At least two companies—Church & Dwight, a producer of baking soda (sodium bicarbonate), and Culligan, a soft water equipment maker—have seen in soap a way to board the antiphosphate bandwagon and use it to boost demand for what they sell.

Church & Dwight has been running an advertising campaign aimed at homemakers who are concerned about the environment. For one thing, the firm reminds housewives that baking soda is good for more than baking. If it isn't "good for everything in the home," it comes close, according to Church & Dwight. The company is distributing colorful cardboard "Dial to Easier Living" guides telling how to use sodium bicarbonate for more than 50 different household tasks, including scouring pots and pans, cleaning false teeth, and deodorizing kitty's litter box. The guides, like the ads, emphasize that Arm & Hammer baking soda, unlike conventional household cleaners and scourers, "contains no phosphates." Church & Dwight stresses that its other main product, sodium carbonate, can also help slow down eutrophication.

"At last," one ad begins, "something you can do about water pollution." By switching from phosphate-containing detergents to soap and sal soda, "you will be helping save our nation's waters because phosphates promote algae pollution—killing fish, stagnating water, and turning lakes into swamps."

Having thus appealed to nobler instincts, the ad gets down to specifics: "Just add ⅓ cup washing soda as machine is filling. Add clothes to washer and then add laundry soap. Use 1½ cups for front loading machines and 1⅔ cups for top loaders. In hard water, add ¼ cup washing soda to first rinse. The results: no polluting phosphates, plenty of white, bright clothes."

Fair enough. Soap is a very good cleaning agent in soft water. Sodium carbonate is a good water softener. Although it works by precipitating the "hardness" ions, rather than by sequestering them (as do the complex phosphates), the precipitate is a granular one that settles harmlessly to the bottom of the washing machine, not a floating curd that gums up the clothes.

The soap/sal soda combination was widely used before synthetic detergents and phosphates came along. It remains to be seen whether very many people nowadays will be willing to go to all the trouble—especially waiting around to toss the extra ¼ cup into the rinse (necessary in hard water; otherwise, the soap remaining in the wet clothing, even after spin-extraction, would still form curds).

The Culligan approach avoids that particular shortcoming. The Northbrook, Ill., firm is now marketing a "phosphate-free" laundry soap as a sideline to its main business of "water quality improvement."

Culligan also points out that soap is an excellent cleaner—in soft water—but that four out of five homes in the U.S. and Canada have hard water.

Culligan offers home-installed water-softening equipment. In an offhand slap at Church & Dwight and other makers of packaged water-softening products, Culligan adds that, "softening water before it is used eliminates hard water problems not only in the washing cycle, but also in rinsing."

Hard water was only one of the reasons, however, that the soap industry went all-out to develop synthetic detergents. Another, equally compelling reason was the increasing competition with the food and feed industries for a limited supply of natural fats and oils.

William C. Krumrei of Procter & Gamble points out that current annual tallow production is about 5 billion pounds per year. To produce soap to satisfy the needs of this country would require more than half this supply, thereby providing a serious interruption in the food supply of humans and animals, he asserts.

One may question the completeness of Mr. Krumrei's statistics—tallow is but one of many natural fats and oils—but as a generalization his point is well taken. With most of the world more concerned about malnutrition than about eutrophication, solving the "phosphate problem" at the expense of the world's food supply is not going to be acceptable. Whether phosphates disappear or not from detergents, it's unlikely that soap will rise again.

environmental contamination by metals

Earth is a metal-rich planet in a metal-poor universe. The core of our planet, by all evidence, is mainly metal—iron and nickel. The crust of earth is nearly one-quarter metal. This metal-laden spaceship is a mere speck, all but lost in a vast universe composed principally of the nonmetals hydrogen and helium.

Metals may not dominate outer space, but they dominate the chemical space of the periodic table. Of 105 known elements, 83 are metals (see following periodic table).

Some 68 of the metals have a density five or more times greater than water. These are the so-called heavy metals. On the whole these are far less common in the earth's crust than are the 15 lighter metals.

Many of the heavy metals have a voracious chemical appetite for sulfur, as was noted in Article 4. They are largely combined with sulfur in the earth's natural ore bodies, and when they inadvertently enter a living organism they relentlessly seek out the sulfur of that organism. Enzymes, the crucial catalyst-regulators of life chemistry, are dotted with sulfur atoms, and thus become the natural targets of heavy metals. The subsequent chemical bonding between enzyme sulfur and the heavy-metal intruders destroys enzyme function and thereby sickens and kills.

For us the rich metal environment of earth is a two-edged sword. The positive side has long been recognized: metals give civilization its building blocks—bridges, automobiles, airplanes, power lines, and more. Only recently have we been made aware of the negative side: some metals, when released widely to the environment, can be dangerous and ecologically disrupting. The following articles describe this threat. Article 19, "Trace Metals: Unknown, Unseen Pollution Threat," outlines the scope of the problem. Articles 20 and 21, from two different perspectives, focus on lead, one of the oldest heavy-metal contaminants. Articles 22 and 23 provide, respectively, a short summary and a more complete chronicle on the origin and magnitude of the mercury pollution problem. Article 24 throws light on the most recent heavy metals threat—cadmium.

Together these articles show us that the metal content of our environment has changed significantly and threateningly at the hand of man. We are only now groping for solutions to this long overlooked threat. Our likelihood for success will be explored in the articles to follow.

Non-metals

Light metals

Heavy metals

1 H																	2 He
3 Li	4 Be											5 B	6 C	7 N	8 O	9 F	10 Ne
11 Na	12 Mg											13 Al	14 Si	15 P	16 S	17 Cl	18 Ar
19 K	20 Ca	21 Sc	22 Ti	23 V	24 Cr	25 Mn	26 Fe	27 Co	28 Ni	29 Cu	30 Zn	31 Ga	32 Ge	33 As	34 Se	35 Br	36 Kr
37 Rb	38 Sr	39 Y	40 Zr	41 Nb	42 Mo	43 Tc	44 Ru	45 Rh	46 Pd	47 Ag	48 Cd	49 In	50 Sn	51 Sb	52 Te	53 I	54 Xe
55 Cs	56 Ba	57 La	58 Ce → 71 Lu	72 Hf	73 Ta	74 W	75 Re	76 Os	77 Ir	78 Pt	79 Au	80 Hg	81 Tl	82 Pb	83 Bi	84 Po	85 At	86 Rn
87 Fr	88 Ra	89 Ac	90 Th → 103 Lr	104 Ku	105 Ha												

trace metals: unknown, unseen pollution threat

staff of chemical & engineering news

Many chemical companies are now conducting internal surveys to hunt down possibly harmful trace elements in their processes.

Pollution of the environment with mercury, which seemed to burst into public view as a fullblown crisis, has now been shown to be a slowly unfolding saga of missed warning signals, painstaking laboratory research, and gradual enlightenment. . . . Summing up the lesson to be learned, Sen. Winston L. Prouty (R.-Vt.) has said, "What we have learned about mercury recently indicates that what we see and know about pollution is not as frightening perhaps as the unknown and unseen."

Efforts are now being made to detect the unseen and learn the unknown, but the task is formidable and likely to be tempered with the sentiment recently expressed by University of California's Dr. Garrett Hardin. . . . "It is difficult to believe in bad news until ruin is fully upon us."

Nevertheless, several chemical companies have decided to ferret out "bad news"—if it exists—by launching internal surveys to pinpoint other trace element pollutants which may be involved in their processes. Dow Chemical, BASF Wyandotte, Georgia-Pacific, Kaiser Aluminum & Chemical, and Weyerhaeuser all have such surveys under way. In Dow's case, 30 elements are on the check list, indicating the diversity of trace elements that may be involved in typical chemical processes. In most cases little is known about the environmental hazards these elements may pose.

The elements on Dow's list are chromium, cadmium, zinc, arsenic, nickel, lead, antimony, copper, thorium, cobalt, ruthenium, selenium, tellurium, boron, tin, strontium, cesium, barium, manganese, silver, beryllium, magnesium, thallium, yttrium, rubidium, cerium, molybdenum, osmium, vanadium, and bismuth.

Already Dow has made some changes as the result of its survey, which is still under way. Some metal compounds used as corrosion inhibitors or antimicrobials are being eliminated, the company says, by substituting other materials. Process and catalyst changes, elimination of use (even though efficiencies may be reduced), improved housekeeping, handling, and waste treatment procedures will all probably come into play as Dow learns more from its survey.

toxicity

The toxicity of trace metals is well documented. Arsenic, for example, has long been used as an instrument of murder and suicide. Lead poisoning may have affected as many as 1% of urban slum children, according to Dr. L. B. Tepper of University of Cincinnati's Kettering Laboratories. Lead, cadmium, arsenic, antimony, and beryllium have all caused accidental deaths in industry.

The most critical concern to public health experts today, however, is for subtle physiological changes caused by trace metals that may go completely undetected or, if detected, be attributed to other causes. How can scientists detect harmful responses to very low doses of trace metals? And once detected how can responses which are simply adaptive or homeostatic be differentiated from those which represent the first stages of disease? Also, synergistic and antagonistic relationships among trace metals must be defined, scientists active in trace metals research believe.

Until these questions and relationships are more thoroughly explored and answers found, air, water, and food residue standards are likely to be based on little more than guesses. As Dr. Emil Pfitzer, a University of Cincinnati environmental scientist jestingly puts it, some standards are first calculated by "a prominent scientist riding in a taxi on the way to a meeting."

Current confusion surrounding standards for trace metals is illustrated by the wide gap between U.S. and Soviet industrial standards for metals, according to Dr. Pfitzer. Often U.S. standards are a hundredfold higher than those in the U.S.S.R., he points out. In the U.S.S.R. subtle changes in conditioned reflex response are used to detect the lowest level at which an environmental agent has an effect on humans or animals. If the Soviet method is accurately picking up early signals of long-term chronic poisoning, then the U.S. standards are obviously too high, he reasons. But if the Soviets merely are measuring adaptive response to environmental change, as some U.S. experts argue they are doing, conditioned reflex response may be a largely useless tool, he adds.

Dr. Henry A. Shroeder, a physiologist in Dartmouth medical school's trace element laboratory, has spent much of his career seeking answers to the riddle of trace metals toxicity. Dr. Shroeder notes that it has been only for the past 100 years that man has been polluting his environment with metals in large amounts, from industrialization, smelting, refining, and burning of coal and oil for energy.

hazards

In the air, Dr. Shroeder says, "cadmium is a present and real hazard." Lead is a potential and imminent hazard, he adds. Nickel carbonyl—formed when finely divided nickel is emitted in an atmosphere of carbon monoxide during combustion of coal, petroleum, diesel fuel, and residual oils—is another potential danger. Dr. Shroeder and his coworkers have calculated that the annual global emission of nickel from fossil fuels into the air amounts to 70,000 tons, or 14.5% of commercial production. And in 1967, Battelle Memorial Institute cited nickel isodecylorthophosphate—a gasoline additive—as a possible environmental hazard.

Dr. Shroeder believes that toxic metals in the environment are a more insidious problem than pollution by pesticides, sulfur dioxide, nitrogen oxides, carbon monoxide, and other gross contaminants. No metal is degradable, he notes. To maintain the present environmental balance of trace elements, Dr. Shroeder urges that cadmium in air be eliminated by controlling emissions from zinc smelting, the lead be eliminated from gasoline, that nickel carbonyl be specifically treated to decompose this compound and that no nickel compounds be allowed in gasoline, and that beryllium and antimony in air be controlled by reducing particulate emissions from coal smokes.

Although burning of fossil fuels (including gasoline with additives) appears to be the largest source of trace element emissions to the air, other sources exist that may prove to be important. The Texas Water Quality Board has found, for example, that 1600 pounds per day of lead, 7900 pounds per day of zinc, 5000 pounds per day of cadmium, and 300 pounds per day of chromium were discharged primarily to the Houston Ship Channel in 1969. The observed concentrations were grossly in excess of those occurring in nature—more than 63,000 times for lead, 15 for cadmium, and 108,000 for chromium.

samples

Sediment samples showed "significant quantities of cadmium, lead, tin," and mercury, according to Texas officials. Toxic compounds were present in concentrations three times greater than those which can be tolerated for normal algal growth. Fish collected near the channel's mouth were generally very small, many were missing tail fins, and some were blinded with hard white crusts covering their eyes, Texas officials report.

In 1967, the Public Health Service analyzed shellfish taken from Raritan Bay, N.J., and adjacent interstate waters and found from 0.8 to 6.2 mg. of lead per kg. of tissue with an average value of 3.2 mg. per kg., a tenfold elevation compared to a normal range of 0 to 0.3 mg., PHS says. The results for nickel were about the same as for lead, that is, a tenfold elevation. PHS also analyzed shellfish for copper, chromium, and zinc; concentrations of these three elements, however, were not significantly above those in nature.

Carl Klein, assistant secretary of interior for water quality and research, told Congress last year [1970] that 4800 pounds of lead per day were being discharged to the Mississippi River between Baton Rouge and New Orleans. In the same area about 100 pounds per day of arsenic were also being discharged. Sen. Philip A. Hart's (D.-Mich.) subcommittee on Energy, Natural Resources and the Environment was told by Murray Stein, head of enforcement of the Environmental Protection Agency's water pollution control efforts, that the offending firms were Kaiser Aluminum & Chemical, Allied Chemical, and Ethyl Corp.

Arsenic occurs in phosphate rock used to make fertilizers and detergents and thus may end up in both rural and urban waterways. Tests by the Federal Water Quality Administration have shown up to 36 p.p.m. arsenic in laundry products.

In a study completed last spring [1971], the U.S. Geological Survey found 4% of 720 waterways sampled to have cadmium levels above PHS standards (10 micrograms per liter or 1 p.p.b.). 2% of the samples were above PHS's standard of 50 p.p.b. for arsenic. A few samples were also above standards for lead and mercury. The USGS survey concentrated on waterways used as sources for metropolitan water supplies.

Without a better grasp of what constitutes toxic levels and how trace metals may be transformed and accumulated in the environment, no hard and fast conclusions can be drawn concerning dangers to the public at current levels of exposure. Work is being done in this area, however, and—in the case of arsenic—early results have not been particularly comforting.

mechanism

At the University of Illinois, where biochemist John Wood has worked out the mechanism for the methylation of mercury, recent work by Dr. B. C. McBride (now at the University of British Columbia, Vancouver) and Dr. R. S. Wolfe indicates that arsenic, as well as selenium and tellurium, may be acted on by bacteria in nature to produce highly poisonous compounds.

Microorganisms in sediments that contain arsenic "convert the arsenic into the deadly poisonous dimethyl arsine," Dr. Wood told Sen. Hart's subcommittee. "This methyl arsenic compound will go through the water just the same as methylmercury does, [accumulate in fish, and] cause another problem," Dr. Wood says.

The work done by Dr. McBride and Dr. Wolfe indicates that methanobacteria act upon a variety of arsenic compounds to produce dimethyl arsine. Methyl cobalamin serves as the methyl donor in the reaction system. As^5+ is first reduced to As^3+. Arsenite is then methylated to form methyl arsonic acid. Methyl arsonic acid is reduced and methylated to form dimethyl arsinic acid ($As+$) and this product is further reduced to form dimethyl arsine (As^3-).

From their work, Dr. McBride and Dr. Wolfe conclude that pollution hazards exist when arsenic and its derivatives are introduced into an environment where anaerobic organisms are growing. Arsenic pesticides such as sodium methyl arsenate and calcium and lead arsenate "may be applied over large areas," the Illinois scientists note, "and eventually find their way into anaerobic aquatic or terrestrial environments where they can be converted to arsine derivatives." The importance of the methylation mechanism in "converting toxic molecules to more toxic derivatives should not be underestimated," they warn.

Virtually all the arsenic produced is recovered as by-product of lead, copper, and gold extraction. Because much more is produced as by-product than demand calls for (one gold mine in the West, for example, has produced 14,600 tons in a single year, an amount equal to demand in 1959), disposal is a nagging problem.

131

Table 4-1. Trace Metals May Pose Health Hazards in the Environment

ELEMENT	SOURCES	HEALTH EFFECTS
Nickel	Diesel oil, residual oil, coal, tobacco smoke, chemicals and catalysts, steel and nonferrous alloys	Lung cancer (as carbonyl)
Beryllium	Coal, industry (new uses proposed in nuclear power industry, as rocket fuel)	Acute and chronic system poison, cancer
Boron	Coal, cleaning agents, medicinals, glass making, other industrial	Nontoxic except as boran
Germa-nium	Coal	Little innate toxicity
Arsenic	Coal, petroleum, detergents, pesti-cides, mine tailings	Hazard disputed, may cause cancer
Selenium	Coal, sulfur	May cause dental caries, car-cinogenic in rats, essential to mammals in low doses
Yttrium	Coal, petroleum	Carcinogenic in mice over long-term exposure
Mercury	Coal, electrical batteries, other indus-trial	Nerve damage and death
Vanadium	Petroleum (Venezuela, Iran), chemicals and catalysts, steel and nonferrous alloys	Probably no hazard at cur-rent levels
Cadmium	Coal, zinc mining, water mains and pipes, tobacco smoke	Cardiovascular disease and hypertension in humans suspected, interferes with zinc and copper metabolism
Antimony	Industry	Shortened life span in rats
Lead	Auto exhaust (from gasoline), paints (prior to about 1948)	Brain damage, convulsions, behavioral disorders, death

Note: Bismuth, tin, and zirconium are also present as pollutants from industry, coal, and petroleum, respectively. C&EN has no data on their possible health effects. Titanium, alumi-num, barium, strontium, and iron are air pollutants that occur naturally in dust from soils. Other metals known to be in the environment—chromium, manganese, cobalt, copper, zinc, and molybdenum—are essential to human health and probably pose no danger at current levels.

Sources: Battelle Memorial Institute, Dartmouth Medical School

by-product

Like arsenic, cadmium is a by-product, occurring in phosphate, zinc, and other mineral deposits. The white metal, used principally in electrical batteries, is concentrated in shellfish in nature by a factor of 900 to 1600 times, according to the University of Cincinnati's Dr. H. G. Petering. In man, cadmium levels have been found to reach 30 mg. total body burden in 50 years from a starting point of about 1 microgram at birth.

Cadmium can cause emphysema when inhaled (as Cd) and is known to be present at levels of about 1 p.p.m. in cigarette smoke. It also causes renal damage, and may cause hypertension and cardiovascular disease.

Its physiological effects are complex and only partly understood. Cadmium mimics lead and mercury in its reaction with sulfhydryl groups, and zinc in its reactions with nitrogen and oxygen. It also affects copper metabolism in ways that are as yet unclear, Dr. Petering says.

In Japan, cadmium intoxication with kidney damage and a painful alteration in bone metabolism known as "itai-itai byo" (ouch-ouch disease) have resulted apparently from industrial contamination of water-ways used to flood rice paddies. . . . Though severe contamination in the past may have led to the disease, experts have not ruled out poor nutritional habits, such as low intake of calcium, protein and vitamin D as possible factors. This latter hypothesis focuses once again on the complex role that deleterious trace metals may play in altering the functioning of essential micronutrients.

At a recent [1971] symposium on the environmental effects of cadmium held at the University of Rochester, under auspices of the Environmental Protection Agency, the wide-scale contamination with cadmium in Japan was spotlighted as a unique opportunity for studies on dose-reponse relationships. Virtually nothing is known at present about dysfunctions at very low concentrations on the cellular level nor about teratogenic and genetic effects of cadmium. In addition, the long-term effects of cadmium when present in combination with chelating agents such as nitrilotriacetic acid (NTA) and ethylenediaminetetraacetic acid (EDTA) should be studied, the Rochester group concluded.

benefits

Another factor which must be added to this tangled riddle is that of the still unknown health benefits of trace elements and combinations of these. Recent comparison of cardiovascular death rates in Georgia, by USGS's Dr. Hansford T. Shacklette and coworkers, for example, indicates that nine high death rate counties (higher by a factor of two than nine low death rate counties) have a relative deficiency in most of the more than two dozen elements for which soils in the 18 counties were analyzed.

Surgeon General Jesse L. Steinfeld noted before Sen. Hart's subcommittee that "knowledge is our primary need." Through basic research," he says, we need to know much more about levels of trace elements essential for health, levels which can be tolerated without health hazards, the pathenogenesis of toxicity, interactions, and repair and defense mechanisms at the cellular, organ, and body level.

"The problem of the health effects of toxic metals is a legitimate area for concern," he summarizes. "In the final analysis there are no nonhazardous substances. There are only nonhazardous ways to use substances."

lead, the inexcusable pollutant

paul p. craig

Americans today are carrying around in their bodies one hundred times the amount of lead they would have absorbed from a primitive environment.

If the crust of planet earth were to be chopped into a million pieces, somewhere between ten and fifteen of them would consist of the chemical element lead. As far as scientists have been able to discover up to now, lead contributes nothing to the development or maintenance of life, either in plants, or in animals, or in man. On the contrary, the evolutionary process that brought forth the human species seems to have recognized long ago that lead is poisonous to life; the farther upward one searches in the chain of species that feed upon other species, the less lead is found.

Yet, within the degree of accuracy to which such matters have been measured, the scientific indications are that the surface waters of earth's oceans today contain ten times as much lead as they did before the human animal emerged.

And the American people today are carrying around in their bodies one hundred times the amount of lead they would have absorbed from a primitive environment.

What does this mean?

Simply that man has changed his natural environment to such an extent and has employed lead in making the changes in such a way as to systematically poison himself.

Originally, all the lead on earth was buried in the planetary crust. Man began digging out the metal about 5,000 years ago, probably after finding it accidentally in the ores from which he obtained silver. Tin also was present in silver-bearing rock, and could be mixed with lead to form pewter and so provide a protective coating for copper pots and pans that otherwise poisoned the food prepared in them. Lead was likewise popular with potters, who used it as glazing for ceramic vessels.

Reprinted from *Saturday Review*, October 2, 1971, pp. 68–75. Copyright 1971 Saturday Review, Inc. The author is a physicist at the U. S. Atomic Energy Commission's Brookhaven National Laboratory. He is a member of the board of trustees of the Environmental Defense Fund and chairman of its Committee on the Environmental Impact of the Automobile.

The poisonous effects of lead on the human organism have long been recognized. The early Romans, in their quest for silver, smelted large amounts of ore that contained lead. About 400 tons of lead were recovered for each ton of silver. The mining and smelting were performed by slaves, who undoubtedly often died of lead poisoning.

The lead was used for a wide variety of purposes, including roof sheathing, and cooking and wine vessels. Democritus noted that the acidity of wine could be reduced by the addition of lead oxide. Pliny specified that leaden pots must be used in making grape syrup; dissolved lead apparently improved the flavor of the syrup.

Since the ruling classes had most access to leaden vessels, they constituted the group that was most poisoned. The resulting decline in their birth rate and in their creative and governing ability has been documented impressively by Dr. S. C. Gilfillan in an ingenious piece of detective work. . . .

Centuries after the Roman Empire collapsed, apparently without understanding what had happened to it, pioneers of modern American civilization acted to prevent a repetition of the performance. Governors of the Massachusetts Bay Colony in New England outlawed the distillation of rum in leaded vessels in order to prevent what were then called "the dry gripes."

Generations of boys on both sides of the Atlantic played with toy lead soldiers until the toys were shown to be connected with sickness and the death of children who nibbled on them.

During the early years of the twentieth century, lead poisoning was common among house painters. The most characteristic symptom was wrist drop, a tendency of the wrist muscles to sag. The sagging resulted from lead interference with the nerves that control the muscles.

The early mortality of painters and workers in the lead processing industry was relatively high and easily identified. On diagnosis, action could be taken to eliminate the sources of exposure. The most decisive action was banning lead from interior paint some years ago. This protected the painters, but not the infants and toddling children who picked off and ate paint peeling from neglected walls. New coats of lead-free paints blocked off the danger residing in the old leaded paints, but when the new coats wore thin and were not in their turn covered, the underlying lead paints again came within reach of the children's hands.

Convulsions, delirium, coma, severe and irreversible brain damage, blindness, paralysis, mental retardation, and death can result from lead poisoning. In children, the early symptoms are particularly subtle. Victims become irritable, sleepy, or cranky. They may be troubled either with diarrhea or its opposite, constipation. Only if a pediatrician is looking for lead poisoning is he likely to identify it in a child, for most children are frequently irritable, sleepy, or cranky. So, although lead poisoning is known to be one of the major sources of injury to young children in low-income families (two hundred die every year in America alone), lead's impact on other children can only be surmised.

Most lead that enters the human body does so through food. This lead, which enters the stomach, is rather inefficiently absorbed by the body, and only about 5 to 10 per cent of the lead ingested actually enters the blood stream. Inhaled lead is far more serious, for the fine particles emitted by automobiles are retained within the alveoli of the lungs and are absorbed by the body with an efficiency of about 40 per cent. Thus, a small quantity of lead inhaled can do far more damage than a large quantity consumed. By emitting lead into the atmosphere, man has bypassed complex and effective mechanisms designed by nature to keep the lead burden of humans low.

Because of these circumstances, the emission of lead through the exhaust pipes of internal combustion-engined automobiles has become man's greatest worry in connection with lead poisoning—greatest because it has been growing constantly since 1923, when lead was first introduced as an additive to automotive fuel. Although concentrated in the cities and hence visited most heavily on city dwellers, atmospheric lead is carried by the winds and deposited all over the globe. The index of its presence is the lead content of the Greenland icecap, which has been traced back to 800 B.C. and shown to have been explosively accelerated during the last half century.

The total daily intake of lead in the food and drink of an individual American is typically about 300 micrograms, of which 15 to 30 micrograms is absorbed. The average city dweller experiences an atmospheric lead level of about 2 micrograms per cubic meter. He inhales about 20 cubic meters of air per day, of which 40 per cent, or 16 micrograms, is absorbed. Thus, at least one-third of the total lead absorbed by average American urban dwellers arises directly from atmospheric lead.

In unfavorably situated cities, the concentration of atmospheric lead can be substantially higher than the levels just mentioned. In midtown Manhattan, for example, average values of 7.5 micrograms of lead per cubic meter of air have been reported. Lead content of some city dust approaches 1 per cent, which is equal to the proportion of lead found in some ores. Grass harvested from alongside highways has been found to contain as much as one hundred times the lead concentration of grass not exposed to automobile exhaust. Recently, at the Staten Island Zoo, two leopards were paralyzed, a horned owl's feathers dropped out, and a number of captive snakes lost their ability to slither. All proved to be victims of lead poisoning, and the source of the lead was the grass, leaves, and soil in outdoor cages, as well as the paint on the cage bars. Dr. T. J. Chow of Scripps Oceanographic Institute recently reported that in San Diego average values of lead are now 8 micrograms per cubic meter of air; he noted that the concentrations are rising at a rate of 5 per cent per year. There can no longer be any question that atmospheric lead is at a dangerous level.

The degree of the danger cannot be stated precisely without an accurate measure of the amount of the lead burden now being carried by the bodies of Americans and of the margin between this level and that known to produce crippling or fatal effects. If the margin is small, it is important to search for subtle effects that would not be noticed in a conventional public health survey.

The most commonly used indicator of exposure to lead is the concentration of lead in the blood. There is at present a narrow margin between the average blood lead level in Americans and the level associated with severe poisoning. The level considered diagnostic of lead poisoning in healthy males is 0.8 parts of lead per million (ppm) parts of blood. Today the average American's blood lead concentration is about 0.2 ppm—one-fourth of the amount commonly considered hazardous to adults and almost half the level indicative of acute poisoning in children.

At best, the margin of safety concept is questionable; at worst, it can be disastrous. The definition of the margin depends in large degree upon the sophistication of diagnosis. Safety levels are set so that known deleterious effects do not occur—at least not often. As diagnostic techniques improve, effects in individuals can be detected at lower levels. As statistical techniques improve, it becomes possible to search for subtle effects in large populations, as well as for synergistic effects in which the sensitivity of the body to a particular insult is increased due to the presence of some other pollutant, dietary deficiency, or the like. With increased sophistication, one also can detect groups of people who are especially sensitive. In the case of lead, it is essential that the most sensitive group—the children—be given particular emphasis in setting permissible criteria and standards.

There has developed in recent years a considerable body of data indicating that a margin of safety for lead exposure may not exist at all and that damage may occur even at low exposure levels. If this is the case, it is imperative that unnecessary exposure to all types of lead be held to an absolute minimum.

Experiments with animals offer an excellent approach to the search for low-level effects. In an elegant series of tests carried out over many years in a special low-lead-level laboratory, Dr. Henry Schroeder of Dartmouth College has found that chromium-deficient mice carrying lead burdens typical of those found in the American people have reduced life spans and increased susceptibility to disease. Chromium deficiency is thought to occur in many humans. Recent experiments in Russia have shown that rabbits exposed to atmospheric lead at levels not much different from those found in some U. S. cities exhibit various functional disabilities and pathological anomalies.

Detailed statistical studies are necessary to delineate the extent of these subtle effects, which may consist of a diminishing of intelligence by a few points, a decrease in nervous coordination and mechanical dexterity, or a general rundown feeling.

In contrast to many other pollutants, lead is a cumulative poison. Studies of Americans show that the older a person is, the more lead is concentrated in his body. (A slight decrease occurs in persons over sixty years of age.) The total body burden of lead in middle-aged Americans is about 200 milligrams, of which about 90 per cent is concentrated in the skeletal structure.

As the impact of lead effluent upon our health and our economy becomes recognized, the need for controls is increasingly evident. The most stringent of these will have to be adopted by the United States, which now consumes about 1.3 million of the total world lead consumption of 2.2-million tons. Some of this consumption—the part that goes into electric batteries, solder, and pewter—can be recycled at the end of the useful lifetimes of those products, but lead used as a gasoline additive cannot be recovered. It can only be prevented from entering the atmosphere in the first place.

The impact of atmospheric lead emitted from automobile exhausts constitutes a threat to health so severe that on this count alone lead emissions should be prohibited. However, the major pressures for the elimination of lead from gasoline so far have not resulted primarily from this important concern, but rather from the fact that lead in gasoline interferes with the control of many other automobile emissions.

Of the many methods proposed to control the amount of hydrocarbons, carbon monoxide, and oxides of nitrogen leaving the exhaust pipes of automobiles, one of the most discussed is the catalytic converter. The catalytic converter depends on the filtering capability of porous material with a large surface area in proportion to the volume occupied. The pores in the material fill rapidly with lead particles when leaded gasoline is used, and the process of converting the other pollutants to their harmless constituents is blocked.

To end the blockage, major auto makers equipped most of their 1971 models with low-compression engines able to operate on 91-octane lead-free gasoline. This surprise action forced the oil companies to shift petroleum refining methods. Several of them have introduced low-lead and lead-free gasoline throughout the country.

Low-compression engines get fewer high-speed miles per gallon of fuel. Also, there is some evidence that emission of aromatic hydrocarbons increases as lead content of fuel falls. These points have been argued forcefully by the Ethyl Corporation and by Du Pont, the primary makers of tetraethyl lead, the gasoline additive. Pollution control devices that will operate on leaded gasoline can be built, they say. As alternatives to catalytic converters, they have demonstrated prototype thermo-reactors, which are claimed not to foul when leaded gasoline is used. Theoretically (but not yet practically), lead particulates can be removed from the exhaust stream by special filters and separation devices. Continued use of lead in gasoline, Ethyl and Du Pont contend, will provide needed engine lubrication and avoid a controversial phenomenon called "valve seat pound-in," which may cause rapid wear of valve seats in cars using unleaded gas.

From an environmental point of view, the Ethyl and Du Pont approaches to the lead problem cannot be rejected or ignored. The environmentalist is primarily concerned with what comes out of the exhaust pipe rather than what goes into the gasoline. Reaction processes occurring in the internal combustion engine are complex and poorly understood. What is essential is that automotive emissions be controlled as expeditiously as possible, using the best technology currently available.

While the gasoline suppliers are now providing low-lead gasoline, it costs several cents per gallon more than leaded gasoline of the same octane rating. Cost-conscious motorists therefore are avoiding the new fuel. They will have to be encouraged to buy it. The encouragement could come through governmental regulation. With official standards in force, all manufacturers would compete on an equal footing. Unfortunately, such standards have yet to be set, although the Environmental Protection Agency has promised them for mid-December [1971]. By that time a year and a half will have passed since the Environmental Defense Fund's petition to the U.S. Department of Health, Education, and Welfare for establishment of criteria and standards for lead.

President Nixon has demonstrated his concern over lead poisoning by ordering all federally owned vehicles to operate on unleaded gasoline; however, because of bulk buying under long-term contract, the order cannot take practical effect until the next fiscal year [beginning July 1972]. The President has also proposed a tax on lead, but Congress has not been enthusiastic about enacting one.

Spurred by the 1970 Clean Air Act amendments sponsored by Senator Edmund S. Muskie of Maine (they authorized consideration of environmental health effects of fuel additives), the Environmental Protection Agency has issued several reports on the danger of lead pollution and on the economics of its removal. One recent document, published in August [1971], said lead-free gasoline could be made available across the country by 1975 at an additional cost to the motorist of between 0.2 and 0.9 cents per gallon of fuel.

The EPA published in June [1971] an interim report on a massive study of lead in several major cities. A comparison between atmospheric lead levels measured in 1961–62 and again in 1968–69 showed that ambient levels had increased by 13 to 33 per cent in Cincinnati, by 33 to 64 per cent in Los Angeles, and by 2 to 36 per cent in Philadelphia. The results of this important and alarming EPA study were unfortunately omitted from a National Academy of Sciences' study of lead released early in September [1971], which concluded from older information that "the lead content of the air over most major cities has not changed over the last fifteen years." The omission of the most recent and best study from the NAS report led the Academy to recommend in its final conclusions only that more research is required on the health impact of automotive lead. Subsequently, the press reported that the Academy study showed that "lead is an overstated peril" (*The Wall Street Journal*, September 7). Meanwhile, the President's Council on Environmental Quality reported that there is little doubt that, at the present rate of pollution, diseases due to lead toxicity will emerge within a few years. The National Academy lead study is a dramatic example of how our most prestigious scientific body is incapable of taking a stand regarding the risks associated with introduction into the environment of substances that damage people in insidious epidemiological ways.

It seems fair to say that if we did not now have lead in our gasoline, and if some gasoline manufacturer proposed to add lead to his product, his proposal would be denied. We are clearly risking our health for the sake of cheap speed on the road. Although lead in gasoline does not constitute the most severe threat to health and well-being confronting society, it is one of the most unnecessary threats–hence an unforgiveable one; yet, one we must all bear.

lead pollution—a growing hazard to public health

d. bryce-smith

Lead is ubiquitous: it is in the food we eat, the water we drink and the air we breathe. Yet it is one of the most insidiously toxic of the heavy metals to which we are exposed, particularly in its ability to accumulate in the body and to damage the central nervous system, including the brain. This article draws attention to some recent evidence that blood lead levels among the general population approach close to, and even exceed, those at which interference with metabolic processes can occur; and points out that a major cause of these high body burdens appears to be the inhalation of airborne lead resulting from combustion of the lead alkyl antiknock agents in gasoline.

The toxicology of lead is very complex. Inorganic lead (Pb^{2+}) is a general metabolic poison and is cumulative in man. It inhibits enzyme systems necessary for the formation of haemoglobin through its strong interaction with –SH groups, and has been said to interfere with practically any life-process one chooses to study.[1] Children and young people appear specially liable to suffer more or less permanent brain damage, leading *inter alia* to mental retardation, irritability and bizarre behaviour patterns. Lead-induced psychosis is said to show striking similarities to the manic-depressive type,[1a] Pb^{2+} can replace Ca^{2+} in bone, so tends to accumulate there; but an unpleasant feature is that it may be remobilized long after the initial absorption, *e.g.* under conditions of abnormally high calcium metabolism such as feverish illness, during cortisone therapy, and also in old age. It can cross the placental barrier, and thereby enter the foetus.

Lead alkyls such as tetraethyl-lead are even more poisonous than Pb^{2+},

Reprinted from *Chemistry in Britain*, February 2, 1971, pp. 54–56. The author is professor of Organic Chemistry at The University, Whiteknights Park, Reading, Great Britain. He is chairman of the European Photochemistry Association.

and are handled quite differently in the body: the effects are probably due to the derived R_3Pb^+ species. Urban atmospheres can contain *ca* 2 per cent—at most 10 per cent—of their lead in this 'organic' form.[1] The earliest toxic symptoms which, one must emphasize, have been observed in men and experimental animals at air concentrations much higher than those now normally found in cities, are psychical, *e.g.* excitement, depression, irritability. More serious occupational exposure can lead to insanity and death: cases have been recently reported from Greece.[2] Oddly enough, it is not apparently known whether children are more sensitive than adults to lead alkyls; but experience with the related alkyl-mercury compounds,[3] and with Pb^{2+},[1] suggests that it would be prudent to assume greater sensitivity in the absence of contrary evidence. It therefore remains to be established whether the present environmental exposure of children to 'organic' lead is safe or harmful.

Man has evolved in the presence of a certain amount of inorganic lead from natural sources, to which he might have adapted, so any assessment of the threat from environmental pollution must consider the increase above natural background levels during biologically recent time. To begin with, we know that over 2000kt of lead is mined each year, in comparison with about 180kt estimated to be naturally mobilized and discharged into the oceans from rivers. A recent examination by Japanese and American workers of annual snow strata in N. Greenland has revealed most elegantly that levels of airborne lead have increased markedly since the Industrial Revolution, and very sharply since about 1940: the findings are illustrated in Figure 4-1.[4] The increase in airborne lead is particularly important because *ca* 50 per cent of this lead can be absorbed on inhalation, in contrast with the 5–10 per cent absorbed from lead-contaminated food and water

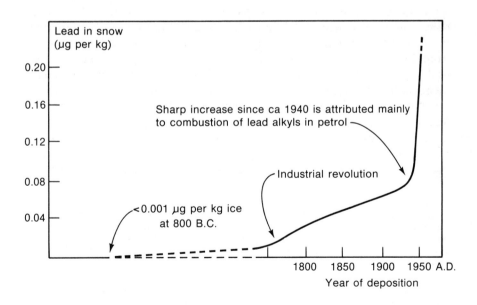

Figure 4-1. Lead content of snow layers (¬ice) in Northern Greenland.[4] Lead levels in South Polar icesheets were too low for detection before 1940, but have now risen to about 0.02μg per kg.

through the alimentary tract.* (Of course, fallout of airborne lead also adds to the lead present in food and water.[1])

Several studies have shown that the principal source of airborne lead in urban environments is the lead-containing aerosol emitted with exhaust fumes from motor vehicles running on petrol containing lead alkyl antiknock agents, *see e.g.* refs 1, 5, 6.

The question remains whether lead is being absorbed by man from the environment in amounts which could hazard public health. And one must remember that the lead absorbed in seemingly harmless trace amounts over a long period can accumulate in the body to levels which exceed the 'threshold level' for potential poisoning, and thereby produce long delayed toxic symptoms.[7] Even the present *average* blood lead levels of adults in industrialized countries are not far below those which can lead to overt clinical symptoms of poisoning: and it has been authoritatively reported that actual levels are related *inter alia* to the opportunity for exposure to the exhaust fumes from motor vehicles.[6] Figure 4–2 illustrates these points by reference to the various termed threshold levels for potential poisoning which have been given by different workers. For comparison, the present body fat levels of DDT (plus its metabolic product DDE) are also shown.

It is clear from Figure 4–2 that present body burdens of lead pose a far greater threat to human health than those of DDT. And to place the effect of lead in even better perspective, to my best knowledge no other toxic chemical pollutant has accumulated in man to average levels so close to the threshold for overt clinical poisoning.

The results illustrated in Figure 4–2 were obtained in the United States.[6] No comparable study with lead seems to have been made in Britain, although the levels of atmospheric lead in London appear to be of the same order as those found for comparable areas in the United States and elsewhere,[12] and lead levels in Warrington (Lancs), for example, are reported to be even higher than those found in California.[13] A recent [1970] survey from Liverpool University of lead in public water supplies showed that of 47 samples, 22 had lead levels at or above the internationally recommended maximum, and 3 had twice this amount.[14] The authors remarked that '. . . two million people were being regularly exposed to the risk of lead poisoning' from lead in water supplies.'†

Examination of a control group of Manchester children showed an average blood lead level of 0.309 ppm,[15] slightly higher than the average figures for American adults illustrated in Figure 4–2, and 17 per cent of

---

*This difference in absorption has led to confusion about the relative importance of airborne and dietary lead. Typically, an urban adult breathing air containing, say, $3\mu g$ m^{-3} of lead and respiring about 15 m^3 of air per day will *absorb* $20-25\mu g$ of lead per day from this source. Roughly the same amount ($15-30\mu g$) will be absorbed from a normal daily diet containing *ca.* $300\mu g$ of lead.

†Lead in drinking water appears to come partly from the still-continuing use of lead water pipes and soldered joints, and partly from atmospheric fallout. A new reservoir to serve the London area is now under construction at Datchett on a site adjacent to the M4 motorway.

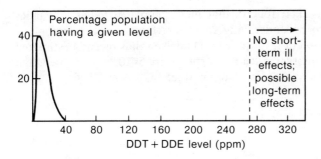

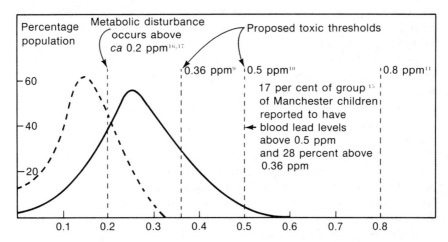

Figure 4-2. Relation between accumulated pollutant levels in man and threshold levels for potential poisoning: *(left)* levels of DDT + DDE in body fat;[8] *(below)* lead levels in blood for Philadelphia males 1961–2—dashed line for suburban inhabitants and full line for downtown inhabitants.[6] 'Kehoes' toxic threshold figure of 0.8 ppm[11] is considered in ref. 1 to be inapplicable to the question of public health in cities. Moncrieff's threshold level of 0.36 ppm[9] is based on studies with children.

these children were reported to have levels above 0.5 ppm.* Thus there is evidence that lead pollution is at least as serious a problem in Britain as in comparable regions in the United States.

Within the last year, Hernberg and Nikkanen (Helsinki)[16] and Millar *et al.* (Glasgow)[17] have independently presented most significant evidence that enzyme inhibition by inorganic lead occurs even over the range 0.2–0.4 ppm in blood, *i.e.* at the levels now present among the general urban

---

*The authors of ref. 9 reported that nearly half of a group of mentally retarded children had blood lead levels above the maximum level of 0.36 ppm found in a control group of normal children; see also similar work in ref. 18. Another recent study[17] found a much smaller proportion of raised blood lead levels in a group of mentally retarded children. The authors wrote that 'even modest elevations of blood lead may be associated with biochemical abnormalities in the child brain'.[17] Although a proportion of the raised lead levels may result from pica, *e.g.* the gnawing of paint, there is abundant clinical evidence that children are more prone than adults to suffer lead poisoning, with damage to the central nervous system: *see e.g.* refs 19, 20.

143

population (Figure 4–2). It follows that most people in towns and cities can already expect to be undergoing some interference with metabolism through their absorption of lead. Indeed, Danielson[1] has recently estimated that present levels of inorganic lead absorption are 5–10 times higher than that which might be toxicologically acceptable.

legislative and economic aspects

Legislation designed to reduce the amounts of lead alkyls added to petrol is in force or under high level discussion in the United States, Japan, France, W. Germany and Sweden. United States government cars are required to use no-lead or low-lead petrol. The use of leaded petrol is prohibited in Moscow. The Soviet Union has set a maximum permissible figure of 0.7μg m^{-3} of lead for the general atmosphere: most of the values measured during a prolonged survey of air pollution in the City of London were higher than this, ranging up to 4.8μg m^{-3}.

There is no legislation in Britain to control the amount of lead which may be added to petrol or present in the general atmosphere. In fact, the British Standard Specification concerned with petrol (BSS 4040) was recently revised, but no change in the lead content was recommended. The extra cost of producing lead-free petrol would be *ca* 2d per gallon, possibly less,[21] and Shell and British Petroleum have separately announced recently that they are ready to provide such petrol for sale in Britain, as and when required. I venture to hope that the companies concerned will soon feel encouraged to implement their public-spirited offer.

references

1. L. Danielson, *Bulletin No. 6, Ecological Research Committee.* Stockholm: Swedish Natural Science Research Council, 1970: see also refs. therein.
1a. H. Stern, *Chicago med. Sch. Q.,* 1969, 3, 87.
2. *The Times,* 7 December 1968.
3. Reviewed by G. Löfroth, *Bulletin No. 4, Ecological Research Committee.* Stockholm: Swedish Natural Science Research Council, 1969.
4. M. Murozumi, T. J. Chow and C. C. Patterson, *Geochim. cosmochim. Acta,* 1969, 33, 1247.
5. T. J. Chow, *Nature, Lond.,* 1970, 225, 295, and references therein: see also *Chem. engng News,* 9 March 1970, p. 42.
6. J. H. Ludwig, D. R. Diggs, H. E. Hesselberg and J. A. Maga, *Am. ind. Hyg. Ass. J.,* 1965, 26, 270.
7. E. Browning, *Toxicity of industrial metals,* 149. London: Butterworths, 1961.
8. K. A. Hassall (University of Reading) kindly provided this graph.
9. A. A. Moncrieff, O. P. Koumides, B. E. Clayton, A. D. Patrick, A. G. C. Renwick and G. E. Roberts, *Archs Dis. Childh.,* 1964, 39, 1:*cf. Br. Med. J.,* 1967, 3, 174.
10. R. Egli, E. Grandjean, J. Marmet and H. Kapp, *Schweiz. med. Wschr.,* 1957, 87, 1171.

11. R. A. Kehoe, *J. R. Inst. publ. Hlth Hyg.,* 1961, 24, 177.

12. R. E. Waller, B. T. Commins and P. J. Lowther, *Br. J. ind. Med.,* 1965, 22, 128.

13. E. Ward (Chief Public Health Inspector, Warrington), quoted in *The Guardian,* 15 May 1970.

14. J. A. Tolley and C. D. Reed, *Ecologist,* 1970, 1 (4), 31.

15. N. Gordon, E. King and R. I. Mackay, *Br. Med. J.,* 1967, 2, 480.

16. S. Hernberg and J. Nikkanen, *Lancet,* 10 January 1970, p. 63.

17. J. A. Miller, V. Battistini, R. L. C. Cumming, F. Carswell and A. Goldberg, *Lancet,* 3 October 1970, p. 695.

18. S. L. M. Gibson, C. N. Lam, W. M. McCrae and A. Goldberg, *Archs Dis. Childh.,* 1967, 42, 573.

19. E. M. Rathus, *Med. J. Aust.,* 1967, 19, 371.

20. M. A. Perlstein and R. Attala, *Clin. Pediat.,* 1966, 5, 292.

21. *Manufacture of unleaded gasoline,* US motor gasoline economics, vol. 1. Houston, Texas: Bonner and Moore Associates, 1967.

methyl mercury

philip h. abelson

Methyl mercury causes neurological damage, produces chromosomal aberrations, and has teratogenic effects.

During this century, in the United States, about 75 million kilograms
of mercury have been consumed; little information is available on its final
disposition or on the concentration of the element at specific points in
the environment. Recently, it has become clear that compounds of mercury
present a substantial hazard. Of particular significance is methyl mercury,
a highly toxic substance that causes neurological damage, produces chromosomal aberrations, and has teratogenic effects. It is mainly in this form
that mercury is found in food fishes. Recent [1969] studies have elucidated
some of the steps in the accumulation.*

Industrial wastes containing inorganic mercury or phenyl mercury find
their way into bottom muds of lakes. There they are converted by anaerobes
into CH_3Hg^+ or $(CH_3)_2Hg$. The latter compound is volatile, and it escapes
into the water column from the sediment. Though quite stable in alkaline
solutions, $(CH_3)_2Hg$ is converted to CH_3Hg^+ at low pH. This ion is soluble
in water, and it is concentrated by living things, usually appearing in the
body lipids. In part, the concentration may come by way of the food chain,
but apparently fishes may also accumulate the toxic ion directly. The
concentration factor from water to pike is of the order of 3000 or more.

Substantial mercury pollution in the Great Lakes became apparent in
March of [1970]. Mercury concentrations as high as 5 parts per million
were reported in some pickerel shipped from Canada. Typical concentrations
in fish taken from Lake Erie were 1 part per million or less. Further
investigations have confirmed the existence of a major environmental problem traceable to the dumping of large amounts of mercury-containing liquid
wastes. This discovery comes as a surprise to most scientists and apparently
to federal authorities. However, there was ample reason for looking for

*S. Jensen and A. Jernelöv, "Biological methylation of mercury in aquatic organisms,"
Nature **223**, 753 (1969).

Reprinted from *Science,* Vol. 169, p. 237, 17 July 1970. Copyright 1970 by the American
Association for the Advancement of Science. The author, a distinguished American scientist,
is the editor of *Science.*

such a phenomenon. Episodes in Sweden* and Japan had pointed to dangers arising when large quantities of mercury are discharged into the environment. In Sweden the use of methyl mercury in a seed dressing had led to a drastic decrease in wild bird populations. Near Minamata, Japan, between 1953 and 1960, 111 persons were reported to have been killed or to have suffered serious neurological damage as a result of eating fish and shellfish caught in mercury-contaminated areas. Among the 111 were 19 congenitally defective babies born of mothers who had eaten the fish and shellfish. Later, at Niigata, Japan, 26 cases of methyl mercury poisoning were noted. The affected persons and their families ate fish with a frequency of 0.5 time to 3 times a day; the fish contained mercury at concentrations of about 5 to 20 parts per million.

Physiological and cytological studies have revealed some of the behavior of methyl mercury. It tends to be associated with red blood cells and nervous tissue, and it easily passes the placental barrier, becoming moderately concentrated in the fetus. It can cause chromosomal disorders. Fruit flies consuming food containing methyl mercury at a concentration of 0.25 part per million had offspring carrying one extra chromosome.

It seems unlikely that anything approaching the Japanese observations will be seen in the region of the Great Lakes. There the concentrations of methyl mercury in fish are lower and fish are a less important part of the diet. Nevertheless, we have a substantial and long-enduring problem; even if fresh pollution were stopped, it would be many years before natural processes could cleanse the lakes.

This episode has not led to demonstrable tragedy, but it should remind us how much we risk when we convert our rivers to sewers and our lakes to cesspools.

---

*Report of an International Committee, "Maximum allowable concentrations of mercury compounds," *Arch. Environ. Health* **19,** 891 (1969).

mercury: anatomy of a pollution problem

lloyd dunlap

Government and industry will have to work together more openly and effectively if other mercurylike surprises are to be averted.

"Nature usually knows best," ecologist Barry Commoner is fond of telling audiences on lecture tours. Dr. Commoner follows this dictum with his second law of ecology: "Everything has to go somewhere."

These simple observations go far to explain man's current problems with mercury (and perhaps lead, cadmium, arsenic, and other trace environment contaminants). For the most part, mercury and other trace elements are found concentrated in various mineral ores and fossil fuels. Nature, as it were, has kept these elements locked away out of reach.

As industrialization has proceeded, however, mercury and other possibly harmful elements have been mined. 163 million pounds of mercury have been consumed in the U.S. in this century, for example. An additional 1 million pounds per year slip into the ecosphere through the burning of coal, investigators believe. Many petroleum deposits contain mercury in the parts-per-million range of concentration, and petroleum is therefore another important source of environmental mercury.

As Dr. Commoner points out, all of this has had to go somewhere. In March 1970, the full impact that mercury's final destination may have on the industrialized world began to be a matter of critical concern to scientists, physicians, and government officials.

Norvald Fimreite, though not the first scientist to discern that mercury, fish, and man are linked in the food chain, will almost certainly occupy much the same spot in the environmental revolution as Paul Revere does in the American Revolution. Mr. Fimreite sounded the alarm, loudly, in March 1970.

Reprinted from *Chemical & Engineering News,* Vol. 49, July 5, 1971, pp. 22–34. Copyright 1971 by the American Chemical Society and reprinted by permission of the copyright owner. The author is affiliated with *Chemical & Engineering News.*

dangerous levels

It was Mr. Fimreite who, while a graduate student at the University of Western Ontario, analyzed fish from Lake St. Clair and reported that dangerous levels of mercury were present in many of them. Dr. A. Jernelöv, of the University of Stockholm, Sweden, who happened to be in the U.S. at the time, was called to Ontario by Canadian authorities, where he informed them that methylation of inorganic mercury was undoubtedly responsible for the high levels in fish.

Quickly government units on both sides of the U.S.-Canadian border began investigations that led to the finding that Dow Chemical's Canadian subsidiary, Wyandotte Chemical (now BASF Wyandotte), and virtually every other concern using the mercury cell route to chlorine-caustic soda manufacture were releasing mercury to the environment. Depending on the plant, mercury discharges typically ranged from 5 to 60 pounds per day. In some instances, plants had been in operation 20 years.

In short order and as a direct effect, fishing restrictions (closure, embargo, warning, or catch-release orders) were issued by state governments. By September of 1970, investigators at Oak Ridge National Laboratory had tabulated 18 states where some such restriction had been put into effect. Elevated mercury levels were found in the waterways of 33 states. Commercial fisheries were particularly hard hit by the restrictions and embargoes.

A question that occurred early to many chemically trained observers was how could an element whose compounds long have been known to be poisonous be released into waterways by technically sophisticated chemical companies? With the waters as muddied as they now are and with lawsuits in some cases still pending, no clear-cut answer to that question is ever likely to emerge. Some industry critics are prone to take the cynical view that chlorine-caustic makers knew the dangers involved, but went ahead anyway simply to save a buck. Others point out that some firms had already initiated mercury audits and process changes based on internally generated evidence that mercury losses were substantial. Thus, while industry may not be the total villain, it isn't a complete hero, either.

Some companies—such as Dow Chemical, BASF Wyandotte, and B. F. Goodrich—while reacting with pained alacrity, have talked fairly freely of what went wrong. Others have tended to clam up, in some cases because their legal departments have told them to. (Dow, BASF Wyandotte, Allied Chemical, Diamond Shamrock, Georgia-Pacific, International Mining & Chemical, Olin, Oxford Paper, Pennwalt, Kaiser Aluminum & Chemical, and Weyerhaeuser have all been sued at one time or another for mercury pollution, and some of the cases are still pending. In addition, it is not at all unlikely that new litigation may crop up.)

informed ignorance

The general corporate reaction has been to plead "informed ignorance." Weyerhaeuser, Allied, Pennwalt, Goodrich, and BASF Wyandotte joined Dow in telling *Chemical & Engineering News* that they simply did not know that inorganic mercury could be methylated and concentrated in biological systems until Mr. Fimreite's alert in March 1970. As Herbert D. Doan, then president of Dow Chemical, put it, "No one realized until recent research in Sweden brought it to light, that mercury itself or inorganic mercury could be biologically converted to organic dimethylmercury, which is the form predominantly found in fish. When I say no one, I mean no one in Dow, no one in industry, no one in the government or the universities."

With the benefit of hindsight, it might now be said that chlorine-caustic soda makers should have known that mercury can be methylated in rivers and lakes. In 1960, L. T. Kurland of the Mayo Clinic speculated that biologic methylation of mercury might have been involved in the Minamata Bay, Japan, disaster. In this diaster, more than 40 persons died of mercury poisoning and more than 100 were seriously affected. Dr. Kurland's work was apparently discounted, however, when an investigation showed that the acetaldehyde and vinyl chloride facilities implicated in the Minamata Bay incident were emitting methylmercury formed from inorganic catalysts during the manufacturing process.

By late 1967, however, Dr. Jernelöv had demonstrated mercury methylation in aquaria sludge. The next year, Dr. John M. Wood, a University of Illinois biochemist, demonstrated that the methylation reaction can take place in natural systems and began working out the biochemistry involved.

Dr. Wood has told Sen. Philip A. Hart's (D.-Mich.) subcommittee on Energy, Natural Resources and the Environment that he tried to sound the alarm by alerting "all the people I thought might be able to influence developments in this area in Washington," but that he was unsuccessful in his efforts. He says that he also contacted a few companies without any apparent success in impressing upon them the gravity of the problem. Had he to do it over again, Dr. Wood says, he might well take his story directly to the press.

little learned

Dr. David Klein, a professor of chemistry at Hope College, expressed dismay when he testified before Sen. Hart's subcommittee that so little had been learned from the Minamata Bay incident, from a similar crisis at Niigata, Japan, and from problems of a less severe but nevertheless critical nature in Sweden, where alkyl mercury compounds used as agricultural seed dressings had been implicated in decreased bird populations. U.S. government scientists attended conferences on mercury in Sweden in 1966, Dr. Klein says, and one in May 1967 sponsored by the International Atomic Energy Agency, without any visible effects on the level of concern in the U.S.

Even a study performed for a government agency (the U.S. Public Health Service) was ineffective. In July 1967 Battelle Memorial Institute, Columbus, Ohio, operating under contract No. Ph-86-66-165 issued its final report on "Design of an Overview System for Evaluating Health Hazards of Chemicals in the Environment." In this report, Battelle notes both the Minamata disaster and the problems in Sweden, where mercury had been found in fish as well as birds. "These observations indicate that mercury from environmental sources can accumulate in the food chain and be transferred to man," Battelle says.

"Mercury contamination in chlorine production is especially important," the report adds. In summary, the Battelle group says that "significant quantities of mercury are released to the environment each year [from chlorine-caustic production] which apparently cannot be traced and which to date cannot be accounted for. There exists a striking lack of fundamental information on national levels of mercury in our air, water, and food."

By May 1969, news of inorganic mercury's transformation in nature and accumulation in food chains had hit the press in the form of a three-article series in *Environment* magazine, a monthly published by the St. Louis-based Committee for Environmental Information.

In response to Sen. Hart's criticism of lack of government awareness, Carl Klein, assistant secretary of the interior for water quality and research, told the Senator's subcommittee that at the time "people were in the middle of worrying about, first, sewage and, second, major industrial items."

who pays?

The failure by both government and corporate officials to recognize the mercury problem has resulted in what Ralph Nader has called "victims without crimes." Certainly fishing interests—sporting and commercial—ranging down to bait sellers and resort town entrepreneurs, have been among the victims of mercury pollution from chlor-alkali plants. Who is to pay the bill, which probably reaches into the billions of dollars in lost income?

Organic chemist Albert J. Fritsch, who accompanied Mr. Nader to testify before Sen. Hart, believes it should be chemical companies. "No company," he told Sen. Hart's subcommittee, "which has caused this desecration should be allowed to report profits until the waterways are again free of their junk [mercury]."

In their favor, chlor-alkali makers have cooperated without exception in lowering mercury output according to government stipulations and many of them—Dow foremost of all—have helped lead the way in developing abatement programs and conducting research on mercury's environmental impact.

Dow, for example, has agreed to dredge up the mercury in the area downstream from its Sarnia, Ont., plant if authorities decide that dredging would be effective. The company has also helped fund Dr. Wood's work at the University of Illinois and has provided sulfhydryl resins to the University of Rochester's Dr. Thomas Clarkson. These resins may be effective in binding and rendering inactive methylmercury that is ingested while, at the same time, speeding the rate of mercury excretion. . . . Dow is currently attempting to modify such resins to increase the effectiveness they have already shown in animal tests at Rochester.

In addition, Dow, BASF Wyandotte, Georgia-Pacific, Kaiser Aluminum & Chemical, and Weyerhaeuser have all initiated trace metals surveys in an attempt to pinpoint any sources of environmental contamination that may have escaped notice until now. Dow has openly committed itself to a policy of "zero emissions" of all pollutants. The company confesses that it does not expect to reach this goal overnight, but that all processes should be engineered with it in mind.

151

mercury sources

Just as early warnings from abroad of hazardous levels of envionmental mercury had their roots in agricultural as well as industrial sources, so too has the problem in the U.S. broadened far beyond a concern centered on chlor-alkali emissions alone.

The first word that mercurials used as fungicides on seed might be an environmental risk came out of Sweden at about the same time (1955) that residents of the Minamata Bay area began to come down with the then-mysterious "Minamata disease." Swedish ornithologists observed a decrease in population of seed-eating and predatory birds, and by 1958 high mercury residues (4 to 200 p.p.m.) had been found in the liver and kidneys of dead birds. Further study revealed that feathers of museum avian specimens contained fairly constant, low levels of mercury until 1940. Specimens taken since 1940 show mercury levels 10 to 20 times higher. It was shortly after 1940 that methylmercury and ethylmercury were introduced as seed dressings.

In contrast to land feeders, fish-eating birds showed a relatively constant increase in mercury content of their feathers throughout the 1900's, suggesting that in Sweden, at least, mercury water pollution has increased at a rate proportional to general industrialization.

In February 1966, alkyl mercury compounds were banned from general use in Sweden and bird populations have responded favorably, according to Swedish reports. In the U.S., however, unhappy foreign experience with alkyl mercurials apparently was again discounted. Disaster was to strike an Alamogordo, N.M., family, the Hucklebys, before the U.S. Government, through the Department of Agriculture, took action.

Though the facts of the matter have not been legally established, Ernest Huckleby apparently acquired mercury fungicide-treated grain and used it as hog feed (though label warnings on bags of such material clearly forbid such use). After some time, one of the hogs was butchered and eaten; the Huckleby family apparently continued to eat the tainted meat even after several other hogs became sick and died. By December 1969, some three to four months after the grain had first been fed to the animals, three of the Huckleby children had been permanently injured from mercury poisoning. Following a Huntley-Brinkley newscast describing the incident on Feb. 17, 1970, the Department of Agriculture notified Nor-Am Agricultural Products, Inc. (a company in which Morton International is a major shareholder), maker of the seed dressing, that registration of its Panogen mercury seed dressing products was suspended and that such products were to be recalled from the market with further shipments unlawful.

imminent hazard

In contrast to the Swedish case history, Agriculture's move to ban alkyl mercury seed dressings did not go very smoothly. Nor-Am quickly sought and got an injunction in District Court for the Northern District of Illinois in Chicago lifting the ban on the basis that it was arbitrary and capricious. The government suspension was ordered on the basis that such action was necessary to prevent an imminent hazard to the public, which is the only

152

basis upon which such suspension can be legally ordered. Though the Government did not pin its move solely to the Huckleby case, no other instances of "public hazard" were cited.

Also, the Secretary of Agriculture's order of Feb. 18 applied only to Nor-Am's Panogen. Alkyl mercury products made by Du Pont and Merck continued to be sold for more than a month.

Moreover, Agriculture's interpretation of the Federal Insecticide, Fungicide, and Rodenticide Act under which the suspension order was made appears to have been somewhat loose, according to Nor-Am. In its letter of suspension to Nor-Am, the department said "the directions for use and warning and caution statements on labels of the products were *inadequate to prevent* [italics added] the treated seed screenings and sweepings from being fed to hogs." But section 2.z(2) (c) and (d) of the act states that "the term misbranded shall apply . . . if the labeling . . . does not contain directions for use which are necessary *and if complied with* adequate for the protection of the public," and "if the label does not contain a warning . . . which may be necessary *and if complied with* adequate to prevent injury" to man, useful animals, and vegetation.

Nor-Am first decided to carry its case to the U.S. Supreme Court. Though the company claimed that it never expected to sell another dollop of Panogen, the battle had become a matter of principle. At issue was whether industry is to be subject to control by administrative fiat, a company spokesman says.

Nor-Am's preliminary injunction was overturned in the U.S. Court of Appeals (7th circuit) on the basis that the courts had no jurisdiction to grant relief until recourse through administrative channels had been exhausted. Thus Nor-Am saw itself as being caught in the middle, its product line banished on questionable grounds prior to any hearing, and its recourse to the courts blocked by the circuit court judgment. Though Nor-Am did proceed as far as filing its writ requesting review in the U.S. Supreme Court, the company has since dropped the case.

Table 4-2. Preparation of Chlor-alkali Is Biggest User of Mercury

	1969 CONSUMPTION[a]
Chlor-alkali production	1575
Electrical apparatus	1417
Paints	739
Industrial and control instruments	531
Dental preparations	232
Catalysts	225
Agriculture[b]	204
General laboratory use	155
Pharmaceuticals	55
Pulp- and papermaking	42
Other uses[c]	736
Total	5911

[a]Thousands of pounds. [b]Includes fungicides and bactericides for industrial purposes. [c]Includes university and other research, and government allocation for military and scientific purposes.

Source: U.S. Bureau of Mines

Summing up the U.S. experience as of May 1970, R. W. Purdy, deputy director of the Michigan Department of Natural Resources, says that "the contamination of the environment by mercury compounds represents a serious fault in our present environmental protection programs. Looking back on the serious incidents that occurred in Japan and Sweden, our lack of knowledge about the use, disposal, effects, and other characteristics of mercury compounds now appears incredible."

mercury sources

Since Alamogordo and Lake St. Clair there has been a flurry of activity aimed at detailing the extent of the danger posed by mercury and other trace elements. Where environmental mercury comes from, how to analyze for it, where it goes, how it is transformed, what constitutes a toxic level in man, and what may be done to remove or neutralize existing concentrations have all been investigated and debated.

Though sources of environmental mercury are easy enough to document and reel off, close examination of these sources reveals how complex may be the task of dealing with mercury pollution. Little of the mercury in fossil fuels, for example, is trapped with the fly ash; instead it apparently is a gaseous product of combustion. Evidence now exists that this gaseous mercury is washed from the air by rain, with portions of it being cycled to rivers, lakes, and oceans, where it is, of course, methylated.

Mercury in rainfall over land is apparently bound to the soil where, again, it may be methylated, though as yet this process has not been clearly proved. Rainwater averages about 0.2 p.p.b. mercury, the U.S. Geological Survey finds.

Equally problematical is the use of mercurial mildewicides in paints. Here, as was true of seed treatment compounds, mercury is intentionally placed in the environment via use in paints, their application to building exteriors, boats, and the like, and consequent weathering.

Electrical equipment is another area of growing mercury use. Alkaline batteries, for example, contain about 8% mercury and these are often burned in municipal incinerators. The biggest user of mercury is the chlor-alkali industry, where the element is not only present in effluent discharges but, in some cases, in the caustic soda as well.

Mercury from these and other sources has apparently become very widely distributed. Tuna and swordfish taken from ocean waters off Malaya and Africa have shown levels of mercury in excess of the FDA recommended maximum of 0.5 p.p.m. 10.5 million tins of tuna have been recalled on FDA order, and swordfish has been banished from U.S. foodshelfs. Tablets prepared from seal livers—popular with health food faddists—contain very high mercury levels. Preliminary research indicates that mercury may be detrimentally affecting growth rates of phytoplankton and diatoms at concentrations in sea water as low as 0.1 p.p.b. [*Science,* **170**, 737 (1970)].

thin margin

For humans, the margin of safety between current levels of mercury in water, fish, and other foods, and levels which would have major, overt effects on public health may be harrowingly thin.

154

The lowest whole-blood concentration at which toxic symptoms have occurred in humans is 0.2 microgram per gram (at Niigata, Japan). The Swedes have associated this with the steady intake of 0.3 mg. per day for a 70-kg. man. Using a safety factor of only 10, the Swedish Commission on Evaluating the Toxicity of Mercury in Fish calculates that the allowable daily intake (ADI) of mercury is 0.03 mg. per 70 kg. or 0.4 microgram per kg. The safe level in whole blood, calculated on the same basis, would be 0.02 microgram per gram.

Already, Dr. Bruce McDuffie, a chemist at the State University of New York, Binghamton, has analytically confirmed cases where diet club members on fish diets have shown blood mercury levels of up to 0.06 microgram per gram, a level three times the "safe" limit and within a factor of less than four from the level where toxic symptoms have occurred. Simple computation shows that if fish containing the 0.5-p.p.m. limit were eaten daily, only 60 grams could be consumed each day without blood mercury levels being elevated over the safe limit.

Overt neurological symptoms of mercury intoxication—numbness and tingling of hands, feet, or lips, ataxia, constricted visual field, emotional disturbances, and others—may or may not occur at the 0.2 microgram-per-gram blood level. Wide variation in individual susceptibility apparently exists. Fetuses and children are most sensitive, whereas some adults may lack symptoms at 10 or even 100 times the level used by the Swedes for calculating an ADI.

No one knows, at this point, what effects low-level chronic exposure to methylmercury may have. Because methylmercury's deleterious effects strike mainly at the brain and central nervous system, low-order effects might well be misdiagnosed as psychological disorders. In a report to the Department of Health, Education, and Welfare's Pesticide Advisory Committee, a study group on mercury hazards called for animal experiments to determine maternal-fetal effects, including genetic abnormalities, chromosomal aberrations, and teratogenic effects in relation to long- and short-term exposure at various levels. Studies of possible synergisms of methylmercury with other neurotoxic chemicals (such as DDT, polychlorinated biphenyls, and lead) were also urged.

third law

Harking back to Dr. Barry Commoner's "laws of ecology," the third law states that "everything is connected to everything else" and in the case of mercury this law appears to be unbreachable. The only known way to break the cycle that finds mercury working its way into human tissue is to bury the victims in indestructible sealed vaults. Short of this unsatisfying solution, the first step would appear to be to stop immediately mercury's release to the environment.

To accomplish this, the HEW study group has recommended that "all controllable sources of mercury contamination should be either eliminated or maximally reduced." The group urges elimination of alkyl mercury pesticides and severe restriction of the use of other mercurial pesticides (such as phenyl mercurials). The study group also urges reduction of discharges from chlor-alkali and plastic plants to "levels approximating background levels." In addition to steps taken to this end by manufacturers themselves, several chemical companies now offer technology and processes designed to reduce or eliminate such discharges.

Texas, Arizona, Oklahoma, Vermont, Florida, Massachusetts, and other states have moved to legally restrict mercury discharges and, in some cases, use. Illinois regulations limit total plant discharge to 5 pounds per year and mercury concentration in effluents to 0.5 p.p.b. Massachusetts has banned mercury in marine paints. New York is expected to prohibit the use of mercury in all paints.

Other sources of contamination—chemicals, cosmetics, pharmaceuticals, sewage, and fossil fuels—must also be brought under control, the HEW study group on mercury hazards concludes.

Even if all sources of additional contamination could be instantly eliminated, accumulations already in place are more than enough to be potential troublemakers for years to come. Dr. John Wood points out, for example, that mercury levels in fish in the St. Clair River area contaminated by Dow's Sarnia plant effluent account for no more than 100 pounds of mercury taken up by all the fish in the basin. "This means that less than 0.2% of the mercury deposited in this system has gone through food chains to make this area very dangerous in terms of fish consumption."

Several means of removing existing mercury accumulations have been suggested, with dredging and burying being mentioned most often. Oak Ridge National Laboratory, in its study of the problem, listed several "decontamination" techniques, but all either have known drawbacks or are plagued by unknowns concerning effectiveness or "ancillary ecological effects."

Dr. Wood, who has emerged as the U.S.'s foremost authority on mercury methylation, has made a provocative observation concerning decontamination as well. Apparently, DDT—that bane of environmentalists—inhibits enzymes from synthesizing methylmercury so that in areas polluted with DDT, there is no mercury problem. DDT may therefore be essential in decontaminating the Great Lakes, for example, he says.

In any event, Dr. Wood believes the wise approach is to work at eliminating, or at least greatly reducing, the microbial populations in sediments. "If we starve the bugs (by eliminating essential nutrients), then the rate of formation of methylmercury will be decreased and we won't have a problem in fish any more," he says.

everything related

Thus the concern about mercury in the environment may lead to increased concern for "first, sewage," the area that was occupying so much of Carl Klein's attention way back when. Everything—mercury and other trace metal contaminants included—may indeed be related to everything else and the complexities of these relationships, the state of toxicological homeostasis, will undoubtedly take years to unravel.

In the course of time, chemical processes will have to be redesigned. In the case of mercury, for example, a number of process changes have been cited by the HEW study group as necessary to eliminate discharges from chlor-alkali plants. Raw material utilization will change (replacing acetylene with ethylene as a raw material in acetaldehyde manufacture results in elimination of mercurial catalysts). Geologists, oceanographers, ecologists, zoologists, biochemists, and others will have to team up to clarify the mechanisms by which elements such as mercury move through the ecosphere. Toxicologists will have to refine the very basis of their science to include more and more information concerning long-term effects upon living organisms of elements and compounds and combinations of trace environmental constituents about which little is known at present.

Government and industry will have to work together with increased candor and effectiveness if other surprises like mercury are to be avoided. Finally, citizens in general will have to learn that the mining, processing, and consumption of natural resources involve hidden burdens of responsibility and hidden costs. It's Dr. Commoner again, with his fourth and final law: "There's no such thing as a free lunch."

metals focus shifts to cadmium

staff of environmental science & technology

Although it's a potentially hazardous pollutant and many questions remain to be answered, there will probably be no "cadmium crisis."

The Japanese call it "itai-itai byo"—the ouch-ouch disease—because of the excruciating pain accompanying a bizarre skeletal disorder known as osteomalacia. In those afflicted with itai-itai, bones may become so fragile that mere coughing is sufficiently traumatic to fracture ribs.

For years in the aftermath of World War II, farmers in Japan's Jintsu River Basin, where itai-itai was most prevalent, had complained that waste water from a zinc mine, discharging directly into the river used for irrigating rice paddies, was spoiling crops. But it wasn't until last year that Okayama University's Jun Kobayashi established the common denominator between the frequently fatal itai-itai and failing rice crops. The culprit was cadmium—a metal intimately associated with lead and zinc deposits and long known to be harmful to man.

Although toxicologists now believe that various nutritional deficiencies play a critical role in the full-blown itai-itai syndrome, the discovery that populations could be exposed to toxic quantities of cadmium by contaminated water caused a nation still jittery over the mercury pollution of Minamata Bay to shudder anew at the prospect of yet another heavy metal disaster. And more than a little concern was expressed in the U.S. last year over findings that showed many municipal water supplies contain significantly more than the 0.1 parts per million of cadmium considered to be "safe" for drinking.

As with mercury, very little was known about the fate and distribution of cadmium in the environment. What was known was scary enough. What was not known was even scarier.

It was known, for example, that cadmium has a very long biological half-life in man and therefore tends to accumulate in the body. Estimates ranged from 10–25 years, compared with about 70 days for methyl mercury. It was also known from industrial toxicology that cadmium could cause severe liver and kidney damage, pulmonary disease, and death.

In the absence of solid toxicological data, speculative analogies between mercury and cadmium were common. Was there, for example, a process similar to the microbial methylation of mercury which would concentrate cadmium in the food chain? Fortunately, that hypothesis appears to be incorrect. Nevertheless, disturbing questions about the amount of cadmium discharged into air and water and the effects of chronic exposure to cadmium remained.

In an effort to answer some of those questions the Environmental Protection Agency (EPA) commissioned studies to determine just how serious a threat cadmium poses. Although more work remains to be done, a picture is beginning to develop that is not quite so black as might have been imagined. The consensus of opinion is that although cadmium is a potentially dangerous pollutant, there is no reason to believe that a "cadmium crisis" is imminent. Cadmium is not "another mercury."

distribution

Cadmium is a relatively rare metal—the earth's crust contains an average of only 0.5 ppm. It occurs chiefly as the sulfide, greenockite, in various zinc, lead, and copper ores. Nearly all the cadmium produced in the world is a by-product of zinc smelting. Recycling is virtually nonexistent. Only 4% of the 10.6 million pounds of cadmium produced in the U.S. during 1968 was derived from reprocessing cadmium-containing scrap.

Cadmium does not degrade in the environment. As greater quantities of cadmium are refined, more and more of it becomes available to interact with man. Domestic consumption of cadmium was more than 15 million tons in 1969 (the last year for which official statistics are available). That's a whopping 13% jump over the figure for 1968. All indications point to further sharp increases in consumption for the foreseeable future. And because nearly everything produced by cadmium-using industries sooner or later winds up on the junk pile, the potential for environmental contamination is considerable.

Studies funded by the EPA provide a fairly complete inventory of sources and amounts of cadmium emissions into the atmosphere. Parallel studies for cadmium in water supplies, however, are lacking. Nearly 4.6 million pounds of cadmium were emitted into the atmosphere in the U.S. during 1968, according to a study prepared for the National Air Pollution Control Administration in 1970. Lee J. McCabe, director of Epidemiology and Biometrics for EPA's Office of Water Programs says there's "some but not much" cadmium in drinking water. Just how much is discharged into waterways is not known.

By far the largest single user of cadmium is the electroplating industry. The metal imparts an attractive, corrosion-resistant finish to ferrous metals. Virtually no cadmium escapes into the atmosphere from electroplating operations; how much gets into water from plating baths is anybody's guess.

159

Table 4-3. Pounds of Cadmium Emitted to Atmosphere in U.S. in 1968

Mining and metallurgical processing		2,100,530
mining	530	
Cd separation from ore	2,100,000	
Incineration and disposal		2,440,000
plated metal	2,000,000	
radiators	250,000	
other	190,000	
Industrial reprocessing		33,528
pigments	21,000	
plastics	6,000	
alloys	5,000	
batteries	400	
miscellaneous	1,128	
Consumptive uses		14,630
rubber tires	11,400	
motor oil	1,820	
fertilizers	910	
fungicides	500	
	Total	4,588,688

Source: National Inventory of Sources and Emissions

Hopefully, says McCabe, such information will be forthcoming in the next couple of years as discharge permits, required by the Army Corps of Engineers, are processed. . . .

Other important applications for cadmium include pigments, plastics stablizers, alloys, and batteries. Together with electroplating, these five product groups account for more than 90% of the cadmium used domestically. A wide variety of minor applications—television picture tube phosphors, fungicides for golf courses, control rods and shields in nuclear reactors, and curing agents for rubber, among others—accounts for the remaining 9–10%.

emissions

Most cadmium emissions into the atmosphere fall into two general categories—disposal and metallurgical processing. Disposal includes incineration and recycling of ferrous scrap and accounts for more than half the cadmium put into the air each year. The biggest chunk is lost in reclamation of scrap steel and recovery of copper from automobile radiators. Incineration of plastic products—ranging from bottles to baby pants—also adds cadmium to the atmosphere.

Metallurgical processing emits nearly as much cadmium to the air as disposal does. Although actual mining operations contribute only slightly to atmospheric cadmium levels, roasting and sintering of ore release vast quantities of cadmium into the air. Smaller amounts of cadmium in the air come from a variety of manufacturing processes as well as the use of certain fertilizers, fungicides, motor oils, and rubber tires.

Against this backdrop of emissions data, EPA commissioned three Swedish veteran cadmium watchers from Stockholm's Karolinska Institute to

160

prepare a report on the health effects of cadmium in the environment. The trio, Lars Friberg, Magnus Piscator, and Gunnar Nordberg, recently presented the results of their review to a symposium at the University of Rochester School of Medicine.

The Swedish report says that although the body contains only $1\mu g$ of cadmium at birth, a 50-year old, 70-kg (155-lb) "standard man" has a body burden 30,000 times that amount (30 mg). Excessive exposure to cadmium can damage the liver, kidneys, spleen, or thyroid, but the amount of cadmium needed to produce severe damage is not known.

Ambient air contains only a small amount of cadmium, the report says, but in the vicinity of certain factories, concentrations can be much higher. Cadmium is absorbed either by inhalation or ingestion and human beings are exposed to substantial amounts in food, according to the report. A differential absorption rate, however, makes inhalation of cadmium more dangerous than ingestion. Only about 5% of ingested cadmium is absorbed by the body; estimates for absorption of inhaled cadmium run as high as 40%, but actual amounts are probably lower. Recent work by Harold G. Petering at the University of Cincinnati indicates that people who smoke as few as 10 cigarettes per day—or the equivalent in other tobacco products—are exposed to concentrations of cadmium from 10-100 times greater than those in the ambient air. Worse yet, smoke from smoldering tobacco that is not inhaled—the sidestream—contains more cadmium than the mainstream inhaled by the smoker. Thus, everyone in the same room with a smoker is exposed to elevated cadmium levels.

Cadmium has also been implicated in cardiovascular disorders and cancer, although the Swedish team emphasizes that there is no conclusive statistical evidence linking cadmium with these diseases.

research needs

The Friberg-Piscator-Nordberg report lists several research priorities including:

• The "urgent and immediate" need for experiments on dose-response relationships considering absorption and excretion rates, particle size, and exposure routes;

• Studies on concentration of cadmium in various organs relative to total body burden;

• Development of better indicators of cadmium levels in the body;

• Further work on teratogenic or carcinogenic effects of cadmium, both alone and in combination with naturally occurring chelating agents such as EDTA and NTA;

• The definition of mechanisms for accumulation in food chains; and

• Metabolic studies establishing the role of essential trace metals in cadmium accumulation.

There is no doubt that cadmium has "caused trouble," according to Robert J. M. Horton, senior research advisor for EPA's Air Programs Office, Division of Effects Research. But, he adds, "I can't think of any reason why there should be a panic reaction." What steps will be taken by the EPA to control cadmium remain uncertain, but Friberg offers some advice: "All such long half-life substances should be controlled to the greatest extent possible."

pesticides everywhere

Of all the chemical changes suffered by the environment in the 20th century, pesticide contamination is in a class of its own. While many destructive chemicals have been discarded into the environment as waste, pesticides have been intentionally released over vast areas of our planet. More than twenty billion pounds of pesticides have been sprayed over farmlands, forests, and swamps—certainly man's most arrogant attempt to subdue nature.

At the beginning of the era of synthetic pesticides (mid-'40s), the extermination of all major insect pests was a goal optimistically predicted. Armed with exotic insect-killing chemicals, man tried very hard to achieve this goal, but in the process he contaminated all the living things on earth, including himself. Ironically, the insects are much better off than when the battle started; many of them are virtually unaffected by pesticides owing to growing genetic resistance. The dream of mankind that synthetic chemicals could dismantle the universal scourge of insects now lies shattered—a monumental ecological absurdity.

Rachel Carson was the first to publicize the destructive repercussions of the chemical campaign against insects in her book *Silent Spring*. Although this book was severely criticized by many experts, its message about the enormous complexity of nature's machinery marked a turning point in man's simplistic thinking of chemical extermination. Now, finally, the profound scope of the problem is widely recognized.

To increase one's awareness of the pesticide problem, six diverse essays are presented. A general background on pesticides is provided in Louis Lykken's "Chemical Control of Pests," Article 25. This is followed by Article 26, Eugenia Keller's "The DDT Story," which relates the painfully evolving awareness of what DDT is doing to our world. Article 27, "Pesticides Cutting into Seafood Resources," is Robert C. Cowen's interpretation of studies on seafood depletion by insecticides, and the likely repercussions. Article 28, by Philip H. Abelson, "Pollution by Organic Chemicals," shows pesticides in the context of a wider class of organic pollutants. Irma West, in her "Biological Effects of Pesticides in the Environment," Article 29, gives the most detailed account of the pesticide effects on man and the environment. To end this section, we get a glimpse of other options to insect control in Carol Knapp's "Choices Are in the Offing," Article 30.

chemical control of pests

louis lykken

Our policy should be concerned with the amount and type of pest control that improves utilization of the nation's resources within realizable and tolerable limits of environmental contamination.

Although man has used chemicals to control pests since the 18th century, the most important developments have occurred during the past 50 years. Beginning in the second decade of this century, arsenicals as insecticides came into use, reaching a peak in the early 1940's; other inorganic compounds used included those of copper and mercury. Also, during this period, some organic compounds derived from plants, such as rotenone and pyrethrum, were used.

But beginning in the late 1940's, use of inorganic and naturally derived insecticides leveled off, and synthetic pesticides came into use, being paced by a variety of insecticide chemicals including chlorinated hydrocarbons, such as DDT, benzene hexachloride, toxaphene, and aldrin (Figure 5–1). Somewhat later, herbicides also appeared and by 1966, in terms of sales value but not in pounds, herbicides had surpassed insecticides. At present, in terms of pounds, they account for a little less than half of the total chemical pesticides sold.

The new pesticides proved to be both economical and effective. Because farmers demanded better crop yields, consumers insisted on filth-free high-quality foods, and public health officials needed disease-control measures, over 500 pesticide chemicals were developed, and federal registration labels were provided for over 50,000 formulations. In the U.S., total annual consumption of unformulated chemicals reached about 1 billion pounds. By 1968, total annual sales in this country had reached some $996 million: nematocides, $13 million; fungicides, $71 million; insecticides, $333 million; and herbicides, $529 million. However, because of cost for formulation,

Reprinted with permission from *Chemistry,* Vol. 44, July-August 1971, pp. 18–21. Copyright by the American Chemical Society. The author, formerly with Shell Chemical Co., is now a specialist in the Division of Entomology and Acarology at the University of California at Berkeley.

Chlorinated Hydrocarbons

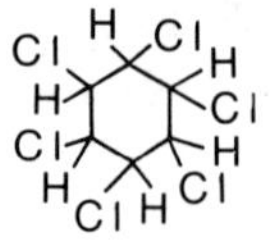

BHC

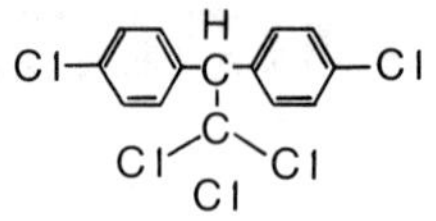

P,P/DDT

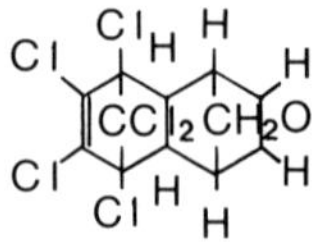

Dieldrin

Organophosphorus Compounds

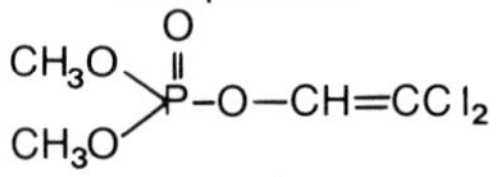

Dichlorous

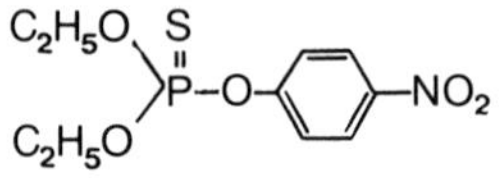

Parathion

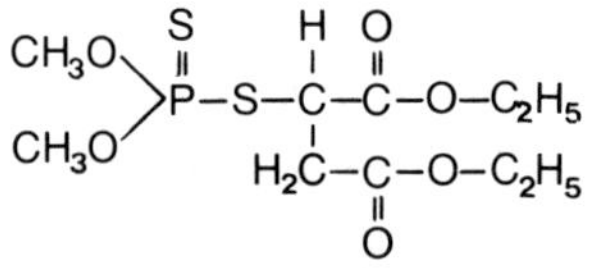

Malathion

Herbicides

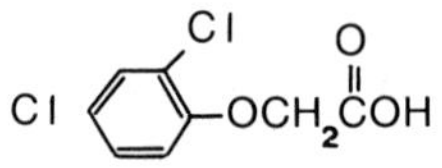

2,4-D

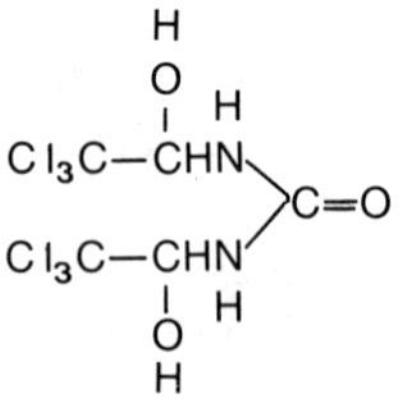

DCU

Figure 5-1. Some pesticide chemicals.

packaging, shipping, and application, expense to the farmer was about four times these amounts.

Although nonchemical means of pest control were investigated (biological, cultural, mechanical), the emphasis at first was on compounds that were extremely toxic to major insect pests and not harmful to plants or animals under conditions of use. Entomologists encouraged development of persistent chemicals, toxic to a broad range of insects. But later, because of regulatory laws and development of pesticide-resistant strains of insects, the trend changed in favor of chemicals that give residues which persist for only a few days. However, for reasons of economy and effectiveness, several persistent insecticide chemicals are still in demand for controlling certain insects of agricultural or public health importance. In fact, over a dozen insect species can be controlled adequately only by persistent chemicals.

The trend also has been toward chemicals that are less toxic to man and useful animals, effective against resistant insect species, and toxic to selected insect species only. As a result, only a fraction of the several hundred pesticides introduced to the market remained for an important length of time. Of the chlorinated hydrocarbons, this fraction includes DDT and about 20 others. In all, about a dozen classes of chemicals now are used as pesticides and their structures are varied, as shown in Figure 5–2. Some of the compounds contain lead, arsenic, copper, iron, mercury, and tin.

The annual production of DDT in this country reached a maximum in 1963 but, by 1968, had declined almost to the 1955 level (Table 5–1). In contrast, its annal consumption in the U.S. had declined to about half the 1950 level (Table 5–2). For the aldrin-toxaphene group, production in 1968 had increased considerably over that for 1955 but, because of increased exports, consumption in this country had dropped to well below 1955 levels. In other words, total use of the principal chlorinated hydrocarbon insecticide chemicals in this country had declined to less than half of the maximum annual usage.

This development probably has resulted from changes in government regulations and recommendations, public pressure against release of persistent pesticides to the environment, development of pesticide-resistant strains of insects, and availability of new insecticide chemicals. Unfortunately, reliable data on the use of persistent insecticides in foreign countries are not available, but the use of DDT abroad has increased.

safety

Pesticide chemicals vary greatly in toxicity to man and animals. Only a few, such as tetraethyl pyrophosphate (TEPP), fall in the extremely toxic category. Approximately 20 are highly toxic, many of which are organophosphorus compounds such as parathion; endrin is the only chlorinated hydrocarbon in this category which in toxicity compares with hydrogen cyanide and arsenic oxide.

The chlorinated hydrocarbons are the most numerous in the moderately toxic group which compares in toxicity to nicotine, copper sulfates, and rotenone. The slightly toxic class contains a variety of chemical types,

167

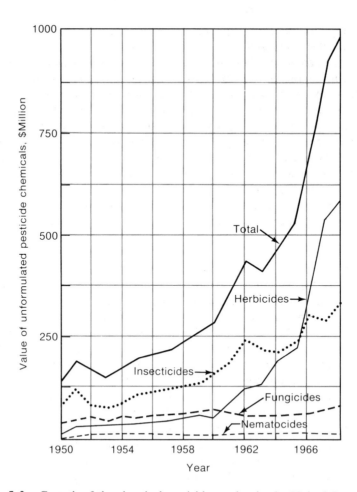

Figure 5-2. Growth of the chemical pesticide market in the United States.

herbicides being prominent; it includes DDT, malathion, and lead arsenate. Only about a dozen pesticide chemicals are practically nontoxic; these include methoxychlor and piperonyl butoxide. A few in this category, such as sulfur, are harmless.

Pesticide chemicals are safe to use, provided common-sense safety is practiced and provided they are used in accordance with instructions on the label, including keeping them away from children and illiterate or mentally incompetent persons.

use

Pesticide chemicals often give an impressive increase in yield and quality of crops to decrease unit cost of production; also they conserve certain resources, such as labor and plant nutrients. For example, in 1963, the use of approximately $450 million worth of formulated pesticides gave an estimated increased yield of about $1.8 billion more than that realizable without pesticides. This amount is equivalent to the total value of the agricultural production in the state of Minnesota for that year or almost half that in California for the same year. In spite of this high expenditure

168

Table 5-1. Production of Certain Pesticide Chemicals in the U.S., Million Pounds

	1950	1955	1960	1963	1965	1967	1968
DDT	80	130	160	179	141		139
Aldrin-toxaphene group		78	90		119	120	116
All insecticides	250	300	460		502		577
Organic pesticides[a]	400	520	660		875		1192
All pesticides	550	640	750		875		1160

[a]Includes small production of soil conditioners.

Table 5-2. Consumption of Certain Insecticide Chemicals in the U.S., Million Pounds

	1950	1955	1959	1960	1965	1966	1968
DDT	58	62	79	71	53		33
Aldrin-toxaphene group		55		76	81	86	39
Total		117		147	134		72

for pesticides, farmers still lost several times this cost to pests and diseases of plants and animals. Hence, much can still be gained by complete control of agricultural pests.

Use of insecticide chemicals, mainly persistent ones, has contributed to the control of several diseases which are transmitted by insects (vector-borne), such as malaria, viral encephalitis, cholera, Rocky Mountain fever, and tularemia. The benefits derived from this use of pesticides include saving the lives of at least 10 million people, preventing 100 million illnesses, and rehabilitating countless millions of persons whose productivity was low because of chronic vector-borne disease. Thus, human resources were conserved and certain areas of the world became more productive of needed commodities. This use of pesticides continues; DDT is considered to be the most important lifesaver known to man, and the Food and Agricultural Organization of the United Nations considers this pesticide essential in developing countries for controlling crop pests or disease.

According to estimates, 75% of chemical pesticides are applied to less than 2% of the land; they are used on approximately 15% of the farm land and less than 0.3% of forest land. About 75% of the total land area has not been treated with pesticides. About half of the agricultural pesticides go on cotton, a fifth on grain crops, a tenth on fruit and nut crops, and the remainder on vegetables, forage and sugar crops, livestock, and farm buildings. Often, the cost of pesticide application is as great as the cost of the products, thereby putting a practical limit on the amount used.

properties

Like many other compounds, pesticide chemicals vaporize, dissolve, hydrolyze, photodegrade, and are oxidized and metabolized. Their effectiveness, persistence, and fate in the environment are governed by the rates at which these reactions occur.

The persistent chlorinated hydrocarbons such as DDT have a low vapor pressure, low solubility in water, high solubility in fats and oils, and a high affinity for colloidal surfaces. They vaporize slowly from plant surfaces, dissolve in waxy surfaces of plants, are stored in fatty tissues of animals, migrate slowly into plant tissue, resist leaching, and move short distances in normal soil.

environmental accumulation

The general environmental contamination by pesticide chemicals results from air convection currents, wind and water erosion of soil, and by transport as molecules adsorbed on soil particles in the silt of streams, estuaries, and the sea. Also, to a lesser extent, they move as residues in plants and animals, especially in fish and wild fowl.

As a result, DDT and dieldrin have spread throughout the environment. Indications are that presence of DDT in the diet of certain species of predatory and fish-eating birds produces thinning of egg shells with consequent reduction in reproduction rates. Certain insecticides apparently present complex hazards to some fish and aquatic organisms. Fish and bird kills from excessive application or accidental spills of a variety of insecticide chemicals are on record.

Chlorinated hydrocarbons accumulate in the fatty tissues of animals, including man, but, when an equilibrium point is reached, they are metabolized or excreted. This high concentration in fat can result in magnification of residues along the food chain; harmful levels in animals at the head of the food chain can accumulate. Harmful levels in human beings and farm animals have not been identified—government regulations impose strict tolerances on residues in food and ingested residues are eventually metabolized and excreted.

degradation

Chlorinated hydrocarbon pesticides degrade in a number of ways. They are subject to photochemical reactions as are some to chemical reactions. All are degraded biologically through enzymatic processes, but some degrade more slowly than others. The rate and type of degradation depend to some extent on the system where this takes place—for example, 80 to 90% of DDT added to fertile, moist agricultural soil generally is lost in 10 years. However, when added to dry, nonfertile soils, 50% of such residue sometimes remains for 10 years or more. In any event, continued use of these insecticides does not result in an ever-increasing accumulation of their residues.

A vast amount of information exists on the biological degradation of chlorinated hydrocarbons, and their major metabolic pathways are known. But information on photochemical degradation pathways is incomplete, and relatively little is known about their ultimate fate in soil and some other parts of the ecosystem. This remains true even though metabolism, degradation, and biochemistry of pesticide chemicals are being studied intensively by several hundred scientists. Also, an effort is under way by state and federal analysts to determine the trend of pesticide chemical residues in various parts of the environment, especially in waterways, soil, and certain plants and animals. Only when reliable data of this kind are available can estimates be made regarding the amount and rate of change in residues in the biosphere. This monitoring activity needs to cover air, water courses, soils, land, aquatic life, and man.

hazard

The hazard to man from long-term ingestion of DDT has been studied for some time, and more is known about the possible medical hazard of this pesticide than any other. In the last two decades, millions of pounds of DDT have been dispersed in the environment but no cases of chronic poisoning have been detected, not even among formulators and malaria-program spray men who have been heavily exposed to DDT for years. Also, no case of harm to man or domestic animals has been traced to DDT residues in food and feed nor has evidence been found to indicate that DDT or other chlorinated hydrocarbon pesticides are carcinogenic in man and domestic animals. Investigators in this field have concluded that pesticide residues and normal exposure to pesticides are not health hazards.

policy

Pesticide chemicals are toxic and, therefore, their use should be minimized or eliminated, provided alternative, known-to-be safe approaches exist which will give adequate pest control under practical conditions. Judgment should enter this consideration because the issues generally are by no means clear-cut and indisputable; emotional appeal or arbitrary legislative action should not be allowed to influence these considerations.

What should our policy for pest control be? It should be concerned with the amount and type of pest control that improves utilization of the nation's resources within realizable and tolerable limits of environmental contamination. Unquestionably, maximum realization of benefits from pesticides entails some risk to society and some adverse effects have to be tolerated, at least for the foreseeable future. This will be so until chemicals cease to be the best means of pest control and cease to bear the brunt of such control. In any event, our policy must relate to the important problem of maintaining a safe, habitable environment in which the overall goal and desires of society are most effectively and easily achieved.

suggested reading

1. "Cleaning Our Environment—The Chemical Basis for Action," Section 4, American Chemical Society, Washington, D. C. 1969.
2. Gillett, J. W., Ed., "The Biological Impact of Pesticides in the Environment," Environment Health Series, No. 1, Oregon State University Press, Corvallis, Ore., 1970.
3. Hansberry, R., "Values and Hazards—DDT and Related Compounds," presented at Ecological Conference, Oakland, Calif., Sept. 27, 1969.
4. Kraybill, H. F., Ed., "Biological Effects of Pesticides in Mammalian Systems," *Annals N.Y. Acad. Sci., 1969,* 100(1), 1–422.

5. Lake States Agriculture Committee, John Osmun, Chm., "Pesticide Report," Purdue University, Lafayette, Ind., 1969.
6. Lykken, L., "The Safe Use of Pesticides," *Agric. Chem., 1967,* 22(8), 14–16; 22(9), 35–36; 22(10), 38, 40, 44.
7. Lykken, L., Casida, J. E., "Metabolism of Organic Insecticide Chemicals," *J. Can. Med. Assoc., 1969,* 100, 145–54.
8. "The Pesticide Review—1969," U. S. Department of Agriculture, Washington, D. C., 1969.
9. "Principles of Plant Management and Animal Pest Control," Vol. 3, Publication 1695, National Academy of Sciences, Washington, D. C., 1969.
10. "Report of Committee on Persistent Pesticides," Division of Biology and Agriculture, National Research Council, Washington, D. C., 1969.
11. "Report of the Secretary's Commission on Pesticides and Their Relationship to Environmental Health, Parts I and II," U. S. Department of Health, Education, and Welfare, Washington, D.C., 1969.
12. Rodda, J., "Pesticides—Past, Present, and Future," Agric. Chem., *1970,* 25(2), 18–20; 25(3), 26, 29, 47.
13. Rosen, A. A., Kraybill, H. F., "Organic Pesticides in the Environment," Advances in Chemistry Series No. 60, American Chemical Society, Washington, D.C., 1966.
14. Zavon, M. R., "Pesticides in Perspective," *Trans. N. Y. Acad. Sci.,* Series II, *1970,* 32, 586–93.

172

the ddt story

eugenia keller

In assessing the behavior of DDT in the animal organism, it should be remembered that man is not far removed from his fellow species.

In 1874, Othmar Zeidler, a German chemist working on his doctoral thesis, synthesized a compound, dichlorodiphenyltrichloroethane. But few people noticed until nearly 60 years later when Paul Mueller, during a search of the literature, found reference to a similar compound, diphenyltrichloroethane. Mueller, a chemist with the Swiss firm, J. R. Geigy, A.G., was seeking a moth preventative—an insecticide that would kill on contact. He synthesized the chemical and found it to be extremely toxic to houseflies. This work led to his synthesis of Zeidler's compound.

Shortly before World War II, the chemical was tested on wine grape pests and American striped potato beetles that had infested Europe. It performed beautifully in both instances and the Swiss company undertook manufacture on a commercial scale. That chemical, useless in 1874, became known as DDT, the first of a series of chlorinated hydrocarbons to be synthesized (see Figure 5–3).

At the beginning of 1942, after Japan attacked Pearl Harbor, this country was in dire need of an insecticide to replace those available at that time. Their main ingredients—arsenic, copper, and lead—were needed for other military uses. Also, an anti-louse product was needed to protect soldiers— during World War I, louse infestation was the curse of the doughboys.

That year, the Swiss firm delivered six pounds of DDT to this country for testing. Again the material proved extremely effective, and soon mass quantities were being manufactured. The next year a spectacular performance launched DDT on its career. After Naples, Italy, was liberated, a massive typhus epidemic broke out. Within a few days after dusting the inhabitants themselves and spraying DDT about generally, the epidemic practically disappeared. This was a tremendous achievement. Later DDT was sprayed from airplanes in the South Pacific to control malaria.

It is said that during the bombing of Okinawa and Iwo Jima, every sixth carrier-based plane laid down a blanket of DDT. As a louse powder

---

Reprinted with permission of *Chemistry*, Vol. 43, February 1970, pp. 8–12, and copyright by the American Chemical Society. The author is managing editor of *Chemistry*.

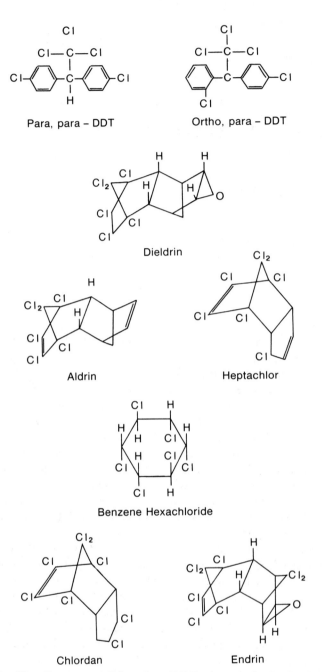

Figure 5-3. The dirty seven. Other than DDT, the principal offenders among insecticidal chlorinated hydrocarbons are dieldrin, aldrin, heptachlor, lindane (benzene hexachloride), chlordane, and endrin. These compounds, sometimes called the dirty seven, are practically insoluble in water and, when discharged into the environment, they resist decomposition. For example, the half life of DDT in the soil is estimated at 10 to 15 years. Also, they are broad spectrum, meaning that in terms of insects they kill friends as well as foes. How they kill insects is not known precisely, but in some manner they attack the nervous system. Some are much more toxic than DDT.

it was combined with talcum—World War II is said to be the first war in history where more soldiers died from bullets than from typhus, a louse-born disease.

In 1948 Paul Mueller was awarded the Nobel Prize for discovering the insecticidal properties of DDT. In November of that year, *Chemistry* said, in announcing the prize, "the boundary-crossing benefits of DDT continue and increase . . . it aids mightily in the efforts of entomologists to prevent the spread of insect pests of cultivated plants and domestic plants. If it could only be used to delouse political heads of their crawling fears, suspicions and hatreds, the peace dream of Alfred Nobel might come closer to realization."

In the developed countries, at least, people seemed to bask contentedly in their freedom from insects and insect-born disease—the ideal pesticide had been found at last. In June of 1947, *Chemistry* had given some 24 pages to DDT. It deplored the fact that this excellent pesticide, which had solved one of mankind's oldest problems (how to get rid of flies) had remained unappreciated for 74 years. Then, *Chemistry* advised its readers: "You can play a trick on them [flies]. Dip lengths of net cord . . . in a DDT solution . . . and after they have dried, hang them from the ceiling . . . Flies will not be able to resist these alighting places [the cords], and every fly that alights will surely die." However, said *Chemistry*, when you use DDT aerosol bombs in a room, be sure that fish bowls and aquariums are removed, because DDT is toxic to fish, especially tropical fish.

Other insecticidal chlorinated hydrocarbons were synthesized and, although articles pointing out their toxicity to other animals began to appear, most people seemed to assume that, when discharged into the environment, this toxicity would automatically disappear. Also, as early as 1946, houseflies resistant to DDT had been noted and by 1948 the list of resistant insects had grown to 12.

Nevertheless, DDT (it is cheaper than other insecticidal chlorinated hydrocarbons) continued to be poured into the environment. By 1962, U.S. production had reached some 167 million pounds per year, and 75 million pounds were sprayed in Asia alone to control malaria. In California 12 million acres of land were sprayed. Marshes and water resources were sprayed to control nuisance pests such as gnats and mosquitoes.

Also in 1962, a bomb was dropped in the midst of this unbridled activity—Rachel Carson, a physically small and rather fragile marine biologist, published her book, *Silent Spring*. Its title implied that unless the use of pesticides was curtailed, someday a spring would arrive when no birds sang and no fish leaped in streams because all had been killed. Her book was well documented with published accounts.

A storm of controversy began to rage immediately. On one side were conservationists, resource analysts, biologists, and sociologists. On the other were factions such as the pesticide industry and agricultural interests. Miss Carson was accused of fomenting hysteria and playing on the fears of the public. Even when publishing her obituary in April 1964, *Time* could not resist an editorial punch. It said, ". . . and despite her scientific training, she rejected facts that weakened her case while using almost any material regardless of authenticity, that seemed to support her thesis." Her critics, who included many eminent scientists, objected to the book's exaggeration.

By 1963, massive fish kills, especially in the lower Mississippi River, caused much concern. Large amounts of endrin were found in bodies of the dead fish. Also discovery that DDT accumulates in the fatty tissue of man and animals was of concern. But opponents to restrictions on its use said that during the 25 years of mass DDT applications, made for public health purposes, no proof has been established that accretion in the human system has caused disease.

Nevertheless, in that same year, President Kennedy's Science Advisory Committee recommended reduction in use of DDT and its related products. Soon thereafter, Secretary of the Interior Stewart L. Udall banned use of DDT on federal lands where another insecticide would be adequate. The governor of New Hampshire banned its use on state lands and New York prohibited its application on its lake-trout watersheds. Michigan and Minnesota reduced its use on state lands and Connecticut prohibited all aerial spraying. But lavish use continued in other quarters. The philosophy seemed to be that if a little spraying does good, then more spraying will do more good.

By 1964, according to one estimate, some 3.5 billion pounds of DDT had been produced, of which 1.8 billion was in this country, and an amount equivalent to 1.5 pounds for each acre of the world's arable land had been applied. Also it became apparent that, because of its stability and insolubility, as much as 50% of DDT applied can still remain in the soil 10 to 15 years after application.

The entire globe was said to be contaminated, and evidence against DDT continued to accumulate. Tests at Texas A&M University in 1965 showed that cotton bollworms were 30,000 times more resistant than they were in 1960. In 1943, before pesticides were introduced into the fertile Cannete Valley in Peru, the average yield of cotton was about 406 pounds per acre. Then in 1949 DDT was introduced and, by 1954, yields had risen to 649 pounds. But by 1965, the harvest had dropped to 296 pounds. One reason was ecological—growing resistance of insects and killing of natural predators of the insects.

Congress, however, paid little attention. The June 24, 1967, issue of the *New Republic* presented an article entitled the "Gathering Storm Over DDT." The first paragraph read, "Again this year Wisconsin's Senator Gaylord Nelson has introduced a long-shot bill to ban the manufacture of the pesticide DDT for use in this country. It languishes in the Agriculture Committee. No hearings have been scheduled."

mode of transport

DDT can wander to far corners of the globe by several pathways. One is air currents. According to estimates, only half the pesticide sprayed from an airplane reaches its destination. The other half drifts and settles over adjacent lands; or it is carried by up-drafts into the upper atmosphere, ultimately to be washed down by rain into oceans and inland waterways. Often rainwater contains more DDT than river waters.

Although streams receive a heavy burden of DDT through drainage from forests and agricultural lands, marine life near the mouth of a river does not always contain more DDT than that at considerable distance. One reason is that the pesticide is adsorbed on particles of soil which, when washed into streams, settle to the bottom. Another, perhaps, is that ocean surface currents can carry the material away. But they cannot account for contamination of Antarctica because that continent is surrounded by up-welling deep waters.

DDT can also reach underground waters. For instance, endrin when discharged by a manufacturer into a sewer survived the sewage treatment plant and, percolating through the soil, rendered a city well unusable.

Two particularly interesting modes of transport have been described—a chemist, on learning that his dry cleaner added DDT as a moth preventative to his solvents, extracted 30 mg. of the pesticide from his suit that had been cleaned at that establishment. Also, the Food and Drug Administration recently banned shelf paper products impregnated with lindane or chlordane because residues can build up in home-stored foods.

concentration in living organisms

One of the most disturbing pathways by which DDT wanders is through concentration in living organisms—the higher the link in the food chain, the greater the concentration. For example, in Antarctica, krill, a small shrimp-like creature, taken from the stomachs of penguins, contained less DDT than the penguins themselves. Plankton that have absorbed DDT are eaten by the krill where DDT is further concentrated and the krill in turn are eaten by the penguins, which concentrates the pesticide still more. A classic example of concentration is provided in California. In 1957, California's Clear Lake, after spraying with DDT for gnat control, contained only 0.02 parts per million of DDT. Microscopic life contained 5 ppm, and fish feeding on these organisms contained as much as 2000 ppm. Grebes, diving birds that fed on fish, died in great numbers.

Oysters absorb DDT in high concentrations. For example, after being placed in waters containing only 10 parts per billion, some contained 151 ppm after only seven days. Much higher concentrations in oysters have been reported. Some species of fish absorb more than others. Last year, a shipment of 28,000 pounds of coho salmon taken from Lake Michigan was embargoed because the fish contained 19 parts per million of DDT. However, other fish in the lake, such as herring and whitefish, have not carried high residues.

Birds seem to be suffering acutely from accumulation of DDT in their bodies, through both poisoning and interference with their calcium metabolism, which in turn causes their egg shells to be too fragile to survive the incubation period. The bald eagle, our national bird, is in danger of extinction. Their egg shells are said to have become some 19% thinner and eggs have been found which were surrounded only by a membrane. In some areas in England, thickness of peregrine falcon egg shells has decreased by about 20%.

Robin populations have been severely depleted. Earthworms, which

177

comprise their major diet, are concentrators of DDT. At Michigan State University, robins continued to die 1½ years after the last application of DDT on the campus. Also deaths of robins have been reported when food supplies became short and the birds were forced to metabolize their fat. For the same reason fish also have died three months after exposure to DDT.

DDT and its analogs have even been found in eggs and in vegetables, especially carrots, potatoes, and leafy vegetables. Shipments of peanuts have been embargoed because of their DDT content.

effect on metabolism

In assessing the behavior of DDT in the animal organism, it should be remembered that Man is not far removed from his fellow species, although experimental proof of ill effects has not been reported. In one program, the average DDT in 800 samples of human fat from Americans was 12 ppm. Samples of human fat taken from other geographic areas showed the following levels:

	PPM		PPM
Arctic regions	3	Hungary	12.4
Canada	4.9	India (New Delhi)	26
Germany	2.3	Israel	19.2
England	3.9		
France	5.2		

DDT is said to concentrate in the brain also. In one Florida study, made between 1964 and 1967, all autopsies on persons showing a history of liver, brain, or neurological disease were compared with controls. DDT levels in liver, fat, and brain were consistently higher, but whether this was significant in cause of the diseases is unknown.

However, some data of possible significance regarding mutation has been obtained. In 1967, two British geneticists studied the genetic effects of alkylating agents—in both animal and human organisms DDT can be converted to this type of product. In fruit flies the scientists found increased mutations, but actual DDT byproducts were not studied because they would have been lethal to the flies. The effects, said the scientists, are accumulative, just as mutation can be caused by several small doses of radioactive radiation. The alkylating agents interfere with the structure of DNA and also can kill cells by interfering with enzymatic activity.

Other evidence of enzymatic interference has been obtained. In one test, houseflies made resistant to DDT were found to contain an enzyme, DDT-dehydrochlorinase which converts DDT to the noninsecticidal, DDE, but not all insects have this pathway. Some convert to an analog where a hydroxyl group replaces the tertiary hydrogen.

In animals evidence of hormonal disturbance has been found. In female rats, chlordane increased estradiol production by 385% and, in male pigeons, testosterone metabolism was increased twofold. When chickens were injected

178

with three consecutive daily doses of 50 mg of the *o,p* form of DDT, weight and glycogen content of the oviduct was increased equivalent to three injections of estradiol. The *p,p'* form had no effect. (Commercial DDT is usually composed of 15 to 20% of the *o,p* form and 80% of the *p,p* form.) When an unidentified form was given to young roosters, it was found that, compared to controls, adult testicular weight was five times smaller. The effect was as though the birds had been given an estrogen. An explanation might be that behavior of DDT is similar to that of stilbesterol (diethylstilbesterol), a female sex hormone.

In addition to possible harmful metabolic effects on man and animals, the list of resistant insects has grown to some 224 of which 27 are of public health and veterinary importance and 127 are predators of crops or forests. Even so, in 1968, some 125 million pounds were produced in this country and although most was shipped abroad, much will drift back through winds and ocean currents. According to a recent estimate, about 1 billion pounds of DDT are circulating in the biosphere. Even if its use were discontinued tomorrow, said *National Parks Magazine,* in its November 1969 issue, concentrations in the world's waters would continue to rise for some time.

federal action

At last, in November of last year [1969], Robert Finch, Secretary of Health, Education, and Welfare called for elimination within two years of all uses of DDT and DDD in this country except those essential to human health. At the same time he said that sensitivity of measuring techniques has increased 1000-fold during the last 11 years, and setting zero tolerances for widely distributed pesticides could have a disastrous effect on our national supply of essential foods.

Hence for the present, starvation seems to be the only alternative to ingesting pesticide residues in our food. But for the future, many types of research are being done to find other methods of insect control. One approach is based on sex attractants where insects, once attracted to a particular spot, can be caught in traps. . . . Another approach is based on unleashing natural predators of the pest, or perhaps microorganisms which infect and kill the insects. Also, a method of sterilization might be found, or resistant crops might be grown. Certainly, with world food shortages threatened, something must be done.

pesticides cutting into seafood resources

robert c. cowen

Fish and shrimp must be considered endangered species in some American estuaries.

Pollution by DDT and related bug poisons is beginning to hit men where it hurts—in their food baskets. Evidence is growing that diluted amounts of these poisons are seriously damaging some coastal seafood resources.

Those who call the DDT family of pesticides "essential to maintain world food supplies" seem thus to be on a collision course with those who look to the sea for new supplies of badly needed protein.

Dr. P.A. Butler, research consultant at the Biological Field Station of the U.S. Bureau of Fisheries, Gulf Breeze, Florida, reviewed the situation for a recent meeting on marine pollution called by Britain's Royal Society.

"fish and shrimp endangered"

Summarizing his talk in the meeting program, he bluntly declared that "pesticide pollution is causing significant changes in mortality, growth rates, or resistance to disease in some marine populations. . . . Fish and shrimp must be considered endangered species in some American estuaries."

For five years, his laboratory has tracked pesticide pollution along both United States coasts. It uses oysters and clams as indicators. These mollusks concentrate the poisons by hundreds, even thousands of times.

High up both coasts, off the states of Washington and Maine, pollution has been minimal. But it rises as you drop southward, Dr. Butler told the meeting.

Some of it comes from industry and municipal sewers. Some comes from such operations as beach spraying. Much comes from farming. This accounts for sharp rises in pesticides in estuaries every spring.

level not heavy

Nowhere has the pollution been heavy. It is generally only a few parts per million in the water or less. This still is dangerous for marine life.

For one thing, many organisms concentrate the poisons, passing them up the food chain to higher animals. Dr. Butler cited his home estuary. There, 70 parts per billion (ppb) in the drifting microscopic plants and animals at the base of the food chain become 800 parts per million (ppm) in the fat of porpoises. That's a ten-thousandfold concentration.

Then too, even a few ppm of poison can kill. Dr. Butler told of several laboratory populations of important food fish, shrimp, and crabs that died off in water with a few ppm of DDT.

They died over several months. Only a few percent went in any one week. Even experts would be unlikely to notice this mortality rate in the wild, Dr. Butler said. They would only know, eventually, that the fish had "gone somewhere else." He cited several cases to illustrate them.

"sublethal effects" deadly

Even so-called "sublethal" effects of pesticides can ultimately be deadly. Dr. J.M. Anderson reported a striking example. Now director of the biological station of the Fisheries Research Board of Canada, St. Andrews, New Brunswick, he investigated a mysterious spring die-off of salmon in New Brunswick streams.

The die-off occurred in spring in a region earlier sprayed with DDT. It happened after sudden rain lowered water temperature by about five degrees C. This shouldn't have hurt the fish. But tests showed that even brief exposure to very low levels of DDT would alter the fish's temperature sensitivity to make such a five-degree drop fatal.

Referring to this kind of effect, Dr. Butler said, "I don't believe there is such a thing as a sublethal toxic effect. I'm quite sure any toxic effect will, in the long run, lead to a lethal effect." This is why he worries about pesticide pollution even though it hasn't yet made seafood inedible or threatened man directly.

He thinks a worldwide ban on DDT and similar poisons is urgently needed. To ban them locally or in a few countries while everyone else uses them, he says is "to blow into the wind."

But what of protests that poorer countries can't afford to give up DDT? Both the United Nations World Health Organization and the Food and Agricultural Organization have been trying to tone down demands for a ban on these grounds.

protein resources at stake

Dr. Butler said flatly that such arguments fall by the way when you realize the poisons are probably killing off protein resources these countries also need.

Dr. Norman W. Moore, who heads the toxic chemicals and wildlife division of Britain's Nature Conservancy, took a somewhat more reserved

181

position when asked about this. As he has in the past, he pointed out the expense a country like India would incur by suddenly dropping so cheap and effective a pesticide as DDT.

Yet he too worries about fisheries. He told of an instance in India where endrin used on rice was ruining a fish resource. He said even some of the fisheries people didn't know the chemical would harm the fish. Many of the farmers couldn't read the warning labels or didn't care.

"It's criminal," he said, "that people who so badly need this marine protein are deprived of it in this way."

pollution by organic chemicals

philip h. abelson

We are manufacturing thousands of chemicals. In their preparation, side reactions are producing many thousands of unwanted and even unidentified substances. To what extent are these strangers being discarded into rivers, lakes, and the sea?

A survey of efforts to secure a livable environment leaves one with the impression that progress is being made in a number of respects. One area that has not received as much attention as it should is pollution by organic chemicals. Of particular concern should be the large group of molecules that are fat-soluble and only slowly biodegradable. Organic chemicals that are fat-soluble often tend to be accumulated in living systems. If not biodegradable, they may be concentrated by the food chain or other mechanisms so that their level in tissue comes to exceed that in the environment by orders of magnitude.

An example of a fat-soluble, slowly degradable compound is DDT. Its tendency to be accumulated by fish, birds, and humans has been repeatedly discussed. A large number of chlorinated aromatic hydrocarbons and chlorinated phenols and their derivatives are also concentrated in living forms. Many of these chemicals are known to have adverse biological effects. The most toxic chlorine-containing compound known is 2,3,7,8-tetrachlorodibenzodioxine ($C_{12}H_4O_2Cl_4$), often called dioxin. The acute oral LD_{50} dose of dioxin in male guinea pigs is about 10^{-6} g/kg. Other animal experiments have resulted in a variety of pathologic phenomena, including neurological disturbances and birth defects. Dioxin is an unwanted contaminant* of the herbicide 2,4,5-T. When manufacture of the herbicide is carefully controlled, the dioxin content is less than 1 part per million. Higher concentrations have been noted, however. Dioxin was identified in 1962, after

*Effects of 2,4,5-T on Man and the Environment, Hearings before the Subcommittee on Energy, Natural Resources, and the Environment of the Committee on Commerce, United States Senate, Ninety-first Congress, Second Session, 7 and 15 April (Serial 91-60, U.S. Government Printing Office, Washington, D.C., 1970).

5 years of dedicated research. In 1957 a mysterious disease had caused millions of dollars of damage and the death of uncounted numbers of chicks. Careful chemical detective work ultimately pointed to dioxin as the culprit. Apparently the herbicide 2,4,5-T or derivatives of it had been taken into plants and had ultimately appeared in vegetable oils. These were processed at high temperatures to liberate fatty acids, but inadvertently some dioxin, which has extreme thermal stability, was formed. Once the problem was identified, the chemical process was modified. Oddly enough, in spite of its great toxicity, the behavior of dioxin in the food chain has not been worked out.

The broad-scale and dramatic deleterious effects of dioxin were manifested in chicks. How much damage has this substance caused in humans? We know that all of us carry substantial quantities of DDT. How much damage has been caused by other related fat-soluble compounds?

When we use DDT and 2,4,5-T, presumably we obtain benefits that tend to balance, or even more than compensate for, the hazards attending them. Moreover, we can test the toxicity of manufacturers' products and be alert to possible problems. However, how do we cope with other possible dioxins? We are manufacturing thousands of chemicals. In their preparation, side reactions are producing many thousands of unwanted and even unidentified substances. To what extent are these strangers being discarded into rivers, lakes, and the sea? To what extent are such substances finding their way into humans? Modern analytical techniques could furnish at least part of the answer. We need much better monitoring of food, water, and human body constituents.

Companies producing fat-soluble, nonbiodegradable, organic chemicals should give careful attention to the question of what they may responsibly set loose on the environment. Failure to act now will surely lead to some new tragedy, aroused public opinion, and harsh federal regulations.

biological effects of pesticides in the environment

irma west

An adequate understanding of the biological effects of pesticides upon people and their living environment requires a synthesis of two important categories of scientific information: (1) the biology, biochemistry, and ecology of the human being and his environment, and (2) the action and effect of each pesticide, over the full course of its influence, as it impinges upon the human being and invades the environment. That we have something less than a full complement of this basic knowledge should be obvious. Undertaking to acquire this information is a monumental and never-ending task. Nevertheless, there is no choice but to pursue it and make much more substantial inroads into it. Introducing new chemicals should be a scientific enterprise based on knowledge and subject to continuous evaluation, criticism, and correction if it is to contribute effectively to human welfare.

There is no question of the great need for effective pest control. There is no question of the immediate efficiency and economic value of modern pesticides in producing food and fiber and in controlling vector-borne disease. There is also no question about the ease of using hindsight to comment on pesticide problems compared with the difficulties of exercising foresight a decade or more ago in predicting these problems. The problems which have arisen with modern pesticides stem from their ability to do much more than is expected or desired of them. The fact that stable pesticides

Reprinted from "Organic Pesticides in the Environment," *Advances in Chemistry Series,* 60, 1966, and copyright 1966 by the American Chemical Society. Reproduced by permission of the copyright owner. The author is with the Bureau of Occupational Health, California State Department of Public Health, Berkeley, California.

contaminate, accumulate, and move about in the environment has taken time to be realized. Neither the chemical nor the environment in which it is applied is a simple arrangement. Even the successful immediate control of a target pest can be diminished by a chain of events where the pesticide eventually causes an increase in the pest. The pace of application has long ago exceeded our ability to investigate and comprehend the ultimate results. Regardless of whether we do or do not escape various small and large disasters potential to this kind of adventure, proceeding so far ahead of understanding is not in the best traditions of science.

A society which expects to reap the benefits of its technological tools must learn to control the adverse side effects of these tools, whatever they may be. To control adverse side effects arising from pesticides better, the needs are most evident in research, field testing, in monitoring the environment, in human health surveillance, and in limiting the use of pesticides to persons who are competent by knowledge, training, and equipment. Introducing synthetic chemicals into people and their environment before the course of their action and significant effects were adequately understood has resulted in unexpected and undesirable side effects. Furthermore, procedures to control known undesirable side effects have often been deficient, either because of short-term economic influences or because these materials were rushed into the hands of the technically unprepared. These inadequacies have aroused considerable criticism and reservation. Either the standards for research, field testing, and control must be raised and broadened in scope or we must curtail the introduction of new materials. Introducing new chemicals should be a scientific enterprise, based on knowledge and dedicated to the long range benefit of mankind, not short range economic interests. It should be subject to continuous evaluation, criticism, and correction if it is to contribute the most to human welfare.

Technology is not an end in itself but a means to an end, which is public welfare. Scientists tend to forget that it is the public which in the final analysis has the responsibility to decide what it considers to be in its best interest. One of the most important duties of the scientist is to communicate his knowledge to the public. Too often the scientist sees his role as a decision-making one and often even without explanation. Subsequent public protest is then labelled "emotional" or worse. Incidentally, the term "emotional" is, in my opinion, the most misused word in the pesticide controversy. The word which should be substituted for emotional is "irrational," for we must not be irrational about a subject as important as pesticides. At the same time we should be, and cannot escape being, emotional as well.

In using pesticides, I believe the public wants continuing factual evidence that it is proceeding with the greatest care and the widest margin of safety. It does not want to be patted on the head periodically and told that the food supply, or whatever, is perfectly "safe." Public distrust of such pronouncements seems to be obvious to almost everyone but the people making the pronouncements. A primitive state of communication exists between the scientific community and the public, particularly on the subject of pesticides. The scientific community does a lot of communicating, but mostly within itself. Important initial steps toward better communications call for scientists to do more listening to the public and to develop a greater sense of humility. Until the scientists and the public learn to operate in greater understanding and harmony, much valuable effort will be wasted.

I do not believe the scientific community has ever really faced the issue of what would be necessary to prevent the undesirable side effects from using pesticides and still enjoy their benefits. First, it would be necessary to know in advance what these undesirable effects are through research and adequate field tests. Second, their use must be controlled to prevent adverse effects. Third, because methods for predicting adverse effects must be continually evaluated and because they cannot be expected to be perfect, a monitoring system for the environment and for human health must be established with built-in power to stop and revise pesticide uses when they are suspected of producing undesirable effects. This kind of system may seem insurmountably difficult, but only because our administrative thinking has never been big enough for our environmental health problems. A good control program is technically feasible. It has been routine, for example, in developing our space program. However, when it comes to down-to-earth matters involving the general population, too little too late is more often the case. Air pollution is another example of our administrative imagination and machinery not being big enough to catch up and come to grips with the problem.

Some distinguished investigators are less than optimistic about our ability to control unwanted effects arising from our technological tools. Rene Dubos is quoted as follows (*13*):

> *Present programs for controlling potential threats to health from new substances and technological innovations are doomed to failure because we lack the scientific knowledge to provide a sound basis for control.*
>
> *Current testing techniques have been developed almost exclusively for the study of acute, direct toxic effects.*
>
> *In contrast, most untoward effects of the technological environment are delayed and indirect. . . . Yet little is being done in schools of medicine and public health or in research institutes or government laboratories to develop the kind of knowledge that is needed for evaluating the long-range effects on man of modern ways of life.*
>
> *The dangers associated with ionizing radiation, or with cigarette smoking, should have sensitized the public as well as scientists to the importance of delayed effects. But, surprisingly, this knowledge has not increased awareness of the fact that most other technological innovations also have delayed effects.*
>
> *The slow evolution of chronic bronchitis from air pollutants, the late ocular lesions following use of chloroquine, the accumulation of the tetracyclines in the fetus, and of course all the carcinogenic effects, are but a few of the countless objectionable results of new substances or technologies which appeared at first essentially safe.*

He elaborates further in another statement (*14*):

> *There is no need to belabor the obvious truth that, while modern science has been highly productive of isolated fragments of knowledge, it has been far less successful in dealing with the complexity of natural phenom-*

ena, especially those involving life. In order to deal with problems of organized complexity, it is therefore essential to investigate situations in which several interrelated systems function in an integrated manner. Multifactorial investigations will naturally demand entirely new conceptual and experimental methods, very different from those involving only one variable, which have been the stock in trade of experimental science during the past 300 years and to which there is an increasing tendency to limit biological research.

Dubos is saying that our scientific comprehension, imagination, and methodology do not match the problems we face in dealing with complex interrelating biological phenomena. In fact, some of our traditional assumptions and methods may be actual barriers to the kind of new thinking which must be developed.

Let us look at three assumptions which have been accepted in at least some quarters in regard to pesticides.

Threshold dose level. The first assumption states that the effects of a chemical upon human beings are in proportion to dose and that there is a threshold dose level below which there is no effect. However, this is not the safe assumption. Even a few exceptions could lead to serious mistakes. No large group of diverse and sometimes multiple chemicals interacting with complex living matter can be expected to add up to such a consistent, simple, and convenient formula. Human experience with chemicals for the past 100 or more years has been in industry and through the use of therapeutic drugs. Here the data do not support such an assumption. Those empowered to make decisions about pesticides often do not take advantage of this wealth of human experience which clearly demonstrates the diversity of human effects from chemicals and how they do not always relate to animal data.

This is not to say that there may not be many chemical effects in proportion to dose and there may not be many "no effect" levels. However, we're hardly in a position to state this is always the case, nor that we necessarily have enough basic knowledge to find whatever "no effect" levels exist.

The possibilities for synergism, antagonism, and potentiation among chemicals, the allergic type responses, and the impaired detoxification and excretion mechanisms in substantial groups of people all call for less rigid assumptions. Data on carcinogenesis alone should give pause for reflection *(16, 28)*. The concept of threshold level may need re-examination and modification with pesticides as it has in the field of ionizing radiation.

Animal data. The second assumption states that the traditional toxicological tests involving rats and mice consistently reflect human response to chemicals.

Since we must use animal data, three points should be emphasized. First, there are qualitative and quantitative species differences among animals and human beings in reactions to chemicals. We don't necessarily know which we are dealing with when we extrapolate toxicological data from animals to man. Second, we use the most convenient and economically feasible animals—not necessarily those known to reflect best the human biochemistry which is deranged by the chemical being tested. Unfortunately we do not even know the mechanism of action most of the time. (However, when we do know the mechanism of action, specific effects can be determined at lower dose levels than would otherwise be the case—for example, cholinesterase levels for phosphate ester pesticides (*21*)). Third, we may not know enough about the biochemistry of the experimental animal to recognize variations produced by chemicals.

Relying heavily on animal data and considering them the final rather than the first step in developing toxicological information has not encouraged the necessary human studies and field tests. Careful observations of those persons who are exposed to pesticides in their work, for example, have not been incorporated into a system for careful transition of the chemical from the laboratory into general use.

Sufficient evidence. The third assumption states that it isn't scientifically proper to state that a chemical is producing harmful effects until all the evidence thoroughly verifies it.

When man is inventing potential sources of human disease and placing them in the general environment, he must be on the alert for adverse effects and be able to withdraw the chemical when he suspects unpredicted serious effects. However, the concept of waiting for proof beyond doubt today in regard to man-made diseases is not tenable. It places the burden of proof on the population and its environment. Furthermore, our lack of basic knowledge severely limits our ability to prove or disprove much in the individual case where new alleged effects may have occurred. Waiting for a sufficient number of dead bodies to provide the proof is crassly immoral and certainly aids and abets the distrust which often exists between the public and the scientific community.

pesticides in the environment

There are few places where residues of pesticides have not been found. They are present in water, soil, air, animals, people, food, and many commodities. Although we are adept at detecting and measuring the most minute amounts, we are not as adept at the more difficult task of determining the significance of pesticide residues in the environment. It is only when effects are immediate and substantial that they are likely to be recognized. However, it is a misconception to point only to the known fatal poisonings from pesticides and consider them the extent of the public health problem. Like air pollution and ionizing radiation, pesticide environmental contamination problems must not be considered in such narrow perspective. It is not valid to compare the number of fatal pesticide poisonings with traffic fatalities and conclude that pesticides are therefore a minor problem. Using the same spurious reasoning we could conclude that air pollution and ionizing radiation are much less a hazard than pesticides because there are fewer fatalities attributed to them.

An increasing number of reports in the literature describe the presence of chlorinated hydrocarbon pesticides, particularly DDT, . . . in surface waters, in well waters, and in marine life in the oceans.

Waters may be contaminated by dumping a large amount of chemical into a water system either by accident or unauthorized disposal. For example, a truck trailer carrying arsenic weed killer was involved in a traffic accident (*53*). The contents spilled over the highway and were washed subsequently into the river. Pesticides disposed by the manufacturer into the sewer survived the treatment plant and were percolated into the ground water, rendering a city well unfit for use *(53)*. An agricultural aircraft operator placed "used" pesticide containers in an irrigation ditch, which drained into a larger water system where many fish died *(99)*. Another sprayed a city reservoir with a defoliant. He was treating the surrounding fields and didn't shut off his apparatus as he criss-crossed the reservoir. This type of substantial contamination can have both long range and immediate significance depending upon the chemical involved. Acute emergencies arise if water for drinking, recreation, irrigation, commercial use, or water supporting wildlife is contaminated.

Another kind of contamination results when pesticides are applied to water or land for other pest control or agricultural purposes. Runoff from agricultural land is the greatest source of pesticides reaching the waters in California. Immediate effects occur most often from pesticides with a higher degree of acute toxicity and long range effects from pesticides which persist or remain. Some pesticides can produce both types and others, neither. The killing of fish has been a dramatic direct effect. Endrin, . . . a persistent and highly toxic pesticide, will kill fish at 0.5 p.p.b. (parts per billion) *(49)*. Holden *(26)* noted that fish took up the DDT in water rapidly by virtue of their external mucus coating and that DDT disappears when added to water. His report suggests that measuring water for the water-insoluble pesticides may not necessarily reflect the amount passing into organic matter.

The long range or indirect effects have been most disturbing. The most widely used pesticides, the chlorinated hydrocarbons, are concentrated by living matter in the aquatic environment. An increasing build-up of the pesticide may occur in each link of the food chain. These effects may not be discovered for some time after initial contact, particularly if acute toxicity of the pesticide is low. Multiple contacts may increase the amount of the chemical accumulating in the animal tissues over the years. The amounts tolerated before noticeable effects vary with the particular animal species and the pesticide. Some species can tolerate larger amounts, but sooner or later are affected by decreased fertility, interference with normal food sources, and eventually death *(29)*. The oyster is particularly efficient in its ability to concentrate chlorinated hydrocarbon pesticides. After seven days in water at 10 p.p.b. of DDT, eastern oysters were analyzed and found to contain 151 p.p.m. (parts per million) DDT *(52)*.

There are too many documented instances where food chain build-up of pesticides has occurred to list them all *(29, 30, 35, 47)*. The most minute amounts can be concentrated a thousandfold *(30)*, and there is no predictable safe level for them in waters where food chain build-up can occur. The literature also reports pesticide contamination of waters and aquatic life over the surface of this country into the oceans and Antarctic, *(2, 3, 19, 32, 39, 42, 48, 51, 52, 56)*. Blubber and oil from two whales washed up on the California coast contained DDE, . . . DDD, . . . and DDT. The highest value in the oil of one whale was 11 p.p.m. DDE, 6 p.p.m. DDT, and 8 p.p.m. DDD *(38)*.

Drinking water has been assayed as extensively as raw water. The levels of pesticides found in raw waters have been considerably below levels

190

considered hazardous to humans. Present knowledge indicates that long before the water becomes hazardous for humans to drink, it is potentially hazardous for aquatic life and fish-eating birds in the area. Biologists tell me that the food chain build-up of these persistent fat-soluble chemicals was predictable. Apparently the biologists were not consulted when the massive applications were initiated. This omission should be carefully noted for it points up an important fact. Knowledge from a much broader base of scientific disciplines must be used to plan and control our technological tools which affect people and their environment. No one group of scientists is capable of encompassing the knowledge vital to this kind of enterprise.

Arsenic and certain chlorinated hydrocarbons may accumulate in the soil and injure plants. Although carrots, potatoes, and leafy plants touching the ground will pick up DDT from the soil, most crops subsequently grown on soil in which DDT has accumulated apparently do not pick up the DDT. The chlorinated hydrocarbons in the soil are reduced by about 30% per year (1) after the last application. Parathion . . . was found to persist in soils for 9 months in a peach orchard in South Carolina. Rotenone, applied to kill fish in the autumn, unexpectedly weathered a winter's freeze and killed fish the next spring. (Rotenone is an older botanical pesticide extracted from derris root. It usually decomposes rapidly in air and light and is considered a little less toxic to humans than DDT. It is highly toxic to fish.) A child was poisoned almost fatally from parathion which had survived the winter snow and rain after being spilled in the driveway of his home. The child had eaten mud pies made from contaminated soil which was found to contain 1% parathion (43).

Marth, in his summary of the literature (35), states that most of the chlorinated hydrocarbons persist in the soil from several to many years. Temperature, moisture, type of soil, amount, and volatility of the compound influence the duration. Soil microflura are not appreciably altered, but fauna are modified as to kind and number.

Carson has postulated that some of the small particles of pesticides, released as sprays or dust, when applied to agricultural land may become airborne for some time and distance, eventually producing fall-out (6). Yates and Akkeson point out (60):

> There is no known way in which drift of agricultural chemicals can be entirely eliminated, whether applied by ground or aircraft. Drift of tracers used in air pollution studies have been authenticated as far as 22 miles, and further distances could be expected, depending on the accuracy of the means for sensing tracer chemicals. Symptoms of 2,4-D drift have been noted on grapes 8 to 12 miles from the point of application and lawsuits in Texas and Washington have been based on greater drift distance.

A series of exploratory determinations involving air collected from four California cities was made in autumn of 1963. All but two showed measurable amounts of DDT (4). A variety of pesticides has been found in the air in several urban communities in the United States (51).

Pesticides have been found in minute to substantial amounts in several strange and miscellaneous locations in the environment and in people. A

191

leaky drum of Phosdrin concentrate spilled on a bale of blue-jeans during transit by truck. Phosdrin, . . . which can be readily absorbed through the skin, is a highly toxic phosphate ester pesticide. Eight months later six boys who wore unwashed jeans from this bale were poisoned (*54*).

A chemist discovered that his neighborhood dry cleaner had routinely added DDT to the cleaning solvent for mothproofing since 1956. He extracted 30 mg. of DDT from his suit which had been cleaned at this establishment. Additional miscellaneous garments were analyzed, and the DDT extracted varied from 20–565 p.p.m. (*50*). In one experiment 3.3 mg. dieldrin . . . also used at one time for mothproofing was removed by 1 liter of sweat from treated woolen cloth (*35*).

Contamination of peach orchards with parathion and possibly its more toxic degradation product, paroxon, sent over 90 poisoned peach pickers to physicians in California in August 1963. Heavy spraying of the orchards in the spring and summer had resulted in a substantial deposit of parathion on the leaves, which were contacted later by the pickers (*37*). About 400 cases of parathion poisoning have occurred in California in sporadic outbreaks among fruit pickers and others who have worked in heavy foliage which had been sprayed with parathion. Because the crop was considered safe to eat since pesticide residues were below legal tolerance, it was assumed that it was safe to go into the orchard and harvest the crop. This assumption is obviously false.

Home and garden contamination from pesticides have received little attention. An increasing variety of products and applications raises questions. Lindane-impregnated shelf paper is available for the cupboard. Pesticides in paints and shellac, furnace filters, swimming pool chemicals for algae control, and in an endless variety of sprays, dusts, and pellets for home, for garden, and for pets can be purchased. Dispensers which continuously or intermittently release pesticides into the air are available. Applications of persistent pesticides by pest control operators into living quarters can remain for some time, recirculating and vaporizing through furnaces and ventilating equipment as well as by normal air motion. We know less about environmental contamination from pesticides in the home than we do about pesticides in penguins in the Antarctic (*19*) despite the fact that the home is the most frequent location from which morbidity and mortality from pesticides is reported.

All samples of human fat tested and reported in the United States show storage of DDT and its metabolite DDE. . . . Residue from food, particularly meat (*5*), is considered the most likely source of stored material. The average fat storage level of DDT plus derived material is about 12 p.p.m. for the approximately 800 samples from the general population which have been reported. For workers with occupational exposure, storage levels over 1000 p.p.m. DDT and DDE are on record. Other chlorinated hydrocarbons have been detected in human fat in Europe as well as in this country. . . . The significance of this stored material to human health has yet to be determined. There are three possibilities: (1) there are no effects; (2) there are effects we're not yet able to detect; (3) there are effects, but they have yet to manifest themselves.

In 1962 human milk analyzed by the California Department of Public

Health ranged from 0 to 0.12 p.p.m. DDT and 0 to 0.25 p.p.m. DDE. The highest total of DDT plus DDE was 0.37 p.p.m. (56).

The one by-product of pesticide use which has received the most research attention and regulative control is the residue of pesticide applied to foods. Focusing attention on food residues for so long has led some to assume it is the only problem. This assumption has made it more difficult to see the other compelling problems arising from using pesticides.

Pesticide residue tolerances on food are based upon the maximum level of pesticide in food which has no discernible effect on test animals, usually rats, during their lifetimes. This "no-effect" level is divided by 100 and sometimes less to provide a margin of safety. When good agricultural practices allow a lower tolerance, it may be set accordingly. The contribution to the human diet that a particular food makes is also considered in deciding the amount of pesticide residue allowed. Tolerances are therefore reliable to the degree that the test animal and humans react with no more than a hundredfold quantitative difference to the same level of lifelong feeding exposure to the pesticides in question. When important human effects are not reflected or detected in rats or when other simultaneous chemical exposures alter results, then the safety of the tolerance must rest on the small magnitude characteristic of tolerances. An additional margin of safety arises from the fact that residues actually found on edible crops are about 1% of the legal tolerance (17). However, there is considerable room for improvement in the surveillance of animal-derived foods which are the major source of pesticides stored in human fat (5, 20). Surveillance of fish and game for pesticide residues also deserves more attention (56).

If there is no choice in using pesticides in agriculture, there is also no choice about adequate monitoring of all of our foodstuffs or about setting valid tolerances for pesticides on foods. We cannot afford even one mistake which involves all or most of the population.

The increasing opportunities for accidental contamination of food and other commodities from spills during storage or transit should not be overlooked. In California recently several persons became ill after eating doughnuts made at one bakery. It was only late in the investigation that the true cause was discovered somewhat by chance. A concentrate of diazinon . . . had been spilled on the doughnut mix through alleged carelessness in pest control operations (57).

One of the delayed effects of exposure to certain chemicals is the production of tumors, some of which are cancerous. Our state of knowledge in this area is growing rapidly but is most difficult to interpret. Chemical carcinogenesis was first reported in 1775 when Sir Percival Pott, an English physician, discovered that the prevalent scrotal cancers of chimney sweeps were caused by the soot. Many additional industrial carcinogens have since been described. It is therefore not surprising that certain pesticides are suspected of producing cancer since it has been demonstrated in animals under certain experimental conditions (16, 18, 28, 59). Arsenic has long been a suspected carcinogen in people, and only recently have arsenic cancers in fish been reported (32). Also suspected are aminotriazole, aramite, dithiocarbamates, DDT, aldrin, heptachlor, dieldrin, endrin, 8-hydroxy-quinoline, ethylene oxide, propylene oxide, and piperonyl compounds and certain chemosterilants (aziridine derivatives) (*9, 14*). The evidence which places lindane suspect as a delayed bone marrow toxicant has been reviewed by West (*57, 58*).

summary

Widespread substantial contamination of the environment has arisen primarily from the massive use of the persistent chlorinated hydrocarbon pesticides. The extent and significance of this contamination is only partly known. Our limited knowledge is most apparent in two areas. First, there is no organized environmental monitoring and human surveillance system to provide comprehensive and representative data about the locations, amounts, and trends of this contamination; second, we are technically unprepared to predict the significant long term effects of this contamination on animal and human life.

In a few areas of scientific concern, knowledge is developing at a faster pace. . . . It is important that this new knowledge be interpreted, integrated, and organized into information which can be put into practical use. Rather than remaining aloof, scientists should interpret their work more freely, comment candidly on its scientific, social, and ethical implications in language which the public as well as the scientific community understands. Furthermore, controversy among different groups of scientists, the public, and the chemical industry should be welcomed. Only out of such controversy can be generated and synthesized the broad panorama of knowledge, ideas and viewpoints which are capable of developing technology for optimal human welfare.

literature cited

1. Anderson, L. D., Deal, A. S., Gunther, F. A., *Proc. Ann. Conf. Use Agr. Chemicals Calif. 2nd*, Davis, Calif., 1963.
2. Breidenbach, A. W., *Arch. Environ. Health 10*, 827 (1965).
3. Breidenbach, A. W., Lichtenberg, J. J., Report of National Water Quality Network, Division of Water Supply and Pollution Control, Public Health Service (July 17, 1963).
4. California Department of Public Health, Bureau of Sanitation, unpublished data, preliminary report, January 1964.
5. Campbell, J. E., *Arch. Environ. Health 10*, 831 (1965).
6. Carson, R.: Testimony before U.S. Senate Subcommittee on Reorganization and International Organizations, Part I, p. 214, 1963.
7. Clayson, D. B., "Chemical Carcinogenesis," p. 114. Little Brown & Company, Boston, 1962.
8. Dale, W. E. *et al., Bull. World Health Org. 33*, 471 (1965).
9. Dale, W. E., Quinby, G., *Science 142*, 593 (1963).
10. Denes, A., *Nahrung 6*, 48 (1962).
11. Durham, W., Armstrong, J., *Science 134*, 1880 (1961).
12. DuBois, K. P., *Arch. Environ. Health 10*, 847 (1965).
13. Dubos, R., *Medical Tribune,* October 28, 1964.
14. Dubos, R., *Bioscience 14*, 11 (1964).
15. Egan, H., *Brit. Med. J. 2*, 66 (1965).

194

16. Falk, H. L. *et al., Arch. Environ. Health 10,* 847 (1965).
17. Food and Drug Administration, Press release, April 9, 1965.
18. Food Protection Committee, *Nat. Acad. Sci. Publ. 749,* (1959).
19. George, J. L., *San Francisco Chronicle* July 11, 1965.
20. Hayes, W. J. *et al., Arch. Ind. Health 18,* 398 (1958).
21. Hayes, W. J. *et al., J. Am. Med. Assoc. 162,* 890 (1956).
22. Hayes, W. J. *et al., Nature 199,* 1189 (1963).
23. Hayes, W. J. *et al., Life Sci. 4,* 1611 (1965).
24. Hoffman, W. S. *et al., Arch. Environ. Health 9,* 398 (1964).
25. Hoffman, W. S. *et al., J. Am. Med. Assoc. 188,* 819 (1964).
26. Holden, A. V., *Ann. Appl. Biol. 50,* 476 (1962).
27. Howell, D. E., *Proc. Oklahoma Acad. Sci. 28–32,* 31 (1948).
28. Heuper, W.E., Conway, W. D., "Chemical Carcinogenesis and Cancers," Charles Thomas, Springfield, Ill. 1964.
29. Hunt, E. G., Bishoff, A. I., *Calif. Fish Game 46,* 91 (1960).
30. Hunt, E. G., Keith, J. O., Proceedings of the Second Annual Conference on Use of Agricultural Chemicals in California, Davis, January 1963, p. 13.
31. Hunter, C. G. *et al., Brit. Med. J. 5325,* 221 (1963).
32. Kraybill, H. F., Presented at Washington State Horticultural Association Meeting, Wenatchee, December 1963.
33. Laug, E. P. *et al., Arch. Ind. Hyg. Occ. Med. 3,* 245 (1951).
34. Maier-Bode, H., *Med. Exptl. 1,* 146 (1960).
35. Marth, E. H., "Residue Reviews," Vol. 9, Springer Verlag, New York, 1965.
36. Mattson, A. M., *Anal. Chem. 25,* 1065 (1953).
37. Milby, T. H., Ottoboni, F., Mitchell, H., *J. Am. Med. Assoc. 189,* 351 (1964).
38. Navonne, R., California State Health Department Branch Laboratory, Los Angeles, personal communication, 1965.
39. Paul, R. M., *Am. J. Public Health 55,* 16 (1965).
40. Pearce, G. W. *et al., Science 116,* 254 (1952).
41. Perry, W. J., Bodenlos, L. J., *Mosquito News 9–11,* 1 (1950).
42. President's Science Advisory Committee Report, "Use of Pesticides," White House, Washington, D.C., 1963.
43. Quinby, G. E., Clappison, G. B., *Arch. Environ. Health 3,* 538 (1961).
44. Quinby, G. *et al., J. Am. Med. Assoc. 191,* 175 (1965).
45. Read, S., McKinley, W. P., *Arch. Environ. Health 3,* 209 (1961).
46. Robinson, J. *et al., Brit. J. Med. 22,* 220 (1965).
47. Rudd, R. L., "Pesticides and the Living Landscape," Chap. 20, University of Wisconsin Press, Madison, 1964.
48. Rudd, R. L., Genelly, R. E., *Calif. Dept. Fish Game, Game Bull. 7* (1956).
49. Shannon, W. T., Testimony before California Senate Fact Finding Committee on Agriculture, Sacramento, October 22–23, 1963.
50. Stanford Research Institute, Pesticide Research Bulletin, Menlo Park, California, November 1963.
51. Tabor, E. C., *J. Air Pollution Control Assoc. 15,* 9 (1965).
52. Udall, S., Testimony before U. S. Senate Subcommittee on Reorganization and International Organizations, Part I, pp. 71–72, May 1963.

53. Warne, W., Testimony before California Senate Fact Finding Committee on Agriculture, Sacramento, October 22–23, 1963.
54. Warren, M. C. *et al., J. Am. Med. Assoc. 184,* 266 (1963).
55. Wasserman, M. *et al., Arch. Environ. Health 11,* 375 (1965).
56. West, I., *Arch. Environ. Health 9,* 626 (1964).
57. West, I., *Calif. Health 23,* 11 (1965).
58. West, I., submitted for publication, 1966.
59. World Health Organization Expert Committee on Food Additives, *World Health Org. Tech. Rept. Ser. 220* (1961).
60. Yates, W. E., Akesson, N. B., *Proc. Ann. Conf. Use Agr. Chemicals Calif.,* 2nd, Davis, Calif., 1963.
61. Zavon, M. *et al., J. Am. Med. Assoc. 193,* 837 (1965).

choices are in the offing

carol knapp

The problem really facing us now is how can we move forward more rapidly to find alternative methods to replace chemicals where they have become objectionable.

In the recent [1971] Senate hearings on new pesticide legislation, Sen. Bob Packwood (R.-Ore.) declared "the crux of the whole (pesticide) problem—research!" The emphasis has always been on research or the lack of it because of too little money, personnel, or facilities. However, research for alternative pest control methods has been given emphasis in the Entomology Research Division of the Agricultural Research Service (ARS) in the U.S. Department of Agriculture (USDA) since 1955 when USDA scientists recognized the many complex residue and environmental pollution problems resulting from broad spectrum (wide range) pesticides.

Packwood and other committees and commissions point out that more research is needed, but the general economic squeeze is also felt in the research area. In other words, there has been a reduction in research programs and increased costs for the past four years.

The restrictions placed on pesticides are creating a demand for alternative methods, and it takes a lot more time and effort to develop biological control methods. With the growing awareness of broad spectrum chemicals creating certain problems and with public pressure, the Environmental Protection Agency is certain to take a hard look at pesticides as a hazard to environmental quality.

"That adequate pest control is an essential practice in modern agriculture hardly needs to be defended," states Edward F. Knipling, science advisor, ARS.

"Unfortunately, however, pest control today is being largely accomplished with pesticides that are responsible for certain known and potential threats to the quality of our environment." Today, over three fourths of the entomology division's effort is devoted to developing alternative selective biological control procedures.

"The problem really facing us now is how can we move forward more rapidly to find alternative methods to replace chemicals where they have become objectionable," Knipling explains. There are several reasons why this effort is moving slowly. At present, about 10,000 insect species in the U.S. are considered pests at one time or another, although most are minor sporadic pests whose numbers increase in intermittent surges. Nevertheless, about 100 species are a problem. These 100 insect types cause 80–90% of the damage. Therefore, 80–90% of the total chemical pesticides is used for their control. Since alternative methods are designed to be as selective as possible against the target pest, avoiding the objectionable features of the broad spectrum pesticide, 100 alternate methods for 100 different insects would have to be developed. While one pesticide, with little modification, could control a dozen or more pests, the very nature of alternative methods does not allow "the same degree of progress that occurs with developing a wide range chemical pesticide," says Knipling.

However, much has been done in the line of alternative biological controls. Promising pest control methods now under study include:
- attractants,
- genetic changes,
- sterility, and
- combinations of these methods.

Not to be forgotten, although still in the category of chemicals, is ultralow volume (ULV) aerial spraying of pesticides. Sprayed in amounts as low as one ounce per acre, the ULV technique is effective in controlling such pests as the mosquito and grasshopper. For example, pesticide, undiluted, is sprayed as a very fine mist; therefore, only a small amount is needed; time and cost of pest control operations are reduced.

attractants

A pest control method that has been gaining recognition is the use of chemical attractants to lure insects. Insects respond to many attractants—sound, light, or chemicals. Light traps have not been too successful thus far, and the use of sound is still experimental. Baits are being used in traps to attract the insects and bring them in contact with toxic chemicals. However, the attractants under the most study are natural attractants that insects produce in communication for mating. This involves using one sex of an insect to attract and destroy the opposite sex. Females produce chemicals called pheromones that attract males for mating, or vice versa. These extremely active compounds are also quite selective, usually for the insect that produces it. The goal is to produce a synthetic chemical based on the structure of the natural attractant.

Sex attractants for pest control look very promising. The chemical methyl euginol has an extremely high attractancy for oriental fruit fly males, an important tropical and citrus fruit pest. A USDA laboratory in Hawaii has applied methyl euginol to one-inch cardboard squares impregnated with a toxicant and demonstrated the eradication of the oriental fruit fly from isolated areas.

Entomologists eventually hope to use sex attractants in two ways. First, the sex attractant might be used to trap insects in sufficient numbers to prevent populations from increasing. The other method confuses males in an area saturated with a chemical attractant where they cannot find females; therefore, "the females just don't get mated," explains Knipling. Since most insects have very short life cycles (two to three weeks), reproduction must take place in that period of time or there are no progeny produced to increase the population.

genetic techniques

Insect geneticists are looking into mechanisms that do not harm or kill (as may sterilization treatments) insects being reared for release. Such insects will transmit characteristics that will eventually lead to death of progeny carrying the genetic defects. For instance, perhaps a strain of insects cannot go into diapause. This pest may develop throughout the summer but lacks the mechanism for going into winter hibernation. This method is just as good as killing insects, but delays it for a season. Normally, the ability to diapause for winter survival is triggered by exposure to less light or to fewer hours of light and cooler temperatures. Also, treating insects with hormone-type chemicals can break diapause.

sterility

Another genetic control, sterility, has been used to control several destructive pests. For this control, millions of insects are exposed to radiation that renders them sterile. When released to mate with insects in the environment, no progeny are produced. Sterility eradicated the screwworm (a serious pest of livestock and wild animals) from the southeastern U.S. and controls 99% of the screwworms in the southwestern U.S. The screwworm program covers a 300,000 square mile area with 150 million screwworm flies released each week. "We have demonstrated," Knipling points out, "that the sterile insect method can be useful in eliminating low level populations of tropical fruit flies, also."

integrated programs

Combinations of treatments with or without chemical pesticides are often more effective than any one method alone. One system may lower the population, and the other(s) will eliminate the remaining few.

In the western states, for example, the codling moth is a serious pest of apples and pears. In fact, more insecticides are used in apple orchards than any other individual use. The approach for elimination of this pest will be reducing the codling moth to the lowest possible level with chemical sprays. Scientists hope that the last few can be overflooded with sterile moths and continuously controlled with sterile moths. In Washington, such pilot tests are taking place now. The results will be definite in the next year or so, at which time a major codling moth eradication program may be started.

Causing $200-million damage to cotton each year, the boll weevil also will be attacked by the sterile male method somewhat like the codling moth program. First, pesticides will reduce the boll weevil population to the lowest possible level (by spraying in the fall). Then in the spring, sex attractant traps will eradicate those not destroyed by insecticides. This treatment will be followed by liberation of sterile males. "When the populations are low enough, we hope that the attractants and sterile males will eliminate the few remaining insects," Knipling explains. This fall, a pilot test for boll weevil eradication will begin in Mississippi, involving 25,000 acres of cotton. In about one and one-half years, the final results will be compiled. If successful, the boll weevil problem in the entire southern U.S. could be tackled.

cultural measures

Other natural biological pest control measures are available and under further development. These include:
- Cultural measures,
- Resistant crops,
- Predators, pathogens, parasites.

Cultural measures or sanitation practices are designed to prevent insect breeding in excessive numbers. Destroying cotton stalks prevents overwintering populations of the boll weevil and pink bollworm to develop; likewise, sanitation measures in tobacco reduce tobacco hornworm and tobacco bud worm numbers. Sanitation is also basic in the control of houseflies, cockroaches, and rodents. Mosquitoes can be more adequately controlled in areas with proper drainage. Cultural methods also include soil tillage, rotation of crops, and early or delayed planting. All these practices help destroy insects or prevent their breeding, but "by themselves, they seldom provide a dependable solution to insect problems," Knipling advises.

resistant crops

One of the more fruitful, long-range approaches to pest control not involving chemicals is developing crop varieties resistant to insect attack. "There has been more progress made in this direction than any alternative method, with the exception of chemicals, of course," says Knipling, "this is one of the more productive alternatives."

Four or five important pests (Hessian fly, corn borer, aphid, loop worm, weevil) are being controlled by resistant crop varieties (wheat, corn, alfalfa). For example, the Hessian fly, once a major pest of wheat, causing several hundred million dollars losses each year, is now reduced to levels that make the insect of relatively minor importance. The reason: there are millions of acres of wheat growing today that are virtually immune to Hessian fly attack.

This desirable pest control method causes no adverse side effects or residues, except to the insect pest, and it costs no more to grow a resistant crop variety than a susceptible one. This method is not used more extensively because of the long, tedious research necessary to develop resistant plants.

three p's

Aside from the above, natural biological agents, the so-called three P's—pathogens, parasites, predators—are often used to control pests. "With-

200

out these natural biological agents, we would be helpless to deal with insects," emphasizes Knipling; "they keep many kinds of insect populations in balance, even repressing those that are highly destructive." However, biological control agents themselves do not take care of pest problems to the degree that society demands.

For example, the "balance-of-nature" allows plants to produce a certain amount while insects feed and exist on them. "As far as nature is concerned, that's successful; however, a half a yield in nature does not satisfy our requirements and quality," Knipling continues. "Yet, without them, we would be helpless, for many alien insect pests have been brought into this country without their natural enemies." The first step in pest control is to find native enemies and release them in the problem areas.

One biological control method—the first of the three P's—uses pathogens (diseases of insects caused by fungi, bacteria, or viruses). Nearly all pests have some organism that affects their well-being. Again, diseases do not do the complete job of pest control that is desirable, but insect pathologists hope to find ways of using these disease organisms to keep the insect population under control.

The best example of success with pathogens is the milky spore disease of the Japanese beetle. "This organism has done a remarkable job in reducing and stabilizing the Japanese beetle," says Knipling. The only limiting feature of this program is that the disease is really not effective until the Japanese beetle has developed to high numbers. However, when the organism is introduced and attacks the beetles, the spores survive in the soil to suppress the beetle for years.

Control of several pests may come by use of a bacterium (*Bacillus thuringiensis*). New strains are being developed to control the cabbage looper, cotton bollworm, cotton bud worm, and tobacco bud worm. In addition to this organism, there are a dozen other promising insect pathogens (mostly viruses).

Control by parasites looks promising. For the past ten years, the alfalfa weevil has caused much damage in New Jersey, Delaware, and Pennsylvania. Weevil parasites (tiny wasps) were brought in from Europe and released. In the past few years, the pest has been decreasing and reduced to the point that less chemical control is required—in some cases, none at all. "Although we don't anticipate that the parasite will necessarily eliminate the pest, the use of chemicals can be reduced by 75%, which is a tremendous gain, and the crop losses will be reduced correspondingly," Knipling stresses.

Noteworthy examples of predators for pest control are the preying mantis and lady bug. These "beneficial" insects do not destroy the crop, just their natural enemies. Eventually, perhaps, both parasites or predators could be mass produced and released into the environment to help attack various pests. Scientists in California are adding supplemental food to crop areas for the predators. Then they will be more productive, lay more eggs, and produce more progeny to prey on harmful insects.

A major problem in developing biological and other alternative controls centers around adequate field tests to see whether alternative methods are effective and ready to use. Even if such methods are deemed feasible and successful, drastic changes in approach may be necessary. With pesticides,

201

individual farmers can control their own problems. Most of the alternative methods, to be successful, will require an attack on the pest problem in its entirety. Programs may have to be regionally or nationally organized—with cooperation among individual farmers and state and federal agencies.

Although many of the alternative controls have shown promise in limited tests or practical use, the majority of pest control methods is still relatively in the future. "We still need to rely on proved pesticides," says Knipling. "The alternatives are going to come slow and will take time. But in the end I'm hoping that we can truly manage a number of key insects effectively and economically."

food additives

Man's altered chemical environment does not end with his protective cover of skin. He is a dynamic component of the environment, constantly exchanging materials with his surroundings. Man alters the environment and the environment alters man—that much is and always will be inevitable.

Food is a component of our personal chemical environment which has an overwhelming impact. It is the fuel that, in combination with inhaled oxygen, provides the energy of life. It also supplies the atomic and molecular building blocks from which our tissues are made. Quite literally, we are products of the food we eat.

Natural food is chemically complex. It contains an enormous variety of organic substances, most of them broadly classed as carbohydrates, proteins, or fats. Individually, these substances vary widely in nutritional value and biochemical role. A few of them are toxic (recall Article 4). On the whole, however, the human organism has adapted beautifully to this chemical hodgepodge.

In only a few decades out of man's long biological history,

there has been a drastic change in the chemical content of foods—much of it owing to chemical additives. Now many people are questioning the wisdom of adding to foods so many chemicals new to human experience. The issue has provoked great controversy, and it is so complex that even specialists frequently disagree on its merits. In view of this, the layman can hardly be expected to reach a final conclusion after reading a few brief essays. However, the layman can, by understanding the issues and arguments more completely, better wield his influence as a consumer and a voter.

The following articles point out the major facts and issues in the raging food-additives controversy. Johnathan Spivak in (Article 31) "Use of Chemicals in Food Stirs Controversy," leads off with a concise summary of the problem and its unexpected magnitude. In Article 32, "Food Additive Makers Face Intensified Attack," Howard J. Sanders provides an in-depth study of food additives, pinpointing such controversial chemicals as monosodium glutamate (MSG), saccharin, the cyclamates, and sodium nitrite. Finally, Article 33, "Even Some Chemicals That Occur Naturally in Foods Can Be Harmful," reminds us that not all questionable chemicals are synthetic; nature is well able to provide her own arsenal of threatening compounds.

use of chemicals in food stirs controversy

jonathan spivak

"We can never, never equate usage with safety," insists Marvin Legator, head of the FDA's cell biology work. One reason: it could take decades before additive-caused health hazards like chronic disease developed; by then it would be too late for precautions.

There's polysorbate 60 in your pickles. There's ethylenediamine tetracetate in your mayonnaise. There's butylated hydroxytoluene in your breakfast cereal.

These complex chemical names are hardly household words. But hundreds of chemicals are being used more and more to flavor, color, fortify, preserve and otherwise alter everyday foods. This chemical influx into the American diet is kicking up fierce controversy that may affect both the safety of foods available to the U. S. public and the operations of food producing companies.

The advocates of food additives insist they are safe, nutritious, and essential for satisfying consumers' taste and convenience. "It's almost impossible for me to conceive of meeting the demands of a country like ours without food additives," declares A. S. Clausi, vice president of General Foods.

The critics contend that some food chemicals are clearly hazardous to humans, others are suspect, and most are needless additions designed to deceive the food purchaser. Ralph Nader accuses industry of "manipulating the content of food as dictated by corporate greed and irresponsibility."

Amid the smoke of controversy, some realities seem clear. Additives furnish vitamins and minerals to replace essential nutrients lost in processing and to prevent deficiency diseases such as rickets and pellagra; synthetic flavors to imitate or supplement scarce natural flavors; antioxidants to keep fatty foods fresh; growth inhibitors to prevent mold or bacteria from infest-

Reprinted with permission of *The Wall Street Journal* from its publication of January 13, 1971, as condensed in the April 1971 issue of *Chemical Technology*. The author is a staff reporter of *The Wall Street Journal*.

ing fruit juices and other products; thickening agents to give body and consistency; and emulsifiers to keep ingredients from separating.

Proponents insist that additives are essential for producing innovative, popular new items: "instant thirst-quenchers," simulated whipped-cream, and "nondairy" creamers. Says Mr. Clausi "we are just on the edge of a whole new plateau of product development."

Critics point to a lengthening list of additives banned by the Food and Drug Administration. These include coumarin, a vanilla flavor; safrole, the primary root-beer flavor; red and yellow food colors derived from coal tars, and, of course, cyclamates.

The primary concern is that these compounds could cause cancer if ingested in large quantities over a long period of time. But some additives have also been shown to cause heart, liver, brain, and other damage in experiments on animals. Although it's difficult to prove hazard to humans, some scientists insist that even the faintest suspicion of risk requires Government limitations.

Despite FDA's safety moves, James Turner, principal author of the Nader group's FDA study "The Chemical Feast," adds that "the FDA has allowed a massive market in food additives to develop with no significant regulation." Many agency officials understandably take a different view. "I think consumers are being unduly concerned by a lot of chemical names they don't understand," argues Virgil Wodicka, director of the FDA's Bureau of Food.

But Democratic Sen. Gaylord Nelson of Wisconsin will prod the Senate Labor Committee to hold food-additive hearings. He'll push bills to ban any chemical that produces an adverse effect in animals, require retesting of hundreds of commonly used additives now assumed to be safe, and enlarge Federal control over testing, which is mainly done by the food companies themselves. The Nelson proposals are sure to be roundly opposed by the food industry, which fears a crippling political attack. But there's little likelihood that Congress will adopt any legislative solution to the food-additive controversy; if anything, further FDA action seems more probable. For the scientific issues are highly complicated and necessary information is often lacking; moreover, experts frequently disagree over the meaning of data and the standards to be applied.

A major problem stems from uncertainty over the meaning of animal tests. Man may respond to particular chemicals quite differently from mice, rats, monkeys, and other animals. "Most of our decisions are based on studies in animals; we may not be able to find from such studies everything that may happen with humans," notes Leo Friedman, director of FDA's Division of Toxicology. Some scientists hope the "minipig," a specially bred hog about 20% smaller than other pigs and resembling man in bone density and certain other ways, will provide the ideal model.

Whatever the outcome, the stakes in this squabble are sizable. Experts estimate that at least 2,000 chemicals are deliberately added to food; probably another 1,500 wind up in products as a result of packaging or processing. All told, there are 30 different categories of additives. The largest consists of 1,200 flavoring agents; sometimes more than a dozen are needed to provide proper taste. Other major categories are vitamins and minerals, emulsifiers, stabilizers, coloring agents, and preservatives.

Most of the 1,000 to 1,500 new food products introduced annually, particularly convenience foods, rely heavily on additives; they are the key to shorter preparation time and extended shelf life. And more of these products are on the way. "Like every other food company, we will be paying attention . . . to any product in which we can save the housewife preparation time or do something her skills are not up to," says Richard Hall, vice president for research and development of McCormick & Co., a seasoning producer that has been diversifying into other food products.

McCormick recently introduced butter-flavored salt for popcorn, has synthesized a bell-pepper flavor, and is working on simulating coffee and bread flavors.

Advancing food technology is even making possible the fabrication of artificial meats and seafoods based on inexpensive vegetable protein like soybeans. The protein is spun into thin filaments that simulate the texture of such foods as bacon, ground beef, or scallops. The FDA is planning a standard for "textured protein products," prescribing the official name and required components. The standard offers the manufacturers a major promotional advantage: They will not have to label meat analogues "imitation," as the FDA required in the past.

Some versions of the analogues have already reached the market as convenient bacon "bits" and components of other products like Lipton's beef stroganoff dinner. Food-industry experts estimate that the analogues now cost about 10% less than meats and the savings could be far more substantial in the future as volume increases. The major uncertainty is whether consumers will accept them as meat substitutes.

Farther in the future is the possibility of fabricating artificial fruits and vegetables and even inventing new ones, says General Foods. Alina S. Szczesniak, a GF researcher, has patented a process for producing such products from alginate, a seaweed protein that has the desired consistency and texture.

"Different additives can be chosen, to produce predetermined cellular structures which resemble the properties of potatoes, water chestnuts, turnips, cucumbers, apples, pears, watermelons, honeydews, and other fruits and vegetables," claims scientist Szczesniak. "The additives can also be chosen to produce cellular textures which represent combinations of desirable characteristics not presently found in nature."

Expanding food technology is also permitting alteration of natural foods to improve their palatability and consumer appeal and to lower their cost.

USDA scientists have perfected a process for defatting peanuts by extracting 40% of the oil for diet-conscious consumers. But producers want a more appealing name than "partially defatted" peanuts.

Other researchers have found promising nonnutritive sweeteners called dihydrochalcones, in citrus fruits. These appear to be nontoxic, and one form is seven times as sweet as saccharin. At its Pasadena, Calif., research laboratories the Agriculture Department is conducting the necessary safety studies, but it says several years of testing will be required. The first commercial use may be as sweeteners for toothpastes.

Many food additives, it should be noted, are naturally occurring substances like sugar and pepper, that have long been safely used. Others are used so sparingly that serious risks are unlikely. Flavoring agents, for example, are generally considered safe and self-limiting; more than a little is distasteful to consumers.

Moreover, food-industry scientists are increasingly conscious of consumers' safety concerns and have developed highly sophisticated laboratory tests to detect dangerous compounds. Nonetheless, there are several chemicals not yet banned which are suspect as possible health hazards. Among these are: Saccharin, an artificial sweetener, which has produced tumors in test animals; monosodium glutamate, a flavor-enchancer, which has caused lesions in the brains of new-born rats; brominated vegetable oils, used to keep coloring agents dispersed in orange drinks, which have produced heart lesions in rats; carageenan, a thickening agent, which has produced ulcers in guinea pigs.

These test findings, of course, come only from experiments on animals and they are usually based on much higher doses of the additives than humans normally consume. Moreover, the chemicals are frequently administered to the animals in unusual ways. Saccharin was implanted with cholesterol in animal kidneys, and monosodium glutamate was injected directly into the animal brains.

Yet many scientists insist the evidence argues for restrictions on use of such chemicals until all doubts about safety are resolved. The FDA is moving in this direction. The agency intends to impose temporary restrictions on additives whose safety has not yet been adequately demonstrated. And even where there's little current concern, the FDA wants to establish limitations to prevent problems from arising.

One candidate for such control is saccharin, which can now be added without limit to food and drinks. The FDA is expected to take action soon to limit adults' saccharin intake to about one gram a day. A heated fight with food firms could ensue because saccharin is contained in a wide array of diet foods and drinks—and no suitable substitute is now available.

The FDA is also reviewing the safety of hundreds of additives, like saccharin, now on a list "generally recognized as safe." This list was established in 1958 when Congress authorized the FDA to require manufacturers to prove the safety of their additives before human use. It was then assumed that a history of safe use satisfied the law, but now there's increasing doubt.

"We can never, never equate usage with safety," insists Marvin Legator, head of the FDA's cell biology work. One reason: It could take decades before additive-caused health hazards like chronic disease, developed; by then it would be too late for precautions.

The FDA is now surveying food manufacturers to determine what safety data are available and which additives are most widely used. Then FDA will impose limitations on many items.

A likely FDA move will be tightening of safety test requirements for new additives. The agency is attempting to develop more specific and exacting standards aimed largely at detecting such long-run risks as reproductive hazards and genetic damage. It's known that in animals some chemicals, like the pesticide 2, 4, 5-T, cause birth defects or harm chromosomes, the carriers of genetic material. The FDA's major problem is selecting a laboratory test that will accurately indicate such hazards for humans; there's intense scientific disagreement over various methods.

210

FDA officials argue that additional tests will mean greater consumer protection. But the changes also promise substantial increases in industry's additive testing costs, now estimated at $250,000 for each new substance, and will make Federal approval harder to get. Some companies already complain that FDA requirements are unduly burdensome, and they worry about restrictions on the use of important additives, like the oil-soluble coal-tar colors used in fatty foods.

Under its new commissioner, Dr. Charles Edwards, the FDA is emphasizing additive efficacy as well as safety. Officials want new food chemicals to provide proven benefits, such as nutritional quality, consumer convenience or lower cost. "If the additive has no definite benefit, why use it at all?" asks Ogden Johnson, head of the FDA's Division of Nutrition.

The FDA may also promote wider use of enriched flour, which contains thiamin, riboflavin, niacin, iron, calcium, and vitamin D. Though enriched flour is now required only in bread, some bakers are using it in other products.

The FDA also intends to establish nutritional guidelines for meat analogues, frozen foods, prepared main dishes, and other products. FDA does not want consumers to suffer nutritionally if they use convenience foods.

In addition, officials plan to require food companies to provide consumers with more information about the nutritional value of their products in easy-to-understand form. Labels will probably have to show the percentage of protein, carbohydrates and fats, and the proportion of recommended daily consumption of important nutrients that is contained in each serving. Some companies already furnish such information, but the FDA requirements would go farther, seeking to prevent consumer confusion over conflicting food claims.

food additive makers face intensified attack

howard j. sanders

"Scare" stories have shaken public confidence in safety of additives; FDA requires more testing, restricts use of some.

Never before have food additives been under such sharp, incessant attack. In recent months [in 1971], scarcely a week has gone by without some new warning being sounded about the possible health hazards of chemical additives in foods. Public confidence in the safety of foods has been shaken by consumer groups, university scientists, government agencies, legislative committees, and newspaper and magazine writers alarmed about food additives.

Many developments reflect the growing public and governmental concern about food additives:

• Last year [1970], a Ralph Nader study group issued a report called "The Chemical Feast," written by James S. Turner. The report contains a scathing preface by Mr. Nader. He writes, "The failure of [governmental] regulation to ensure safe, pure, and nutritious food in the world's largest breadbasket has been in step with each new, ingenious technique for manipulating the content of food products as dictated by corporate greed and irresponsibility. Making food appear [to be] what it is not is an integral part of the $125 billion food industry." Because of "the cosmetic treatment of food" with chemical additives, he says, the purity, wholesomeness, safety, and nutritional value of foods are being seriously degraded.

• On April 6 [1971], the Senate's Executive Reorganization and Government Research Subcommittee, headed by Sen. Abraham Ribicoff (D.-Conn.), began a series of hearings about the effects on man of chemicals present in foods, drugs, and the environment. The opening hearings dealt with the possible link between food additives and such threats as birth defects, genetic damage, and cancer. A month earlier, the House Subcommittee on Intergovernmental Relations, headed by Rep. Lawrence H. Fountain (D.-N.C.), held similar hearings.

• According to a recent [1971] issue of *Time,* the selling of so-called "health

Reprinted from *Chemical & Engineering News,* Vol. 49, July 12, 1971, pp. 16–23. Copyright 1971 by the American Chemical Society and reprinted by permission of the copyright owner. The author is a senior associate editor of *Chemical & Engineering News.*

foods" or "organic foods" (foods grown without the use of chemical fertilizers and pesticides and containing no emulsifiers, mold inhibitors, antioxidants, maturing agents, thickeners, stabilizers, preservatives, artificial
flavorings and sweeteners, synthetic coloring agents, synthetic nutritional
supplements, and other additives) is "one of the nation's fastest rising
businesses." Reportedly, the U.S. now has some 2500 health food stores,
with estimated annual sales of $200 million. To put this last figure in
perspective, it should be pointed out that if the U.S. food industry has
annual sales of $125 billion, as Mr. Nader says, health foods have captured
only 0.16% of the market.

• The May 2, 1971, issue of *The New York Times Book Review* contains
a full-page advertisement that, in bold letters, carries the title "Food Pollution." The ad promotes a new book, *Consumer Beware! Your Food and
What's Been Done to It,* by Beatrice Trum Hunter, author of *The Natural
Foods Cookbook.* Her latest volume, the ad declares, "charges that the
food industry—protected by timid, vague laws and the lax enforcement
of even these—is free to serve up virtually anything it chooses to an unsuspecting public. . . . What it chooses is cause for national alarm and
immediate action." The book's "carefully documented analysis" covers
such topics as the "unholy alliance [between] science and the food industry."

• Since January 1968, the magazine *Prevention,* published by Rodale Press,
has doubled its circulation to more than 1 million. Although the magazine
is strenuously opposed to many things, such as DDT, chemical fertilizers,
phosphate detergents, water fluoridation, high-cholesterol diets, and aluminum kitchen utensils, one of its main targets is food additives.

The public, argued the magazine's founder Jerome I. Rodale (described
in a recent article in *The New York Times* as the "guru of the organic
food cult"), should eat only "pure foods"—that is, foods in their natural
state, without additives. Mr. Rodale, who died last month at the age of
72, let it be known that he regularly ate sunflower seeds and assiduously
avoided refined white sugar. He had once announced that he expected
to live to 100—"unless I'm run over by a sugar-crazed taxi driver."

• Some food companies are now getting more mail than ever from consumers either complaining about the use of chemical additives or (in fewer
cases) asking for information about these additives. General Foods Corp.
reports that the number of such letters it received in its fiscal year ending
March 31, 1971, for example, was three times the number it received in
the similar period two years earlier.

The company also reports that there has been a small but noticeable
increase in the number of such letters that contain four-letter obscenities,
or what one General Foods spokesman refers to more delicately as the
"new-wave vocabulary."

• In their advertising, some food companies are now making a major
point of the fact that their products contain no chemical additives. In some
of its recent television commercials, Dannon Milk Products, for example,
has been strongly emphasizing that there are no chemical additives in its
yogurt. Sealtest Foods has run major ads to promote its Breyers "all-natural
ice cream." Breyers is superior, the ads assert, because it has "all-natural
ingredients for all-natural flavor."

Because of the mounting public clamor about food additives, stimulated

213

by the growing publicity about the alleged hazards of these chemicals, the food additives industry today is described by some industry people as edgy and apprehensive. One additives producer says, "Nobody knows where the ax will fall next, or when one of your products may be ruthlessly maligned by some alarmist report in the press." A Monsanto spokesman declares, "We have a very deep and growing concern over the emotional impact that a few preliminary, unconfirmed but widely publicized experiments in laboratory animals can have on the public's confidence in the safety of food additives."

In contrast, a spokesman for Atlas Chemical Industries says, "You never really know whether all the scare headlines reflect the genuine apprehension of a large segment of the general population or of only a relatively few people, most of whom are not well informed and are readily inflamed by sensational reports of 'poisons in our foods.' I am inclined to believe that the vast majority of people are not being carried away by the hysteria in some quarters, and thus continue to have great confidence in the safety of the foods they eat."

Quite plainly, the food additive companies are fully convinced that their products are safe. The Food and Drug Administration, moreover, would not allow these chemicals to be added to food if FDA did not also consider them safe by present standards.

Some months ago, Dr. Fredrick J. Stare, head of Harvard's department of nutrition, wrote in *Life:* "As a physician and a student of nutrition for the past 30 years, I am convinced that food additives are far safer in actual use than the basic natural foods themselves . . . ." The many beneficial effects of food chemicals, he believes, far outweigh "the very, very few instances of harm [resulting] from excessive or careless use of additives."

If the majority of experts in the field are convinced—as they are—that, with few exceptions, food additives are safe at their present permitted levels of use, why are some food additive manufacturers so edgy? One reason is that many people can be readily swayed by shock headlines, by provocative articles in newspapers and magazines, by muck-raking books, and by preliminary reports of unconfirmed experiments.

msg

A case in point is that of the flavor enhancer monosodium glutamate (MSG). In May 1969, Dr. John W. Olney of Washington University, St. Louis, Mo., reported that brain damage resulted when high doses of MSG were injected under the skin of two- to 10-day-old mice. He speculated that similar damage might be produced in human infants receiving MSG in their food.

When this report hit the newspapers, many mothers became deeply disturbed about the use of baby foods containing MSG. Furthermore, the value of MSG in these foods was questioned by some scientists on the grounds that babies may be far less sensitive to taste than are adults. Thus, MSG does not make the food taste significantly better to babies, these scientists believe, although it does make the food more appealing to mothers who sample it.

Because of the public alarm about MSG in baby foods and the great uncertainty about its taste-enhancing value for infants, the producers of these foods (chiefly to allay public fears, and not because they felt that MSG was unsafe) voluntarily stopped using the additive. Contrary to some published reports, the baby food companies were not forced to do so by FDA. In fact, FDA has never banned the use of MSG, in reasonable concentrations, in any food.

FDA did, however, ask the National Academy of Sciences-National Research Council to investigate the safety and usefulness of MSG in foods. The NAS-NRC committee concluded in its July 1970 report that the risk associated with use of MSG in baby foods is extremely small. But the group could not find that MSG confers any benefit to the child and therefore recommended that it not be added to foods for infants.

beneficial

In addition, the committee reports that it found no evidence that reasonable use of MSG in foods is hazardous to older children or to adults, except to those persons unusually sensitive to the additive. Moreover, the committee points out, the flavor-enhancing ability of MSG is definitely beneficial to the general consumer in these age groups.

According to Dr. Lloyd J. Filer, Jr., chairman of the NAS-NRC committee, the "Chinese Restaurant Syndrome" experienced by some people after eating MSG-containing foods is merely a hypersensitivity response of a small percentage of the population. This syndrome, which manifests itself as a numbness, a tingling sensation, a flushed feeling, or a tightening in the chest, is little different from the hypersensitivity of some people to tomatoes or strawberries, he says. And no one is about to ban tomatoes or strawberries.

One would think, then, that the public would be satisfied that MSG is a safe food additive—except for those relatively few people peculiarly sensitive to it. But is the general public satisfied? Not really.

The typical consumer who two years ago read about the "perils" of MSG has probably never heard of the more recent findings about its safety. He has probably never heard of the more than 25 years of safety testing that preceded this work. All he can remember is talk of that mysterious malady called Chinese Restaurant Syndrome, or reports of the "banning" of MSG from baby foods, or ominous findings of brain damage in newborn mice.

suspicions

The lurking suspicions about MSG have had a profound impact on the sales of this product. International Minerals & Chemical Corp., which makes about 80% of the MSG produced in the U.S., reports that its sales of MSG have dropped precipitously in the past two years, mainly because of the adverse publicity. In its fiscal 1968, which ended June 30, 1968, the company's food products division, whose principal product is MSG, had an operating income of $3 million. In fiscal 1970, this division suffered an operating loss of $2.3 million, largely because of sharply reduced sales of MSG. Part of this sales decline, however, was caused by increasing competition from MSG made by other U.S. producers and by companies abroad.

This case history partially explains why some of the nation's producers of food additives are so edgy today—because unfavorable publicity can have such a devastating effect on the sales of a product, even when the publicity is false or utterly misleading. Not only must a product be safe but the general public must believe that it is safe. It is in a world of increasing uncertainty, trial-by-newspaper, and growing public mistrust that U.S. food additive producers must live.

cyclamates

Many people in the food additives field believe that the current widespread public concern about food additives was touched off by the Government's 1969 announcement that the nonnutritive sweetener cyclamate was no longer to be classified in the GRAS category (generally recognized as safe).

GRAS substances are compounds, such as salt, pepper, baking powder, citric acid, and MSG, that are exempted from the safety provisions of the 1958 Food Additives Amendment because of their long history of safe use. GRAS substances legally are not food additives, since they are not regulated by the amendment. Nevertheless, most people still think of GRAS substances as food additives.

The original GRAS list was compiled by asking numerous experts in toxicology, food technology, and related fields to give their opinions about the safety of a great many chemicals used in foods. These experts considered not only the history of use and possible natural occurrence of the additives in foods, but also the often extensive published results of toxicity testing.

When the GRAS list was published in several installments during 1959 and 1960, it included about 600 substances, of which about 280 were flavoring agents. Since then, no substances have been added to the list, and a few have been removed.

For some GRAS substances, FDA specifies the maximum allowable concentration (the tolerance) of the chemicals and the foods in which they can be used. The agency is much less specific for most GRAS substances, however. It requires only that a food company follow good manufacturing practice in using the additive and that the concentration used be the smallest required to produce the intended effect.

The removal of cyclamate from the GRAS list in 1969 and the eventual ban against its use in foods were prompted by the finding that this sweetener causes bladder cancer when fed to rats in large amounts over long periods of time. A subsequent study showed the same effects in rats at cyclamate levels more comparable to the average human intake. FDA was required to prohibit the use of cyclamate in foods because the Delaney clause of the Food Additives Amendment forbids the use in foods of any additive known to produce cancer when ingested in any amount by man or animals.

The company most seriously affected by FDA's decision was Abbott Laboratories, the nation's biggest producer of cyclamate. In 1969, Abbott's sales of this artificial sweetener in all its forms totaled about $16 million.

Subsequently, these sales plummeted essentially to zero. Abbott has stopped making the compound, but still sells a small quantity abroad.

The furor over cyclamate, which dragged on for almost a year after the compound was removed from the GRAS list, had repercussions throughout the food additives industry. If cyclamate could produce cancer in animals and possibly in man, the public reasoned, might not other food additives "generally recognized as safe" also be threats to human health? Was FDA too lax in regulating the chemicals (sometimes referred to damningly as "those noxious chemicals") used in foods? In the minds of many people, these questions still persist.

saccharin

One of the first chemicals to be viewed with alarm after the demise of cyclamate was saccharin, the only other nonnutritive sweetener used in the U.S. Prior to the FDA ban, cyclamate was generally used in combination with saccharin, each compound supplying about half of the total artificial sweetening power. Now, with cyclamate gone, saccharin is providing the entire nonnutritive sweetening power in low-calorie foods. It will continue to do so until a new compound is developed and approved or unless, for some reason, the use of saccharin is restricted or banned. Over the years, various scientists have questioned the safety of saccharin. As recently as April [1971], Dr. George T. Bryan of the University of Wisconsin told an American Cancer Society press seminar that saccharin is a potential carcinogen in man. The test method he uses indicates, he says, that saccharin can cause bladder cancer in mice. Other scientists, however, doubt the validity of Dr. Bryan's test procedure, which involves the implantation of a cholesterol pellet containing 20% saccharin in the bladder of mice.

Despite the heated controversy about saccharin, Monsanto, the nation's leading producer of this additive, says that it is not currently carrying out tests to determine the safety of saccharin because eight major studies to determine its safety are now under way in the U.S. and abroad. This research is being done by FDA, the National Cancer Institute, the Wisconsin Alumni Research Foundation, and the Canadian government, as well as by laboratories in Germany and Japan.

Monsanto believes that its own additional safety testing of saccharin would be a needless duplication of effort. The studies now in progress, it says, should provide the answers that scientists and others are seeking. The company also points out (no doubt, as a result of unfortunate experience) that today's ultraskeptical public is much more apt to accept the findings of independent laboratories than any findings that Monsanto itself might report.

hazardless

In July 1970, an NAS-NRC committee told FDA that "the present and projected use of saccharin in the U.S. does not pose a hazard" to human health. As a result, saccharin remained on the GRAS list.

Last month, however, FDA announced plans to remove saccharin from the GRAS list in the near future and limit its use to specified maximum concentrations in various types of foods, such as soft drinks, fruit juices, and processed food. Since the present concentrations of saccharin in foods are much lower than these limits, no changes in existing foods will be required.

At the time of the recent announcement, FDA Commissioner Charles C. Edwards pointed out that the latest FDA action "will not affect any of the current uses of saccharin." The action was taken, he says, "to assure the continued safety of saccharin's use within specific limitations, pending the outcome of current research."

The objective of the FDA action is to hold the intake of saccharin to a maximum of 1 gram per day for an average adult, as recommended by the NAS-NRC committee. Few people, however, presently consume more than 0.2 gram of saccharin per day. Even heavy users take less than 0.5 gram daily.

Contrary to a recent headline in *The Washington Post* ("Saccharin Off 'Safe' List"), FDA does not now regard saccharin as unsafe. As an FDA spokesman explains, however; "Obviously, the degree of risk acceptable for saccharin in 1959 when it was placed on the GRAS list—at a time when the consumption of this compound was relatively small—must be re-examined in the light of its use pattern today." He adds that FDA's current studies involving the long-term feeding of saccharin to rats and hamsters will not be completed for at least another year.

others

Many other food additives have also become subjects of growing public concern about their safety. One is nordihydroguaiaretic acid. Another is sodium nitrite, which is used in such foods as frankfurters, bologna, spiced ham, Vienna sausage, and smoked salmon.

Sodium nitrite serves two functions. It maintains the color of meat by converting red myoglobin to another red compound, nitrosomyoglobin. Nitrosomyoglobin is less reactive with oxygen, so that formation of brown metmyoglobin is retarded. Nitrite also acts as a preservative by preventing the growth of *Clostridium botulinum* spores, which produce lethal botulinus toxin.

In March, Dr. William Lijinski of the University of Nebraska told the House Subcommittee on Intergovernmental Relations that FDA should forbid the "cosmetic use" of nitrite as a color fixation in food. But FDA should, he agreed, permit continued use of nitrite as a preservative. Such action, he says, would reduce the present permissible levels of this compound in foods by 90 to 95%.

Apprehension about sodium nitrite in foods stems from the fact that nitrite, when fed to experimental animals in large amounts and in combination with secondary amines, reacts with these amines to form nitrosamines, which are carcinogenic. For the present, however, FDA says that fears about nitrite are greatly exaggerated and that no reduction in the allowable levels is necessary. FDA Commissioner Edwards told the House Subcommittee on Intergovernmental Relations: "No one has yet established [whether nitrite is or is not carcinogenic]. . . . Additional data must be developed. We are trying to develop this evidence."

218

nitrate

Similar research is under way on the food additive sodium nitrate. Like nitrite, nitrate is used in foods as a color fixative and a preservative. Unlike nitrite, however, nitrate does not react with amines to form nitrosamines. Nevertheless, a problem may arise if nitrate is converted to nitrite in the stomach. Such a conversion can occur under some conditions.

One other compound that has drawn fire is the food color FD&C Red No. 4. FDA banned this color additive in 1964 when it was shown to damage the adrenal glands and urinary bladders of dogs that were fed the compound at high concentrations.

On the basis of further toxicity testing at lower concentrations, however, FDA later gave provisional approval to continued use of FD&C Red No. 4—but only in maraschino cherries. For people other than habitual Manhattan drinkers, maraschino cherries are, of course, only a very minor food item.

How has the increasing governmental and public concern about food additives affected the producers of these chemicals? One effect is that food additive companies are supporting more research on the safety of these compounds. They are doing this research for a number of reasons:

• To satisfy themselves that the products they market are safe—that the additives do not have chronic toxicity at the levels used in foods and that they are not potential carcinogens or teratogens. Says one company spokesman, "Certainly no responsible manufacturer wants to sell a food additive that might possibly cause cancer or other harmful effects in humans."

• To satisfy their customers in the food industry that the additives are safe. More and more food companies are demanding that suppliers of food additives furnish them with scientific data establishing the safety of these chemicals.

• To meet the requirements of FDA.

• To ensure continued public and governmental acceptance of food additives in which the producer may have a sizable financial investment.

In most cases, only the larger chemical firms can afford the safety testing. This testing is often done for them, at considerable cost, by outside laboratories.

Even some of the larger chemical firms, however, are not supporting such testing at the moment. One reason is that the food additives they sell have already been approved by FDA, and the companies are confident that FDA will continue to allow these additives to be used in foods. Another reason is that, in some cases (such as Monsanto and its saccharin), the company would be duplicating independent studies being carried out by other organizations.

But many companies are actively sponsoring studies of the safety of their food additives. IMC, for example, says that it is continuing to support outside research on the safety of MSG, even though repeated studies have shown that the additive is safe. Research procedures are being expanded and improved, IMC says, and the company believes that all of its food products should be studied by the most sophisticated methods available.

Similarly, Atlas—which makes such food additives as emulsifiers and humectants—points out that it is continuing to test the safety of the chemicals it produces for use in foods. This work is being done on the company's

219

own initiative, Atlas says, because the company believes that its products should be checked by the newest and best methods.

cooperative

Some companies say that, because safety testing is so expensive, they cannot afford to pay the full cost—particularly if the product has only limited sales. In such cases, some companies join with others that make the same additive and jointly sponsor the required research. Some of the safety testing of synthetic food colors, for example, has been cosponsored by the nation's six producers of these additives.

In other cases, a food additives producer may obtain help in sponsoring the studies from a food industry customer or from a food trade association, such as the Grocery Manufacturers of America or the International Association of Ice Cream Manufacturers. If outside assistance is unobtainable, however, the company may simply decide to stop making the additive altogether.

One chemical executive tells C&EN: "There is probably a lot more safety testing going on today than we are aware of. Many companies are doing this research, but are deliberately not talking about it. The reason is that, if some chemical firm announces that it is rechecking the safety of compound X, some incorrigible cynics are sure to say, 'Aha, there must be something definitely and ominously suspect about chemical X, or else the company wouldn't be doing all that testing.' That's the sort of wild conjecturing that most chemical firms can very well do without."

cautious

Most firms were also unusually cautious in replying to questions. "You'd be cautious too," says one observer, "if you had been so repeatedly kicked in the teeth by the public."

Many observers, however, feel that this is clearly no time for food additive companies to retreat into sullen silence in the face of blunderbuss attacks. It is especially important to reply, they say, when the food additives industry can convincingly document the safety, efficacy, and value of its products.

Many companies who will talk about their additives stress the fact that FDA's increasingly strict regulations are resulting in the development and marketing of fewer new food additives. One reason is the high cost of documenting the safety of new additives.

Allied Chemical Corp., for example, has been developing and testing a new synthetic food color, Allura Red AC, since 1964. FDA recently approved Allura Red AC for use in foods, and the company will begin marketing it in October. The total cost of developing and testing this color (the first completely new one to be offered for use in foods since 1938) was about $500,000—about half of which represents the cost of safety testing. According to some other companies, the cost of safety testing a new food additive may, in some cases, run as high as $1 million.

One industry observer gives another reason why he expects fewer new food additives to be introduced in the future. "Companies," he says, "are too much at the mercy of any scandalmonger. . . . For the would-be manufacturer of a new food additive, the risks of capricious public opinion are just too great."

question

A major question confronting food additives producers is: What will FDA do next? One thing seems certain. FDA will be asking for more and more tests to determine the safety of food additives.

This testing is hindered, however, by the lack of agreement about which laboratory tests are the most meaningful to determine, for example, the potential mutagenicity of a food additive. Says one food additives scientist, "No one knows for sure which of the proposed mutagenicity tests are most relevant to human safety or how the results of such testing should be translated into regulatory action. . . . The situation is further complicated by the difficulty of judging the implications to human safety of chemicals used at normal levels, when the actual animal testing is done with chemicals fed in very high, if not near-lethal, doses."

In addition to requiring greater testing of new additives, FDA plans to review in detail the safety studies of some food additives that have been in widespread use for many years. Among these compounds are saccharin, nitrite, nitrate, sulfur dioxide (a preservative used in dried fruits, corn sirup, wines, and other foods), butylated hydroxyanisole and butylated hydroxytoluene (antioxidants used to retard the formation of rancid fats), and all synthetic food colors.

Furthermore, FDA may require testing of metabolic products of food additives. There is growing awareness that an additive may itself be safe, but that it may be converted to an unsafe product in an animal or human body. Such testing is complicated, however, by the fact that these reaction products may or may not be the same in animals and man.

nitrosamines

A case in point is the reaction between nitrite and secondary amines to form nitrosamines, which may produce cancer in laboratory animals. This reaction has been shown to occur under certain conditions in experimental animals, but has not been demonstrated in man. The conversion of a variable but significant percentage of cyclamate to cyclohexylamine, however, has been found to occur in both laboratory animals and man. In 1968, FDA scientists showed that cyclohexylamine can cause chromosome breaks in vivo in the germinal cells of male rats.

Another significant development is FDA's growing belief that some chemicals now on the GRAS list should be removed from the list and placed under more rigid control. This removal, FDA says, will be necessary in the light of new scientific knowledge, the development of new methods of toxicological testing, and the expanded consumption of some GRAS substances in recent years.

questionnaire

As part of a pilot study last year [1970], NAS-NRC's Food Protection Committee sent a questionnaire to 47 food and food additive producers, requesting information about their use of additives now on the GRAS list. Because of the good response to the pilot project, the NAS-NRC committee will this year perform a vastly enlarged survey.

The results of this study, in addition to other information, will be used in a program to re-evaluate the safety of food chemicals now on the GRAS list and to determine which of these should be more closely regulated. To assist in this re-evaluation, FDA last month established specific criteria for classifying food substances as either GRAS compounds or regulated food additives.

Which additives will be removed from the GRAS list is not yet known. Some manufacturers predict that those removed will include such amino acid nutritional supplements as lysine and histidine. These amino acids are expected to be more closely regulated because, even though they are natural components of proteins, they can be toxic when eaten in excessive quantities. Moreover, they can upset the nutritionally balanced pattern of amino acids in the diet.

Some companies also predict that the fat-soluble vitamins (A, D, and E) will be taken off the GRAS list. These vitamins, unlike the readily excreted water-soluble vitamins, can build up to toxic levels in the body if they are consumed in inordinately large amounts.

climbing

Despite the clamor about food additives, the sales of these products are climbing. Dr. Jules Blake of Mallinckrodt predicts that in the next five years, U.S. sales of food additives will grow about 6% per year, not counting inflation. (In the recent past, these sales have risen about 5% per year.) Total 1970 sales of food additives made and used in the U.S., he estimates, were $484 million. This figure will climb to $756 million in 1980, according to Richard L. Hughes of Arthur D. Little, Inc.

The demand for food additives, Dr. Blake says, will be accelerated by the mounting demand for highly processed convenience foods, which typically use relatively large amounts of additives. These convenience foods will be used more and more by housewives and by restaurants, hotels, and institutions. Demand will also be spurred by the growing use of nutritional food supplements.

In years past, FDA was highly skeptical about the use of nutritional supplements, which it regarded as largely unnecessary. But now, Dr. Blake says, FDA is actively encouraging the use of these additives.

deficiencies

Part of this change in FDA's attitude stems from studies by the Public Health Service and others. These studies show that many Americans (especially teenagers and elderly people, even in above-average income groups) do not eat "normal, balanced diets" and, therefore, suffer nutritional deficiencies. A significant number of teen-age girls, for example, don't get enough iron, calcium, and vitamin C—partly because their diets consist largely of such things as hamburgers, hot dogs, French fries, and soft drinks.

Says one company spokesman, "In the past, it was axiomatic in the food industry that you sold foods primarily on the basis of their taste, color, texture, and convenience. Although food companies sometimes fortified their products with special nutrients, this generally had little effect on the public's acceptance of these products.

"Now that consumers are becoming more and more concerned about nutrition, however, food companies are placing greater stress on the nutritional content of their products. This should lead to increased sales of vitamin and mineral additives and other nutritional supplements in foods."

Producers of these supplements and of virtually all other types of food additives can thus look forward to expanding markets. Although these producers can expect intensified safety evaluation, growing consumer concern about potential hazards (real or imagined), and greater governmental control, they can also expect a significant rise in the demand for these valuable food components.

even some chemicals that occur naturally in foods can be harmful

staff of chemical & engineering news

Many chemicals that occur naturally in foods—caffeine, oxalic acid in rhubarb—can, if consumed in excess, be harmful.

One food additive whose use has bothered some scientists is nordi-hydroguaiaretic acid (NDGA), an antioxidant that inhibits the development of rancidity in fats. Canada banned NDGA in 1967 after it was shown to cause cysts and kidney damage in a large percentage of rats to which it was fed.

FDA removed the compound from the GRAS list in 1968 and prohibited its use in foods over which FDA has jurisdiction. But the U.S. Department of Agriculture, which controls antioxidants used in lard and animal shortening, allowed its continued use in these products. In recent months, however, USDA has been in the process of banning NDGA use in animal fats.

Much of the controversy surrounding NDGA has actually been something of a tempest in a teapot, since its use in recent years has been quite limited. Nonetheless, some people who vociferously oppose the use of food additives continue to point to NDGA as a prime example of an additive that is a dire threat to public health and whose continued use represents gross negligence on the part of the government agencies.

The story of NDGA may come as a severe jolt to natural food enthusiasts whose central dogma is that food components from living things are inherently superior to those made by the chemical industry. NDGA is obtained from the creosote bush, the guaiac plant, or other plants, and is not one of "those dreadful synthetics."

In fact, many chemicals that occur naturally in foods—caffeine in coffee, theobromine in cocoa, oxalic acid in rhubarb—can, if consumed in excess, be harmful. Some people have been poisoned by eating large amounts of dark Lima beans, grown in the Far East, that contain unusually high concentrations of specific glycosides that, when digested, can produce dangerous amounts of hydrogen cyanide. (American Lima beans have been bred to reduce their content of cyanide-producing glycosides.)

The contention that all natural foods are inherently more healthful than foods containing synthetic additives, therefore, does not hold up in all cases. Moreover, many food additives made by the chemical industry are identical to compounds present in natural foods. These chemicals include, for example, citric acid, acetic acid, vitamin C, and sorbitol. Hence, the distinction between natural and synthetic compounds is blurred.

solid wastes

The effluents of civilization, like other chemical matter, may be gas, liquid, or solid. Only the first two tend to disappear by natural means: gases are blown away by the winds, and liquids are carried off by water. Solids are unique in that they stay largely in place until they are intentionally moved. Ancient cities where garbage was thrown in the streets left solid deposits that archeologists now carve through. The air and water once surrounding ancient dwellings long since mixed with world currents, but the solids are still there to remind us that early man was a polluter too—only the scale of pollution has changed.

Indeed the present scale of discarded solids is staggering. Roughly four billion tons are generated in this country every year—enough to bury a thousand ancient villages. Instead of burying villages, we now bury marshes, estuaries, and farmland—all priceless ecological commodities.

The problem of solid waste reflects the bankruptcy of our throw-away economy. We cannot go on indefinitely extracting resources from the earth with one hand, and throwing them away with the other. We would create ecological havoc, both in extracting the resources and in filling our land with its discards. Even today the problems are becoming serious.

Every atom now in solid waste was once an atom in a sought-after resource. These atoms are inherently as valuable as ever. All that has changed is the chemical and physical form of the material they are in. Society must find ways to reclaim these materials—to recycle them. This is the only logical means of avoiding the double damage caused by extracting new materials and dumping old ones.

The U.S. Bureau of Mines (USBM) is making a broad study on recycling, and, in Article 34, Charles B. Kenahan tells about these studies under the appropriate title "Solid Waste: Resources Out of Place." Following this, Article 35 describes the potential for salvaging a very large class of solid wastes in "Process Converts Animal Wastes to Oil." Finally, one of the unique solid-waste problems of our age is discussed briefly in Article 36, "Plastics Face Growing Pressure from Ecologists."

solid waste: resources out of place

charles b. kenahan

A pioneer in secondary metals recovery, the U.S. Bureau of Mines possesses the technical know-how to reclaim solid waste effectively.

The constant increase in per capita generation of solid waste, stimulated by production growth and coupled with a rapidly increasing population concentrated in urban areas, is responsible for the nation's present environmental crisis. Increased demand and the increased production to meet it are the basic causes of increased pollution. This is confirmed by the fact that the real output of goods and services in the U.S. has grown as much since 1950 as it grew in the entire period from the landing of the Pilgrims up to 1950.

To add fuel to the fire—or waste to the pile—consider that a similar growth period is predicted between 1970 and 1980, which can easily be translated into more junk cars, cans, bottles, plastics, fly ash, and paper products. If the present production of solid waste is not managed, what of the future?

solid waste

The terminology and characteristics of this solid waste that is causing such a furor must be examined. Where does it come from? How much of it is there? Where is its final resting place? And, what is being done about it?

Solid waste falls into three major source categories. The first is urban refuse, which includes domestic, commercial, municipal, and industrial waste products; the second category contains the mineral waste which results from mining and mineral processing operations; and the last, agricultural waste, includes farming, animal, and crop waste.

Reprinted from *Environmental Science & Technology,* Vol. 5, July 1971, pp. 594–600. Copyright 1971 by the American Chemical Society. Reprinted by permission of the copyright owner. The author joined the U.S. Bureau of Mines in 1953, and is presently chief of the bureau's Division of Solid Wastes.

A further breakdown of urban refuse shows that the nation generates about 400 million tons each year. This includes 60 billion cans, 36 billion bottles, 58 million tons of paper and paper products, 4 million tons of plastics, over 1 million abandoned automobiles, mountains of demolition debris, 180 million tires, and countless millions of tons of refrigerators, stoves, TV sets, and like items. The cost to collect and dispose of urban solid waste alone is about $6 billion annually. Where does it all go? About half is burned in some manner, and the other half is buried in landfills and dumps, with the values it contains lost forever.

The second category, mineral waste, is larger—about 1.7 billion tons each year. The production of 1 ton of copper results in about 500 tons of waste earth and rock. Additionally, a past accumulation of about 23 billion tons of mineral waste is scattered across the nation.

The final category, agricultural waste, is even more awesome—over 2 billion tons annually—including farming, slaughterhouse, and animal waste. An average-sized steer generates about 10 tons of solid waste each year.

Furthermore, over 100 lb of solid waste daily is generated for every man, woman, and child in the country. By 1980, this is expected to increase to 150 lb per day.

The importance of secondary metals—which represent the only growing metal resource—can best be assessed by comparing the gross production of major metals with quantities reclaimed from secondary sources. According to production estimates (on an annual basis), over 50% of the lead, 40% of the copper, 45% of the iron and steel, and 25% of the zinc and aluminum made available for new products last year were derived from secondary sources. Equally important are the estimated quantities of these metals accumulating in the "in-use" channels of the economy. Nearly 40 million tons of copper, over 3.5 million tons of lead, and about 4 million tons of zinc are presently in this category, which represents a constantly growing man-made mine of future raw materials.

These figures are indeed impressive, but the amounts of metals still being wasted are equally impressive. Annually discarded in municipal dumps are 11 million tons of ferrous metals and over 1 million tons of nonferrous metals, including copper, aluminum, tin, lead, and zinc. An estimated 12 million junk cars still remain to be reclaimed from auto graveyards across the nation. In addition, automotive scrappage has now reached a rate that can provide over 10 million tons of ferrous and a half million tons of nonferrous metals annually. Nearly 400,000 tons of aluminum was used for manufacturing cans, lids, and caps in 1970; only a small percentage of this was reclaimed. Thrown away each year in city dumps is 25,000 tons of tin in tin-coated steel cans, which is equivalent to the amount of tin salvaged from all other secondary sources. These are just a few opportunities.

bu mines research

The Department of the Interior's Bureau of Mines has always considered waste products and scrap generated by the mineral and metals industry and the consuming public as potential resources. In the business of reclaiming values from metal and mineral-based by-products for over 30 years,

230

the bureau has been a pioneer in the field of secondary metals recovery and solid waste research. The authority and responsibility for conducting research on separation, recovery, and recycling of metal, mineral, and energy-based by-products, however generated, are inherent in the Organic Act of May 16, 1910, as amended in 1913, which established the Bureau of Mines. Congress assigned a major role to the Department of the Interior in the Solid Waste Disposal Act of 1965, and more recently in the Resource Recovery Act of 1970.

Under the original Solid Waste Act, the Department of the Interior was authorized $32.3 million over a 3-year period for research relating to metal and mineral waste. Only $11 million was appropriated to the Bureau of Mines under this law. The Resource Recovery Act of 1970 authorizes funding of $8.75 million for fiscal year (FY) 1971, $20 million for FY 1972, and $22.5 million for FY 1973 to the Department of the Interior.

The bureau's Metallurgy Research Activity, equipped for metal and mineral waste problems, includes the Divisions of Metallurgy and Solid Wastes with 777 full-time employees at eight research centers across the country. About half are professionally trained in metallurgy, chemical engineering, chemistry and physics, and mineral engineering. The bureau's coal and petroleum research activities also deal with solid waste problems relating to energy recovery.

The bureau has already laid valuable groundwork in several solid waste research areas, including urban refuse, junk cars, mining and processing waste, and industrial waste products.

For over a year the bureau has operated a pilot plant at the College Park (Md.) Metallurgy Research Center which separates and recovers, in much the same way that minerals are separated from their ores, the major metal and mineral values contained in municipal incinerator residues. The process, which employs conventional mineral engineering equipment such as magnetic separation, screening, grinding, and shredding procedures, separates the ferrous and nonferrous metals and glass from the burned refuse on a continuous basis. . . . The plant, which can process one-half ton of residues per hour, is sophisticated enough to separate glass into clear and colored components. Based on the engineering data developed from the pilot-plant operation, estimates for capital and operating costs for a 1000-ton-per-day plant show a cost of about $2 per ton of residue. Each ton of residue processed through the plant yields 700 lb of iron, 40 lb of nonferrous metals including aluminum, copper, lead, tin, and zinc, small amounts of silver, and a half ton of glass. The total value is $10 to $12 per ton of residues. The remainder is finely powdered ash, which makes excellent fill material and also has agricultural nutrient value. . . .

An air classification system to recover the metal and mineral values from raw, unburned refuse is also being investigated. The bureau has developed an experimental, simple, horizontal air classifier with a feed rate of over 1 ton per hour, which produces a concentrate from shredded municipal refuse assaying 65% metal and 85% paper, with high metal and paper recovery. Potential uses for the paper and plastics are also being examined.

Significant progress has also been made in developing processes for refining ferrous and nonferrous products reclaimed from refuse. High-purity zinc and an alluminum alloy having utility in the secondary aluminum industry have been produced in the laboratory. Tin cans and other iron products can be used for precipitating copper from waste copper dump leach solutions, which is an established practice, or used as feed material for steelmaking after removing deleterious contaminants.

The bureau has been successful in producing standard bricks from various grades of glass recovered from refuse. The bricks, made by dry pressing or extruding mixes of 70% glass and 30% clay and firing at 1000°C, meet or exceed ASTM specifications for severe weathering, FBS brick.

Another use for glass from refuse is mineral wool production. By fusing glass with about 50% dolomite and blowing, an excellent grade of colorless glass wool, having a bulk density of 2.5 lb per ft³ and an average fiber diameter of 6 μ, is produced. The fibers are shorter and softer than typical commercial slag wools tested. . . .

Another development that could significantly affect the disposal or utilization of urban solid waste is a process recently developed by the bureau's Pittsburgh Coal Research Center for converting garbage and waste paper into crude petroleum. In the process, the combustible material from refuse, including garbage, is hydrogenated by reaction with carbon monoxide and steam at 500 psi. The resulting product is a heavy paraffinic oil, that is low in sulfur. It is estimated that each ton of dry refuse would yield over two barrels of this crude petroleum. The same process has been applied to wood by-products, sewage sludge, and animal manure to yield a crude oil. Based on current generated domestic refuse and animal manures, this represents a potential equivalent to 2 billion barrels of oil annually.

Other research has demonstrated that organic fractions of wastes can be pyrolyzed thermally (destructive distillation in the absence of oxygen) to yield liquid and gaseous hydrocarbons, tar, and valuable chemicals. . . . Worn-out rubber tires, for example, are a nationwide waste product that can be disposed of by pyrolysis.

About 180 million tires containing nearly 2 million tons of rubber are scrapped yearly. Tire disposal by burning causes serious air pollution by the billowing, acrid, black smoke produced. Disposal in landfills or open dumps is less than desirable because tires are difficult to compact and are essentially not biodegradable. Bureau research on pyrolysis of tires has shown that 1500 ft³ of high-quality gas (800 to 1200 Btu per ft³) and 140 gallons of hydrocarbon liquid oil can be produced per ton of tires treated. The Firestone Tire and Rubber Co. has constructed a pilot plant to prove out the technical and economic feasibility of the bureau-developed process. In other research, the pyrolysis process has been applied successfully on a laboratory scale to urban refuse, wood bark and sawdust, plastics, and discarded battery cases to produce a variety of useful products.

The bureau is also investigating vortex incineration to solve problems encountered in conventional furnaces. The vortex incinerator is more compact, has a lower capital cost, and greater potential for cleaner effluents than the conventional grate-type incinerator commonly used to burn refuse. A pilot-scale vortex unit, incinerating combustible solids ranging from high-moisture-content sludge to industrial and domestic refuse, is currently under evaluation at the bureau's Coal Research Center in Pittsburgh.

Bureau of Mines researchers at the Twin Cities Metallurgy Research Center in Minneapolis, Minn., have found another novel use for the mounting avalanche of trash from this affluent society. The refuse, traditionally posing a costly disposal problem to every municipality, has proved to be an effective reductant for converting nonmagnetic taconite ore (a waste product of iron ore mining) into high-quality magnetic iron ore in a reduction–roasting process developed by the bureau. The average composition of raw refuse includes about 8% metallics, 42% paper, and 22% other combustible rubbish such as wood, rags, rubber, grass, leaves, and plastics. These supply both fuel and metal for the reduction process. The nonmagnetic taconite ore, containing about 30% iron, is roasted with the refuse in a large rotary kiln furnace at 1000°C. The final recovered product analyzes 70% iron—a high-grade iron ore suitable for smelting in the blast furnace.

junk cars

Another problem to which the bureau's Salt Lake City, Utah, research center has been devoting a considerable research effort is junk cars. Although discarded auto hulks constitute only a small fraction of the waste disposal problem in terms of tonnage, they are higher in metal values than most waste materials.

As a result of recent research by the bureau, practical and economic methods have been developed for dismantling junk automobiles to produce high-quality scrap. All components of 15 scrap automobiles procured from auto-wrecking yards, scrap processors, and insurance salvage firms—cars manufactured between 1954 and 1965—were dismantled, separated into various components, and analyzed. Alternative means and methods of stripping and dismantling the cars were employed to determine the fastest and most practical technique. Derived from the information obtained, a representative junk automobile weighing 3600 lb could yield approximately 2500 lb of steel, 500 lb of cast iron, 32 lb of copper, 54 lb of zinc, 51 lb of aluminum, and 20 lb of lead. The remaining 400 lb consisted of nonmetallics.

The bureau conducted time and motion studies on the 15 scrap cars using various dismantling procedures (cutting torches, hand-stripping, and cut-off saws) and found that a typical vehicle could be economically burned in a smokeless incinerator and hand-dismantled, and the steel could be baled into a high-quality bundle containing less than 0.1% copper. A cost evaluation study showed that such an operation could provide an annual return rate on investment of 25%.

In a cooperative effort with the Wasatch Metal and Salvage Co. (Salt Lake City, Utah), the bureau developed, constructed, and is presently operating a practical, smokeless junk car incinerator. . . . It is relatively inexpensive and can efficiently process as many as 80 cars in an eight-hour period. Also, the combustion gases are smokeless and meet or exceed most clean air standards.

The new incinerator's principle attraction is its $22,000 construction cost (roughly one-tenth the cost of smokeless models now commercially available) and a relatively low operating cost of about $2 per car. The incinerator has stimulated wide interest among scrap processors whose open-air burning practices are being increasingly restricted. At least nine scrap car processors are constructing auto incinerators which are based on the bureau design.

Bureau engineers are also working on the problem of upgrading the nonmetallic and nonferrous rejects from junk car shredding operations. Such rejects are currently being generated at the rate of about 1 million tons annually. Aluminum, copper, zinc, and lead constitute over 30% of this reject. For the most part, these valuable nonferrous metals are being wasted because no practical method has been devised to separate and recover them.

Recently, the bureau's Salt Lake City research center developed an air separation method that yields a concentrate of the metallic constituents from this residue. This air classifier has a 16-ton-per-hour capacity for shredded residue. The concentrate, which is 84% metal, contains 97% of the nonferrous content of the residue. This metallic concentrate can be refined into some of its constituent parts by physical concentration methods and pyrometallurgical processing.

Other bureau research aimed at developing a continuous process for steelmaking in the electric furnace promises to have an impact on automotive scrap consumption that makes an ideal feed for such a process. Test results to date indicate that the steel produced will be suitable for teeming into ingots and rolling into a variety of finished structural products.

A relatively simple technique was developed at the Twin Cities, Minn., research center, for recovering copper from starters, generators, armatures, and similar high-copper automotive components. This process may offer the solution to a troublesome and time-consuming problem for scrap processors. In this process, copper-containing scrap is dipped in a molten salt (calcium chloride) and agitated briefly. The bath does not affect the iron and steel scrap but quickly melts the copper, even in inaccessible small holes and crevices. The molten copper collects in the bottom of the vessel and can easily be tapped off. About 99% of the copper can be reclaimed in this manner. The process is economical because the salt is cheap and can be reused.

Bureau research on utilization of auto scrap as a reductant for converting currently nonexploitable, nonmagnetic taconite ores to a commercially attractive iron resource has been given much attention. In this process, the nonmagnetic taconites, rejected as waste during mining and beneficiation of the magnetic taconites and analyzing about 30% iron, are mixed with unburned auto scrap. This material is heated in a rotary kiln at 1000°C to reduce simultaneously the nonmagnetic oxide iron in the ore to the magnetic form and oxidize the scrap iron to the magnetic oxide. The final product is a high-grade ore that analyzes about 70% iron. Tin cans, borings and turnings, and other low-grade ferrous scrap are also ideal raw materials for this process.

mineral waste

The bureau has also been active in reclaiming values from mining, metallurgical, chemical, and industrial processing operations. This work not only includes salvage and reuse, but also stabilizing nonusable mineral waste.

A large-scale effort has been made to stabilize the waste tailing piles from mining operations that have no mineral or utilization values. . . . These wastes are often air, water, and land pollution sources. Successful chemical and vegetative techniques have been demonstrated on copper and uranium-mill tailing piles.

Thirty-four acres of uranium leach plant residues, located on the Navajo Indian Reservation in Arizona, have been effectively stabilized against wind erosion using a low-cost chemical method developed by bureau scientists. In Durango, Colo., another 13-acre plot of waste uranium tailings was stabilized by a vegetative cover under bureau supervision. The procedure has been so successful that a stalk of wheat grown on the waste pile, where formerly nothing would germinate, won second prize in a local flower and garden show.

Engineers have also demonstrated that mineral waste such as copper and gold mill tailings, coal washer rejects, and power plant bottom and fly ash can be converted into useful finished products.

The bureau also initiated a modest contract and grant program under authority of the Solid Waste Disposal Act of 1965. Under the contract and grant program, the University of Utah made significant progress producing crystallized glass and ceramic tile and pipe from copper tailings, fabricating a promising refractory and tile from asbestos tailing waste, and producing high-quality ferrites from mill scale.

West Virginia University, under a bureau grant, developed a process producing rock wool insulation from coal ash slag, a waste product from coal-fired central power plants. Commercially competitive structural concrete blocks also have been fabricated from the power plant fly ash. Stanford University researchers, under another bureau grant, demonstrated the technical and economic feasibility of producing steam-cured, calcium-silicate bricks from California gold mine waste. A preliminary report indicates that the calcium silicate bricks can be produced from the tailings and delivered to the market areas at costs below the existing lowest quoted selling price of standard clay bricks.

Research conducted by the IIT Research Institute, Chicago, Ill., on red mud has shown that this waste material can be fabricated into a variety of potentially useful commercial products. Red mud is a slimy, high-iron content reject resulting from processing bauxite to produce alumina for making aluminum. Ceramic articles such as tile pipe, wall and floor tile, and lightweight building blocks have been fabricated from the mud which otherwise poses an acute disposal and impounding problem.

Processes have been developed by bureau scientists to convert asbestos mining waste, phosphorus furnace slags, and mine and mill tailings into raw materials for manufacture of wall tile and bricks.

industrial waste

In the industrial waste area, the bureau has developed several promising methods to convert waste materials into useful resources. A unique method for reclaiming valuable cobalt from sintered carbide scrap was developed at the research center in Rolla, Mo. The process involves the use of molten zinc, which forms an alloy with the cobalt binder. The zinc is then recovered by distillation techniques. Over 99% of the tungsten carbide and over 98% of the cobalt can be recovered and reused. Virtually all of the zinc is recovered and can be reused to reclaim additional scrap. The process yields products that are directly reusable without further treatment. Evaluating the products made from recycled materials shows that there is no difference between the properties of those made from used material and those made from virgin sources. The treatment is unique in that virtually all components of the process are recovered and can be reused. The technique is believed to be a breakthrough in the recycling of cemented carbides, which is a $250 million business nationally. The Wendt-Sonis United Greenfield Division of TRW Inc. is presently testing the bureau process on a pilot-size scale.

Other research has focused on developing methods that may alleviate serious water pollution problems for the nearly 20,000 metal-plating and coating facilities across the nation. Electroplating and metal-finishing wastes are significant stream pollutants—either directly, owing to their content of toxic and corrosive materials such as cyanide, acids, and metals, or indirectly, owing to the deleterious effect of these components on sewage treatment systems. Bureau scientists have shown that reducing an organic-cyanide electroplating waste with formaldehyde will cause metallic copper and silver to coprecipitate while destroying all of the poisonous cyanides. Another method, which is even more promising, employs two plating waste solutions to recover metals and chemicals and leaves behind a harmless liquid free of toxic metal ions and hazardous cyanides.

Bureau researchers have developed processes for recovering expensive metals from cuttings and grindings left over when "superalloy" jet engine parts are machined. Such scrap, containing nickel, cobalt, molybdenum, and chromium, has a metal content worth nearly $1000 per ton. It is regularly sold to overseas markets for far less, because of the high cost of separating and recovering the metals by methods now available in the U.S.

Remelting the material for reuse as alloy is impractical because oil, rags, abrasive grit, and other contaminants are mixed with the alloy, and its alloying metals content is not uniform. In the bureau process, the scrap is cleaned by screening, burning, and magnetic separation, and dissolved in hot acid. Molybdenum, cobalt, chromium, and nickel are removed from the hot acid solution in successive operations by solvent extraction, followed by selective precipitation of the valuable metals.

The bureau is working on recovering and reusing waste materials that are being ejected in the stack gases generated by the minerals and metal industries during smelting and chemical processing. Good progress is being made by removing these waste materials in a form that will permit their recycling and reuse. For example, fluorine liberated in processing phosphate rock to phosphoric acid has been converted to synthetic fluorite or calcium fluoride, which is a raw material in short supply for steel and aluminum manufacturing.

There has been exceptional success in developing a process for removing sulfur dioxide from copper and other base-metal smelter gases. The process not only effectively removes all of the sulfur dioxide from the gases but converts the sulfur dioxide to elemental sulfur that can be stored for indefinite periods or easily shipped over long distances to consumer points. Currently, a major copper producer is constructing a pilot plant at a smelter in Arizona to test the process and obtain detailed operating and cost figures preparatory to design and construction of a full-sized facility.

236

These are some of the uses the bureau has found for solid wastes. Several of the processes developed have already attracted wide interest by the industrial sector and probably will be adopted.

It is not inconceivable that the present-day mine tailing dumps, municipal landfills, and junk car graveyards may be looked upon in the future as "man-made mines" for minerals whose natural ores have been depleted or remain in deposits that can be mined only at greater cost than required for recycling waste. The Bureau of Mines considers solid waste as resources out of place—and is simply trying to put it back where it belongs.

additional reading

1. Appell, H. R., Wender, I., Miller, R. D., *Conversion of Urban Refuse to Oil,* Bureau of Mines Technical Progress Rept. 25, May 1970.
2. Chindgren, C. J., Dean, K. C., Sterner, J. W., *Construction and Testing of a Junk Auto Incinerator,* Bureau of Mines Technical Progress Rept. 21, February 1970.
3. Cservenyak, F. J., Kenahan, C. B., *Bureau of Mines Research and Accomplishments in Utilization of Solid Wastes,* Information Circ. 8460, March 1970.
4. George, L. C., Cochran, A. A., *Recovery of Metals From Electroplating Wastes by the Waste-Plus-Waste Method,* Bureau of Mines Technical Progress Rept. 27, August 1970.
5. IIT Research Institute, *Continuous Physical Beneficiation of Metals and Minerals Contained in Municipal Incinerator Residues,* Proceedings of the Second Mineral Waste Utilization Symposium, March 18–19, 1970, Chicago, Ill.
6. IIT Research Institute, *Recovery of Metallurgical Values from Industrial Wastes, ibid.*
7. Sanner, W. S., Ortuglio, C., Walters, J. G., Wolfson, D. E., *Conversion of Municipal and Industrial Refuse Into Useful Materials by Pyrolysis,* Bureau of Mines Report of Investigations 7428, August 1970.

process converts animal wastes to oil

staff of chemical & engineering news

Conversion of all domestic animal waste to oil would provide equivalent of half of U. S. oil supply.

When one observer, admiring the efficiency of turn-of-the-century meat packers, wrote that they use everything from the pig "but the squeal," he overlooked one important by-product—manure. Today, it is nearly impossible to overlook animal wastes, for they total nearly 2 billion tons annually, dwarfing the 250 million tons of household, commercial, and municipal solid wastes generated yearly and creating a disposal problem of great magnitude.

Now, scientists at the U.S. Bureau of Mines' Pittsburgh Energy Research Center have developed a scheme that not only would dispose of these wastes, but also would provide an important new source of energy and contribute to the abatement of air pollution. Their scheme: Convert the wastes to oil.

The center began its work in an attempt to convert coal into oil, Dr. G. Alex Mills, chief of BuMines' division of coal, explains. Along the way, Dr. Herbert R. Appell and Dr. Irving Wender discovered that one of the processes they were investigating could be used to dispose of urban wastes—garbage—by converting it to oil. . . .

deluge

After the center publicized its findings, Dr. Mills tells *Chemical & Engineering News,* it was deluged with a variety of other materials for testing. But, "We came to realize that the [quantity of] so-called agricultural waste was about 10 times larger than [urban] waste, and this brings a new dimension—not so much getting rid of an unwanted thing as the possibility of providing a fuel oil in significant dimensions."

The process is simple. Manure (or any cellulosic waste) is placed in a reaction vessel with carbon monoxide at an initial pressure of 1200 p.s.i.

and heated at 380° C. for 20 minutes. Based on dry manure, the yield of oil is 47% (3 barrels per ton). But, Dr. Mills notes, "if you consider sugar or cellulose and calculate how it should break down, you get a 50% yield of water and a 50% yield of hydrocarbon, so that this 47% in these terms represents maybe a 96% theoretical yield." This was the highest yield from any of the materials examined.

The center has begun to study the mechanism of the reaction and current thinking is that the reaction proceeds through a formate ion, "But we really don't know yet," says the division of coal's staff research coordinator, Dr. John S. Tosh. They do know, however, that the combination of carbon monoxide and steam is far more effective in the processing than is direct hydrogenation.

constant

Whatever the mechanism, the reaction produces a remarkably constant product from a wide variety of cellulosic materials. That product is a heavy oil with an energy content of 14,000 to 16,000 B.t.u. per pound. For comparison, normal oil has a B.t.u. value of about 20,000, and coal's is between 7000 and 12,000, depending on the type; the energy content of manure ranges from 5000 to 7000 B.t.u. per pound.

The oil is largely paraffinic, with virtually no aromatics present. It has a nitrogen content of about 2% and an oxygen content of about 9%, which makes it difficult to refine the material into gasoline, Dr. Tosh says. But the oil also has a sulfur content of less than 0.35%. And that, Dr. Mills contends, is one of its most important properties in light of the growing need for low-sulfur oils to prevent urban air pollution.

Dr. Mills is very enthusiastic about the future of the process. The Bu-Mines process is, in effect, a way to harness the sun's energy, he says, and to do so in a manner that is economically viable. The cost of disposing of the urban and agricultural wastes, he adds, provides a strong economic driving force. And the low temperature required in the process means that only a small amount of energy is necessary for the conversion—energy that can be provided by burning either manure or a small amount of the product. (Burning manure directly for heat is impractical and expensive, Dr. Mills notes, because of its low energy content and the problems of handling it.)

And then there is the large supply of raw material: "It's been pointed out," Dr. Mills notes, for example, "that there are more chickens in the U.S. than there are people in the world." If all of the so-called agricultural wastes were collected and converted, "You'd make about half this country's oil supply—in other words, about 2.45 billion barrels of oil per year. You're not going to collect it all," he concludes, "but at least this shows it's of a significant dimension."

plastics face growing pressure from ecologists

staff of chemical & engineering news

Packages made of plastics, particularly polyvinyl chloride, create tough waste disposal problem for many municipalities.

"You're kidding yourselves if you think you can tell us there's no problem or let's study the problem, because that kind of thing doesn't work anymore. We will never believe you. You will always have to live under the pressure. And even after you get done [attempting to solve disposal problems] we'll still believe you're a bunch of liars."

With this verbal blast, leveled at plastics producers at the recent [1971] Plastics Institute of America meeting, New York City air resources commissioner Dr. Robert N. Rickles stopped short of calling for an outright ban on the use of plastics. This was scant comfort, however, for those attending the session on plastics waste disposal problems.

No doubt about it, the problems are formidable. Methods currently available for disposing of plastics all have their shortcomings. Incineration of plastics is feasible, but hydrogen chloride gas, generated in burning polyvinyl chloride, is an air pollutant. Sanitary landfill can be used but land for this approach is becoming scarce. A third approach, degradable plastics, is still in the developmental phase. So until the problem of disposal can be solved, Dr. Rickles told the meeting, some restrictions on the use of plastics will have to be imposed.

incineration

Although plastics turn up in many forms for disposal, packaging materials are the biggest problem today, critics of plastics use feel. The plastic that has come under the most fire as a disposal problem is PVC. "It is a fact that when PVC is made to burn it emits hydrogen chloride gas," says George A. Fowles, marketing vice president at B. F. Goodrich Chemical Co. "And this has been related to possible air pollution or corrosion damage to incinerators. It has been demonstrated, however, that properly designed and operated incinerators will easily handle PVC in the typical municipal waste load without damage either to the incinerator or to the environment," he claims.

Counters Dr. Rickles, "There are no well-run ones [incinerators]—certainly we don't have any in New York City." Properly operating pollution control equipment and competent personnel are tough to obtain even in model incineration programs, he explains.

Although incineration is the apparent answer to waste disposal in land-scarce New York City and other urban centers, sanitary landfill is the solution for 90% of municipal waste, Arthur J. Warner, president of Debell & Richardson, told the meeting. Landfill disposal raises the problem, however, of whether plastics should be biodegradable. If plastics remain indefinitely in filled land, then settling will be minimal and the land can be used for parking lots and other purposes, says Ralph L. Harding, Jr., of the Society of the Plastics Industry.

Another approach, suggests Mr. Warner, would be to design embrittlement into plastics that would be triggered by air, wind, and sun. Embrittlement would reduce plastics to inert particles. Although it would be a fairly easy property to impart to polyolefins, embrittlement would be almost impossible to design into PVC, he adds.

Some progress has been made in developing degradable plastics . . . , and SPI has granted $83,000 to Dr. Elmer R. Kaiser and Dr. Arrigo A. Carotti of New York University to study efficient incineration of plastics. Although research goes on, however, public officials feel that they must act now.

bills pending

Some bills now in state legislatures involve bans on metal, glass, plastics, and paper containers, unless these containers are recyclable, biodegradable, or returnable for a deposit. Two bills, for instance, are currently [as of March 1971] before the New York City council concerning plastic packaging materials. Under one bill, containers weighing more than 4 ounces would require a 2-cent deposit on purchase, and would be redeemed for 4 cents on return. The difference would be made up from public funds.

The other New York City bill would levy a tax (payable at the wholesale level) of 1.35 cents on each glass bottle, 0.5 cent on steel cans, 0.25 cent on aluminum cans, and 2 cents on plastic bottles. The same bill would impose a 2.3 cent-per-pound tax on paper packaging, and 3.8 cents per pound on plastic packaging other than bottles.

Plastic producers fear that such hefty deposits and taxes on plastic packages will price plastics out of the market for packaging materials. Plastics are at a disadvantage by weight, along with metal and glass, compared to paper in any system of taxing by weight.

Nevertheless, governmental action is necessary, Dr. Rickles feels. He believes that selective taxation rather than bans are needed to help control the problem. "The city of the future is going to have a lot of plastics in it," Dr. Rickles points out. "The only thing we want is for the plastics industry to do its part to minimize these problems."

population
and
environmental
impact

A burgeoning population and technological advances are at the root of today's environmental woes. More people naturally generate more air pollution, more solid wastes, and more heavy-metal contamination. They devour more food, thus more intensive agriculture is needed, which in turn requires heavier applications of pesticides and fertilizers. They consume more energy and dissipate more resources. They release more phosphorus to waterways, thus adding to the toll of euthophic lakes. In short, almost every adverse change in chemical environment mentioned in this book is intensified by population growth. In this sense, population is the central topic of the book—all other topics being connected to it by the unfailing relationship of population and environmental impact.

Man's growing energy consumption and the inevitable flavor of the atomic nucleus in our future are two topics most critically related to long-term population growth. We will examine these issues in the next two sections.

Population is an indirect and sometimes hidden variable in

man's environmental impact. The owner of a factory smoke-stack which belches toxic substances into the atmosphere is commonly blamed for intensive pollution, or shares the blame with local air pollution authorities. Rarely is the blame put on the teeming millions eagerly waiting to consume the goods produced in the factory beneath the smokestack. Phosphate pollution in our lakes is blamed on the detergent manufacturers rather than on the excessive population which is releasing them into our waterways. These cases are relatively obvious, but the links between population and environmental impact are often much more subtle. No better example of this exists than in Garrett Hardin's "Nobody Ever Dies of Overpopulation," Article 37. This short and surprising article stimulates one to think of other heretofore unsuspected consequences of too many people.

Environmental degradation in the advanced countries is multiplied by the effects of unwise technology and economics. In fact, Ansley J. Coale, in Article 38, "Man and His environment," argues convincingly that faulty economic organization, much more than population, is the prime element in environmental decay. However, this view is disputed by Paul R. Ehrlich and John P. Holdren in Article 39, "Impact of Population Growth." Ehrlich and Holdren develop cogent arguments to the effect that population is indeed a major factor in environmental quality.

One of the most thoughtful essays ever written on population is Garrett Hardin's "The Tragedy of the Commons," Article 40. Here, Hardin shows how uncontrolled reproduction can lead to tragic consequences for all those who share a common earth.

nobody ever dies of overpopulation

garrett hardin

Go, go, go, said the bird: human kind
Cannot bear very much reality.

Those of us who are deeply concerned about population and the environment—"econuts," we're called—are accused of seeing herbicides in trees, pollution in running brooks, radiation in rocks, and overpopulation everywhere. There is merit in the accusation.

I was in Calcutta when the cyclone struck East Bengal in November 1970. Early dispatches spoke of 15,000 dead, but the estimates rapidly escalated to 2,000,000 and then dropped back to 500,000. A nice round number: it will do as well as any, for we will never know. The nameless ones who died, "unimportant" people far beyond the fringes of the social power structure, left no trace of their existence. Pakistani parents repaired the population loss in just 40 days, and the world turned its attention to other matters.

What killed those unfortunate people? The cyclone, newspapers said. But one can just as logically say that overpopulation killed them. The Gangetic delta is barely above sea level. Every year several thousand people are killed in quite ordinary storms. If Pakistan were not overcrowded, no sane man would bring his family to such a place. Ecologically speaking, a delta belongs to the river and the sea; man obtrudes there at his peril.

In the web of life every event has many antecedents. Only by an arbitrary decision can we designate a single antecedent as "cause." Our choice is biased—biased to protect our egos against the onslaught of unwelcome truths. As T. S. Eliot put it in *Burnt Norton*:

Go, go, go, said the bird: human kind
Cannot bear very much reality.

Were we to identify overpopulation as the cause of a half-million deaths, we would threaten ourselves with a question to which we do not know

Reprinted from *Science*, Vol. 171, editorial page, 12 February 1971. Copyright 1971 by the American Association for the Advancement of Science. The author is professor of biology, University of California, Santa Barbara.

the answer: *How can we control population without recourse to repugnant measures?* Fearfully we close our minds to an inventory of possibilities. Instead, we say that a cyclone caused the deaths, thus relieving ourselves of responsibility for this and future catastrophes. "Fate" is *so* comforting.

Every year we list tuberculosis, leprosy, enteric diseases, or animal parasites as the "cause of death" of millions of people. It is well known that malnutrition is an important antecedent of death in all these categories; and that malnutrition is connected with overpopulation. But overpopulation is not called the cause of death. We cannot bear the thought.

People are dying now of respiratory diseases in Tokyo, Birmingham, and Gary, because of the "need" for more industry. The "need" for more food justifies overfertilization of the land, leading to eutrophication of the waters, and lessened fish production—which leads to more "need" for food.

What will we say when the power shuts down some fine summer on our eastern seaboard and several thousand people die of heat prostration? Will we blame the weather? Or the power companies for not building enough generators? Or the econuts for insisting on pollution controls?

One thing is certain: we won't blame the deaths on overpopulation. No one ever dies of overpopulation. It is unthinkable.

man and his environment

ansley j. coale

Economic factors are more important than population growth in threatening the quality of American life.

The way our economy is organized is an essential cause, if not *the* essential cause, of air and water pollution, and of the ugly and sometimes destructive accumulation of trash. I believe it is also an important element in such dangerous human ecological interventions as changes in the biosphere resulting from the wholesale use of inorganic fertilizers, of the accumulation in various dangerous places such as the fatty tissue of fish and birds and mammals of incredibly stable insecticides. We can properly attribute such adverse effects to a combination of a high level of economic activity and the use of harmful technological practices that are inconsistent with such a high level.

The economist would say that harmful practices have occurred because of a disregard of what he would call *externalities.* An externality is defined as a consequence (good or bad) that does not enter the calculations of gain or loss by the person who undertakes an economic activity. It is typically a cost (or a benefit) of an activity that accrues to someone else. A fence erected in a suburban neighborhood for privacy also affords a measure of privacy to the neighbor—a cost or a benefit depending on how he feels about privacy versus keeping track of what goes on next door. Air pollution created by an industrial plant is a classic case of an externality; the operator of a factory producing noxious smoke imposes costs on everyone downwind, and pays none of these costs himself—they do not affect his balance sheet at all. This, I believe, is the basic economic factor that has a degrading effect on the environment: we have in general permitted economic activities without assessing the operator for their adverse effects. There has been no attempt to evaluate—and to charge for—externalities. As [economist Ken-

Reprinted from *Science,* Vol. 170, 9 October 1970, pp. 132–136. Copyright 1970 by the American Association for the Advancement of Science. This article is adapted from a talk given 19 March 1970 at a symposium devoted to "Man and Environment" at the University of North Carolina, Chapel Hill. The author is director of the Office of Population Research at Princeton University, Princeton, New Jersey 03540.

neth] Boulding says, we pay people for the goods they produce, but do not make them pay for the bads.

To put the same point more simply: environmental deterioration has arisen to a large extent because we have treated pure air, pure water, and the disposal of waste as if they were free. They cannot be treated as free in a modern, urban, industrial society.

There are a number of different kinds of policies that would prevent, or at least reduce, the harmful side effects of some of our economic activities, either by preventing or reducing the volume of the harmful activity, or by inducing a change in technique. Other policies might involve curative rather than preventive steps, such as cleaning up trash along the highways, if we cannot prevent people from depositing it there.

Among the possibilities are steps that would make externalities internal. An example that I find appealing, although it is perhaps not widely practical, is to require users of flowing water to take in the water downstream of their operation and discharge it upstream. A more general measure is to require the recycling of air or water used in industrial processes, rather than permitting the free use of fresh water and clean air, combined with the unmonitored discharge of exhaust products.

Public authorities can charge for unfavorable external effects by imposing a tax on operations that are harmful to the environment. The purpose of such taxes is to reduce the volume of adverse effects by inducing a shift in technique or by reducing the volume of production by causing a rise in price. Also, the tax receipts could be used to pay for mitigating the effect. An example of a desirable tax is one imposed to minimize the use of disposable cans and bottles for soft drinks and beer. Not long ago the majority of manufacturers produced these commodities in containers that were to be returned. The producer offered a modest price for returning bottles as an inducement. It has proven cheaper to use disposable glass bottles and cans; recently aluminum cans have rapidly increased in popularity, substituting a container that lasts indefinitely for the tin cans that would sooner or later rust away. Everyone is familiar with the resultant clutter on beaches, in parks, and along the highways. If a tax of 10 cents per unit were imposed on each disposable container, it would clearly be cheaper to go back to returnables. If some manufacturers found it advantageous to pay the 10-cent tax, the receipts could be used to pay for cleaning up highways and beaches.

Another approach that would induce people to give up economic activities with harmful effects on others is to make individuals and corporations financially liable for any damage caused by their operations. The resultant litigation would be an unwarranted windfall for lawyers, but financial liability might be a very potent factor in reducing pollution.

There is general agreement that our knowledge of what affects the environment is wholly inadequate. Because of inadequate monitoring and measurement, we do not know what is happening to the atmosphere or the biosphere; we need research to keep track of what is going on as well as to develop the techniques that will produce the goods we want with fewer of the bads we do not want.

an economist's review of resource exhaustion

One of the questions most frequently raised about the environmental effects of modern life is the rapid and rising rate of extraction of raw materials. Are we running out of resources?

I would first like to note that the distinction between renewable and nonrenewable resources is not a clear one. There are, of course, instances of nonrenewable resources in the form of concentrated sources of energy, such as the fossil fuels. These are reservoirs of reduced carbon embodying radiant energy from the sun that accumulated over many thousands of years. When these fuels are used, the energy that is released is to a large extent radiated into space, and we have no way of reclaiming it. The geological processes that are constantly renewing the fossil deposits of carbon are so slow compared to the rate at which we are burning the fuels that the designation "nonrenewable" is appropriate.

On the other hand, when we think of our resources of such useful materials as the metallic elements of iron, copper, nickel, lead, and so forth, we should realize that spaceship Earth has the same amount of each element as it had a million years ago, and will have the same amount a million years from now. All we do with these resources is to move them around. The energy we use is lost, but the minerals we find useful are still with us. It does not pay to recycle these minerals (that is, to use them repeatedly by reclaiming scrap) because the deposits of minerals in the ground or in the ocean are still such a cheap source. It must be noted that the mining of fresh ore is cheaper than the use of scrap in part because miners are not charged for their "externalities." If harmful by-products of mining could not be discharged into streams, if mine tailings were regulated, and erosion-producing or even unesthetic practices forbidden, minerals would be more expensive and recycling more attractive. In the production of any metallic element, the easier sources are exploited first. As mining gets more difficult, the ore gets more expensive, and recycling becomes more nearly competitive. It seems wholly probable that the technology of recycling will be improved.

The surprising fact is that raw materials are not at the moment very costly, and moreover their cost relative to the cost of finished goods has not been increasing. The gross national product in the United States is more than $4500 per capita and the raw materials component per capita is less than $100. The price of raw materials relative to the price of finished goods is no higher now than at the beginning of the century, and if we were running out of raw materials, they would surely be rising in relative expensiveness. A prominent exception is saw lumber, which is substantially more expensive relative to the cost of finished wooden products than it used to be.

The reason that the future of our resource situation always seems so bleak and the past seems quite comfortable is that we can readily construct a plausible sounding estimate of the future demand for a particular raw material, but cannot form such a plausible picture of the future supply. To estimate the future demand, we need merely note the recent trends in the per capita consumption of whatever it is we are concerned about, utilize whatever plausible projection of population we are prepared to accept, multiply the two together and project an astonishingly high rate of usage 50 years in the future. If this demand does not seem overwhelming, we need only make a projection 100 years in the future. What we cannot so readily foresee is the discovery of new sources and of new techniques of extraction, and, in particular, the substitution of other raw materials or the substitution of other industrial processes which change the demand away from the raw material we are considering. Hence it can always be made to appear that in the future we are going to run out of any given material, but that at present we never have.

It is possible to set plausible limits to the stores of fossil fuels that we are likely to discover, and with the very rapid rise in the use of these fuels they will surely become more expensive in some not too distant time. It should be noted, however, that we will not suddenly "run out" of fossil fuels. Long before the last drop of oil is used, oil will have become much more expensive. If gasoline were $5 or $10 a gallon, we would utilize it much more sparingly, with small economical automobile engines, or perhaps the substitution of some non-petroleum-based fuel altogether. In fact, the principal user of our petroleum deposits may be the petrochemical industries. I have given this special attention to fossil fuels because there is no substitute in prospect for such fuels in small mobile units such as automobiles. On the other hand, the supply of overall energy seems to pose no problem. There seems to be ample fissionable material to supply rising energy needs for many centuries, if breeding reactors are perfected. If fusion proves a practical source, the supply of energy can properly be considered limitless.

Another aspect of the relation of the United States economy to resources that is much publicized today is the fact that we are consuming such a large fraction of the current annual extraction of raw materials in the world. A much quoted figure is that 6 percent of the world's population is using 30 percent of the resources. It is concluded from figures such as these that we are robbing the low-income countries of the world of the basis of their future prosperity—that we are using up not only our resources, but theirs as well. Most economists would find this a very erroneous picture of the effect of our demand for the raw materials extracted in the less developed parts of the world. The spokesmen for the less developed countries themselves constantly complain about the adverse terms of trade that they face on world markets. The principal source of their concern is the low price of raw materials and the high price of finished goods. The most effective forms of assistance that the developed countries (including the United States) give to the less developed countries are the purchases they make from the less developed countries in international trade. A developing country needs receipts from exports in order to finance the purchase of the things they need for economic development. For example, in order to industrialize, a nonindustrialized country must for a long time purchase capital equipment from more advanced countries, and the funds for such purchases come from exports—principally of raw materials. Economists in the developing countries feel that the demand for raw materials is inadequate. Perhaps the most important adverse effect of slowing down the growth of the gross national product in the United States would be that it would diminish the demand for primary products that we would otherwise import from the less developed countries. After all, if a developing country wants to retain its raw materials at home, it can always place an embargo on their export. However, it would be a policy very damaging to economic progress of that very country.

Note that the effect of our high demand for raw materials is a different matter from the desirability of the domestic control of mineral resources within the developing countries. Selling oil on the world market provides immense economic advantages to a developing country. Whether foreign interests should be represented in the extraction of raw materials is another question.

population growth in the united states

I shall begin a discussion of population with a brief description of recent, current, and future population trends in the United States. Our population today is a little over 200 million, having increased by slightly more than 50 percent since 1940. I think it is likely to increase by nearly 50 percent again in the 30 years before the end of the century.

This rate of increase cannot continue long. If it endured throughout the next century, the population would reach a billion shortly before the year 2100. Within six or seven more centuries we would reach one person per square foot of land area in the United States, and after about 1500 years our descendants would outweigh the earth if they continued to increase by 50 percent every 30 years. We can even calculate that, at that rate of increase, our descendants would, in a few thousand years, form a sphere of flesh whose radius would, neglecting relativity, expand at the velocity of light.

Every demographer knows that we cannot continue a positive rate of increase indefinitely. The inexorable arithmetic of compound interest leads us to absurd conditions within a calculable period of time. Logically we must, and in fact we will, have a rate of growth very close to zero in the long run. The average rate of increase of mankind from the inception of the species until the present is zero to many decimal places. If we agree that 10,000 years from now we can have no more than one person per square foot, and that the population of the world will at a minimum exceed that of Richmond, Virginia, we can say that the average annual growth of population will be within one per thousand of zero.

The only questions about attaining a zero rate of increase for any population are when and how such a rate is attained. A zero rate of increase implies a balance between the average birth and death rates, so the choice of how to attain a zero rate of increase is a choice between low birth and death rates that are approximately equal. The average growth rate very near to zero during mankind's past history has been attained with high birth and death rates—with an average duration of life that until recently was no more than 30 or 35 years. I have no difficulty in deciding that I would prefer a zero rate of growth with low rather than high birth and death rates, or with an average duration of life in excess of 70 years, as has been achieved in all of the more advanced countries of the world, rather than the life that is "nasty, brutish, and short." The remaining question then is *when* should our population growth level off.

A popular answer today is "immediately." In fact a zero rate of increase in the United States starting immediately is not feasible and I believe not desirable. The reason is the age composition of the population that our past history of birth and death rates has left to us. We have an especially young population now because of the postwar baby boom. One consequence is that our death rate is much lower than it would be in a population that had long had low fertility. That is, because our population is young, a high proportion of it is concentrated in ages where the risk of mortality is small. Therefore, if we were to attain a zero growth rate immediately, it would be necessary to cut the birth rate about in half. For the next 15 or 20 years, women would have to bear children at a rate that would produce only a little over one child per completed family. At the end of that time we would have a very peculiar age distribution with a great shortage of young people. The attendant social and economic disruptions represent too large a cost to pay for the advantages that we might derive from reducing growth to zero right away.

In fact, a more reasonable goal would be to reduce fertility as soon as possible to a level where couples produced just enough children to insure that each generation exactly replaced itself. If this goal (early attainment of fertility at a replacement level) were reached immediately, our population would increase 35 to 40 percent before it stabilized. The reason that fertility at the mere replacement level would produce such a large increase in population is again the age distribution we have today. There are many more people today under 20 than 20 to 40, and when the relatively numerous children have moved into the childbearing ages, they will greatly outnumber the persons now at those ages, and when the current population under age 20 moves into the old ages, they will be far more numerous than the people now at the old ages. Thus to move the population to replacement would be to insure approximately that the number of children under 20 will be about the same as it is today, but that the number above that age will be substantially higher. The net effect is the increase of 35 to 40 percent mentioned just above. It is the built-in growth in our age composition that led me to state earlier that I think an increase in the order of 50 percent of the U. S. population is not unlikely.

A sensible choice in reducing our growth rate to zero then is between early or late attainment of fertility at the replacement level. Is there any reason that we should not attempt to attain a fertility at replacement as soon as possible? My own opinion is that an early move in that direction is desirable, but for the sake of completeness, I must point out that there is a nonnegligible cost associated with attaining a stationary population—the population that will exist with fertility at replacement after the age distribution left over from the past has worked out its transitory consequences.

A stationary population with the mortality levels that we have already attained has a much older age distribution than any the United States has ever experienced. It has more people over 60 than under 15, and half the population would be over 37 rather than over 27, as is the case today. It would be an age distribution much like that of a health resort.

Moreover, if we view the age pyramid in the conventional way, with the number of males and females being drawn out as in the branches of a Christmas tree (age representing altitude of the tree) the pyramid for the stationary population is virtually vertical until age 50 because of the small number of deaths under the favorable mortality conditions we have attained. In contrast, the age distribution of the United States to date has always tapered more or less sharply with increasing age. The stationary population with its vertical sides would no longer conform in age composition to the shape of the social structure—to the pyramid of privilege and responsibility. In a growing population, the age pyramid does conform, so there is a rough consonance of shape between diminishing numbers at higher ages and the smaller number of high positions relative to low positions. In a stationary population there would no longer be a reasonable expectation of advancement as a person moves through life. I have indicated that sooner or later we must have a stationary population, so that sooner or later we must adjust to such an age composition. I am pointing to this disadvantage to show that there is a choice between moving more gradually to a stationary population at the expense of a larger ultimate population size in order to continue to enjoy for a longer time the more desirable age distribution of a growing population.

connection between population and pollution

The connection between the current growth in our population and the deterioration of our environment of which we have all become aware is largely an indirect one. The problem has arisen because we are permitting the production of bads (pollution, or negative externalities) along with goods. There seems little doubt that the rapid increase in the production of goods has been responsible for the rapid increase in the production of bads, since we have made no effective effort to prevent the latter from accompanying the former. But per capita increase in production has been more important than population growth. It has been calculated that if we were to duplicate the total production of electricity in the United States in 1940 in a population enjoying the 1969 per capita usage of energy, the population could be only 25 million rather than the 132 million people there were in 1940. Population has increased by 50 percent, but per capita use of electricity has been multiplied several times. A similar statement can even be made about the crowding of our national parks. The population has increased by about 50 percent in the last 30 years—attendance in national parks has increased by more than 400 percent.

A wealthy industrial urban population of 100 million persons would have most of the pollution problems we do. In fact, Sydney, Australia, has problems of air and water pollution and of traffic jams, even though the total population of Australia is about 12 million in an area 80 percent as big as the United States. Australia is actually more urbanized than the United States, in spite of its relatively small population and large overall area.

If we have the will and intelligence to devise and apply proper policies, we can improve our environment and can do so either with the current population of 200 million, or with the population that we will probably have in another 50 years of 300 million. On the other hand, if we ignore environmental problems and continue to treat pure air and water and the disposal of trash as if they were free, and if we pay no attention to the effects of the techniques that we employ upon the balance of nature, we

253

will be in trouble whether our population grows or not. There is no doubt that slower population growth would make it easier to improve our environment, but not much easier.

policies that would affect the growth of population

We must, at some time, achieve a zero rate of population, and the balance should surely be achieved at low birth and death rates rather than at high rates. If, as at present, only about 5 percent of women remain single at the end of the childbearing span, and if 96 percent of women survive to the mean age of childbearing, and if finally the sex ratio at birth remains about 105 males for every 100 females, married couples must have an average of about 2.25 children to replace themselves. What kinds of policies might be designed to assure such a level of fertility or, more generally, to produce the fertility level that is at the moment socially desirable?

I begin with a set of policies that are consistent with general democratic and humanitarian principles, although a minority of the population would oppose them on religious grounds. These are policies that would, through education and the provision of clinical services, try to make it possible for every conception to be the result of a deliberate choice, and for every choice to be an informed one, based on an adequate knowledge of the consequences of bearing different numbers of children at different times. A component of such a set of policies would be the development of more effective means of contraception to reduce the number of accidental pregnancies occurring to couples who are trying to avoid conception. These are policies that call for a substantial government role and I think that an effective government program in these areas is already overdue. I personally believe that education in the consequences of childbearing and in the techniques of avoiding pregnancy, combined with the provision of contraceptive services, should be supplemented by the provision of safe and skillful abortion upon request. It is clear that the public consensus in favor of abortion is not nearly as clear-cut as that in favor of contraception, and I know that the extent and the strength of the moral objection to induced abortion is much greater. Nevertheless, I am persuaded by experience in Japan and eastern Europe that the advantages of abortion provided under good medical auspices to cause the early termination of unwanted pregnancies are very important to the women affected, as is evident in the fact that when medically safe abortion has been made available at low cost, the number of abortions has initially been as great or greater than the number of live births. Later there is a typical tendency for women to resort to contraception rather than repeated abortions.

The reason I favor abortion is that such a high proportion of births that occur today are unwanted, and because a large number of desperate pregnant women (probably more than a half million annually) resort to clandestine abortions today, with high rates of serious complications. In contrast, early abortion, under skilled medical auspices, is less dangerous than tonsillectomy, and substantially less dangerous than carrying a child to full term.

In recent years the number of births that were unwanted in the United States constituted about 20 percent of the total (an unwanted birth was defined as one in which the woman said that conception occurred either as a result of a failure of contraception or in the absence of contraception but without the intent to become pregnant as soon as possible, when at the time the conception occurred the husband or wife or both did not want another child then or later). The rate at which women are having children today would lead to a completed family size of slightly under three children. If all unwanted births were eliminated, the number of children born per married woman would be about 2.4 or 2.5 on average. This is very little above replacement, and when allowance is made for the likely possibility that women understated the proportion of births that were unwanted, it is probable that the elimination of unwanted births would bring a fertility at or below replacement.

If it is true that the elimination of unwanted pregnancies would reduce fertility very nearly to replacement, it must be conceded that this outcome is fortuitous. It is highly unlikely that over a substantial period of time the free choice by each couple of the number of children they want would lead exactly to the socially desirable level of fertility. The erratic behavior of fertility in America and in other advanced industrialized countries in the last 30 or 40 years is ample evidence that when fertility is voluntarily controlled, the level of fertility is subject to major fluctuations, and I see no logical reason to expect that on average people would voluntarily choose a number of children that would keep the long-run average a little above two per couple. In other words, we must acknowledge the probable necessity of instituting policies that would influence the number of children people want. However, there is no need for haste in formulating such policy, since, as I have indicated, improved contraceptive services combined with a liberal provision of abortion would probably move our fertility at present quite close to replacement, and a gradual increase in population during the next generation would not be a major addition to the problems we already face.

Policies intended to affect people's preferences for children should be designed within the framework of our democratic traditions. They should be designed, for example, to encourage diversity and permit freedom of choice. An average of 2.25 children does not require that 75 percent of couples have two children and 25 percent three, although that would produce the desired average. Another possibility is a nearly even division of family size among zero, one-, two-, three-, four-, and five-child families. The ideal policy would affect the decision at the margin and not try to impose a uniform pattern on all. I do not think that people who prefer to have more than the average number of children should be subject to ridicule or abuse.

It is particularly difficult to frame acceptable policies influencing the number of children that people want. While it is still true that so many large families result from unwanted pregnancies, the unwanted child that is the most recent birth in a large family already faces many deprivations. The psychological disadvantages of the unwanted child cause some of our most serious social problems. In addition to these psychological disadvantages, the unwanted child in a large impoverished family faces an inadequate diet, much below average chances for schooling, and generally inferior opportunities. I hardly think it a wise or humane policy to handicap him further by imposing a financial burden on his parents as a result of his birth.

When unwanted births have become negligible in number, we could imagine trying to design a policy in which the couple is asked to pay some part of the "externalities" that an additional birth imposes on society. In the meantime, I suggest as a desirable supplement to better contraception and free access to abortion the extension of more nearly equal opportunities in education and employment for women, so that activities outside of the home become a more powerful competitor to a larger family. We should start now devoting careful attention to formulation of policies in this area—policies that could increase fertility when it fell too low as well as policies to induce people to want fewer children.

Some aspects of the deterioration of our environment appear to be critical and call for prompt action. We need to start now to frame and apply actions that would arrest the careless destruction of the world in which we live. We also need policies to reduce promptly the incidence of unwanted births. In the long run we shall also need ways to influence the number of births people want. To design policies consistent with our most cherished social and political values will not be easy, and it is fortunate that there is no valid reason for hasty action.

impact of population growth

paul ehrlich and john holdren

Complacency concerning this component of man's predicament is unjustified and counterproductive.

The interlocking crises in population, resources, and environment have been the focus of countless papers, dozens of prestigious symposia, and a growing avalanche of books. In this wealth of material, several questionable assertions have been appearing with increasing frequency. Perhaps the most serious of these is the notion that the size and growth rate of the U.S. population are only minor contributors to this country's adverse impact on local and global environments (*1, 2*). We propose to deal with this and several related misconceptions here, before persistent and unrebutted repetition entrenches them in the public mind—if not the scientific literature. Our discussion centers around five theorems which we believe are demonstrably true and which provide a framework for realistic analysis:

1) Population growth causes a *disproportionate* negative impact on the environment.

2) Problems of population size and growth, resource utilization and depletion, and environmental deterioration must be considered jointly and on a global basis. In this context, population control is obviously not a panacea—it is necessary but not alone sufficient to see us through the crisis.

3) Population density is a poor measure of population pressure, and redistributing population would be a dangerous pseudosolution to the population problem.

4) "Environment" must be broadly construed to include such things as the physical environment of urban ghettos, the human behavioral environment, and the epidemiological environment.

5) Theoretical solutions to our problems are often not operational and sometimes are not solutions.

We now examine these theorems in some detail.

Reprinted from *Science*, Vol. 171, pp. 1212–1216, 26 March 1971. Copyright 1971. Reprinted by permission of the authors and the editors of *Science*. This article is adapted from a paper presented before the President's Commission on Population Growth and the American Future on 17 November 1970. Dr. Ehrlich is professor of biology at Stanford University, Palo Alto, California, and Dr. Holdren is a physicist at the Lawrence Radiation Laboratory, University of California, Livermore.

population size and per capita impact

In an agricultural or technological society, each human individual has a negative impact on his environment. He is responsible for some of the simplification (and resulting destabilization) of ecological systems which results from the practice of agriculture (*3*). He also participates in the utilization of renewable and nonrenewable resources. The total negative impact of such a society on the environment can be expressed, in the simplest terms, by the relation

$$I = P \cdot F$$

where P is the population, and F is a function which measures the per capita impact. A great deal of complexity is subsumed in this simple relation, however. For example, F increases with per capita consumption if technology is held constant, but may decrease in some cases if more benign technologies are introduced in the provision of a constant level of consumption. (We shall see in connection with theorem 5 that there are limits to the improvements one should anticipate from such "technological fixes.")

Pitfalls abound in the interpretation of manifest increases in the total impact *I*. For instance, it is easy to mistake changes in the composition of resource demand or environmental impact for absolute per capita increases, and thus to underestimate the role of the population multiplier. Moreover, it is often assumed that population size and per capita impact are independent variables, when in fact they are not. Consider, for example, the recent articles by Coale (*1*), in which he disparages the role of U.S. population growth in environmental problems by noting that since 1940 "population has increased by 50 percent, but per capita use of electricity has been multiplied several times." This argument contains both the fallacies to which we have just referred.

First, a closer examination of very rapid increases in many kinds of consumption shows that these changes reflect a shift among alternatives within a larger (and much more slowly growing) category. Thus the 760 percent increase in electricity consumption from 1940 to 1969 (*4*) occurred in large part because the electrical *component* of the energy budget was (and is) increasing much faster than the budget itself. (Electricity comprised 12 percent of the U.S. energy consumption in 1940 versus 22 percent today.) The total energy production, a more important figure than its electrical component in terms of resources and the environment, increased much less dramatically—140 percent from 1940 to 1969. Under the simplest assumption (that is, that a given increase in population size accounts for an exactly proportional increase in production), this would mean that 38 percent of the increase in energy production during this period is explained by population growth (the actual population increase from 1940 to 1969 was 53 percent). Similar considerations reveal the imprudence of citing, say, aluminum consumption to show that population growth is an "unimportant" factor in resource use. Certainly, aluminum consumption has swelled by over 1400 percent since 1940, but much of the increase has been due to the substitution of aluminum for steel in many applications. Thus a fairer measure is combined consumption of aluminum and steel,

258

which has risen only 117 percent since 1940. Again, under the simplest assumption, population growth accounts for 45 percent of the increase.

The "simplest assumption" is not valid, however, and this is the second flaw in Coale's example (and in his thesis). In short, he has failed to recognize that per capita consumption of energy and resources, and the associated per capita impact on the environment, are themselves functions of the population size. Our previous equation is more accurately written

$$I = P \cdot F(P)$$

displaying the fact that impact can increase faster than linearly with population. Of course, whether $F(P)$ is an increasing or decreasing function of P depends in part on whether diminishing returns or economies of scale are dominant in the activities of importance. In populous, industrial nations such as the United States, most economies of scale are already being exploited; we are on the diminishing returns part of most of the important curves.

As one example of diminishing returns, consider the problem of providing nonrenewable resources such as minerals and fossil fuels to a growing population, even at fixed levels of per capita consumption. As the richest supplies of these resources and those nearest to centers of use are consumed, we are obliged to use lower-grade ores, drill deeper, and extend our supply networks. All these activities increase our per capita use of energy and our per capita impact on the environment. In the case of partly renewable resources such as water (which is effectively nonrenewable when groundwater supplies are mined at rates far exceeding natural recharge), per capita costs and environmental impact escalate dramatically when the human population demands more than is locally available. Here the loss of free-flowing rivers and other economic, esthetic, and ecological costs of massive water-movement projects represent increased per capita diseconomies directly stimulated by population growth.

Diminishing returns are also operative in increasing food production to meet the needs of growing populations. Typically, attempts are made both to overproduce on land already farmed and to extend agriculture to marginal land. The former requires disproportionate energy use in obtaining and distributing water, fertilizer, and pesticides. The latter also increases per capita energy use, since the amount of energy invested per unit yield increases as less desirable land is cultivated. Similarly, as the richest fisheries stocks are depleted, the yield per unit effort drops, and more and more energy per capita is required to maintain the supply (5). Once a stock is depleted it may not recover—it may be nonrenewable.

Population size influences per capita impact in ways other than diminishing returns. As one example, consider the oversimplified but instructive situation in which each person in the population has links with every other person—roads, telephone lines, and so forth. These links involve energy and materials in their construction and use. Since the number of links increases much more rapidly than the number of people (6), so does the per capita consumption associated with the links.

Other factors may cause much steeper positive slopes in the per capita impact function, $F(P)$. One such phenomenon is the *threshold effect*. Below a certain level of pollution trees will survive in smog. But, at some point, when a small increment in population produces a small increment in smog, living trees become dead trees. Five hundred people may be able to live around a lake and dump their raw sewage into the lake, and the natural systems of the lake will be able to break down the sewage and keep the lake from undergoing rapid ecological change. Five hundred and five people may overload the system and result in a "polluted" or eutrophic lake. Another phenomenon capable of causing near-discontinuities is the *synergism*. For instance, as cities push out into farmland, air pollution increasingly becomes a mixture of agricultural chemicals with power plant and automobile effluents. Sulfur dioxide from the city paralyzes the cleaning mechanisms of the lungs, thus increasing the residence time of potential carcinogens in the agricultural chemicals. The joint effect may be much more than the sum of the individual effects. Investigation of synergistic effects is one of the most neglected areas of environmental evaluation.

Not only is there a connection between population size and per capita damage to the environment, but the cost of maintaining environmental quality at a given level escalates disproportionately as population size increases. This effect occurs in part because costs increase very rapidly as one tries to reduce contaminants per unit volume of effluent to lower and lower levels (diminishing returns again!). Consider municipal sewage, for example. The cost of removing 80 to 90 percent of the biochemical and chemical oxygen demand, 90 percent of the suspended solids, and 60 percent of the resistant organic material by means of secondary treatment is about 8 cents per 1000 gallons (3785 liters) in a large plant (7). But if the volume of sewage is such that its nutrient content creates a serious eutrophication problem (as is the case in the United States today), or if supply considerations dictate the reuse of sewage water for industry, agriculture, or groundwater recharge, advanced treatment is necessary. The cost ranges from two to four times as much as for secondary treatment (17 cents per 1000 gallons for carbon absorption; 34 cents per 1000 gallons for disinfection to yield a potable supply). This dramatic example of diminishing returns in pollution control could be repeated for stack gases, automobile exhausts, and so forth.

Now consider a situation in which the limited capacity of the environment to absorb abuse requires that we hold man's impact in some sector constant as population doubles. This means *per capita effectiveness* of pollution control in this sector must double (that is, effluent per person must be halved). In a typical situation, this would yield doubled per capita costs, or quadrupled total costs (and probably energy consumption) in this sector for a doubling of population. Of course, diminishing returns and threshold effects may be still more serious: we may easily have an eightfold increase in control costs for a doubling of population. Such arguments leave little ground for the assumption, popularized by Barry Commoner (2, 8) and others, that a 1 percent rate of population growth spawns only 1 percent effects.

It is to be emphasized that the possible existence of "economies of scale" does not invalidate these arguments. Such savings, if available at all, would apply in the case of our sewage example to a change in the amount of effluent to be handled at an installation of a given type. For most technologies, the United States is already more than populous enough to achieve such economies and is doing so. They are accounted for in our example by citing figures for the largest treatment plants of each type. Population growth; on the other hand, forces us into quantitative *and* qualitative changes in how we handle each unit volume of effluent—what fraction and what kinds of material we remove. Here economies of scale do not apply at all, and diminishing returns are the rule.

global context

We will not deal in detail with the best example of the global nature and interconnections of population resource and environmental problems—namely, the problems involved in feeding a world in which 10 to 20 million people starve to death annually (*9*), and in which the population is growing by some 70 million people per year. The ecological problems created by high-yield agriculture are awesome (*3, 10*) and are bound to have a negative feedback on food production. Indeed, the Food and Agriculture Organization of the United Nations has reported that in 1969 the world suffered its first absolute decline in fisheries yield since 1950. It seems likely that part of this decline is attributable to pollution originating in terrestrial agriculture.

A second source of the fisheries decline is, of course, overexploitation of fisheries by the developed countries. This problem, in turn, is illustrative of the situation in regard to many other resources, where similarly rapacious and shortsighted behavior by the developed nations is compromising the aspirations of the bulk of humanity to a decent existence. It is now becoming more widely comprehended that the United States alone accounts for perhaps 30 percent of the nonrenewable resources consumed in the world each year (for example, 37 percent of the energy, 25 percent of the steel, 28 percent of the tin, and 33 percent of the synthetic rubber) (*11*). This behavior is in large part inconsistent with American rhetoric about "developing" the countries of the Third World. *We* may be able to afford the technology to mine lower grade deposits when we have squandered the world's rich ores, but the underdeveloped countries, as their needs grow and their means remain meager, will not be able to do so. Some observers argue that the poor countries are today economically dependent on our use of their resources, and indeed that economists in these countries complain that world demand for their raw materials is too low (*1*). This proves only that their economists are as shortsighted as ours.

It is abundantly clear that the entire context in which we view the world resource pool and the relationships between developed and underdeveloped countries must be changed, if we are to have any hope of achieving a stable and prosperous existence for all human beings. It cannot be stated too forcefully that the developed countries (or, more accurately, the overdeveloped countries) are the principal culprits in the consumption and dispersion of the world's nonrenewable resources (*12*) as well as in appropriating much more than their share of the world's protein. Because of this consumption, and because of the enormous negative impact on the global environment accompanying it, the population growth in these countries must be regarded as the most serious in the world today.

In relation to theorem 2 we must emphasize that, even if population growth were halted, the present population of the world could easily destroy civilization as we know it. There is a wide choice of weapons—from unstable plant monocultures and agricultural hazes to DDT, mercury, and thermonuclear bombs. If population size were reduced and per capita consumption remained the same (or increased), we would still quickly run out of vital, high-grade resources or generate conflicts over diminishing supplies. Racism, economic exploitation, and war will not be eliminated by population control (of course, they are unlikely to be eliminated without it).

population density and distribution

Theorem 3 deals with a problem related to the inequitable utilization of world resources. One of the commonest errors made by the uninitiated is to assume that population density (people per square mile) is the critical measure of overpopulation or underpopulation. For instance, Wattenberg states that the United States is not very crowded by "international standards" because Holland has 18 times the population density (*13*). We call this notion "the Netherlands fallacy." The Netherlands actually requires large chunks of the earth's resources and vast areas of land not within its borders to maintain itself. For example, it is the second largest per capita importer of protein in the world, and it imports 63 percent of its cereals, including 100 percent of its corn and rice. It also imports all of its cotton, 77 percent of its wool, and all of its iron ore, antimony, bauxite, chromium, copper, gold, lead, magnesite, manganese, mercury, molybdenum, nickel, silver, tin, tungsten, vanadium, zinc, phosphate rock (fertilizer), potash (fertilizer), asbestos, and diamonds. It produces energy equivalent to some 20 million metric tons of coal and consumes the equivalent of over 47 million metric tons (*14*).

A certain preoccupation with density as a useful measure of overpopulation is apparent in the article by Coale (*1*). He points to the existence of urban problems such as smog in Sydney, Australia, "even though the total population of Australia is about 12 million in an area 80 percent as big as the United States," as evidence that environmental problems are unrelated to population size. His argument would be more persuasive if problems of population *distribution* were the only ones with environmental consequences, and if population distribution were unrelated to resource distribution and population size. Actually, since the carrying capacity of the Australian continent is far below that of the United States, one would *expect* distribution problems—of which Sydney's smog is one symptom—to be encountered at a much lower total population there. Resources, such as water, are in very short supply, and people cluster where resources are available. (Evidently, it cannot be emphasized enough that carrying capacity includes the availability of a wide variety of resources in addition to space itself, and that population pressure is measured relative to the carrying capacity. One would expect water, soils, or the ability of the environment to absorb wastes to be the limiting resource in far more instances than land area.)

In addition, of course, many of the most serious environmental problems are essentially independent of the way in which population is distributed.

These include the global problems of weather modification by carbon dioxide and particulate pollution, and the threats to the biosphere posed by man's massive inputs of pesticides, heavy metals, and oil (*15*). Similarly, the problems of resource depletion and ecosystem simplification by agriculture depend on how many people there are and their patterns of consumption, but not in any major way on how they are distributed.

Naturally, we do not dispute that smog and most other familiar urban ills are serious problems, or that they are related to population distribution. Like many of the difficulties we face, these problems will not be cured simply by stopping population growth; direct and well-conceived assaults on the problems themselves will also be required. Such measures may occasionally include the redistribution of population, but the considerable difficulties and costs of this approach should not be underestimated. People live where they do not because of a perverse intention to add to the problems of their society but for reasons of economic necessity, convenience, and desire for agreeable surroundings. Areas that are uninhabited or sparsely populated today are presumably that way because they are deficient in some of the requisite factors. In many cases, the remedy for such deficiencies—for example, the provision of water and power to the wastelands of central Nevada—would be extraordinarily expensive in dollars, energy, and resources and would probably create environmental havoc. (Will we justify the rape of Canada's rivers to "colonize" more of our western deserts?)

Moving people to more "habitable" areas, such as the central valley of California or, indeed, most suburbs, exacerbates another serious problem—the paving-over of prime farmland. This is already so serious in California that, if current trends continue, about 50 percent of the best acreage in the nation's leading agricultural state will be destroyed by the year 2020 (*16*). Encouraging that trend hardly seems wise.

Whatever attempts may be made to solve distribution-related problems, they will be undermined if population growth continues, for two reasons. First, population growth and the aggravation of distribution problems are correlated—part of the increase will surely be absorbed in urban areas that can least afford the growth. Indeed, barring the unlikely prompt reversal of present trends, most of it will be absorbed there. Second, population growth puts a disproportionate drain on the very financial resources needed to combat its symptoms. Economist Joseph Spengler has estimated that 4 percent of national income goes to support our 1 percent per year rate of population growth in the United States (*17*). The 4 percent figure now amounts to about $30 billion per year. It seems safe to conclude that the faster we grow the less likely it is that we will find the funds either to alter population distribution patterns or to deal more comprehensively and realistically with our problems.

meaning of environment

Theorem 4 emphasizes the comprehensiveness of the environment crisis. All too many people think in terms of national parks and trout streams when they say "environment." For this reason many of the suppressed people of our nation consider ecology to be just one more "racist shuck" (*18*). They are apathetic or even hostile toward efforts to avert further

263

environmental and sociological deterioration, because they have no reason to believe they will share the fruits of success (*19*). Slums, cockroaches, and rats are ecological problems,. too. The correction of ghetto conditions in Detroit is neither more nor less important than saving the Great Lakes— both are imperative.

We must pay careful attention to sources of conflict both within the United States and between nations. Conflict within the United States blocks progress toward solving our problems; conflict among nations can easily "solve" them once and for all. Recent laboratory studies on human beings support the anecdotal evidence that crowding may increase aggressiveness in human males (*20*). These results underscore long-standing suspicions that population growth, translated through the inevitable uneven distribution into physical crowding, will tend to make the solution of all of our problems more difficult.

As a final example of the need to view "environment" broadly, note that human beings live in an epidemiological environment which deteriorates with crowding and malnutrition—both of which increase with population growth. The hazard posed by the prevalence of these conditions in the world today is compounded by man's unprecedented mobility: potential carriers of diseases of every description move routinely and in substantial numbers from continent to continent in a matter of hours. Nor is there any reason to believe that modern medicine has made widespread plague impossible (*21*). The Asian influenza epidemic of 1968 killed relatively few people only because the virus *happened* to be nonfatal to people in otherwise good health, not because of public health measures. Far deadlier viruses, which easily could be scourges without precedent in the population at large, have on more than one occasion been confined to research workers largely by good luck [for example, the Marburgvirus incident of 1967 (*22*) and the Lassa fever incident of 1970 (*21, 23*)].

solutions: theoretical and practical

Theorem 5 states that theoretical solutions to our problems are often not operational, and sometimes are not solutions. In terms of the problem of feeding the world, for example, technological fixes suffer from limitations in scale, lead time, and cost (*24*). Thus potentially attractive theoretical approaches—such as desalting seawater for agriculture, new irrigation systems, high-protein diet supplements—prove inadequate in practice. They are too little, too late, and too expensive, or they have sociological costs which hobble their effectiveness (*25*). Moreover, many aspects of our technological fixes, such as synthetic organic pesticides and inorganic nitrogen fertilizers, have created vast environmental problems which seem certain to erode global productivity and ecosystem stability (*26*). This is not to say that important gains have not been made through the application of technology to agriculture in the poor countries, or that further technological advances are not worth seeking. But it must be stressed that even the most enlightened technology cannot relieve the necessity of grappling forthrightly and promptly with population growth [as Norman Borlaug aptly observed on being notified of his Nobel Prize for development of the new wheats (*27*)].

Technological attempts to ameliorate the environmental impact of population growth and rising per capita affluence in the developed countries suffer from practical limitations similar to those just mentioned. Not only do such measures tend to be slow, costly, and insufficient in scale, but in addition they most often *shift* our impact rather than remove it. For example, our first generation of smog-control devices increased emissions of oxides of nitrogen while reducing those of hydrocarbons and carbon monoxide. Our unhappiness about eutrophication has led to the replacement of phosphates in detergents with compounds like NTA—nitrilotriacetic acid—which has carcinogenic breakdown products and apparently enhances teratogenic effects of heavy metals (28). And our distaste for lung diseases apparently induced by sulfur dioxide inclines us to accept the hazards of radioactive waste disposal, fuel reprocessing, routine low-level emissions of radiation, and an apparently small but finite risk of catastrophic accidents associated with nuclear fission power plants. Similarly, electric automobiles would simply shift part of the environmental burden of personal transportation from the vicinity of highways to the vicinity of power plants.

We are not suggesting here that electric cars, or nuclear power plants, or substitutes for phosphates are inherently bad. We argue rather that they, too, pose environmental costs which must be weighed against those they eliminate. In many cases the choice is not obvious, and in *all* cases there will be some environmental impact. The residual per capita impact, after all the best choices have been made, must then be multiplied by the population engaging in the activity. If there are too many people, even the most wisely managed technology will not keep the environment from being overstressed.

In contending that a change in the way we use technology will invalidate these arguments, Commoner (2, 8) claims that our important environmental problems began in the 1940's with the introduction and rapid spread of certain "synthetic" technologies: pesticides and herbicides, inorganic fertilizers, plastics, nuclear energy, and high-compression gasoline engines. In so arguing, he appears to make two unfounded assumptions. The first is that man's pre-1940 environmental impact was innocuous and, without changes for the worse in technology, would have remained innocuous even at a much larger population size. The second assumption is that the advent of the new technologies was independent of the attempt to meet human needs and desires in a growing population. Actually, man's record as a simplifier of ecosystems and plunderer of resources can be traced from his probable role in the extinction of many Pleistocene mammals (29), through the destruction of the soils of Mesopotamia by salination and erosion, to the deforestation of Europe in the Middle Ages and the American dustbowls of the 1930's, to cite only some highlights. Man's contemporary arsenal of synthetic technological bludgeons indisputably magnifies the potential for disaster, but these were evolved in some measure to *cope* with population pressures, not independently of them. Moreover, it is worth noting that, of the four environmental threats viewed by the prestigious Williamstown study (15) as globally significant, three are associated with pre-1940 technologies which have simply increased in scale [heavy metals, oil in the seas, and carbon dioxide and particulates in the atmosphere, the latter probably due in considerable part to agriculture (30)]. Surely, then, we can anticipate that supplying food, fiber, and metals for a population even larger than today's will have a profound (and destabilizing) effect on the global ecosystem under *any* set of technological assumptions.

conclusion

John Platt has aptly described man's present predicament as "a storm of crisis problems" (*31*). Complacency concerning any component of these problems—sociological, technological, economic, ecological—is unjustified and counterproductive. It is time to admit that there are no monolithic solutions to the problems we face. Indeed, population control, the redirection of technology, the transition from open to closed resource cycles, the equitable distribution of opportunity and the ingredients of prosperity must *all* be accomplished if there is to be a future worth having. Failure in any of these areas will surely sabotage the entire enterprise.

In connection with the five theorems elaborated here, we have dealt at length with the notion that population growth in industrial nations such as the United States is a minor factor, safely ignored. Those who so argue often add that, anyway, population control would be the slowest to take effect of all possible attacks on our various problems, since the inertia in attitudes and in the age structure of the population is so considerable. To conclude that this means population control should be assigned low priority strikes us as curious logic. Precisely because population is the most difficult and slowest to yield among the components of environmental deterioration, we must start on it at once. To ignore population today because the problem is a tough one is to commit ourselves to even gloomier prospects 20 years hence, when most of the "easy" means to reduce per capita impact on the environment will have been exhausted. The desperate and repressive measures for population control which might be contemplated then are reason in themselves to proceed with foresight, alacrity, and compassion today.

references and notes

1. A. J. Coale, *Science 170,* 132 (1970).
2. B. Commoner, *Saturday Rev. 53,* 50 (1970); *Humanist 30,* 10 (1970).
3. For a general discussion, see P. R. Ehrlich and A. H. Ehrlich, *Population, Resources, Environment* (Freeman, San Francisco, 1970), chap. 7. More technical treatments of the relationship between complexity and stability may be found in R. H. MacArthur, *Ecology 36,* 533 (1955); D. R. Margalef, *Gen. Syst. 3,* 3671 (1958); E. G. Leigh, Jr., *Proc. Nat. Acad. Sci. U.S. 53,* 777 (1965); and O. T. Loucks, "Evolution of diversity, efficiency, and stability of a community," paper delivered at AAAS meeting, Dallas, Texas, 30 Dec. 1968.
4. The figures used in this paragraph are all based on data in *Statistical Abstract of the United States 1970* (U.S. Department of Commerce) (Government Printing Office, Washington, D.C., 1970).
5. A dramatic example of this effect is given in R. Payne's analysis of

the whale fisheries [*N.Y. Zool. Soc. Newsl.* (Nov. 1968)]. The graphs in Payne's paper are reproduced in Ehrlich and Ehrlich (*3*).

6. If N is the number of people, then the number of links is $N(N-1)/2$, and the number of links per capita is $(N-1)/2$.

7. These figures and the others in this paragraph are from *Cleaning Our Environment: The Chemical Basis for Action* (American Chemical Society, Washington, D.C., 1969), pp. 95–162.

8. In his unpublished testimony before the President's Commission on Population Growth and the American Future (17 Nov. 1970), Commoner acknowledged the operation of diminishing returns, threshold effects, and so on. Since such factors apparently do not account for *all* of the increase in per capita impact on the environment in recent decades, however, Commoner drew the unwarranted conclusion that they are negligible.

9. R. Dumont and B. Rosier, *The Hungry Future* (Praeger, New York, 1969), pp. 34–35.

10. L. Brown, *Sci. Amer.* 223, 160 (1970); P. R. Ehrlich, *War on Hunger* 4, 1 (1970).

11. These figures are based on data from the *United Nations Statistical Yearbook 1969* (United Nations, New York, 1969), with estimates added for the consumption by Mainland China when none were included.

12. The notion that dispersed resources, because they have not left the planet, are still available to us, and the hope that mineral supplies can be extended indefinitely by the application of vast amounts of energy to common rock have been the subject of lively debate elsewhere. See, for example, the articles by P. Cloud, T. Lovering, A. Weinberg, *Texas Quart. 11,* 103, 127, 90 (Summer 1968); and *Resources and Man* (National Academy of Sciences) (Freeman, San Francisco, 1969). While the pessimists seem to have had the better of this argument, the entire matter is academic in the context of the rate problem we face in the next 30 years. Over that time period, at least, cost, lead time, and logistics will see to it that industrial economies and dreams of development stand or fall with the availability of high-grade resources.

13. B. Wattenberg, *New Republic 162,* 18 (4 Apr. and 11 Apr. 1970).

14. These figures are from (*11*), from the *FAO Trade Yearbook*, the *FAO Production Yearbook* (United Nations, New York, 1968), and from G. Borgstrom, *Too Many* (Collier-Macmillan, Toronto, Ont., 1969).

15. *Man's Impact on the Global Environment, Report of the Study of Critical Environmental Problems* (M.I.T. Press, Cambridge, Mass., 1970).

16. *A Model of Society, Progress Report of the Environmental Systems Group* (Univ. of California Institute of Ecology, Davis, April 1969).

17. J. J. Spengler, in *Population: The Vital Revolution,* R. Freedman, Ed. (Doubleday, New York, 1964) p. 67.

18. R. Chrisman, *Scanlan's 1,* 46 (August 1970).

19. A more extensive discussion of this point is given in an article by P. R. Ehrlich and A. H. Ehrlich, in *Global Ecology: Readings Toward a Rational Strategy for Man,* J. P. Holdren and P. R. Ehrlich, Eds. (Harcourt, Brace, Jovanovich, New York, in press).

20. J. L. Freedman, A. Levy, J. Price, R. Welte, M. Katz, P. R. Ehrlich, in preparation.
21. J. Lederberg, *Washington Post* (15 Mar. and 22 Mar. 1970).
22. C. Smith, D. Simpson, E. Bowen, I. Zlotnik, *Lancet 1967-II,* 1119, 1128 (1967).
23. Associated Press wire service, 2 Feb. 1970.
24. P. R. Ehrlich and J. P. Holdren, *BioScience 19,* 1065 (1969).
25. See L. Brown [*Seeds of Change* (Praeger, New York, 1970)] for a discussion of unemployment problems exacerbated by the Green Revolution.
26. G. Woodwell, *Science 168,* 429 (1970).
27. *New York Times,* 22 Oct. 1970, p. 18; *Newsweek 76,* 50 (2 Nov. 1970).
28. S. S. Epstein, *Environment 12,* No. 7, 2 (Sept. 1970); *New York Times* service, 17 Nov. 1970.
29. G. S. Krantz, *Amer. Sci. 58,* 164 (Mar.-Apr. 1970).
30. R. A. Bryson and W. M. Wendland, in *Global Effects of Environmental Pollution,* S. F. Singer, Ed. (Springer-Verlag, New York, 1970).
31. J. Platt, *Science 166,* 1115 (1969).

the tragedy of the commons

garrett hardin

The population problem has no technical solution: it requires a fundamental extension in morality.

At the end of a thoughtful article on the future of nuclear war, Wiesner and York[1] concluded that: "Both sides in the arms race are . . . confronted by the dilemma of steadily increasing military power and steadily decreasing national security. *It is our considered professional judgment that this dilemma has no technical solution.* If the great powers continue to look for solutions in the area of science and technology only, the result will be to worsen the situation."

I would like to focus your attention not on the subject of the article (national security in a nuclear world) but on the kind of conclusion they reached, namely that there is no technical solution to the problem. An implicit and almost universal assumption of discussions published in professional and semipopular scientific journals is that the problem under discussion has a technical solution. A technical solution may be defined as one that requires a change only in the techniques of the natural sciences, demanding little or nothing in the way of change in human values or ideas of morality.

In our day (though not in earlier times) technical solutions are always welcome. Because of previous failures in prophecy, it takes courage to assert that a desired technical solution is not possible. Wiesner and York exhibited this courage; publishing in a science journal, they insisted that the solution to the problem was not to be found in the natural sciences. They cautiously qualified their statement with the phrase, "It is our considered professional judgement. . . ." Whether they were right or not is not the concern of the present article. Rather, the concern here is with the important concept of a class of human problems which can be called "no technical solution problems," and, more specifically, with the identification and discussion of one of these.

Reprinted from *Science*, Vol. 162, 23 December 1968, pp. 1243-1248. Copyright 1970 by the American Association for the Advancement of Science. This article is based on a presidential address presented before the meeting of the Pacific Division of the American Association for the Advancement of Science at Utah State University, Logan, 25 June 1968. The author is professor of biology, University of California, Santa Barbara.

It is easy to show that the class is not a null class. Recall the game of tick-tack-toe. Consider the problem, "How can I win the game of tick-tack-toe?" It is well known that I cannot, if I assume (in keeping with the conventions of game theory) that my opponent understands the game perfectly. Put another way, there is no "technical solution" to the problem. I can win only by giving a radical meaning to the word "win." I can hit my opponent over the head; or I can drug him; or I can falsify the records. Every way in which I "win" involves, in some sense, an abandonment of the game, as we intuitively understand it. (I can also, of course, openly abandon the game—refuse to play it. This is what most adults do.)

The class of "No technical solution problems" has members. My thesis is that the "population problem," as conventionally conceived, is a member of this class. How it is conventionally conceived needs some comment. It is fair to say that most people who anguish over the population problem are trying to find a way to avoid the evils of over-population without relinquishing any of the privileges they now enjoy. They think that farming the seas or developing new strains of wheat will solve the problem—technologically. I try to show here that the solution they seek cannot be found. The population problem cannot be solved in a technical way, any more than can the problem of winning the game of tick-tack-toe.

what shall we maximize?

Population, as Malthus said, naturally tends to grow "geometrically," or, as we would now say, exponentially. In a finite world this means that the per capita share of the world's goods must steadily decrease. Is ours a finite world?

A fair defense can be put forward for the view that the world is infinite; or that we do not know that it is not. But, in terms of the practical problems that we must face in the next few generations with the foreseeable technology, it is clear that we will greatly increase human misery if we do not, during the immediate future, assume that the world available to the terrestrial human population is finite. "Space" is no escape.[2]

A finite world can support only a finite population; therefore, population growth must eventually equal zero. (The case of perpetual wide fluctuations above and below zero is a trivial variant that need not be discussed.) When this condition is met, what will be the situation of mankind? Specifically, can Bentham's goal of "the greatest good for the greatest number" be realized?

No—for two reasons, each sufficient by itself. The first is a theoretical one. It is not mathematically possible to maximize for two (or more) variables at the same time. This was clearly stated by von Neumann and Morgenstern,[3] but the principle is implicit in the theory of partial differential equations, dating back at least to D'Alembert (1717–1783).

The second reason springs directly from biological facts. To live, any organism must have a source of energy (for example, food). This energy is utilized for two purposes: mere maintenance and work. For man, maintenance of life requires about 1600 kilo-calories a day ("maintenance calories"). Anything that he does over and above merely staying alive will be defined as work, and is supported by "work calories" which he takes in. Work calories are used not only for what we call work in common speech; they are also required for all forms of enjoyment, from swimming and automobile racing to playing music and writing poetry. If our goal is to maximize population it is obvious what we must do: We must make the work calories per person approach as close to zero as possible. No gourmet meals, no vacations, no sports, no music, no literature, no art. . . . I think that everyone will grant, without argument or proof, that maximizing population does not maximize goods. Bentham's goal is impossible.

In reaching this conclusion I have made the usual assumption that it is the acquisition of energy that is the problem. The appearance of atomic energy has led some to question this assumption. However, given an infinite source of energy, population growth still produces an inescapable problem. The problem of the acquisition of energy is replaced by the problem of its dissipation, as J. H. Fremlin has so wittily shown.[4] The arithmetic signs in the analysis are, as it were, reversed; but Bentham's goal is still unobtainable.

The optimum population is, then, less than the maximum. The difficulty of defining the optimum is enormous; so far as I know, no one has seriously tackled this problem. Reaching an acceptable and stable solution will surely require more than one generation of hard analytical work—and much persuasion.

We want the maximum good per person; but what is good? To one person it is wilderness, to another it is ski lodges for thousands. To one it is estuaries to nourish ducks for hunters to shoot; to another it is factory land. Comparing one good with another is, we usually say, impossible because goods are incommensurable. Incommensurables cannot be compared.

Theoretically this may be true; but in real life incommensurables *are* commensurable. Only a criterion of judgment and a system of weighing are needed. In nature the criterion is survival. Is it better for a species to be small and hideable, or large and powerful? Natural selection commensurates the incommensurables. The compromise achieved depends on a natural weighting of the values of the variables.

Man must imitate this process. There is no doubt that in fact he already does, but unconsciously. It is when the hidden decisions are made explicit that the arguments begin. The problem for the years ahead is to work out an acceptable theory of weighting. Synergistic effects, nonlinear variation, and difficulties in discounting the future make the intellectual problem difficult, but not (in principle) insoluble.

Has any cultural group solved this practical problem at the present time, even on an intuitive level? One simple fact proves that none has: there is no prosperous population in the world today that has, and has had for some time, a growth rate of zero. Any people that has intuitively identified its optimum point will soon reach it, after which its growth rate becomes and remains zero.

Of course, a positive growth rate might be taken as evidence that a population is below its optimum. However, by any reasonable standards, the most rapidly growing populations on earth today are (in general) the most miserable. This association (which need not be invariable) casts doubt on the optimistic assumption that the positive growth rate of a population is evidence that it has yet to reach its optimum.

We can make little progress in working toward optimum population size until we explicitly exorcize the spirit of Adam Smith in the field of practical demography. In economic affairs, *The Wealth of Nations* (1776) popularized the "invisible hand," the idea that an individual who "intends only his own gain," is, as it were, "led by an invisible hand to promote . . . the public interest."[5] Adam Smith did not assert that this was invariably true, and perhaps neither did any of his followers. But he contributed to a dominant tendency of thought that has ever since interfered with positive action based on rational analysis, namely, the tendency to assume that decisions reached individually will, in fact, be the best decisions for an entire society. If this assumption is correct it justifies the continuance of our present policy of laissez-faire in reproduction. If it is correct we can assume that men will control their individual fecundity so as to produce the optimum population. If the assumption is not correct, we need to reexamine our individual freedoms to see which ones are defensible.

tragedy of freedom in a commons

The rebuttal to the invisible hand in population control is to be found in a scenario first sketched in a little-known pamphlet[6] in 1833 by a mathematical amateur named William Forster Lloyd (1794–1852). We may well call it "the tragedy of the commons," using the word "tragedy" as the philosopher Whitehead used it:[7] "The essence of dramatic tragedy is not unhappiness. It resides in the solemnity of the remorseless working of things." He then goes on to say, "This inevitableness of destiny can only be illustrated in terms of human life by incidents which in fact involve unhappiness. For it is only by them that the futility of escape can be made evident in the drama."

The tragedy of the commons develops in this way. Picture a pasture open to all. It is to be expected that each herdsman will try to keep as many cattle as possible on the commons. Such an arrangement may work reasonably satisfactorily for centuries because tribal wars, poaching, and disease keep the numbers of both man and beast well below the carrying capacity of the land. Finally, however, comes the day of reckoning, that is, the day when the long-desired goal of social stability becomes a reality. At this point, the inherent logic of the commons remorselessly generates tragedy.

As a rational being, each herdsman seeks to maximize his gain. Explicitly or implicitly, more or less consciously, he asks, "What is the utility *to me* of adding one more animal to my herd?" This utility has one negative and one positive component.

1. The positive component is a function of the increment of one animal. Since the herdsman receives all the proceeds from the sale of the additional animal, the positive utility is nearly $+1$.

2. The negative component is a function of the additional overgrazing created by one more animal. Since, however, the effects of overgrazing

are shared by all the herdsmen, the negative utility for any particular decision-making herdsman is only a fraction of –1.

Adding together the component partial utilities, the rational herdsman concludes that the only sensible course for him to pursue is to add another animal to his herd. And another; and another. . . . But this is the conclusion reached by each and every rational herdsman sharing a commons. Therein is the tragedy. Each man is locked into a system that compels him to increase his herd without limit—in a world that is limited. Ruin is the destination toward which all men rush, each pursuing his own best interest in a society that believes in the freedom of the commons. Freedom in a commons brings ruin to all.

Some would say that this is a platitude. Would that it were! In a sense, it was learned thousands of years ago, but natural selection favors the forces of psychological denial.[8] The individual benefits as an individual from his ability to deny the truth even though society as a whole, of which he is a part, suffers. Education can counteract the natural tendency to do the wrong thing, but the inexorable succession of generations requires that the basis for this knowledge be constantly refreshed.

A simple incident that occurred a few years ago in Leominster, Massachusetts, shows how perishable the knowledge is. During the Christmas shopping season the parking meters downtown were covered with plastic bags that bore tags reading: "Do not open until after Christmas. Free parking courtesy of the mayor and city council." In other words, facing the prospect of an increased demand for already scarce space, the city fathers reinstituted the system of the commons. (Cynically, we suspect that they gained more votes than they lost by this retrogressive act.)

In an approximate way, the logic of the commons has been understood for a long time, perhaps since the discovery of agriculture or the invention of private property in real estate. But it is understood mostly only in special cases which are not sufficiently generalized. Even at this late date, cattlemen leasing national land on the western ranges demonstrate no more than an ambivalent understanding, in constantly pressuring federal authorities to increase the head count to the point where overgrazing produces erosion and weed dominance. Likewise, the oceans of the world continue to suffer from the survival of the philosophy of the commons. Maritime nations still respond automatically to the shibboleth of the "freedom of the seas." Professing to believe in the "inexhaustible resources of the oceans," they bring species after species of fish and whales closer to extinction.[9]

The National Parks present another instance of the working out of the tragedy of the commons. At present, they are open to all, without limit. The parks themselves are limited in extent—there is only one Yosemite Valley—whereas population seems to grow without limit. The values that visitors seek in the parks are steadily eroded. Plainly, we must soon cease to treat the parks as commons or they will be of no value to anyone.

What shall we do? We have several options. We might sell them off as private property. We might keep them as public property, but allocate the right to enter them. The allocation might be on the basis of wealth, by the use of an auction system. It might be on the basis of merit, as defined by some agreed-upon standards. It might be by lottery. Or it might be on a first-come, first-served basis, administered to long queues. These,

I think, are all the reasonable possibilities. They are all objectionable. But we must choose—or acquiesce in the destruction of the commons that we call our National Parks.

pollution

In a reverse way, the tragedy of the commons reappears in problems of pollution. Here it is not a question of taking something out of the commons, but of putting something in—sewage, or chemical, radioactive, and heat wastes into water; noxious and dangerous fumes into the air; and distracting and unpleasant advertising signs into the line of sight. The calculations of utility are much the same as before. The rational man finds that his share of the cost of the wastes he discharges into the commons is less than the cost of purifying his wastes before releasing them. Since this is true for everyone, we are locked into a system of "fouling our own nest," so long as we behave only as independent, rational, free-enterprisers.

The tragedy of the commons as a food basket is averted by private property, or something formally like it. But the air and waters surrounding us cannot readily be fenced, and so the tragedy of the commons as a cesspool must be prevented by different means, by coercive laws or taxing devices that make it cheaper for the polluter to treat his pollutants than to discharge them untreated. We have not progressed as far with the solution of this problem as we have with the first. Indeed, our particular concept of private property, which deters us from exhausting the positive resources of the earth, favors pollution. The owner of a factory on the bank of a stream—whose property extends to the middle of the stream—often has difficulty seeing why it is not his natural right to muddy the waters flowing past his door. The law, always behind the times, requires elaborate stitching and fitting to adapt it to this newly perceived aspect of the commons.

The pollution problem is a consequence of population. It did not much matter how a lonely American frontiersman disposed of his waste. "Flowing water purifies itself every 10 miles," my grandfather used to say, and the myth was near enough to the truth when he was a boy, for there were not too many people. But as population became denser, the natural chemical and biological recycling processes became overloaded, calling for a redefinition of property rights.

how to legislate temperance?

Analysis of the pollution problem as a function of population density uncovers a not generally recognized principle of morality, namely: *the morality of an act is a function of the state of the system at the time it is performed.*[10] Using the commons as a cesspool does not harm the general public under frontier conditions, because there is no public; the same behavior in a metropolis is unbearable. A hundred and fifty years ago a plainsman could kill an American bison, cut out only the tongue for his dinner, and discard the rest of the animal. He was not in any important sense being wasteful. Today, with only a few thousand bison left, we would be appalled at such behavior.

In passing, it is worth noting that the morality of an act cannot be

274

determined from a photograph. One does not know whether a man killing an elephant or setting fire to the grassland is harming others until one knows the total system in which his act appears. "One picture is worth a thousand words," said an ancient Chinese; but it may take 10,000 words to validate it. It is as tempting to ecologists as it is to reformers in general to try to persuade others by way of the photographic shortcut. But the essence of an argument cannot be photographed: it must be presented rationally—in words.

That morality is system-sensitive escaped the attention of most codifiers of ethics in the past. "Thou shalt not . . ." is the form of traditional ethical directives which make no allowance for particular circumstances. The laws of our society follow the pattern of ancient ethics, and therefore are poorly suited to governing a complex, crowded, changeable world. Our epicyclic solution is to augment statutory law with administrative law. Since it is practically impossible to spell out all the conditions under which it is safe to burn trash in the back yard or to run an automobile without smog-control, by law we delegate the details to bureaus. The result is administrative law, which is rightly feared for an ancient reason—*Quis custodiet ipsos custodes?* "Who shall watch the watchers themselves?" John Adams said that we must have "a government of laws and not men." Bureau administrators, trying to evaluate the morality of acts in the total system, are singularly liable to corruption, producing a government by men, not laws.

Prohibition is easy to legislate (though not necessarily to enforce); but how do we legislate temperance? Experience indicates that it can be accomplished best through the mediation of administrative law. We limit possibilities unnecessarily if we suppose that the sentiment of *Quis custodiet* denies us the use of administrative law. We should rather retain the phrase as a perpetual reminder of fearful dangers we cannot avoid. The great challenge facing us now is to invent the corrective feedbacks that are needed to keep custodians honest. We must find ways to legitimate the needed authority of both the custodians and the corrective feedbacks.

freedom to breed is intolerable

The tragedy of the commons is involved in population problems in another way. In a world governed solely by the principle of "dog eat dog"—if indeed there ever was such a world—how many children a family had would not be a matter of public concern. Parents who bred too exuberantly would leave fewer descendants, not more, because they would be unable to care adequately for their children. David Lack and others have found that such a negative feedback demonstrably controls the fecundity of birds.[11] But men are not birds, and have not acted like them for millenniums, at least.

If each human family were dependent only on its own resources; *if* the children of improvident parents starved to death; *if*, thus, overbreeding brought its own "punishment" to the germ line—*then* there would be no public interest in controlling the breeding of families. But our society is deeply committed to the welfare state,[12] and hence is confronted with another aspect of the tragedy of the commons.

In a welfare state, how shall we deal with the family, the religion, the race, or the class (or indeed any distinguishable and cohesive group) that

275

adopts overbreeding as a policy to secure its own aggrandizement[13]? To couple the concept of freedom to breed with the belief that everyone born has an equal right to the commons is to lock the world into a tragic course of action.

Unfortunately this is just the course of action that is being pursued by the United Nations. In late 1967, some 30 nations agreed to the following:[14]

> *The Universal Declaration of Human Rights describes the family as the natural and fundamental unit of society. It follows that any choice and decision with regard to the size of the family must irrevocably rest with the family itself, and cannot be made by someone else.*

It is painful to have to deny categorically the validity of this right; denying it, one feels as uncomfortable as a resident of Salem, Massachusetts, who denied the reality of witches in the 17th century. At the present time, in liberal quarters, something like a taboo acts to inhibit criticism of the United Nations. There is a feeling that the United Nations is "our last and best hope," that we shouldn't find fault with it; we shouldn't play into the hands of the archconservatives. However, let us not forget what Robert Louis Stevenson said: "The truth that is suppressed by friends is the readiest weapon of the enemy." If we love the truth we must openly deny the validity of the Universal Declaration of Human Rights, even though it is promoted by the United Nations. We should also join with Kingsley Davis[15] in attempting to get Planned Parenthood-World Population to see the error of its ways in embracing the same tragic ideal.

conscience is self-eliminating

It is a mistake to think that we can control the breeding of mankind in the long run by an appeal to conscience. Charles Galton Darwin made this point when he spoke on the centennial of the publication of his grandfather's great book. The argument is straight-forward and Darwinian.

People vary. Confronted with appeals to limit breeding, some people will undoubtedly respond to the plea more than others. Those who have more children will produce a larger fraction of the next generation than those with more susceptible consciences. The difference will be accentuated, generation by generation.

In C. G. Darwin's words: "It may well be that it would take hundreds of generations for the progenitive instinct to develop in this way, but if it should do so, nature would have taken her revenge, and the variety *Homo contracipiens* would become extinct and would be replaced by the variety *Homo progenitivus.*"[16]

The argument assumes that conscience or the desire for children (no matter which) is hereditary—but hereditary only in the most general formal sense. The result will be the same whether the attitude is transmitted through germ cells, or exosomatically, to use A. J. Lotka's term. (If one denies the latter possibility as well as the former, then what's the point of education?) The argument has here been stated in the context of the population problem, but it applies equally well to any instance in which society appeals to an individual exploiting a commons to restrain himself for the general good—by means of his conscience. To make such an appeal is to set up a selective system that works toward the elimination of conscience from the race.

pathogenic effects of conscience

The long-term disadvantage of an appeal to conscience should be enough to condemn it; but it has serious short-term disadvantages as well. If we ask a man who is exploiting a commons to desist "in the name of conscience," what are we saying to him? What does he hear?—not only at the moment but also in the wee small hours of the night when, half asleep, he remembers not merely the words we used but also the nonverbal communication cues we gave him unawares? Sooner or later, consciously or subconsciously, he senses that he has received two communications, and that they are contradictory: (i) (intended communication) "If you don't do as we ask, we will openly condemn you for not acting like a responsible citizen"; (ii) (the unintended communication) "If you *do* behave as we ask, we will secretly condemn you for a simpleton who can be shamed into standing aside while the rest of us exploit the commons."

Everyman then is caught in what Bateson has called a "double bind." Bateson and his co-workers have made a plausible case for viewing the double bind as an important causative factor in the genesis of schizophrenia.[17] The double bind may not always be so damaging, but it always endangers the mental health of anyone to whom it is applied. "A bad conscience," said Nietzsche, "is a kind of illness."

To conjure up a conscience in others is tempting to anyone who wishes to extend his control beyond the legal limits. Leaders at the highest level succumb to this temptation. Has any President during the past generation failed to call on labor unions to moderate voluntarily their demands for higher wages, or to steel companies to honor voluntary guidelines on prices? I can recall none. The rhetoric used on such occasions is designed to produce feelings of guilt in noncooperators.

For centuries it was assumed without proof that guilt was a valuable, perhaps even an indispensible, ingredient of the civilized life. Now, in this post-Freudian world, we doubt it.

Paul Goodman speaks from the modern point of view when he says: "No good has ever come from feeling guilty, neither intelligence, policy, nor compassion. The guilty do not pay attention to the object but only to themselves, and not even to their own interests, which might make sense, but to their anxieties."[18]

One does not have to be a professional psychiatrist to see the consequences of anxiety. We in the Western world are just emerging from a dreadful two-centuries-long Dark Ages of Eros that was sustained partly by prohibition laws, but perhaps more effectively by the anxiety-generating mechanisms of education. Alex Comfort has told the story well in *The Anxiety Makers;*[19] it is not a pretty one.

Since proof is difficult, we may even concede that the results of anxiety may sometimes, from certain points of view, be desirable. The larger question we should ask is whether, as a matter of policy, we should ever encourage the use of a technique the tendency (if not the intention) of

277

which is psychologically pathogenic. We hear much talk these days of responsible parenthood; the coupled words are incorporated into the titles of some organizations devoted to birth control. Some people have proposed massive propaganda campaigns to instill responsibility into the nation's (or the world's) breeders. But what is the meaning of the word responsibility in this context? It is not merely a synonym for the word conscience? When we use the word responsibility in the absence of substantial sanctions are we not trying to browbeat a free man in a commons into acting against his own interest? Responsibility is a verbal counterfeit for a substantial *quid pro quo*. It is an attempt to get something for nothing.

If the word responsibility is to be used at all, I suggest that it be in the sense Charles Frankel uses it.[20] "Responsibility," says this philosopher, "is the product of definite social arrangements." Notice that Frankel calls for social arrangements—not propaganda.

mutual coercion mutually agreed upon

The social arrangements that produce responsibility are arrangements that create coercion, of some sort. Consider bank-robbing. The man who takes money from a bank acts as if the bank were a commons. How do we prevent such action? Certainly not by trying to control his behavior solely by a verbal appeal to his sense of responsibility. Rather than rely on propaganda we follow Frankel's lead and insist that a bank is not a commons; we seek the definite social arrangements that will keep it from becoming a commons. That we thereby infringe on the freedom of would-be robbers we neither deny nor regret.

The morality of bank-robbing is particularly easy to understand because we accept complete prohibition of this activity. We are willing to say "Thou shalt not rob banks," without providing for exceptions. But temperance also can be created by coercion. Taxing is a good coercive device. To keep downtown shoppers temperate in their use of parking space we introduce parking meters for short periods, and traffic fines for longer ones. We need not actually forbid a citizen to park as long as he wants to; we need merely make it increasingly expensive for him to do so. Not prohibition, but carefully biased options are what we offer him. A Madison Avenue man might call this persuasion; I prefer the greater candor of the word coercion.

Coercion is a dirty word to most liberals now, but it need not forever be so. As with the four-letter words, its dirtiness can be cleansed away by exposure to the light, by saying it over and over without apology or embarrassment. To many, the word coercion implies arbitrary decisions of distant and irresponsible bureaucrats; but this is not a necessary part of its meaning. The only kind of coercion I recommend is mutual coercion, mutually agreed upon by the majority of the people affected.

To say that we mutually agree to coercion is not to say that we are required to enjoy it, or even to pretend we enjoy it. Who enjoys taxes? We all grumble about them. But we accept compulsory taxes because we recognize that voluntary taxes would favor the conscienceless. We institute and (grumblingly) support taxes and other coercive devices to escape the horror of the commons.

An alternative to the commons need not be perfectly just to be preferable.

With real estate and other material goods, the alternative we have chosen is the institution of private property coupled with legal inheritance. Is this system perfectly just? As a genetically trained biologist I deny that it is. It seems to me that, if there are to be differences in individual inheritance, legal possession should be perfectly correlated with biological inheritance—that those who are biologically more fit to be the custodians of property and power should legally inherit more. But genetic recombination continually makes a mockery of the doctrine of "like father, like son" implicit in our laws of legal inheritance. An idiot can inherit millions, and a trust fund can keep his estate intact. We must admit that our legal system of private property plus inheritance is unjust—but we put up with it because we are not convinced, at the moment, that anyone has invented a better system. The alternative of the commons is too horrifying to contemplate. Injustice is preferable to total ruin.

It is one of the peculiarities of the warfare between reform and the status quo that it is thoughtlessly governed by a double standard. Whenever a reform measure is proposed it is often defeated when its opponents triumphantly discover a flaw in it. As Kingsley Davis has pointed out,[21] worshippers of the status quo sometimes imply that no reform is possible without unanimous agreement, an implication contrary to historical fact. As nearly as I can make out, automatic rejection of proposed reforms is based on one of two unconscious assumptions: (i) that the status quo is perfect; or (ii) that the choice we face is between reform and no action; if the proposed reform is imperfect, we presumably should take no action at all, while we wait for a perfect proposal.

But we can never do nothing. That which we have done for thousands of years is also action. It also produces evils. Once we are aware that the status quo is action, we can then compare its discoverable advantages and disadvantages with the predicted advantages and disadvantages of the proposed reform, discounting as best we can for our lack of experience. On the basis of such a comparison, we can make a rational decision which will not involve the unworkable assumption that only perfect systems are tolerable.

recognition of necessity

Perhaps the simplest summary of this analysis of man's population problems is this: the commons, if justifiable at all, is justifiable only under conditions of low-population density. As the human population has increased, the commons has had to be abandoned in one aspect after another.

First we abandoned the commons in food gathering, enclosing farm land and restricting pastures and hunting and fishing areas. These restrictions are still not complete throughout the world.

Somewhat later we saw that the commons as a place for waste disposal would also have to be abandoned. Restrictions on the disposal of domestic sewage are widely accepted in the Western world; we are still struggling to close the commons to pollution by automobiles, factories, insecticide sprayers, fertilizing operations, and atomic energy installations.

In a still more embryonic state is our recognition of the evils of the

279

commons in matters of pleasure. There is almost no restriction on the propagation of sound waves in the public medium. The shopping public is assaulted with mindless music, without its consent. Our government is paying out billions of dollars to create supersonic transport which will disturb 50,000 people for every one person who is whisked from coast to coast 3 hours faster. Advertisers muddy the airwaves of radio and television and pollute the view of travelers. We are a long way from outlawing the commons in matters of pleasure. Is this because our Puritan inheritance makes us view pleasure as something of a sin, and pain (that is, the pollution of advertising) as the sign of virtue?

Every new enclosure of the commons involves the infringement of somebody's personal liberty. Infringements made in the distant past are accepted because no contemporary complains of a loss. It is the newly proposed infringements that we vigorously oppose; cries of "rights" and "freedom" fill the air. But what does "freedom" mean? When men mutually agreed to pass laws against robbing, mankind became more free, not less so. Individuals locked into the logic of the commons are free only to bring on universal ruin; once they see the necessity of mutual coercion, they become free to pursue other goals. I believe it was Hegel who said, "Freedom is the recognition of necessity."

The most important aspect of necessity that we must now recognize, is the necessity of abandoning the commons in breeding. No technical solution can rescue us from the misery of overpopulation. Freedom to breed will bring ruin to all. At the moment, to avoid hard decisions many of us are tempted to propagandize for conscience and responsible parenthood. The temptation must be resisted, because an appeal to independently acting consciences selects for the disappearance of all conscience in the long run, and an increase in anxiety in the short.

The only way we can preserve and nurture other and more precious freedoms is by relinquishing the freedom to breed, and that very soon. "Freedom is the recognition of necessity"—and it is the role of education to reveal to all the necessity of abandoning the freedom to breed. Only so, can we put an end to this aspect of the tragedy of the commons.

references

1. J. B. Wiesner and H. F. York, *Sci. Amer.* **211** (No. 4), 27 (1964).
2. G. Hardin, *J. Hered.* **50,** 68 (1959); S. von Hoernor, *Science* **137,** 18 (1962).
3. J. von Neumann and O. Morgenstern. *Theory of Games and Economic Behavior* (Princeton Univ. Press, Princeton, N.J., 1947), p. 11.
4. J. H. Fremlin, *New Sci.,* No. 415 (1964), p. 285.
5. A. Smith, *The Wealth of Nations* (Modern Library, New York, 1937), p. 423.
6. W. F. Lloyd, *Two Lectures on the Checks to Population* (Oxford Univ. Press, Oxford, England, 1833), reprinted (in part) in *Population, Evolution, and Birth Control,* G. Hardin, Ed. (Freeman, San Francisco, 1964), p. 37.
7. A. N. Whitehead, *Science and the Modern World* (Mentor, New York, 1948), p. 17.

8. G. Hardin, Ed. *Population, Evolution, and Birth Control* (Freeman, San Francisco, 1964), p. 56.
9. S. McVay, *Sci. Amer.* **216** (No. 8), 13 (1966).
10. J. Fletcher, *Situation Ethics* (Westminster, Philadelphia, 1966).
11. D. Lack, *The Natural Regulation of Animal Numbers* (Clarendon Press, Oxford, 1954).
12. H. Girvetz, *From Wealth to Welfare* (Stanford Univ. Press, Stanford, Calif., 1950).
13. G. Hardin, *Perspec. Biol. Med.* **6,** 366 (1963).
14. U. Thant, *Int. Planned Parenthood News,* No. 168 (February 1968), p. 3.
15. K. Davis, *Science* **158,** 730 (1967).
16. S. Tax, Ed., *Evolution after Darwin* (Univ. of Chicago Press, Chicago, 1960), vol. 2, p. 469.
17. G. Bateson, D. D. Jackson, J. Haley, J. Weakland, *Behav. Sci.* **1,** 251 (1956).
18. P. Goodman, *New York Rev. Books* **10**(8), 22 (23 May 1968).
19. A. Comfort, *The Anxiety Makers* (Nelson, London, 1967).
20. C. Frankel, *The Case for Modern Man* (Harper, New York, 1955), p. 203.
21. J. D. Roslansky, *Genetics and the Future of Man* (Appleton-Century-Crofts, New York, 1966), p. 177.

energy— the basic resource

In this section, we will specifically be talking about *useful energy*—energy that can be harnessed to run machines. Electrical energy, the chemical energy of fuels, and the energy of falling water are examples of useful energy. Useful energy must be distinguished from the more abundant *heat energy*, which warms the environment but is most often useless for the running of machinery. Heat energy is very often a by-product of the generation of useful energy, in which case it is called *thermal pollution.*

Useful energy is one of man's essential resources. It is central among resources because it is needed to run machines, either animal or mechanical, that extract and utilize all other resources. It is also required for the recycling of other resources.

Useful energy itself is the one resource that cannot be recycled. According to the laws of thermodynamics which govern the behavior of energy, useful energy is converted to heat as it does work, and in effect it can never be recovered to do work again. For this reason, we must husband our sources of energy more jealously than any other resource, and we must use utmost care in formulating energy policies for the future lest we someday run out of practical energy sources. Running out is unlikely for the immediate future, but should it occur it would mark the end of civilization.

Man's useful energy is generated mainly by energy-yielding chemical changes (the combustion of fuel) or by the splitting of atoms (nuclear fission). The altered molecules and atoms produced in these processes frequently escape to the surroundings, where they create a large proportion of the total adverse change in the chemical environment of earth. Sulfur dioxide (SO_2), the oxides of nitrogen (NO and NO_2), carbon dioxide (CO_2), and radioactive isotopes are the major chemical wastes. Because thermal pollution accompanies the production and use of energy, it is no wonder that energy production and pollution are so often regarded as synonymous. This further complicates energy management, for we must be concerned about pollution side-effects as well as about the sufficiency of energy itself. Truly energy is a resource of critical environmental concern, a concern reflected in the following articles.

In Article 41, "Continuing Increase in Use of Energy," Philip H. Abelson provides a short overview of energy excesses, repercussions, and cures. Irving Bengelsdorf then summarizes the use and future potential of various sources of energy in Article 42, "Are We Running Out of Fuel?" In Article 43, "Defusing Old Smoky by Plugging into Nature," John Holdren examines the hopeful prospects for tapping direct solar energy (and several lesser sources). Article 44, "Fuels Management in an Environmental Age," is a detailed account by G. Alex Mills, Harry R. Johnson, and Harry Perry on techniques we must use in extracting, altering, and using existing fuels to minimize environmental impact.

We then turn more specifically to important aspects of electrical energy. In Article 45, "Electrical Heating and Thermal Pollution," F. T. Wall shows that electrical heat is *not* clean heat when all environmental consequences are considered. The subject of growth in the electrical power industry along with the implications of continued growth are treated skillfully by Daniel B. Luten in Article 46, "The Electrical Power Industry: Its Prospects for Growth."

Finally in Article 47, "The Power Crisis That Threatens the World," Isaac Asimov tells us about nuclear fusion energy, its prospects for development, and the reasons it is the most logical fuel for man's long-term future. This article forms a bridge to the next section, which treats our nuclear future in detail.

continuing increase in use of energy

philip h. abelson

Atmospheric pollution is not an inevitable consequence of production of energy.

Consumption of energy is the principal source of air pollution, and energy production, transportation, and consumption are responsible for an important fraction of all our environmental problems. Use of energy continues to rise at the rate of 4.5 percent per year. Even if fuel supplies were infinite, such an increase could not be tolerated indefinitely. But fuel supplies are not inexhaustible, and this combined with the need to preserve the environment will force changes in patterns of energy production and use.

Our economy has been geared to profligate expenditure of energy and resources. Much of our pollution problem would disappear if we drove 1-ton instead of 2-ton automobiles. Demand for space heat and cooling could be reduced if buildings were properly insulated. Examples of needless use of electricity are everywhere. Promotional rates and advertising tend to encourage excessive consumption.

Slowing down the rate of increase in use of energy will not be easy. Public habits of energy consumption will not be quickly altered, and a sudden change in the rate of growth of energy consumption would cause major additional unemployment.

Most people are at least somewhat aware that their consumption of various forms of energy adds to pollution. Yet despite all the publicity and exhortations, little effect has been noted in overall energy consumption. Increase in use of energy has not abated. Some signs of impact can be detected. Sales of smaller automobiles have increased somewhat. However, the rate of increase of "clean" electricity was 6 percent last year in spite of brownouts and the economic recession. Consumption of natural gas in the production of electricity rose 11 percent, reflecting in part a desire to use cleaner fuel.

A major factor in the burgeoning use of energy is its low price—one that does not take into account all the costs to society. In the generation of electric power from coal and oil, millions of tons of sulfur dioxide are released, which cause billions of dollars worth of damage to health and property. We are consuming rapidly, at ridiculously low prices, natural gas reserves that accumulated during millions of years. Prices for energy should reflect their full cost to society. The Nixon Adminstration's proposed tax on sulfur in fuel should be enacted. The rate structure for electric power should be modified to discourage excessive use. A substantial increase in the price of natural gas, including a new federal tax, would diminish waste of this resource. Taxes on automobiles should increase sharply with weight and horsepower.

Measures to cut excessive use of energy are likely to come only after a long time, if ever. We should face the possibility that increased consumption of energy will continue and prepare to meet that possibility. Atmospheric pollution is not an inevitable consequence of production of energy. In the use of fossil fuels, production of sulfur dioxide is not an essential by-product. Destruction of the environment is not a necessary consequence of strip mining. Pollution from almost every method of producing and utilizing energy could be sharply attenuated either through better practices or through development of new methods. In view of the importance of energy to society, present expenditures on research and development related to energy are small and these are not well apportioned. Two areas that particularly merit increases in support are thermonuclear research and development of pollution-free means of using coal for electricity, liquid fuels, and methane.

are we running out of fuel?

irving bengelsdorf

All our energy comes from the sun in the form of two energy bank accounts: A renewable account in which energy deposits are made every day, and a nonrenewable account that has a fixed energy deposit which we continuously deplete by our withdrawals.

Love is not all it takes to make the world go round; it also takes energy. Man's pursuit of energy sources has profoundly affected the course of history, it has created severe social problems, and now it threatens our very survival.

The development of agriculture by early hunting and foraging man provided a reliable, steady energy source which allowed civilizations and populations to grow and flourish. It is estimated that without agriculture our planet could support a human population of only about 10 million. This is fewer people than live in London or the entire country of Kenya, and it is only about three-tenths of one percent of the present human population of 3.6 billion.

As man's numbers have increased, so have his energy, or fuel, demands (the words "energy" and "fuel" may be used interchangeably). The insatiable demand for more and more energy by densely populated technological societies is now ripping the thin veneer of our global environment. Moreover, as the aspirations of the so-called underdeveloped nations mount, demands for increased amounts of energy inevitably accompany them.

Consumption of energy pollutes and warms the air above us and the seas around us; it spreads disease and destroys the aesthetic values of land. Men in general, and Americans in particular, are energy profligates and wastrels. We now are engaged in an unprecedented energy-consuming spree.

Though coal has been mined for 800 years, one-half of it has been dug

Reprinted from the February-March, 1971 issued of *National Wildlife Magazine*, pp. 4–8. Copyright 1971 by the National Wildlife Federation. The author, former science editor of *The Los Angeles Times*, was a recipient of journalism awards from the American Chemical Society and the American Association for the Advancement of Science.

in the last 33 years. Petroleum has been pumped out of the ground for about 100 years, but one-half of it has been pumped out in the last 14 years.

Stated another way, most of the world's consumption of energy from fossil fuels—from the beginning of recorded history until today—has taken place in the last 25 years!

The United States is the world's leading energy spendthrift. With less than 6 percent of the world's population, Americans annually consume more than one-third of the world's energy expenditures. In contrast, India, with about 15 percent of the world's population, consumes only about 1.5 percent of the world's energy. What is socially and politically disturbing is that India and the other technologically underdeveloped countries cannot hope to better themselves economically unless they also greatly increase their energy consumption—which in turn causes increased pollution.

Can such an energy binge long continue? And if it can, what are the environmental prices we must pay?

Before we try to answer these questions, we must understand that all our energy comes from the sun in the form of two energy bank accounts: a *renewable* account in which energy deposits are made every day, and a *nonrenewable* account that has a fixed energy deposit which we continuously deplete by our withdrawals.

renewable sources

First, consider the daily renewable energy bank account. Like other stars, the sun is a huge, glowing thermonuclear furnace. Located 93 million miles from the sun, our planet is an infinitesimal speck in the cosmos that intercepts an incredibly tiny fraction of the energy that pours out from the sun. Yet, it is this exceedingly minute fraction of the total solar energy that makes life possible on earth

PHOTOSYNTHESIS

Green plants play key roles in our renewable energy account. They alone have the incredible ability to convert the energy in sunbeams into the energy in wood, rice, corn, wheat, sugar cane, and other natural products. This is the process we call photosynthesis, and an understanding of it is the first basic lesson in ecology. Man produces nothing; he only consumes. It is the green plants that act as intermediary energy brokers between man and the sun to keep man going as an energy consumer.

Of all the forms of energy consumed by man, none is more important— none has more consequences—than food. Historically, an increased food supply has meant an increase in population which, in turn, has increased the need for more food. It is this mutually reinforcing, positive-feedback relationship between food and people that is responsible for the ever-increasing demands on both our energy sources and the planet's environment. (It is interesting to note that there are more human "engines" in the world that burn rice as fuel, than there are engines that run on gasoline.)

Increased food production means more pesticides and fertilizers, and consequent potential pollution. It may also mean the inundation of scenic or historic landscapes by man-made lakes that extend in back of dams built to provide water for irrigation. In tropical countries, moreover, the quiet, fresh water of irrigation channels and ditches sometimes breeds disease. The construction of a dam can be a delight to the ministries of agriculture and power, but a despair to the ministry of health.

In addition to food, other sources of energy in our renewable bank account are direct solar energy, wind power, tidal power, and hydroelectric power. Though these energy sources generally have minimum impact on the environment (with hydroelectric dams the exception), none plays a significant role anymore in the world's overall energy picture, nor will in the future.

SOLAR ENERGY

The enormous amount of sun power intercepted by earth is about 100,000 times greater than the entire world's presently installed electrical power-generating capacity. But it is terribly diffuse and difficult to concentrate. The capital investment for a solar power installation is prohibitive.

Direct solar energy, of course, can be used for small-scale, special-purpose uses such as solar furnaces, solar cooking stoves, water and house heating. The sun's energy also runs our atmospheric "engine," causing winds to blow. Though wind power played a historic role in man's use of energy—windmills and Yankee clippers—it is little used today.

HYDROELECTRIC POWER

The sun's energy evaporates water from the ocean's surface, changing salty water to fresh water in the form of clouds, snow and rain. The snow melts and rain falls, and as the fresh water runs back in the form of a river to the sea, we can harness its energy to turn a turbine to produce electricity. Slightly more than 4 percent of America's total power usage is now met by hydroelectric-produced power. This may increase to about 5 percent by the year 2000.

The world has a hydroelectric power potential comparable to the *total* amount of power consumed today (with most of this potential in Africa and South America). We use only about 8 percent of this potential and any further growth in hydroelectric power must deal with these questions:

1. Does the world want to sacrifice much of its most beautiful natural scenery to dams and the resulting lakes?

2. Would the energy generated by a dam be more valuable than the energy which could be released through foods grown on the lands flooded by dams?

3. Is it worthwhile to build dams if they will last only about 50–100 years before they clog up with silt and sediment carried by the dammed streams?

TIDAL POWER

Instead of using the one-way flow of water from river to sea to generate electricity, why not use the daily two-way movement of water—the ebb and flow of the tides? A major tidal-electric power plant now operates in France, and one was once considered in Maine.

The best that can be said is that if the world's potential tidal power were fully developed, it would amount to only about 1 percent of the world's potential hydroelectric power.

This completes our inventory of our renewable energy bank account. Green plants, we have seen, are responsible for our most important renewable source of energy. But they are constantly being depleted, not only by consumption (trees cut down), but also by pollution (one can no longer grow broad-leaved vegetables in the smog of the Los Angeles basin). Furthermore, prime land to grow crops, orchards and forests is fast disappearing under such land-obliterating "advances" as highway construction, housing developments, airports and dams. Our other renewable energy sources are, for one reason or another, of limited scope.

nonrenewable sources

This takes us to our planetary, nonrenewable energy bank account with finite deposits of coal, oil, natural gas, shale, tar sands, uranium-235 and uranium-238, deuterium and also geothermal energy.

The so-called fossil fuels—coal, oil, natural gas, shale and tar sands—are the subterranean remains of green plants that once grew and then were buried long ago in geological time. Nonrenewable fossil fuels are thus the remnants of ancient sunbeams that slammed into earth aeons ago.

COAL

Of the fossil fuels, coal is in greatest supply. The United States has enough coal to meet industrial energy needs, at present consumption rates, for about 350–450 years. Unfortunately, coal is an "unclean" fuel, and its use leads to air pollution, especially from sulfur oxides.

While engineering research has been preoccupied with the development of novel nuclear energy, research to make commonplace coal available as clean, cheap fuel—to remove its sulfur before or after burning—has been neglected. Some scientists feel that a "massive injection of money into coal engineering could lead to suppression of sulfur dioxide and at the same time to a lower cost of power generated from coal." Research to gasify coal—to convert it into a gaseous fuel—has also lagged badly.

NATURAL GAS

Now obtained from petroleum production, natural gas is the fossil fuel in shortest supply, and demand has tripled in the last 20 years.

Thus, in 1941, if one divided the proved reserves of natural gas by the consumption that year, there was a 33-year supply of natural gas available. But by 1965, the same ratio of proved reserves to consumption had dropped to only a 17-year supply. "Brownouts" due to short supplies of natural gas could become an ever-more frequent occurrence in the next decade.

PETROLEUM

As for petroleum, not only is there less oil than coal, but it is also being consumed at a faster rate. In 1900, America obtained 89 percent of its energy from coal and 7.8 percent from oil. But in 1965, about 68 percent of U.S. energy came from oil and 28 percent from coal.

It is estimated that American oil fields, including the new Alaska find, now have about a 30-35-year supply of petroleum remaining, at current consumption levels. The importation of ever-greater amounts of petroleum and natural gas from foreign countries is dependent upon the international political situation and is in conflict with underdeveloped nations, whose rising economic expectations are dependent upon their own increased energy consumption.

OTHER FOSSIL FUELS

There are, however, two additional fossil fuel sources. Near Fort McMurray in northeastern Alberta, there are large deposits of the *Athabasca tar sands* containing an extremely viscous, nonflowing, petroleumlike liquid fuel. Starting in 1967, a large-scale plant began extracting 45,000 barrels of tar-sand oil daily.

In Colorado, Utah and Wyoming there are deposits of *oil shale* from which a solid fuel called kerogen can be obtained. But the processing of kerogen from oil shale is in an experimental stage; no large-scale production is underway. And the disposal of tons of extracted shale rock could be a serious environmental problem since it would damage wildlife habitat (Colorado, for example, is the wintering ground for the world's largest migrating mule deer herd).

The supply of coal, oil, natural gas, oil shale and tar sands is sufficient, in terms of current consumption levels, to meet immediate future needs, but we must remember that it is finite. Or, as Dr. M. King Hubbert of the U.S. Geological Society writes, "The epoch of fossil fuel can only be a transitory and ephemeral event. . . ."

With the end in sight for some of the fossil fuels in our nonrenewable energy bank account, the world has looked to geothermal energy and nuclear energy.

GEOTHERMAL ENERGY

Using underground heat or hot water heated in the earth's interior by such naturally radioactive atoms as potassium-40, geothermal energy is now being used in Italy, New Zealand, Japan, Mexico, Iceland, the U.S.S.R. and California. But this energy is very limited in scope, suited for only a specific locale where earth's internal heat can be tapped easily.

NUCLEAR ENERGY

Uranium-235 is the only variety of atom found in nature that can fall apart (undergo fission) to release heat to be used to generate electricity, and uranium-235 is rare. Of every 140 uranium atoms in nature, only one is U-235. Moreover, our present-day, pressurized-water nuclear reactors are primitive devices, terribly inefficient, and if they were to be used to produce our future requirements of electricity, *we would use up all our U-235 in 20-30 years.*

Fortunately, there is a more sophisticated, more efficient nuclear reactor called a breeder reactor that could save the day. But breeder reactors are experimental. No large-scale breeder fission reactor is currently in operation, though a crash research program now underway may, if successful, enable us to have it by the 1980s.

Of every 140 uranium atoms in nature, 139 are uranium-238. Though U-238 does not undergo fission as does U-235, it can be changed into another variety of atom called plutonium-239. And Pu-239, like U-235, can undergo fission to produce electricity. Thus, nonfissionable U-238 can "breed" fissionable Pu-239, and U-238 is plentiful in rocks.

But the use of nuclear fission energy to generate electricity involves a radiation hazard to the environment. Proper use of nuclear fission may involve the location of power plants remote from densely populated areas, careful reactor design, establishment of suitable radiation standards, and the regulation of nuclear power plant construction and operation.

The disposal and storage of radioactive wastes from nuclear power plants will, moreover, make radioactive waste our number one garbage problem by the end of this century. Future generations may have to monitor and stand guard over some of our nuclear excreta for about 10,000 years.

THERMONUCLEAR FUSION

Instead of heavyweight nuclei releasing energy by falling apart as in the fission of U-235 or Pu-239, lightweight nuclei can combine or fuse together at extremely high temperatures to release energy by thermonuclear *fusion*. Man has mastered *uncontrolled* thermonuclear fusion, the energy of exploding H-bombs. But he has not mastered *controlled* thermonuclear fusion, the energy that powers the sun and the stars.

Who will be the modern Prometheus who kindles the celestial fires of the stars here on earth? The achievement of controlled thermonuclear fusion to generate electricity is a major engineering challenge of our time. Yet U.S. research funds for controlled thermonuclear fusion are only about $30 million per year. Many scientists feel that such research funds should be at least doubled.

Thus far, controlled thermonuclear fusion is not technically feasible. As yet, it has not even been demonstrated experimentally. But if the controlled thermonuclear fusion of deuterium atoms—a heavyweight variety of hydrogen atoms—to produce electricity becomes technically and economically feasible, it would open up "unlimited" energy vistas for all mankind.

The energy released by the controlled thermonuclear fusion of only 1 percent of the deuterium atoms present in the oceans would be about 500,000 times as much energy as our planet's total fossil fuel energy bank account originally contained. We would enjoy an energy abundance through the "burning of water" with less radiation and thermal pollution than from nuclear fission.

We may run out of certain types of fuel, but we will not run out of energy. I predict the limitations of energy production will not depend on fuel supplies, but on the deterioration of our natural environment.

Besides air, water and land pollution, and contamination by radiation, energy production also gives rise to waste heat. Not only does the river or ocean water used for cooling an electrical power-generating plant become warmer, but so does the air. The electricity that exists from generating plants enters factories, offices and homes and dissipates heat in motors, fluorescent lamps, television sets, toasters, washing machines, dryers, refrigerators and can openers. This leads to warmer and warmer air. In turn, we install more and more air conditioners. They make our air still warmer. And so on. The amount of heat generated by man-made activities in Los Angeles now amounts to about five percent of the total sunlight the city receives daily from the sun.

Not only will it be difficult for our air and water to absorb the diverse and unwanted chemical and thermal by-products of energy production, but also our landscape will be desecrated to accommodate transmission lines, radioactive waste storage and sites for power plants. For example, if the 8.8-percent annual increase in electricity produced in California during the 16-year period 1950-1966 were to continue for the next three decades, California would have to construct 92 additional power plants, each of 4,000-megawatt capacity. That amounts to one power plant for every 10 miles of California coastline!

International agricultural authority Lester R. Brown, commenting on the world's food problems, says: "Whatever measures are taken, there is growing doubt that the agricultural ecosystem will be able to accommodate both the anticipated increase of the human population to seven billion by the end of the century and the universal desire of the world's hungry for a better diet.

"The central question is no longer, Can we produce enough food? but What are the environmental consequences of attempting to do so?"

What goes for food production also goes for energy production. Or, to state the matter another way: How many people can the earth support, at what standard of living, and at what level of environmental deterioration? The central question is no longer, Can we generate enough energy? but, Will we wreck our environment attempting to do so?

additional reading

1. Anthrop, Donald F. *Environmental Side Effects of Energy Production.* Bulletin of Atomic Scientists, October 1970.
2. Brooks, Norman H. *Man, Water and Waste.* Brown, Harrison S. *The Next Ninety Years.* Both in The Next Ninety Years. Pasadena: California Institute of Technology, 1967.
3. Brown, Lester R. *Human Food Production as a Process in the Biosphere.* Scientific American, September 1970.

defusing old smoky by plugging into nature

john holdren

The thermal impact of solar energy will be much smaller than that of any other alternative. And in every other environmental respect, there seems to be very little hazard whatsoever.

In the year 1970, mankind consumed an amount of energy equal only to the amount of solar energy that strikes earth's outer atmosphere in fifteen minutes. Because solar energy is clean, free and abundant, why did we not use it to solve our energy problems long ago? There are two main reasons. First, the solar energy reaching the surface of the earth is dilute: to acquire enough for large projects it must be collected over a large area, which makes solar energy, although free, expensive. Second, solar energy is variable: on cloudy days not much gets through, none at night, and in winter less is available than in summer. Storing large amounts of heat or electricity is difficult and expensive. But these problems are not overwhelming. Much progress has been made during the past few decades, despite woefully inadequate financial support for the research.

Two misconceptions about solar energy should be dismissed at the outset. One that can unfortunately be found in many recent books and articles is that harnessed solar energy would cost "one thousand times as much" as electricity does today. The basis for this statement is the high cost of the sophisticated photovoltaic cells which convert sunlight directly to electricity in running space satellites. These cells cost $175,000 per kwe of capacity, or about one thousand times as much as a coal-burning power plant. But there are dozens of other ways to harness solar energy. The extremely expensive solar cells for space flights are so unrepresentative that one might think this misconception was planted by the coal industry or the nuclear interests.

The second misconception is that harnessing solar energy necessitates covering sixteen square miles of flat land with solar collectors in order

Reprinted from *Sierra Club Bulletin.* Copyright © 1971 by the Sierra Club. The article is from *Energy: A Crisis in Power* by John Holdren and Philip Herrera. A Sierra Club Book. The author is a physicist at the Lawrence Radiation Laboratory, University of California.

to build a single 1 million kwe power plant. Again, the measurement has some technical basis.* But it is misleading because heavy reliance on centralized power plants is not the only way to exploit solar energy. After all, one of the great built-in advantages of energy from the sun is that transmission and distribution are free. Many household, commercial and even industrial consumers of energy could be served by roof-top solar collectors, with the higher construction cost of the numerous small facilities (as opposed to a few centralized ones) being partly offset by savings in transmission and distribution.

Solar energy is already used for domestic water heating in many parts of the world, especially where electricity or fuel is expensive. The usual method exploits the fact that a black surface absorbs almost all the solar energy falling on it. Water pipes are laid over black panels of metal or wood; glass is placed over the pipes to reduce heat loss by radiation and convection. The water is heated while circulating through the pipes and is then stored in an insulated tank. An adequate system for a typical family requires ten to fifty square feet of panels, costs between $100 and $500, and can heat water to 200 degrees Fahrenheit. For decades, a few experimental houses have been successfully heated with solar energy in climates as cold as Boston's. Usually, water or a bed of rocks has served as a storage medium for the heat until needed, but we can probably anticipate important advances in chemical storage.

Larger amounts of energy can be obtained by building collectors that follow the sun in its path across the sky; higher temperatures can be achieved by using lenses and mirrors to concentrate the sun's energy on a small area. Using such techniques, small solar-driven steam engines have been built for $1,000 per kwe—not one thousand but only five times as expensive as a large nuclear or fossil fuel power plant.

A solar unit providing heat in winter and air conditioning in summer is an attractive possibility. A particular virtue of solar air conditioning is that the period of peak demand coincides rather closely with the period of peak solar energy flow. Within ten years, such dual-purpose units could compete with electrical heating and air conditioning in many parts of the United States. They could employ relatively simple collectors like those described above.

New coatings superior to glass in increasing the "greenhouse effect" (solar energy gets in but heat doesn't get out) may put an end to conventional assumptions about the efficiency of solar collectors. Two Arizona astronomers, Drs. Alden Meinel and Marjorie Meinel, have proposed a system in which the solar-to-electrical conversion efficiency would be 25 to 30 percent, making the generation of electricity at even large central power plants a possibility. (*Science* magazine, May 14, 1971, *Power for the People.*) The same materials should vastly upgrade the prospects for local applications of solar energy. The Meinels' proposal also includes advanced methods for chemical storage against energy consumption at night and during poor weather.

Even the solar cell may eventually become an economic proposition for

*kwe—an abbreviation for *kilowatt electrical* (a measure of electric power, i.e., the rate at which electric energy is used or produced). kwht—an abbreviation for *kilowatt hours thermal* (a measure of heat energy).

large-scale terrestrial use. Some experts believe that solar cells manufactured in quantity, with lenses or mirrors to reduce the necessary surface area, could be one hundred times cheaper than they are today. It has also been suggested, for the longer term, that large collectors in earth orbit could tap solar energy before any is lost in reflection and absorption by atmosphere and clouds. While in orbit the energy would be converted to electricity, then beamed to earth on microwaves (*Science*, November 22, 1968). The difficulties of such an enterprise should not be underestimated, but it would be foolish to state flatly that it cannot or will not be done within the next thirty or fifty years.

If solar energy is indeed harnessed through large electric power plants, there will be some esthetic loss in the rather large areas required. Such plants, if they employed the usual steam boiler, turbine and condenser, could cause aquatic thermal pollution by discharging waste heat to local water bodies. This problem could be ameliorated by cooling towers or cooling ponds. In the broader area of regional heat discharge, there would be no thermal pollution from solar power because this heat would have appeared in the system whether man had tapped the energy or not. In the event of collecting vast amounts of solar energy in one geographical area—perhaps the Southwest—and then transmitting it elsewhere as electricity, one could imagine upsetting the natural energy balance enough to influence circulation patterns. Similarly, having solar-collecting satellites provide a large fraction of the future energy demand a century hence could cause climatic perturbations because large amounts of energy that would have been reflected—or not struck the earth at all—would be collected and eventually dissipated on earth as heat. Nevertheless, whatever the assumptions, the thermal impact of solar energy will be much smaller than that of any other alternative. And in every other environmental respect, there seems to be very little hazard whatsoever.

geothermal energy

Heat from the earth's molten core and from chemical and nuclear reactions in the crust is carried to the surface by conduction, and by volcanoes and hot springs. In some circumstances, underground water, trapped in porous rock formations, is heated to extremely high temperatures by this geothermal energy. By concentrating energy, such underground reservoirs make it attractive for man's use. All that is needed is to locate the reservoirs, drill into them, and run the steam thus obtained through a conventional steam-electric power plant. Electricity produced this way is cheap. Furthermore, there are no noxious combustion products or hazardous wastes.

Estimates of how much geothermal energy is exploitable, and for how long, vary widely. The world's total installed geothermal electric capacity is now about 1 million kwe, which is equalled by a single large fossil fuel or nuclear power plant. About 40 percent of the total is found in Italy, with the rest spread over New Zealand, California, the Soviet Union and Iceland. As recently as 1965 some experts argued that the exploitable world capacity was unlikely to exceed 60 million kewe, and that the major underground reservoirs supplying steam were likely to be depleted after 50 or 100 years of exploitation. If true, this would mean the world's geothermal capacity is only about 2 percent of its hydroelectric capacity (itself woefully inadequate to meet projected electricity demand) and would become even smaller after a relatively short time. Other experts are much more optimistic. A single field now being explored extends from the Salton Sea in southern California into northern Mexico, and may be able to provide 20 million kwe for one to three centuries, say the investigators. Much of the western United States may be sitting on reservoirs of geothermal steam that have not been found because we haven't looked very hard.

Even the optimists do not claim that geothermal energy is likely to provide a long-term means of meeting the fantastic electric city demand projected for the future. They do argue, however, that it could provide electricity in many specific locations for a considerable length of time, with environmental advantages superior to most alternatives. The principal environmental problem with geothermal energy may be the possibility of surface subsidence if the water is not pumped back underground after being passed through the turbines. Additionally, the water from underground reservoirs is laden with mineral salts which could constitute a nuisance if not returned underground. The proposal has been advanced that, at seaside locations, waste heat from the generation process could be used to desalt ground water, with the residual brine (augmented by sea water) being pumped back into the ground to prevent subsidence. How all this would work out in practice remains to be seen. It is certainly worth pursuing.

tidal and wind energy

The source of tidal energy is the gravitational force of the moon and the sun acting on the world's oceans. Like solar energy, this source will continue essentially forever. Exploiting the energy of the tides requires a partly enclosed coastal basin, the twice-daily filling and emptying of which can be harnessed by a dam containing two-way turbines. (Without a dam to create a difference in water level between ocean and basin, the force against the turbine would usually be inadequate.) The largest tidal power station now in operation is a 240,000-kwe installation in France. Unlike solar energy, tidal energy is wholly inadequate in magnitude to meet man's needs. All the exploitable tidal sites of the world together could provide an average total power of 13 million kwe, in the estimation of energy specialist M. King Hubbert *(Resources and Man)*. This amounts to less than 1 percent of the world's exploitable conventional hydroelectric power. Thus, while tidal energy may provide appreciable amounts of electricity with rather small environmental intrusion at specific locations, it will never contribute an important fraction of the energy consumption of this country or of the world.

Wind energy is even less promising, as there are few places in the world where the wind is strong enough and steady enough to make harnessing it for the large-scale production of power at all promising. The ultimate source of the energy in the wind is the sun; the prospects for exploiting that directly seem much brighter.

burning garbage

Every American generates an average of five pounds of municipal solid wastes—not including industrial, mineral and agricultural solid wastes—per day. The municipal wastes have a fuel value averaging 1.5 kwht per pound, or more than one-third that of high grade coal *(Environmental Cost of Producing Electric Power)*. For many years the better part of the garbage from the city of Paris has been burned to produce steam for heating and for electric power plants. If all of America's municipal solid wastes had been used in this way in 1969 at 33 percent plant efficiency, they could have supplied about 8 percent of our electrical consumption.

Very few such plants exist in the United States, but several advanced designs are under development. Once such design dispenses with steam and has hot combustion gases drive a gas turbine, which turns the generator. The only effluents from such a plant are warm, filtered, combustion gases, and a solid residue much smaller than the original waste. One potential problem with installations of this sort is the combustion products of the wide variety of plastics in municipal garbage, some of which may not be removed by the usual filtering. The products could have serious effects on human health.

fuels management in an environmental age

g. alex mills, harry r. johnson, and harry perry

New criteria for fuels selection, based on environmental awareness, are replacing the old idea that cheapest is always best.

Until the late 1960's, the selection of a fuel for any use was a matter of choosing one with the lowest overall costs, with little regard for its effects on the environment. The rising concern about the environment, however, has changed the traditional concept of what is desirable.

In selecting a fuel, the effects of production, processing, and utilization of each fuel on the land, water, and air must now be considered. This presents a complex situation, since all the principal energy sources—coal, oil, gas, nuclear, and hydro—have differing environmental effects. Moreover, the severity of the pollution trade-offs must be evaluated and decisions must be made as to which fuel is likely to have the least harmful environmental impact.

Two fuels management problems are particularly urgent. The first, automobile fuels, is undergoing rapid change, and little can be done in the short term to replace gasoline as a fuel. The second, generation of electricity, does have much substitutability from competing energy sources. Both pose unique management problems that must be solved if the nation is to benefit from low-cost energy that is produced and used in a manner that does not further degrade our environment.

energy demand and resources

Energy demand is growing exponentially, and the established trends are expected to continue through 1980. Demand for oil and gas is expected

Reprinted from *Environmental Science and Technology*, Vol. 5, January 1971, pp. 30-38. Copyright 1971 by the American Chemical Society. Reprinted by permission of the copyright owner. G. Alex Mills is Chief, Division of Coal, Energy Research, U. S. Bureau of Mines. Harry R. Johnson is a scientific staff assistant to the Chief, Division of Petroleum and Natural Gas, Energy Research, U. S. Bureau of Mines. Harry Perry is Senior Specialist in Environmental Policy in the Legislative Reference Service, Library of Congress.

to show the greatest increase in absolute terms; however, in relative terms, the increase in nuclear energy is the greatest. Projecting to the year 2000, many technological, economic, environmental, and political factors will influence the demand and supply for various energy sources. These factors have been studied by the Bureau of Mines, with the conclusion that demand for each of the most-used fuels—petroleum, natural gas, and coal—will at least double between 1968 and 2000. Uranium, however, will increase by a factor of about 15.

The cumulative requirements for these energy resources are enormous. However, the nation's resource base is adequate to supply the demand through 2000. But, if these demands are to be met, the nation's coal and oil shale resources will have to play an important role, whether they are used to generate electricity or are converted into gases or liquids and used in these more convenient, pollutant-free forms.

The nation's fossil fuel resources are not unlimited, and a maximum of producibility is expected to be reached early in the next century. Thus, after 2000, the nation's energy demand could set the stage for the emergence of unproved systems, such as nuclear fusion, and the widespread use of solar and geothermal energy.

Imported liquid fuels (crude and residual oils and products) now provide 23% of all liquid petroleum consumed in the U.S. Management of fuel resources to solve environmental problems depends upon policy decisions made with respect to future oil import programs, as well as public land leasing, tax treatment, and prorationing policies which, in turn, are intertwined with other factors of national interest such as military security and balance of payments.

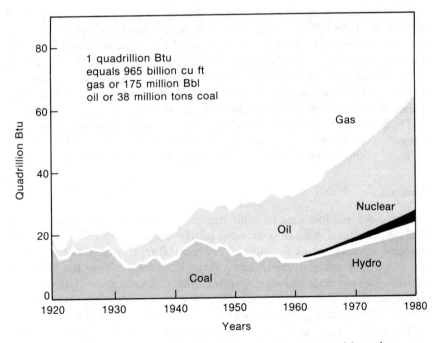

Figure 9-1. U.S. energy consumption is growing by leaps and bounds . . .

301

The consumption of fuels must also be considered according to the use—household and commercial, industrial, transportation, or electricity generation. By comparing the expected fuel consumption in the year 2000 with use patterns for 1968 (see Table 9–1), it can be seen that total gross energy inputs are expected to increase from 62 to 163 quadrillion Btu. Electricity generation will dominate in the future, increasing both absolutely, from 14.0 to 72.3 quadrillion Btu, and as a percent of total gross energy input, from 23 to 44%. Nuclear generation is expected to dominate the generation of electricity, increasing from 0.1 to 38 quadrillion Btu; but coal used for this purpose will increase more than threefold, from 7 to 24 quadrillion Btu.

Table 9–1.   . . . All Types of Consumer Are Sharing in the Increase*

UNITS ARE QUADRILLIONS OF BTU; LOW FUEL USE ESTIMATES USED FOR YEAR 2000

CONSUMER	COAL	GAS	PETROLEUM	HYDRO	NU-CLEAR	GROSS INPUT	ELECTRICITY PURCHASED (SOLD)	NET INPUT
Household and	0.6	6.5	6.6			13.6	2.5	16.1
commercial		**19.1**	**2.0**			**21.1**	**20.0**	**41.0**
Industrial	5.6	9.3	4.5			19.4	2.0	21.4
	2.0	**17.5**	**13.1**			**32.6**	**11.0**	**43.4**
Transportation	0.1	0.6	14.5			15.2		15.2
		1.0	**35.6**			**36.6**	**0.1**	**36.7**
Electricity	7.1	3.2	1.2	2.4	0.13	14.0	(4.5)	
generation	**24.2**	**4.1**	**0.9**	**5.1**	**38.1**	**72.3**	**(30.8)**	
Totals 1968	13.4	19.6	27.1	2.4	0.13	62.4		52.7
2000	**26.2**	**41.7**	**51.6**	**5.1**	**38.1**	**162.6**		**121.1**

*Figures for 1968 in lightface; 2000 in boldface. (Source: U.S. Bureau of Mines.)

Consumption patterns of different fuels up to about 1968 are a good indication of the amounts and types of fuels that would be used if environmental problems could be largely ignored. Environmental considerations, however, have begun to alter these supply patterns sharply. For example, sulfur dioxide emission standards in 1969 caused a shift from coal to residual fuel oil at east coast electricity generating plants. By early 1970, the initial penetration of residual oil into the Chicago market had been approved.

The production, processing, and utilization of fuels cause the most environmental problems for the nation. Let us then look at the most significant of these pollution problems, and the impact on land, water, and air.

land use

About 3.6 million tons of solid wastes are generated each year in the U.S. Agricultural wastes constitute nearly two-thirds of the total, and mineral wastes account for most of the rest. Mineral wastes, not including the large amounts of overburden removed in surface mining but including those wastes generated by mining, processing, and utilization of all minerals and fossil fuels, amount to about 30% of the total wastes. But fuels account for only 125 million tons, or about 3% of all solid wastes generated.

The last complete survey of mining operations in the U.S. indicated that, in 1965, about 3.2 million acres of land had been disturbed by surface mining. Of this total, about 41% resulted from activities associated with coal production.

As yet, only a few tenths of 1% of the total land area of the U.S. has been disturbed by surface mining. Effects of such mining upon the environment, however, vary widely and depend upon such factors as the type of mining, characteristics of overburden, steepness of the terrain, amount of precipitation, and temperature. Where land reclamation is not practiced, water pollution from acid mine drainage and silt damage occur. It is possible, however, to prevent much of this damage through proper land reclamation, adequate drainage, and planting to achieve soil stabilization. In the principal coal mining areas, the average costs of completely reclaiming coals lands range from $169 to $362 per acre, an average cost of 4 to 8 cents per ton.

Underground coal mining can cause subsidence unless the mining systems are designed to prevent deterioration and failure of abandoned mine pillars. Underground fires may weaken or destroy coal pillars that support the surface, causing subsidence with consequent damage to surface structures. An additional threat is the possible collapse of buildings and openings of surface fissures and potholes.

Fuel processing also contributes large quantities of wastes during the washing of coal to improve its quality. Over 62% of all coal mined is washed, producing 90 million tons of waste annually. If not returned to the mine, the water accumulates in piles near the plant and mine. At times, these piles ignite and burn for long periods, thus creating air pollution. Rainwater leaches salts and acid from the piles to contaminate nearby streams.

Utilization of coal also produces solid waste in the form of ash and slag. About 30 million tons of these materials are collected each year; an estimated 8 million tons are discharged into the atmosphere.

Uranium mined by either open pit or underground methods creates similar land problems. However, since uranium mining in quantity is a relatively new industry, the volumes and tonnages involved are only 1% of those for coal, and the adverse effects are much smaller. Estimates of the solid wastes from the mining of ore and the subsequent extraction of the desired uranium product are 38 million tons annually.

Solid wastes resulting from nuclear generation of electricity involve only small tonnages of materials, but have a very great potential for environmental damage for long periods because of their radioactivity. As nuclear plants become more numerous, the magnitude of this problem will grow.

Transportation of oil and gas, which is largely by underground pipelines, does not normally produce land problems. However, the special case of transporting oil from Alaska by pipeline raises numerous and, as yet, unresolved land-use problems.

water problems

Two distinct water problems are of growing concern in fuels management—water quality and water temperature. Questions of quality relate to individual energy sources; thermal problems, however, are common to use of all fuel commodities.

Poor water quality, whether it be through chemical pollution or sedimentation, is a major damage resulting from both surface and underground mining. Available data make no distribution between the two, but it has been estimated that approximately 48% of mine water pollution, primarily sediment, results from surface mining. In the U.S., some 5800 miles of streams and 29,000 surface acres of impoundments and reservoirs are seriously affected by such operations. Acid drainage from underground mines is more difficult to control than that from surface mines, but preventing water from entering the mine and the rapid removal of water which does get into the mine are effective methods for reducing pollution. The effects of acid mine drainage can be reduced by decreasing the amount of acid produced at the source, or by neutralization of the mine water before it is discharged to the streams. The latter technique, though highly effective, is more costly. Erosion and sedimentation from surface mining are serious problems in many areas, but they can be prevented by controlling the surface runoff that follows rainstorms.

In processing uranium ores, some of the potentially hazardous radioactive elements or isotopes, particularly Ra-226 and Th-230, are partly dissolved during the leaching operation used to recover uranium oxide. While most processing plants are located in very isolated areas, steps are taken to avoid pollution of water supplies by radioactive constituents of liquid effluents.

Disposal of the effluent is accomplished principally by impoundment and evaporation, controlled seepage into the ground, and injection through deep wells into saline or nonpotable aquifers. Where ore processing plants are adjacent to rivers or streams, the effluents may be released directly to the streams at controlled rates if, after dilution, the concentration is within predetermined limits. During periods of low stream flow, effluents are impounded or may be chemically treated before release.

Onshore oil production, except for accidental occurrences, does not present any difficult pollution problem. Nevertheless, nearly three barrels of brine must be disposed of for every barrel of oil produced. Accidental pollution may occur from blowouts of wells, dumping of oil-based drilling muds, or losses of oil in production, storage, or transportation. At sea, the blowout at Santa Barbara, the oil slicks and the fires and oil spills in the Gulf of Mexico in recent months have demonstrated that these

Table 9-2. Most Energy Sources Have Significant Environmental Impacts

ENERGY SOURCE	IMPACTS ON LAND RESOURCE			IMPACTS ON WATER RESOURCE			IMPACTS ON AIR RESOURCE		
	PRODUC-TION	PROCESS-ING	UTILIZA-TION	PRODUC-TION	PROCESS-ING	UTILIZA-TION	PRODUC-TION	PROCESS-ING	UTILIZA-TION
Coal	Disturbed Land	Solid Wastes	Ash, slag Disposal	Acid Mine Drainage		Increased Water Temperatures			Sulfur oxides Nitrogen oxides Particulate Matter
Uranium	Disturbed Land		Disposal of radioactive material		Disposal of radioactive material	Increased Water Temperatures			
Oil				Oil spills, transfer, brines		Increased Water Temperatures			Carbon monoxide Nitrogen oxides Hydrocarbons
Natural Gas						Increased Water Temperatures			
Hydro									

dangers are more than academic in offshore operations. Methods must be found for their prevention and control. Spills and discharges from tankers are also important. However, the greatest, if less dramatic, problem is the contamination of inland waterways and harbors resulting from transfer of oil between or from vessels.

thermal pollution

By far the most important water problem resulting from fuel use is thermal pollution. Over 80% of all thermal pollution arises from the generation of electricity. The amount of heat rejected to cooling water represents 45% of the heating value of the fuel used in the most efficient fossil fuel plants, and 55% in nuclear plants. If projected use of electricity is accurate and if nuclear energy, as expected, supplies nearly 50% of the electricity demand, more than 10 times as much heat will be rejected to turbine cooling water in 2000 as is being rejected now. Even with greatly increased use of brines or seawater for cooling, the demands for fresh cooling water will be larger than its supply.

This suggests that the solution is not in treating the heat as a "waste" product. Rather, the heat must be viewed as a resource that can be used. Evolution of such concepts must not be constrained by current uses, for huge amounts of heat may be used in systems not considered practical or feasible at this time. For example, the heating and cooling of whole cities whose environment is controlled by a protective membrane is one possibility.

air pollution

Nearly 80% of all air pollution in the U.S. is caused by fuel combustion. About 95% of all sulfur oxides, 85% of all nitrogen oxides, and over half

Table 9–3. Recoverable Resources Are Adequate for the Next 30 Years

FUEL	FUEL CONSUMPTION PER YEAR 1968	2000	CUMULATIVE DEMAND 1968 to 2000	ESTIMATED RECOVERABLE RESOURCES
Coal (billions of tons)	0.5	0.9–3.0	27–42	773.5 bituminous coal and lignite 6.5 anthracite
Petroleum (billions of barrels)	4.9	7.3–16.4	195–308	532 crude petroleum 600 shale oil 4 in bituminous rocks
Natural gas (trillions of cu ft)	19.0	34.8–55.7	855–1130	2400
Uranium (thousands of tons)	4.0	61.0–69.0	1190–1540	553 as uranium 527 as thorium (estimate based on approximate current prices)

Source: U. S. Bureau of Mines

of the carbon monoxide, hydrocarbons, and particulate matter are produced by fuel use. Management of fuels, therefore, is critical for the minimization of the nation's air pollution problems.

The most competitive market for fuels is the generation of electricity. Not only do the fossil fuels compete with each other, but they also compete with hydropower and, more recently, with nuclear energy. Obviously, from an air pollution standpoint, hydropower is the perfect method of electricity generation. During the generation of electricity from fossil fuels, production of oxides of nitrogen or carbon monoxide is not greatly different for any of the fossil fuels used. The production of electricity using natural gas produces no sulfur oxide emissions, but the use of coal and residual oil in electric generating plants is the source of 74% of all the oxides of sulfur emitted into the air.

About seven times as much coal as oil is used in electricity generating plants. For this reason, and because of its relatively high sulfur content, coal accounts for nearly two-thirds of the sulfur oxides emitted to the atmosphere. In addition, nearly one-third of the particulate matter emitted into the atmosphere is from burning coal for generation of electricity.

About one-half of the coal consumed by industry is used to make coke. Part of the sulfur appears in the coke oven gas and, if this is used as a fuel, it eventually appears as sulfur dioxide. The balance of the sulfur remains in the coke and is released as hydrogen sulfide in the blast furnace gas. When the gas is used as a fuel or flared, the sulfur appears as sulfur dioxide.

Local air pollution problems in the vicinity of plants that make coke are severe. Alternatives to the use of coke for the production of pig iron are available, and these processes might reduce the amount of air pollutants released to the air. Uncontrolled surface and underground coal fires emit smoke, fumes, and noxious gases.

About 17% of all the oil consumed in this country is used by industry. Much of it is residual oil, which in most cases is high in sulfur. Moreover, residual oil is difficult to burn efficiently and is usually burned in large equipment at high temperatures. Because of these two factors, industrial use of oil tends to contribute larger amounts of carbon monoxide, hydrocarbons, and oxides of nitrogen than the household and commercial sector, which consume about 25% of the fuel oil.

The largest use of oil is for gasoline to power the nation's 100 million vehicles. About 42% of each barrel of oil is used in this manner. If we include diesel and jet fuels, about 54% of each barrel of oil is used for transportation.

The use of fuels in transportation causes approximately one-half of all the air pollution in the U.S. There are alternatives to the use of gasoline for automobiles and trucks, such as natural gas and liquefied petroleum gases. But it is doubtful that the massive changeover that would be required by two of the country's largest industries would occur if other solutions could be found to reduce air pollution generated by the transportation sector. Moreover, if a switch to electric cars were made, the total pollution load might actually be increased, although controls would be needed on a relatively few electric power plants, rather than on millions of autos and trucks.

management problems

Ideally, the management of fuels to satisfy environmental requirements should be guided by a system model that relates energy needs to damage, emissions, and fuel availability. Included in the model would be an assessment of the relative damage among dissimilar pollutants, for example, esthetics of land vs. air pollution, as well as comparisons between a small, constant hazard (nitrogen oxide) vs. a large, infrequent hazard (nuclear). Detailed knowledge of what happens to specific pollutants both geographically and over time would also be included in the model. In addition, economics, supply availability, and the broader question of national security would all need to be examined.

No such model now exists. However, many factors can be approximated so that a number of problems associated with fuel use can be examined. Two such problem areas are the automobile and the generation of electricity.

autos and air pollution

Much that is written and said about automotive pollution indicates that very little is really being done to change the pollution characteristics of internal-combustion engines. It is alleged that, in fact, little can be done. Such negative views are unwarranted, since both engines and fuels offer opportunity for modification to reduce markedly the pollution from internal-combustion engines in all applications. Nevertheless, in the long run, other supplementary methods of transporting people may be needed. All of the alternatives proposed to eliminate automobile-caused air pollution have great implications for fuels and materials management.

Some reduction in pollution from the automobile has resulted from federal standards already enacted through 1971. These standards will result in a continuous improvement in air quality through the 1970's as the controlled vehicles comprise an increasingly larger portion of the car population. Unless further progress is made to clean up exhaust emissions, however, an upturn in emission output is expected near the end of the 1970's, as the increasing number of vehicles in use begins to overcome the effects of the standards. Technology is available for continued progress, but lead times of two years or more are required to manufacture and distribute modified fuels and (or) engines. Thus, continued progress will depend upon the decisions made between 1970 and 1975.

The impact of change in fuels and engine design will be far reaching and long lasting. Trends now developing and those established within the next few years will be, in practice, largely irreversible within the next decade. In terms of today's dollar, costs will be higher for each mile driven, and some of the broad options that are now available for fuels manufacture and for designing high-performance engine and fuel systems will be lost.

The types and effectivenesss of control methods depend upon the composition of the automobile population in the 1970's. Early in this decade, pre-1968 cars will represent 50% of the automobile population. Even in the last half of the decade, pre-1968 cars will still be a significant part of the population. These vehicles are important, since they generally do not have exhaust-emission controls.

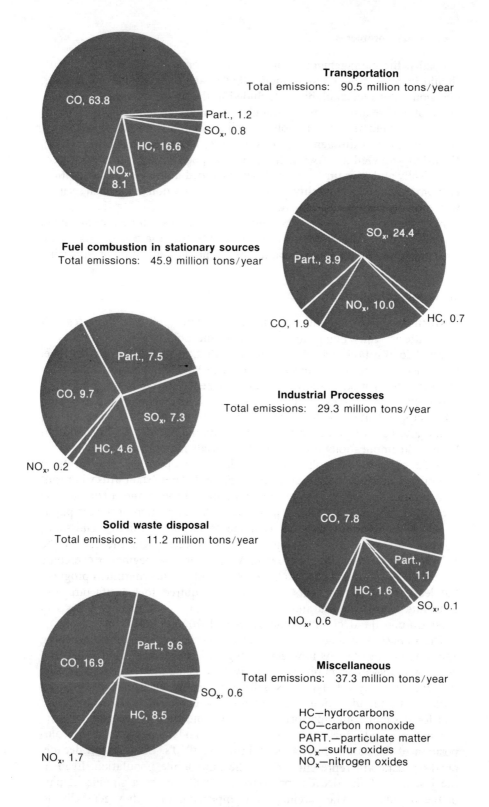

Figure 9-2. Nationwide air pollutant emissions come from many sources. (Source: CEQ First Annual Report. Estimated data for 1968.)

There are options available to reduce pollution from the various automobile populations. Relatively simple engine and fuel-system modifications have been or will be made in 1968–74 model vehicles to meet emission standards. But the major impact of these changes will not be seen until the mid-1970's. Extensive engine redesign and exhaust treatment is expected for the 1975–79 cars. This possibility is widely discussed in the popular press, but the maximum effectiveness of such technology as catalytic conversion of exhaust gases will not be until 1980 or later—a decade away. Gasoline-composition modification is applicable to all cars on the road today, and its effect would be immediate. Engine retuning is mainly for those cars manufactured before 1968, and its effect would also be immediate. Field tests of this control method have met with disappointing public response and, in the absence of compulsory legislation, engine retuning will probably not result in a significant reduction of polluted air.

Changes in the composition of gasoline which limit volatility during the summer months and eliminate C_4 and C_5 olefins would reduce smog by 25% or more, according to recent research by the Bureau of Mines. This is the most rapid solution toward improving air quality, because such modifications can be accomplished quickly and are applicable to all cars now in use, without requiring any changes in the cars themselves. However, the olefins to be replaced have high octane ratings and their removal would make it more difficult to maintain the octane levels of fuels without using lead. Thus, this control method must be carefully coordinated with lead removal if undue losses in engine performance are to be avoided. It has been estimated that the modifications to gasoline can be achieved without significant changes in the product mix from refineries and at a cost to the consumer of less than 1 cent per gallon of gasoline. No estimates are yet available on the cost of accomplishing the same thing with low-lead

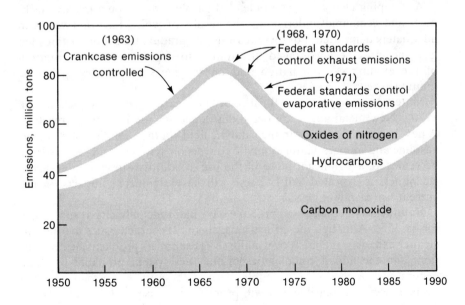

Figure 9-3. Without further restrictions, auto pollution will again increase. (Source: Department of Health, Education, and Welfare.)

309

and unleaded fuels, but the cost should not be significantly higher provided all fuel composition changes are carefully coordinated.

The lead-in-gasoline issue evokes a strange mixture of emotion, politics, and fact. Lead does contribute to the contamination of our environment—nearly 170,000 tons are released annually. It also forms deposits that foul engines and emission-control systems, unless controlled by additives, leading to increased emissions. Of particular importance, it presents difficult problems in developing exhaust-treatment catalysts. For effective use of these advanced control systems, the lead content of gasoline should be near zero.

Any move to modify fuels must be guided by the types of vehicles already in use. Many of these vehicles may have marginal acceptable performance using a low-octane, unleaded gasoline. High-octane unleaded fuels that contain large amounts of aromatics blended into the gasoline could increase the smog-forming potential of the exhaust gases up to as much as 25%, depending on the octane level to be achieved. The cost of manufacturing unleaded gasolines with acceptable octane levels would be reflected in gasoline price increases of 1 to 4 cents per gallon.

The lead issue demonstrates the difficult fuels management problem that has arisen as the result of environmental awareness. For example, if engine compression ratios are lowered to accommodate lower octane unleaded gasoline, the efficiency of the engine may drop and gasoline consumption increase. This would significantly reduce our already declining petroleum reserves. The manufacture of high-octane unleaded gasoline could set up severe competition for the stocks normally used as raw materials for the petrochemical industry. Significantly greater amounts of new oil may be required, and the needed fractions would be stripped from this oil. In this case, large volumes of oil products without aromatics would need to find a market.

A sweeping change-over to unleaded gasoline would be a massive technical and economic undertaking, the results of which have not yet been adequately delineated. For these reasons, the gradual transition to unleaded gasoline must be encouraged, the timing to depend on the distribution of the existing car population and on the types of vehicles yet to be manufactured.

Materials management will also become vastly more complex in the 1970's. New metal alloys are being developed for use in thermal reactors. A new horizon is opening in the catalytic field—both in refining of modified gasoline and in material for catalytic conversion systems. And, as lead may be removed, a significant jump in the use of additives to maintain engine cleanliness is expected. All of these will have significant impacts on the current use of raw materials.

Natural gas (methane) and propane have had wide publicity as substitutes for gasoline. Although these fuels have chemical characteristics that permit cleaner exhausts, the crisis over natural gas supplies, problems of distribution, and the added complexities of the fuel system probably preclude general use by the motoring public. Use of these fuels in urban-operated fleets, however, is feasible and will probably increase in the future. Moreover, synthetic gas from coal or oil shale could be an added source for the needed fuel.

All of the alternatives proposed as substitutes for the internal-combustion engine must meet three key tests: Will there be a significant change in pollution? If so, at what cost? Is near-comparable performance obtained? Ultimately, it may be cheaper to meet air-quality standards by a totally different approach that involves engine systems yet to be developed. Present analyses of all competing systems indicate that, into the 1980's, the best combination of costs, utility, and potential for reduced pollution output is the current gasoline-powered automobile.

The need for further reductions in total pollution output, however, may force a move to limit the size of both the vehicle and the engine. The

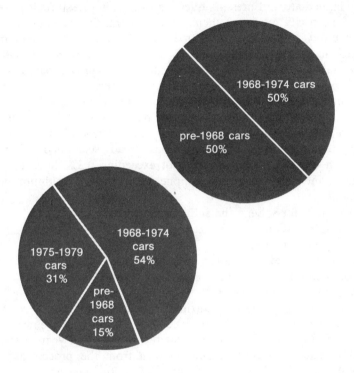

METHODS OF REDUCING AUTO EMISSIONS	APPLICABLE TO	SIGNIFICANT EFFECT BEGINNING
Engine and fuel system modification	1968–74 cars	mid–1970
Engine redesign and exhaust treatment	1975–79 cars	1980 and after
Gasoline composition modification	All cars	Immediate
Engine retune	pre–1968 cars	Immediate

Figure 9-4. Even in late seventies, many pre-'68 cars will be on the road, but emissions can be controlled on both old and new cars. (Source: U.S. Bureau of Mines.)

311

increasingly severe problem of urban traffic congestion will result in increasing efforts to develop mass-transportation systems. These pressures may cause a significant reduction in the demand for gasoline. This, when combined with adoption of proven technology that will enable a 95% reduction in all automobile pollutants, indicates that air pollution caused by automobiles can and will be solved. However, the accomplishment of this task will present a challenge of fuels and materials management unexcelled in a peace-time economy.

sulfur and electricity

The immediate and pressing question concerning fossil fuels for generation of electricity relates to their sulfur content. Of the coals shipped to electric utility plants in the U.S. in 1964, 21% had a sulfur content above 3%, 60% had between 1.1 and 3.0% S, and only 19% had less than 1% S. Regulations being established for sulfur in fuels are based on sulfur dioxide believed allowable in the air. Each community translates its requirements into a certain maximum sulfur content of the fuel. For a number of communities, a 1% sulfur maximum has been established. Obviously, much of the coal being mined and that in the ground cannot meet this requirement. Moreover, some regulations already scheduled call for a fuel having an effective sulfur content not exceeding 0.3%. Such coal is not available, and only exceptional supplies of petroleum residuum meet this requirement.

The options for solving the sulfur problem are:
- Fuel substitution.
- Fuel preparation (coal).
- Stack gas removal of sulfur oxides.
- Coal and oil shale conversion to low-sulfur fuels.
- New combustion methods.

Substitution of naturally occurring low-sulfur fuel (gas for coal) is not practical in the immediate future since adequate supplies are not available in the U.S. Two promising options for the next several years are removal of sulfur before combustion and removal from the process gases after combustion. Conversion of coal to other low-sulfur fuels and new combustion processes are long-range options.

fuel preparation

Improvement in coal preparation involves the removal of iron pyrite from coal. Often, the pyrite content accounts for a half of the sulfur in the coal. However, even with improved pyrite removal, it is evident that the degree of sulfur removal necessary to meet anticipated regulations cannot be achieved by this means alone.

Lignitic coal, mostly located in the West, represents a vast national resource, and it typically has a sulfur content of about 0.6%. (The effective sulfur content is a little higher than this, since lignite contains about 7000 Btu/lb, compared with about 12,500 Btu/lb for bituminous coal.) Moreover, lignite is an inexpensive fuel, priced at only about $1.50 per ton, which is equivalent to about 10 cents per million Btu. Lignitic coals should be helpful in certain areas, but obviously do not solve situations where regulations call for 0.3% S. Moreover, lignite deposits are generally far removed from population centers, and shipping costs can be excessive. One possibility is the generation of electricity in huge plants in the West, coupled with a system of long-range, low-cost electrical transmission through a cable cooled to very low temperature.

stack gas removal

The once-through process for removing sulfur oxides from combustion gases, typified by wet carbonate scrubbing (Combustion Engineering), and being installed in three plants, ranges from 125 to 450 MW. It offers the advantage of relatively low capital investment in plant equipment (perhaps $6 to $13 per kW) and low operating cost ($1.50 per ton of coal). However, it does pose problems in disposal of calcium sulfate (or magnesium sulfate) product—indeed, there is the uneasy fear that an air pollution problem may transform into a land or water pollution problem. It seems likely that with pressure for meeting new regulations, systems such as wet limestone scrubbing will be adopted to some extent in the short-term future.

Regenerative processes for stack gas sulfur removal are expensive to install and to operate. Investments might run from $17 per kW to more than $30 per kW, and operating costs would be in the $3 to $5 per ton of coal range. Such systems involve a solid or liquid which chemically reacts with and removes sulfur oxides. The sorbent is regenerated, in a separate step, usually with the production of sulfur. Included in the "regenerative absorbent" group are potassium bisulfite (Wellman-Lord), magnesia (Chemico), caustic plus electrolytic regeneration (Stone and Webster/Ionic), molten carbonate (North American Rockwell), potassium formate (Consolidation Coal), copper on silica (Houdry), alkalized alumina (Bureau of Mines), and others. Recently, it was announced that a regenerative-type plant, based on magnesia sorbent and costing $5 million, would be installed in the Boston area.

The conversion-type process is typified by the Monsanto Cat-Ox process. Although well defined, it is relatively costly to install and produces sulfuric acid that may not be desired. Bureau of Mines estimates an investment cost of more than $30 per kW for such a process, and an operating cost of about $4 per ton of coal.

New combustion methods, such as fluidized-bed combustion, offer opportunity for some improvement, if not prevention, of air pollution. However, conversion of a high-sulfur to a low-sulfur fuel appears to present the fundamentally best opportunity for a long-term solution.

synthetic fuels

From a supply standpoint, natural gas—essentially methane—is now in the most critical stage of all fossil fuels. For the second consecutive year, recoverable reserves have declined—that is, more gas was used than discovered. Yet the use of gas is the most rapidly growing of all the fossil fuels (about 7% annually) compared with a growth rate for energy as a whole of about 3%.

313

Looking ahead to 1985, projected rates of development will not fulfill the projected need for natural gas, even including importation of gas by pipeline from Canada and Alaska, or by cryogenic tanker from overseas. Anticipating this situation, and in the search for new markets for coal, a vigorous research and development program has been in progress for a number of years to provide processes for conversion of coal to gas. Several processes are currently in advanced stages of development.

Pilot plants are under construction for the Hy-Gas (Institute of Gas Technology) and the CO_2 acceptor processes (Consolidation Coal Co.) under the sponsorship of the Office of Coal Research of the Department of the Interior. Scale-up of the Bureau of Mines steam-oxygen, fluidized-bed coal gasification process has also been initiated.

In the Bureau of Mines process, coal is reacted with steam and oxygen in a fluidized bed at about 600 to 1000 psi, to produce a mixture of CH_4, H_2, CO, H_2S, and CO_2. After the CO_2 and H_2S are removed, the CO and H_2 are reacted to form additional methane. For a 250-million ft^3/day plant, the capital requirement has been estimated to be \$160 to \$180 million, the manufacturing cost 43 cents/ft^3 and selling price 54 cents/1000 ft^3 using utility company-type financing. It now appears that if the price of gas increases enough, or if adequate technologic-economic improvement in coal gasification can be made, synthetic gas from coal may soon become a commercial reality.

The price of synthetic pipeline gas noted above is too high to be used by electrical utilities. However, there is a very interesting related possibility—the production of low-Btu gas from coal using air instead of oxygen, followed by sulfur and ash removal, and generation of electricity by gas turbines. In this case, a high-temperature sulfur removal process is needed, to avoid the inefficiency involved in cooling the gas and heating it up again.

Underground gasification of coal and gasification of oil shale offer additional possibilities for gas supply if new technical advances can be achieved. It should be emphasized that all processes contemplated for manufacture of synthetic gases or liquids from coal result in a low-sulfur product.

It is possible to convert coal to liquid fuels, including high-quality gasoline. Moreover, the cost of doing so is approaching the cost of refining gasoline from petroleum. Therefore, probably within the next 15 years, it will be both necessary and economically feasible to make gasoline synthetically.

Another very important possibility which has not yet received emphasis is the conversion of coal to a low-sulfur, low-cost utility fuel. In such a process, coal is contacted with hydrogen and solvent with or without an added catalyst, thus transforming the coal into a new fuel product low in sulfur and ash. It is not important to upgrade the product by removing asphaltenes as in the case of gasoline production. By operation at relatively low pressure and relatively mild temperature, a minimum of hydrogen is used, so that a low-cost fuel can be manufactured.

petroleum desulfurization

With new regulations and increased demand, it has become necessary to desulfurize petroleum to achieve a more adequate supply. Fortunately,

314

the petroleum industry has developed effective hydrodesulfurization processes. Of a total of about 14 million barrels of oil produced per day, about 4 million are being desulfurized in the U.S. At present, most desulfurized oils consist of lighter petroleum fractions. Significantly, processes for desulfurizing residua are now coming on stream in different parts of the world. The cost of desulfurization ranges from about 20 to 80 cents a barrel. As an example, for a high-sulfur (2.6%) residuum costing 32 cents per million Btu ($2.00 a barrel), it would cost 4 cents per million Btu for each 0.5% by which the sulfur content were reduced. Desulfurization to 0.5% would thus add 16 cents, bringing the cost to 48 cents per million Btu, a 50% increase over the undesulfurized oil. Costs rise sharply, however, below about 0.5% sulfur.

The natural sulfur content of oil varies greatly. For example, residuum from Algeria is low in sulfur, about 0.5%, whereas that from Venzuela is relatively high, about 3%. No large supply of domestic low-sulfur residuum is available. The importation of a high proportion of utility fuel from abroad poses a problem from the viewpoint of national security since the east coast now imports nearly 94% of its requirements. Part of the current shortage in available residuum is due to its increased initial costs and increased tanker rates.

During the past few years, the substitution of low-sulfur petroleum residuum from abroad for high-sulfur domestic coal has been widely adopted on the east coast, where there is no oil import quota on fuel oil. Moreover, governmental approval recently provided for one plant to use imported residuum in the Chicago area. In this instance, the oil, containing 1% sulfur, will replace coal, at a reported cost of 46 cents per million Btu at that location as compared to about 30 cents for coal. This illustrates forcefully that pollution control is expensive.

new technology

Finally, we should not overlook new energy conversion devices which can become important if certain technological breakthroughs are achieved. Specific cases are fuel cells and magnetohydrodynamics. The former would permit the widespread use of gas for the transmission of energy, followed by generation of electricity, in the home or community.

Management of fuels also should take into account one human habit sometimes not recognized in the fuels system—that is, the production of so-called urban and agricultural refuse. Much of this is organic—for example, urban refuse is about half paper. In the U.S., 7 lb of urban refuse is collected per person per day, and nearly 10 times that amount of agricultural wastes is produced. In the past, urban refuse has been used as landfill or incinerated, causing significant air pollution. Now it is possible to recover energy by controlled incineration, by pyrolysis to make gas and oil, or by hydrogenation to produce a low-sulfur oil. Recent experiments by the Bureau of Mines have shown that heating a ton of garbage to 380°C for 20 minutes in the presence of carbon monoxide and water under high pressure produced over two barrels of low-sulfur oil per dry ton of garbage. Perhaps some such novel means will be necessary for conversion of cellulose, grown by solar energy and discarded by man, into a fuel that can be utilized with less pollution.

315

additional reading

1. Elliott, M., *Energy Conversion and Fuel Reserves,* North American Fuel Technology Conference, Ottawa, 1970.
2. U.S. Dept. of Interior, *Surface Mining and Our Environment,* Washington, D.C., 1967.
3. Gakner, A., *Electrical Power and the Environment: Collision or Coexistence?* National Materials Policy Conference, 1970.
4. Eccleston, B.H., et al., *Studies of Vehicle Emissions,* Bureau of Mines Reports of Investigations 7291 and 7390, 1970.
5. DeCarlo, J.A., Sheridan, E.T., Murphy, Z.E., *Sulfur Content of United States Coals,* Bureau of Mines Information Circular 8312, 1965.
6. Lawson, S.D., et al., *Economics of Changing Volatility and Reducing Light Olefins,* American Petroleum Institute preprint, 1968, pp. 41–68.

electrical heating and thermal pollution

f. t. wall

Electrical resistance heaters indirectly cause a substantial amount of unnecessary thermal pollution.

Of the various kinds of pollution confronting the world, one of them, thermal pollution, is relatively little understood. It is easy to see litter or smog and to smell or be irritated by offensive materials. On the other hand, raising the temperature of a river or a lake by several degrees does not produce any immediate human discomfort; hence thermal pollution generally does not excite people as much as the other kinds do. Moreover, a group of volunteers can scarcely go out and extract heat from our lakes or streams as they might pick up empty cans and other debris from our roadsides. Nevertheless, thermal pollution in some specific geographic sectors is a serious problem, a problem that is recognized by ecologists, many of whom have expressed concern about the long-range effects.

But it is not my purpose in writing this editorial to emphasize the gravity of the problem, for I am quite prepared to accept the conclusions of experts in this regard. However, I do want to comment on what I believe to be unnecessary thermal pollution and what steps might be taken to diminish it. By "unnecessary" I refer to that which can be avoided, at least in part, by alternative means for achieving otherwise desirable ends.

For reasons indicated below, it is clear that a substantial amount of unnecessary thermal pollution indirectly accompanies the use of electrical resistance heaters. Examples of offending devices include hot water heaters, stoves and ovens, clothes dryers, and house heaters, excepting, in principle, those using efficient heat pumps. I do not have precise estimates of the extent to which this is going on, but it is certainly substantial. From basic thermodynamic considerations, it follows that electrical resistance heating not only contributes unnecessarily to thermal pollution, but also wastes fuel. Since elimination of unnecessary thermal pollution would also help

Reprinted from *Chemical & Engineering News,* Vol. 48, June 29, 1970, editorial page. Copyright 1970 by the American Chemical Society and reprinted by permission of the copyright owner. The author is Executive Director of the American Chemical Society.

conserve fuel, there is a double reason for initiating appropriate corrective measures.

The specific arguments supporting these assertions follow. Suppose a certain amount of combustible gas would serve to heat some water; then in accordance with the second law of thermodynamics, a much greater quantity of gas or equivalent fuel would have to be burned to produce the electrical energy required to heat that water by the same amount. This follows because no cyclical heat engine, however perfect, can convert more than a fraction of the heat supplied into electrical energy. The most efficient fossil-fueled steam plants convert about 40% of the heat of combustion of the fuel into electricity and the nationwide average is less than 33%. The substantial amount of heat (about two thirds of the total) not converted into electricity at the power plant must be discharged into the surroundings, such as a lake or river. This is the principal source of thermal pollution, which in many instances has serious consequences depending upon where and how the heat is discharged.

Even if the heat effect at the power plant were of no consequence, the overall process still wastes fuel. Accordingly, it is definitely more efficient to burn gas in a hot water heater than to burn gas to generate steam to make electricity for the heater. I use gas as an example, but the argument is valid irrespective of the kind of fuel employed as long as one deals with thermal equivalents. (Through gasification of coal, one can use gas in a home, for example, without depending on natural gas alone.)

People generally think of electric heat as clean and hence desirable from the standpoint of keeping our environment unspoiled. This is true where the electricity is *used* but it is not necessarily true at the power plant. Although there is some compensation in the efficiency attending the operation of a large-scale power plant, the conclusion is still inescapable that, from the standpoints of thermal pollution and fuel conservation, we would be better off using directly the heat resulting from burning a fuel instead of going through an electrical intermediate. (The foregoing argument is not valid if reasonably efficient heat pumps are employed, nor would it apply to hydroelectric power sources, which account for a small fraction of the total.)

It is interesting to note that thermal pollution, like other kinds of pollution, and waste of fuel, like other kinds of waste, correlate rather directly with degree of affluence. Even though electric heat is more costly, an affluent society has no compunctions about using electrical heating devices because of the immediate convenience and apparent local cleanliness. Since, however, a modern electric home is in fact coupled with a power plant located elsewhere, it is the combination that must be judged; unhappily that combination gives rise to more, not less, undesirable effects on our total environment than would direct combustion in a properly designed heating device.

What can be done about this? In the first place, the use of electrical resistance heating should be severely restricted wherever electrical energy is generated by steam plants whose operations seriously affect the environment. Prompt action might give us enough time to determine more precisely what further measures, if any, must be taken to avoid serious, irreversible consequences. The development of means for the direct conversion of nuclear energy into electrical energy might, of course, solve the problem.

A return to individual coal-burning furnaces is not advocated; this can be avoided by gasification of coal, which would make available a convenient, not too costly, and relatively nonpolluting fuel for small heating units.

It should be emphasized that I am not suggesting the elimination of electric lights, minor heating appliances, or electric motors that perform work. I do want to focus attention on space and water heating, since the energy required for such can be very large, with a correspondingly large wasteful thermal discharge in the neighborhood of a power plant. At the same time, the use of heat pumps should be encouraged as an alternative both to cut down on thermal pollution and to save fuel. Finally, our people should be reminded that what they see or feel in their houses does not disclose all of the environmental effects attending living in those houses.

the electrical power industry: its prospects for growth

daniel b. luten

In the short run, nothing seems likely to stop growth; in the middle run, economics will; in the long run, the environment will strike back.

The human use of energy is, of course, exactly as old as man himself. Metabolism has been here as long as we. The growth in the first technology of energy, the burning of fuels, is younger and has been erratic. It has had many peaks, symbolically celebrated by each small boy as he learns the joys of a bonfire and the bitterness of accidental incendiarism.

Growth in the conversion to work of various forms of energy has had its ups and downs, too, but has been steadier simply because no possibilities of magnificent extravagance were ever at hand. So, while increase in the amount of work available per capita during the Christian era could not have increased by as much as 0.3% per year (based on manpower vs U.S. electricity), it is really not surprising to learn that water mills in England increased by about 4% per year during the eleventh century.[1]

A century ago, in the United States, we still had a fuelwood economy [Figure 9-5] and were beginning to shift to coal [Figures 9-5 and 9-6]. If we wish to examine successive fuels separately, we can demonstrate proud rates of growth. Coal's use grew at 6.6% per year[2] during the nineteenth century. Petroleum did even better, close to 9% per year,[3] during its heyday in the first quarter of the twentieth century, but currently it is probably less than 4% and due to stay there. Natural gas over the entire last century has been remarkably steady at 7%[4] and wants to continue. But, if we look at the fuel economy as a whole, growth over the last hundred years is only 2.9% per year. The fluid fuels have grown at the expense of coal, wood, and hydropower.

Reprinted with permission of the author. This paper was presented at the annual meeting of the Association of Pacific Coast Geographers, Santa Cruz, California, June 1970. The author is Lecturer in the Department of Geography at the University of California at Berkeley.

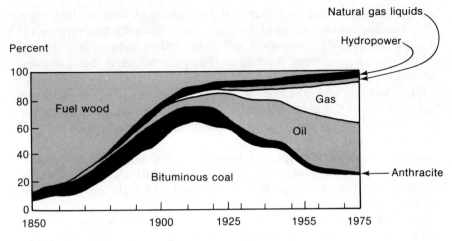

Figure 9-5. Contribution of several energy sources in U.S. consumption.

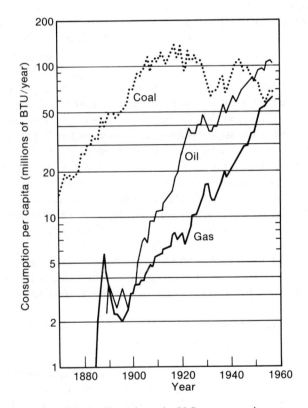

Figure 9-6. Growth of coal, oil, and gas in U.S. consumption.

Some of these effects reflect resource depletion, but more of them the development of a technology for handling and moving fluids: from wooden vats bolted upright on flatcars to four-foot diameter pipelines across Alaska and 400,000 ton supertankers; from local gas mains to cross-country high pressure pipelines and, next, tanker transport of liquid natural gas.

Growth of demand for fluid fuels was associated with the automobile—

321

transportation in small individualized packages, and with an increasing affluence that enabled us to choose automatically controlled furnace oil or natural gas in our homes over shovelling coal or carrying in firewood.

Coal should have been doomed as fuelwood before it, but for three differences:

First, coal was and continues to be the major part of all of the fossil fuel resources in the ground in amounts still almost undiminished by the past few centuries of exploitation, even though the most accessible portions have been mined and burned.

Second, we have also learned how to move solids cheaply. Witness unitized trains that never stop moving and shovels which remove overburden at 250 tons per bucket load. But the economies of scale are now about to run out on this front.

Third, in electricity we found a way to meet our demands for work in the household and in industry without being mechanically tied to the waterfall or steam engine, and for light without a kerosene can.

The electrical industry began small, but by 1902 was worth statistical mention[5] with an annual percapita consumption of 75 kilowatt hours, enough to run a 100 watt bulb ten hours per day in each of our households. However, we didn't have that much light, because most consumption was industrial in 1902.

The earliest steam engines were so inefficient, converting less than 1% of the heat input to work, that it hardly made sense to ask about efficiency. But as efficiency rose, as the amount of work that could be obtained from a ton of coal grew, questions arose where this would end. The development of a unified theory of energy, of an understanding of thermodynamics a little over a century ago showed that indeed limits existed. By the time the electrical power industry got underway, we knew that hydropower plants were highly efficient, certainly exceeding 80%. This was a simple deduction. More difficultly, but just as certainly, we knew that thermal power plants were not as much as 10% efficient. Their efficiency has grown steadily, and today must average close to 35% for the nation, and approaches 40% for the newest plants. This has had the result of extending our fuel resources four-fold. That is, we will get four times as much electricity as if we had effected no increase in efficiency. This has also made electricity progressively cheaper.

No further substantial increase is on the horizon. From now on, increased electrical consumption must be paralleled by increased fuel consumption.

The growth of electrical generation in the United States has been remarkably steady at 8% per year except for a hesitation during the depression. [Figure 9–7]. In 1960, our use of electricity was about half a kilowatt each; today it must be close to a kilowatt. Only about a fourth of this is used in our households; the remainder is mostly classed as industrial or commercial. Our generating capacity is about two kilowatts each; that is, on the average, our power plants run half the time. About a fifth is hydropower, a quarter from natural gas, and a bit more than half from coal. This is why the coal industry has not collapsed.

So much for the past; what of the future?

The curve of electrical energy growth plotted on semi-logarithmic paper

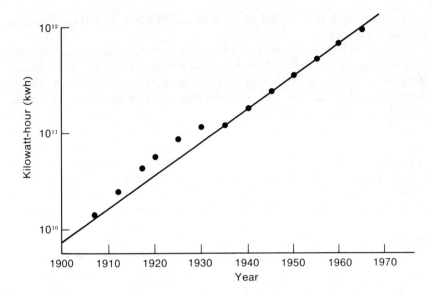

Figure 9-7. Historical growth of electricity consumption in the United States (kwh). (Source: *U.S. Stat. Abstr.* 1966, p. 529; *Hist. Stat. of the U.S.,* p. 506.)

is a straight line, the most seductive of all curves to the forecaster. It takes character to resist the temptation simply to continue the line onward. The act is easy; it seems simple and logical; it is subjective; it is self-serving for the forecaster, for his boss, for the utility employing him, for the industry, for the economy. It may even be self-fulfilling.

And it has been the practice. The literature, everywhere you turn, is full of a general gleeful, thoughtless prostration before the 8% growth curve. Even the Federal Power Commission,[6] in what should be the most thoughtful of all projections, has done little more than obtain the consensus of the utilities. These temper the most extravagant hopes by reducing the 8% to 6, and by limiting the projection to 1980, perhaps as far as is necessary for scheduling construction. Even those few who see[7] reason for alarm must needs go along with the higher rates in order to substantiate their fears. And so must I.

It has been said by an economist, "No obvious reason exists why it should not continue . . . [and] many arguments to prove that technology can overcome increasing shortages of natural resources ad infinitum." But obvious reasons do exist. The first is simply that the earth is finite, a matter more familiar to geographers than to economists; the second is that exponential growth will surpass any finite limits given a little time—a matter still known to too few.

Thus, 8% growth per year leads to a doubling time of nine years, a ten-folding time of 29 years, 2200-fold per century; enough, carefully applied, to vaporize the earth in the year 2370.

To say this is to say simply that growth must end. The question I am trying to force on us is two-fold: shall we let growth continue until "natural forces" bring it to an end, and perhaps us, too; or shall we try to decide where it should end and seek to identify and establish policies to bring it to such an end? Who's in charge around here, anyway?

323

I see three sorts of so-called "natural forces"; I prefer to call them inertial guidance principles.

First: the extractive resource. It is hopeless to evaluate this at the moment. Hubbert[8] has shown clearly that the age of fission nuclear energy is limited. But, fusion energy is beginning to perk up a bit and I think we should assume it will work. If it does, then we can vaporize the earth, and more, with the deuterium in the seas.

Second, let me come up with a new term for a class of resources. I have deliberately used "extractive" just a moment ago. Now, let me use "absorptive resource" for the capacity of the environment to accept the energy we throw away, the waste heat. This is in the area of environmental quality. Energy is less messy than beer cans; energy is radiated from the earth and never returns. But the earth must warm up if it is to radiate more energy; fortunately, the rate goes up (barring albedo changes) as the fourth power of absolute temperature (Wien's Law).

I want to argue some generalities on the absorptive energy resource, and ask your pardon for using some big numbers. The sun's annual input of energy to the earth is 5300 Q where Q is 10^{18} BTU. The human use of energy in 1950 was about 0.1 Q (100 milli Q); I suppose it is about 0.2 Q today. If all men used as much electricity as the American and if American electrical growth continues at 8% per year, the human output of energy in about 2100 AD would be 5300 Q and the earth, according to Wien's Law, would be 100°F hotter. I can't imagine what we would use this power for until close to the end, but then, it is painfully clear we would use it all for air conditioning. In about a century from now, with the same assumptions, the earth would be 10°F hotter and the ice caps would be melting. Gondolas on Fifth Avenue and all that; Cairo, Illinois, a seaport; 30 billion people and a lot less cropland. Before panicking, note that you have seventy years before the warmup reaches 1°F.

Shorter term problems do arise locally. Washburn (California State Senate Commission testimony)[9] has noted that if you believe in such growth, you should anticipate by the end of the century a million kw nuclear power plant every six miles along the California coast.

Jaske and his associates have estimated recently[10] that by 2000, heat rejection from the Atlantic Metropolitan area in January will come to half of the solar input. Microclimatology will be a growing field. While hotspots have long existed where local output exceeded input of heat, any campfire for instance, these will grow; and spread.

New York already has trouble finding enough electricity for existing air conditioning equipment, but the more air conditioning is localized, the hotter the outside air becomes, the more air conditioning is needed and the less effective it becomes. I think I may have been in a few places where air conditioning failed to work because it was warming up the outside air too much. The natural response is for the most heat sensitive occupant to order more equipment, which will force the neighborhood to do the same, which in turn will simply increase the external temperature. Here we have an "externality" with a vengeance, a magnificent example of Garrett Hardin's "Tragedy of the Commons." Those of us who can't stand the heat had better get out of the kitchen.

These heat burdens on the absorptive resource can also be expressed

324

in terms of evaporative load. The sun's input, if all spent in evaporation of water, would vaporize 190″ per year. Current world total energy use, 0.2 Q, would then evaporate 190/5300 × 0.2 = 0.007″ per year, a trivial layer. For the 48 states it is 0.04″ for electricity alone, and would be 0.4″ at the end of the century. Stream runoff in the 48 states is about 8″. But in the metropolitan east, the intensity of energy use must rise to at least a thousand times the national average, or equivalent to 40″ of evaporation. These regions may already be preying on external water supplies for cooling and are compounding their air conditioning problems with increased humidity.

This is why power plants will be seeking the coasts from now on. Washburn, though, concerned for the aesthetic value of the coasts, would require them to be several miles inland, and thinks we might as well admit that cooling water is to be evaporated immediately in cooling towers. Sacramento Municipal Utility District is building a big one now at Rancho Seco near Ione. It is something like 400 feet tall and 400 feet in diameter.

So much for the absorptive resource. We cannot prove that disaster faces us immediately; only presently.

Turning to the next "natural force," the next sort of inertial guidance, what will we do with so much electricity, and can we afford it? Eight percent growth to the end of the century means 8-10 times as much altogether, perhaps five times as much percapita. Does anyone have the ghost of a notion how we will use so much? The plausibility of the exponential projection can be no greater than the plausibility of prospective use. From the point of view of the proponents of growth, yesterday's tomorrow had much more in it than today's tomorrow. In 1930, aluminum, other electrosmelted metals, television, better lighting, a host of appliances and a world of improved electrical industrial equipment were on the horizon. Today, I see little: more air conditioning which is still a long way from saturation and the "all-electric home," already a controversial matter.

On the matter of cost, an older generation was brought up to turn off the lights because electricity cost money; some of us are still compulsive on this score. A younger generation believes electricity is free, and can't be bothered to throw the switch. We even have a mythology which says you shouldn't turn off fluorescent lights; I hope this is about to be smoked out. One utility is said to leave fluorescent lights always on in its own building, for heat as well as light. This is as bad an example as I can imagine for others who must pay for their own lighting as well as for the utility's.

At today's 8,000 kwh per capita, costing perhaps 1.3¢/kwh[11] whether paid directly or indirectly, our annual personal share is $100 each, wholesale. This is less than 5% of income and essentially trivial. Will it continue to be trivial when approaching 10% of income? By the end of the century it would be $1,000 per capita, and in sixty years, $10,000

We believe that electricity has always become cheaper and are told that no reason to believe otherwise exists. But, in fact, the price of electricity, which has been falling throughout our lives, has about hit bottom, and throughout our children's lives, it will be rising. Even if power plants become slightly more efficient, the increasing cost of fuel, of wages, of maintenance and, especially, of administration, will increase costs for the consumer. When will he begin to resist and to insist that the kids turn off the lights? Pacific Gas and Electric Company is even now petitioning for a 10% increase in rates.

Again, so long as costs were declining, return on utility investment should have been good because, in the nature of things, regulatory agencies were slower to reduce rates than utilities were to reduce costs. Under such conditions, expansion of capacity with its increasing proportion of efficient generators make a good thing look even better. With rising costs and with very limited prospective gains in efficiency, will expansion look so good? Will, perhaps, the utilities cease to urge us to use more electricity?

To sum up on inertial guidance: in the short run, nothing seems likely to stop growth; in the middle run, economics will; in the long run, the environment will strike back, if nothing else works.

I should like to close with a few notes on another path. This stems from my belief, presented to you two years ago, that we suffer from having established a resource policy for an empty land and a poor society, a resource policy which won't work in a full land and for a rich society. I have suggested in an intervening paper that we must begin to regard our natural resources as finite and inherently valuable, as the common property of the society, and that we must begin to discourage their exploitation in order to shift the emphasis of our economy from growing extraction to growing service. To this end, I have advocated charging, whether by tax or severance fee, or whatever, for the use of those resources which are in the market, but not for those which are aesthetic.

Before I itemize some recommendations, please consider these items: If you heat a house with natural gas, with coal, with wood, you thermally pollute this world with the heat liberated by the fuel you burn, no more. If you heat the house electrically (except it be by hydroelectricity, an unlikely event), you thermally pollute the environment by three times as much. If you heat your house with a fuel containing sulfur, you pollute the environment with sulfur dioxide; if you heat your house electrically from a power plant using the same fuel, your share of sulfur dioxide pollution is tripled. Next, and quite different, we expect to get lower rates if we are big customers for energy; again, we expect lower tolls if we use the bridge at rush hour. Neither makes any sense today; they are empty land policies. In contrast, we expect to pay higher rates if we use the telephone at rush hour.

Specifically, I recommend that we:

1. Tax the fuel resource so that the tax falls on the consumer and so that it escalates with increasing use.

2. Charge for the privilege of using the absorptive resources, certainly for heat and sulfur dioxide, and perhaps for carbon dioxide, with again escalation, both for total amount and regional intensity.

3. Penalize the power industry for using natural gas for electrical generation. The public welfare will be better served if gas is reserved for domestic heating.

4. Penalize the use of electricity, except hydroelectricity, for domestic heating, especially if natural gas is available. (However, when nuclear energy has become dominant, domestic electric heating may become inescapable.)

5. Substantially abandon the development of additional hydroelectricity;

the slides you have been seeing since the last diagram are intended to suggest to you that moving water is more to be admired than used, that the primary purpose of water is to beautify the earth.

6. Penalize the power industry for advertising for growth.

7. Constrain the siting of thermal power plants to ease and distribute the burden on absorptive resources, and to protect aesthetic resources.

8. In regions of acute air conditioning burden, provide systems for collective heat removal.

9. Do not consider regional integration and pumped storage any boon. They increase the overall absorptive resource burden. Storm King pumped storage, for example, will only aggravate New York City's microclimate.

10. Encourage retirement of old plants, but only modestly. While they aggravate the heat burden, they are trivial.

1. R. J. Forbes and E. J. Dijksterhuis, *A History of Science and Technology,* vol. 1, p. 132. Penguin Books, Baltimore, 1963.
2. Palmer C. Putnam, *Energy in the Future,* p. 82. Van Nostrand, New York, 1953.
3. Neal Potter and Francis T. Christy, Jr., *Trends in Natural Resource Commodities,* p. 33. Resources for the Future/Johns Hopkins Press, Baltimore, 1962.
4. *loc. cit.* p. 34.
5. U.S. Department of Commerce, *Historical Statistics of the United States,* 1960.
6. Federal Power Commission, *National Power Survey,* 1964. Part 1, pp. 35–50.
7. "Engineers project heat rejection requirements"; news report of a paper by R. T. Jaske *et al; Chemical & Engineering News,* 48:9 (March 2, 1970).
8. Committee on Resources and Man, *Resources and Man,* Chapter 8, esp. pp. 205–206. W. H. Freeman and Co., San Francisco, 1969.
9. Personal communication from Charles A. Washburn summarizing testimony before a Commission of the California State Senate *ca.* March 1970.
10. *Chemical & Engineering News, loc. cit.*
11. Bureau of the Census, *Statistical Abstract of the United States,* 1966, pp. 529, 536.

the power crisis that threatens the world

isaac asimov

Earth's fuel supply is starting to run low. The solution: make "hydrogen fusion" work.

It is astonishing but frighteningly true—America is deeply concerned about its energy supply. When the weather gets too hot for too long, electric companies throughout the heavily populated Northeast have to begin rationing electricity. In the winter, we must look forward to a shortage in fuel oil and natural gas.

Can it be that our fuel supply, which we need for providing heat and producing electricity, is running out?

Not just yet. The trouble right now is that tension in the Middle East is reducing oil supplies from there; that difficulties in transportation in the United States are cutting down the fuel supply to the Northeast; that the necessity of clearing pollution agents out of fuel is limiting the supply we can use.

But someday, in the not-too-distant future, the ordinary fuels of today *will* begin to run out.

Ever since primitive man discovered how to make and use a fire, mankind has been burning fuel for warmth, and to cook food. About 6,000 years ago, we began to use the heat of fire to smelt ore and form metal; also to make glass and bake clay. About 200 years ago, we began to use the heat of fire to boil water and run steam engines. About 100 years ago, we began to use the heat of fire to generate electricity and to run internal-combustion engines that eventually powered automobiles and airplanes.

But to make all this possible, mankind needs something that will burn. First we used wood, but in the centers of civilization the forests began to disappear. Then we turned to coal and, still later, for greater convenience, to oil and natural gas.

Every year we have burned more and more of this fuel, and right now

Reprinted with permission of the author and *Boys Life*, 23 November 1971 issue, pp. 33–35. Published by the Boy Scouts of America. The author is a leading writer of science facts and fiction.

we burn enough to produce 20 billion billion calories of energy per year. To get that would mean burning nearly three billion tons of coal.

Nor is this the end. Each year there are more people on earth, more machines, more fuel-consuming devices. It has been found that we are doubling the use of energy every 15 years. By 1985, the world will need all the energy that could be produced by burning nearly six billion tons of coal.

How long can this go on?

It is estimated that there is enough gas, oil, and coal here and there in the earth to keep us going for 7,500 years at our present rate of energy use. Unfortunately, not all of this fuel can be dug or drilled out of the earth. Some of it is so deep, or spread out so thin, it would take more energy to get the fuel than that fuel would yield when burned. The fuel we could get out at an energy-profit would only last us about 1,000 years at the present rate of use.

Gas and oil are present in much smaller quantities than coal and would be used up much faster, in perhaps a hundred years. If the population continues to increase and our needs continue to double every 15 years, all the gas and oil, and coal will be gone in 135 years.

There is more to the problem of burning fuel than just the danger of its running out. The burning of fuel is the main source of air pollution, a problem that is growing more serious each year.

If mankind wishes to maintain the present level of civilization, we must find some alternate sources of energy, sources that will produce no pollution and are plentiful enough to keep us going and supply all our needs even if our population continues to increase for a while. (Of course, no source of energy can fill our needs if population increases forever, but we can suppose that, after a while, population will stop increasing and reach some stable figure.)

One new energy source that became practical only 30 years ago is the fission into smaller atoms of the large atoms of elements such as uranium and thorium.

Uranium and thorium aren't as plentiful as coal, but pound for pound there is much more energy to be obtained from fissioning atoms than from burning coal. It is estimated that the energy available from the uranium and thorium we can mine out of the earth's crust is a hundred times as great as the energy we can get from burning the earth's coal.

There are difficulties, though: Uranium and thorium atoms are spread thin among the rocks and it isn't easy to get them out.

Then, too, the smaller atoms formed by fission are very radioactive and, therefore, dangerous. What does one do with this "radioactive ash"? It can't be allowed to contaminate the environment, for it is a far more dangerous form of pollution than anything produced by the burning of coal or oil. Complicated ways have been worked out to store the radioactive ash in huge drums of liquid, or to combine it with glass, and then place it all in deep salt mines. But scientists continue to be nervous about this solution to the problem.

What's more, there is always a chance of some accident in the very complicated machinery in a fission power-plant, resulting in a bit of runaway reaction. This could spread radioactivity for miles around.

The energy produced by fission is good; but the manner of production is risky.

What else? There is energy produced by moving water (waterfalls or river currents) and moving air (winds), or by the tides as they come and go, or by the heat inside the earth. There is no possible pollution here and such energy never can run out as long as the earth and sun exist. The trouble here is that there are only certain places where waterfalls and hot springs and large tides can be found, and these are not always convenient places. The winds blow everywhere, of course, but they are not reliable.

Moreover, all these forms of energy are not enough. They would be useful to stretch the supply, but mankind could not depend on them alone.

Then what about the heat of the sun, itself? The energy of the sunlight that falls on the earth each year is 60,000 times as great as all the energy we use that year by burning fuel. Couldn't we use a little bit of it for the needs of our industries and homes?

Unfortunately, the sun's energy is spread out so that we would have to collect all of it over 3,000 square miles to satisfy our needs. If all we were able to collect were just one percent of its energy, we would have to spread out our collectors over 300,000 square miles. And that doesn't allow for the fact that clouds would interrupt the energy supply frequently.

The places where the sun shines most steadily and where there is the most room available are the desert areas, which are far removed from the population centers that need the energy. We might imagine huge portions of the Sahara desert filled with special devices that turn sunlight into electricity, but it would be difficult to get that energy from the Sahara, where it is not needed, to New York, say, where it is.

Science-fiction writers have imagined devices out in space (nearer the sun, where the energy is more concentrated) that capture sunlight and beam it down to energy plants in various parts of the earth. However, something like this probably can't be accomplished soon enough for our immediate needs.

That leaves one other energy source—the smashing of very small atoms together to form slightly larger ones. Suppose hydrogen atoms (the smallest of all) are smashed together, or "fused," to form the somewhat larger helium atoms. Such "hydrogen fusion" would release far more energy, pound per pound, than one could get out of uranium fission.

It is hydrogen fusion that results in the vast explosion of the hydrogen bomb. It is hydrogen fusion that keeps the sun and other stars shining and giving off energy for billions of years.

There are three kinds of hydrogen: hydrogen-1; hydrogen-2, or "deuterium"; and hydrogen-3, or "tritium." It is very hard to make hydrogen-1 undergo fusion and scientists consider its use impractical. It would be much easier to work with tritium but that exists in only very tiny quantities.

That leaves deuterium, which is easier to handle than ordinary hydrogen, and is more common than tritium. In all the hydrogen of the world, only one atom out of 6,000 is deuterium, while all the rest are ordinary hydrogen; but even so, that is enough.

Earth's vast oceans are made up almost entirely of water molecules, and each water molecule contains two hydrogen atoms. Even if only one in

6,000 of those hydrogen atoms is deuterium, that still means there are about 35 thousand billion tons of deuterium in the oceans.

What's more, it isn't necessary to dig for that deuterium or to drill for it. If ocean water is allowed to run through separation plants, the deuterium can be extracted without very much trouble. In fact, for the energy you could get out of it, deuterium from the oceans would be only one hundredth as expensive as coal.

The deuterium in the world's oceans, if allowed to undergo fusion little by little, would supply mankind with enough energy to keep going, at the present rate, for 500 billion years. Since the sun won't last nearly that long, we might just as well say that if we are careful, hydrogen fusion will supply mankind with energy for as long as we will exist on earth.

Then, too, there is no danger of hydrogen fusion plants running out of control. They would be simpler than fission plants and if anything at all went wrong, the deuterium supply could be automatically cut off and the fusion process then would stop instantly. Nor is there any pollution problem, for in the fusion process all that is formed is ordinary helium, which is the *least* dangerous substance known.

Well, then, when can we expect to have controlled hydrogen fusion plants supplying mankind with energy?

There is a catch. A big catch. To start the fusion going we need a temperature of a hundred million degrees. At that temperature, all substances become thin vapors that spread out beyond our control at once. Is there a solution?

One thing scientists can do is to try to hold the deuterium together by magnetic fields. But even with magnetic fields, the deuterium is hard to handle—the hot gas wiggles like a fast and furious snake. Magnetic fields of many shapes have been tried to tame that wiggle, and doughnut shapes of one kind or another have proved to be best.

In order to make the hot deuterium easier to hold in place, scientists have had to make it very thin, only about a hundred-thousandth as dense as ordinary air at most. If it is still less dense, it is even easier to handle.

But then, the less dense the deuterium, the longer it must be held at a hundred million degrees before it starts to fuse. If the deuterium is a hundred-thousandth as dense as ordinary air, it must be kept in place at the right temperature for nearly a second.

So we must have a magnetic field of the right shape that can hold enough deuterium in place while it is heated to a hundred million degrees for nearly a second. If this could be done, the fusion reaction would start and energy would pour out of the system. That energy could be used to make the magnetic field more stable and more powerful and to keep the temperature at the proper level.

Once started, such a system would be self-sustaining. The very energy it produced would be enough to keep it going.

How close are we now to starting such a controlled fusion system?

For nearly 20 years, scientists all over the world, particularly in the United States and the Soviet Union, have been working hard on devices for the purpose.

In the Soviet Union, for instance, hopeful results have been achieved with devices called "Tokamak" (an abbreviation of a long, complicated Russian phrase). Soviet scientists have used them to keep a supply of deuterium one millionth as dense as air in place at a hundred million degrees for one hundredth of a second.

This is the best anyone has done yet. If only the deuterium could be made ten times denser, and then held in place at that tremendous temperature for a hundred times longer, fusion would start.

The Soviet Union is building a similar device that will be larger and more powerful. It ought to be finished by 1974 and Soviet scientists are sure that, with that device, they can push the deuterium over the edge and start the fusion process going.

The United States is hot on Soviet heels in this respect and some optimistic scientists think that, by 1980, the world will witness a small power plant somewhere that will be producing electricity from the heat of hydrogen fusion.

If so, and if mankind can solve its other problems, too, then we can envision a future in which nobody need fear energy shortages ever again.

our
nuclear
future

With the unleashing of nuclear energy, man's world will never be the same. There is no single agent in man's technological arsenal so capable of transforming the environment of earth and the future of man. The atomic nucleus is most certainly an appropriate topic for the concluding section of this book.

The one characteristic of the nucleus with overriding importance to the environment and to the affairs of man is its stupendous energy. Over a million times more energy is released in nuclear change than in chemical change. The energy man could once generate with a million tons of coal, he can now obtain with less than one ton of uranium. And all that he could do with a million tons of TNT, he can now do with about one ton of plutonium, deuterium, and lithium. Clearly, the nucleus brings to man both promise and threat on an unprecedented scale. For this reason, nuclear energy has appropriately been called "the honey-venom."

To harvest the honey of abundant nuclear power, we are plunging headlong into the nuclear age without duly considering the associated venom. In weighing nuclear promise against nuclear threat, we should recognize that all the advantages lie on the side of nuclear threat. A million tons of TNT used destructively can never be offset by a million tons of coal used constructively. A single nuclear weapon dropped on target would unleash more environmental and political havoc than could be justified by a hundred nuclear reactors pouring out cheap power. Viewed in this light, our present course is indeed dangerous.

The impingement of the nucleus on man's environment has barely begun. The articles to follow are largely future-oriented—attempts to anticipate the impact and repercussions of nuclear growth. Glenn T. Seaborg, discoverer of plutonium (Pu) and for ten years chairman of the Atomic Energy Commission, begins in article 48, "Nuclear Power—An Environmental Asset," by emphasizing the advantages of nuclear power, especially in the reduction of air pollution. He points to the need for nuclear power to help meet the future's massive energy requirements. In Article 49, "Plutonium and the Energy Decision, begins in Article 48, "Nuclear Power—An Environmental nium—fuel of the future.

Nuclear radiation, a by-product of the enormous energy of the nucleus, is the topic of the next two essays. In Article 50, "Issues in the Radiation Controversy," Arthur R. Tamplin engages a broad spectrum of nuclear questions, including the radiation controversy in which he has been so prominently embroiled. Then, in Article 51, "The Radioactive Risks of Nuclear Pollution," Jerold M. Lowenstein points out the adverse biological impact of radiation.

We end this book with two articles focusing on nuclear weapons—perhaps the most sinister threat of all to man and his environment (see Article 3). Ralph E. Lapp examines the phenomenal and dangerous growth in nuclear weapon firepower in Article 52, "Nuclear Weapons: Past and Present." In Article 53, "Nuclear Tyranny and the Divine Right of Kings," Gale Edward Christianson reminds us of the terrible danger of nuclear destruction in today's moral and political climate. He ends by stating a reality that the whole world must realize and realize soon if we are to have a future at all: "All other social issues including civil rights, poverty and pollution pale in the light of the nuclear threat because they are based upon the promise of a better life—while the single promise of nuclear war is universal death."

nuclear power—an environmental asset

glenn t. seaborg

Nuclear power is needed to help meet massive energy requirements. Without it, the drain on fossil fuel reserves and the air pollution problem would be enormous.

The growing national concern for the environment has resulted in close scrutiny of various power sources as possible purveyors of pollution. Plants powered by nuclear energy have received their share of attention and a number of questions and comments indicate honest concern about radiation levels and waste heat discharges into rivers and lakes. Many comments, however, reflect a lack of understanding of the Atomic Energy Commission's (AEC) comprehensive system of safety review and regulatory controls and the extensive scientific data on which these are based. Taking all factors into account, I feel that nuclear power, in balance, is really an environmental asset.

The major advantage of nuclear power in the environmental context is that it diminishes significantly the air pollution caused by power generation. This advantage cannot be appreciated fully until one considers that a typically modern coal-fired plant of 1000 electrical megawatts capacity released about 750,000 pounds of sulfur dioxide each day of operation. A second advantage of nuclear power is the general cleanliness of the plant and its environs. While it is necessary to refuel a nuclear plant only about once a year, a modern 1000 electrical megawatt coal-fired plant needs about 8000 tons of coal every 24 hours.

A characteristic which nuclear plants share with all steam electric generating plants is that they must release the waste heat of their cooling water to the environment. The thermal effects of this water may be detrimental, beneficial, or insignificant, depending upon the specific site and measures taken in the design and operation of the plant.

Reprinted from *Environmental Science & Technology*, Vol. 4, April 1970, p. 269. Copyright 1970 by the American Chemical Society. Reprinted by permission of the copyright owner. The author was appointed AEC chairman by President Kennedy (1961), and reappointed by Presidents Johnson and Nixon. A discoverer of the transuranium elements (1940–1958), he was awarded the Nobel Prize in Chemistry (1951). He returned to the University of California at Berkeley in 1971.

Today's nuclear power plants produce more waste heat than modern fossil-fueled units of the same generating capacity. But advanced reactors now under development will release substantially less waste heat, reducing the present disparity in thermal effects between nuclear and conventional plants.

The AEC and other federal agencies have been conducting research on the problems associated with the disposal of waste heat. In fiscal year 1970, the AEC anticipates spending more than $1.6 million on the study of thermal effects. The electric utilities also are sponsoring considerable work in this area. Ways to make beneficial uses of heated water in agriculture and aquaculture also are being studied.

Another environmental aspect of nuclear power which has recently been the subject of more public discussion is the radioactivity associated with the production of nuclear power. Nuclear power plants do release, under controlled conditions, very small amounts of low-level radioactive effluents. The maximum amounts allowed to be released are based on radiation protection standards set by the Federal Radiation Council in light of the knowledge of the biological effects of radiation resulting from decades of study by national and international scientific groups, and continuously reevaluated by them. According to the best scientific evidence available today, this tiny increment to the natural background radiation we live with daily creates no significant biological hazard.

A new national effort is underway to convince the public of the environmental assets of nuclear power. Furthermore, the public must be convinced that additional power plants are truly needed. With our current electric generating capacity of about 325 million kilowatts, our requirements are expected to double in about 10 years, and, by the year 2000, our capacity should reach more than 1.5 billion kilowatts.

There is no doubt that nuclear power is needed to help meet these massive energy requirements. Without it, the drain on our fossil fuel reserves and the air pollution problem that would result should we try to meet all our projected requirements only by burning fossil fuels both would be enormous. Fortunately, we have at hand in nuclear energy an abundant source of power that can be advanced with a minimum of environmental impact.

What we need now, in addition to better long-range energy planning, are increased efforts to improve public understanding of the nature of our energy sources, our energy requirements, and our need to utilize all energy resources wisely and with the utmost consideration of their environmental effects.

plutonium and the energy decision

donald p. geesaman

In the final analysis the present generation of light water reactors is a technological cul de sac, with little relevance to a solution of the ultimate energy problem. This technology is probably no more than a final offering at the altar of exponential growth of electric power. The future and the substance of the fission program is the breeder reactor, and the representative fuel of the breeder is plutonium.

In our social climate of aggressive change, technology has evolved to a special station. As a catalyst of change, technology has become a basic implement of economic and political power. As a consequence, technological decisions are made on the limited social and physical scales dictated by specific economic and political responsibilities. This decoupling of decision from the complete world is the indulgence of a society that is socially diffuse and physically confined. It is an indulgence that can no longer be sustained.

The premium value placed by our society on growth and innovation manifests itself in a promotional attitude towards technology. Within this bias, benefits are regarded with indelicate optimism, and detriments as the hobgoblins of small minds. In the absence of any effective institution of contrary bias, the promoter's influence has become the dominant and hence the characteristic influence in our society's attitude toward technology. This situation deprives society of an overall appreciation of alternatives and implications, and hence, in the largest sense, is not beneficial.

Technology has conferred upon our society a way of life. Society is now vaguely coming to realize that something must be done to assure that this way of life is acceptable and sustainable. If these expectations are to be realized, then decisional decoupling and promotional bias must be recognized as defects in the present relationship between society and technology.

Reprinted by permission of *Science and Public Affairs, the Bulletin of the Atomic Scientists,* September 1971, pp. 33–36. Copyright © 1971 by the Educational Foundation for Nuclear Science. The author is a physicist who has been associated with John Gofman and Arthur Tamplin for the last four years.

The energy crisis, the reactor controversy and, more specifically, the proposed plutonium economy of the future are representative of this problem. It is in this context that they will be considered.

The present energy crisis in this country is largely confined to the electrical sector of the energy market. During this century the electric utility industry has enjoyed an uninhibited growth through orders of magnitude. The dilemma in which this industry presently finds itself is a consequence of the intrusion of new growth limiting factors on its former economic isolation. Because of this intrusion the industry has begun to recognize the distinction between markets and needs. It is certainly true that the markets for electric power are not saturated, and to the extent that they are decoupled from the social and physical world, the markets could be expected to grow exponentially for some time to come. But it is naive to believe that saturation of the markets will painlessly place the ultimate limit on the growth of the electric power industry. In fact, what the present crisis demonstrates is that physical limitations such as fuel availability, biological limitations such as air quality, and social limitations such as citing criteria are factors that intercede long before market saturation.

Recognition of this fact would be wider spread if a heavily subsidized nuclear technology had not materialized in the 1960s, and offered the possibility of bypassing these growth limiting factors. The Atomic Energy Commission and the reactor vendors promised clean, safe, cheap, abundant electrical power; and the utility industry accepted the nuclear solution to their restricted responsibilities, and in the years 1964–67, 60 reactors were purchased for some $10 billion in an unprecedented economic commitment to a new technology. As a result of promotional bias and isolation of decision, the determination to implement this major technology was easy for society. Too easy in fact, for now when the reactor arguments are belatedly raised in a larger forum, society is faced with its own *fait accompli,* and technological judgment is further distorted by deep economic involvement.

fission cul de sac

It has been eight years since the sale of the Oyster Creek reactor precipitated the rush to nuclear power. Some 110 commercial reactors are now completed or on order, and only now are the simplest implications of the commitment being widely appreciated. Radiation standards are being contested because of the potential increase in low level radiation exposure. The threat of major reactor accident has become aggravated as reactors have accumulated more rapidly than operating experience. The disposal of high level radioactive waste is an unsolved problem; no disposal site has been finally approved; and the practicality of large scale solidification of wastes is still undemonstrated. But reassessment of the reactor decision is awkward with so much committed, with some tens of thousands employed by the industry, with billions of dollars of reactor-funding utility bonds held by pension funds, insurance companies and foundations, and with the Federal Power Act's tradition of "greatest possible economy" as an added constraint on the production of electrical power.

In the final analysis the present generation of light water reactors is

341

a technological *cul de sac,* with little relevance to a solution of the ultimate energy problem. This technology is probably no more than a final offering at the altar of exponential growth of electric power. The future and the substance of the fission program is the breeder reactor, and the representative fuel of the breeder is plutonium.

Plutonium is an element virtually nonexistent in the earth's natural crust; for all practical purposes it is of man's doing. It has several long-lived isotopes, the most significant being plutonium-239, which because of its fissionable properties and ease of production is potentially the best of the three fission fuels. Plutonium-239 is an alpha emitter with a half-life of 24,000 years, hence its activity is undiminished within human time scales. It is 30 years since plutonium was first produced and isolated by Glenn T. Seaborg, now chairman of the AEC, and his colleagues. Until recently it was significant only as a nuclear explosive. Now, the Atomic Energy Commission is promoting it as the energy source of the not too distant future. How is this new technology to be assessed and appreciated by society? From Chairman Seaborg's "child-in-the-manger" descriptions of plutonium's origin; from romanticizations of the future, reminiscent of Jules Verne; from speculative projections of energy needs and markets to the year 2020? The more favorable side of the picture will assuredly be there; but is that enough for society or even utilities to judge by responsibly when considering the conjectured primary energy source of the future.

If the liquid metal fast breeder reactor is developed and implemented according to AEC projections, then by the year 1980 commercial plutonium production will be 30 tons annually, and in excess of 100 tons by the year 2000.

Plutonium is a fuel that is toxic beyond human experience. It is demonstrably carcinogenic to animals in microgram quantities. (Pure plutonium-239 in this amount would be roughly the size of a pollen grain.) One millionth of a gram injected intradermally in mice has caused local cancer. A similar amount injected into the blood system of dogs has induced a substantial incidence of bone cancer because of the element's affinity for bone tissue. It is fortunate that the body maintains a relatively effective barrier against the entry of plutonium into the blood system.

Under a number of probable conditions plutonium forms aerosols of micron-sized particulates. When lost into uncontrolled air these particulates can remain suspended for a significant time, and if inhaled they are preferentially deposited in the deep lung tissue, where their long residence time and high alpha activity can result in a locally intense tissue exposure. The lung cancer risk associated with these radiologically unique aerosols is unknown to orders of magnitude. Present plutonium standards are certainly irrelevant and probably not conservative. Even so, the fact that under present standards, the permissible air concentrations are about one part per million billion is a commentary on plutonium's potential as a pollutant. Its insolubility and long half-life make the continuing resuspension of particulate contamination another unresolved concern of serious proportions.

Nor is plutonium contamination an academic question. In May 1969 the most costly industrial fire in history occurred in Colorado at Rocky Flats, the weapons-making plant operated for the Atomic Energy Commission by Dow Chemical. This major plutonium handling facility lies 10 miles west of Denver. A subsequent environmental study by an independent party, E. A. Martell, revealed that off site plutonium contamination was two to three orders of magnitude greater than would have been expected from measured plutonium losses in the heavily filtered air effluent of the plant. After-the-fact explanations seemed to fix the source of this anomalous contamination as wind blown plutonium that had leaked from openly stored barrels of contaminated oil. The plutonium involved in the fire was largely contained and apparently was not implicated in the off-site contamination. Nevertheless, it is hardly reassuring that consequent to this fire Congress voted a special appropriation of $25.5 million (of a projected $118 million) for the upgrading of "fire protection, safety and operating conditions" at Rocky Flats and similar facilities. And there is little comfort to be found in the irresponsible waste disposal practices which were revealed by the investigation after the fire. The leakage of plutonium from the contaminated oil led to an uncontrolled source of plutonium which was some orders of magnitude larger than the integrated effluent loss during the 17 years of plant operation. As a result of this source, tens to hundreds of grams of plutonium went off site, 10 miles upwind from a metropolitan area. The loss was internally unnoticed, the ultimate deposition is now speculative, as is its human significance.

Is present society so psychically stable, so civilly docile that it can have its energy addiction based on a material whose radiological toxicity is such that a few ounces might cause a million undetected and irremediable fatal injuries? A complex and sophisticated society must bear the burdens of vulnerability and constraint that are inherent in its technologies.

Implicit in the present nuclear industry is the production of fissionable material. Our transition to plutonium as a major energy source will inextricably involve our society with the large scale commercial production of a substance that is a suitable nuclear explosive. A mystique of scientific accomplishment surrounded the development of nuclear weapons during World War II. That mystique has become illusory. The main practical impasse to nuclear weapon manufacture was perfecting and implementing the expensive technologies for manufacture of fissionable material. Gaseous diffusion enrichment of uranium and reactor breeding of plutonium were major industrial projects in their own rights, but they are now implicit in the nuclear power industry. A reactor of even the present generation will produce some 250 kilograms of plutonium per year, and since the amount necessary for an explosive device is described by Theodore Taylor as "a few kilograms," the substantial weapon capability of one commercial reactor can be inferred.

By the year 2000 plutonium is conjectured to be a major energy source with an annual production in excess of 100 tons. Can these quantities be handled without internal subversion? Underworld involvement in the transportation industry is legendary, and theft in the industry is epidemic. University unrest is ubiquitous, radical activism is a reality. So far as accountability experience is concerned, Nuclear Materials and Equipment Corporation (NUMEC), over several years of operation, was unable to account for six per cent (100 kilograms) of the highly enriched uranium that passed through its plant; and at a recent safeguards symposium the director of the AEC's Office of Safeguards and Materials Management observed that "we have a long way to go to get into that happy land where one can measure scrap effluents, products, inputs and discards to a one per cent accuracy."

[A number of "misroutings" of special nuclear materials has occurred and these have pointed clearly to the need for enhanced safeguards to prevent loss by theft of hijacking.

On March 5, 1969, a container of highly enriched UF-6 (uranium hexafluoride) was shipped from Portsmouth, Ohio, to Hematite, Missouri. It did not reach its destination in Missouri. The AEC, the Federal Bureau of Investigations and many individuals searched intensively. Finally, on March 19, the shipment was found in Boston.

In the same month of 1969, a shipment of highly enriched uranium destined for delivery at Frankfurt, Germany, wound up in London. In April 1970, a drum of waste containing some 70 per cent enriched uranium which was being shipped locally from one firm to another in the same California city ended up in Tijuana, Mexico. U.S. Representative Craig Hosmer of California, a member of the Congressional Joint Committee on Atomic Energy who described these incidents in a talk last year, recalled that the report on the Tijuana diversion was entitled: "Inadvertent export of special nuclear materials." Bulletin Ed. Note]

When plutonium commonly exists, the possibility of theft will exist, and accountability will be difficult, and the technology needed to make an explosive device will be available in textbooks, as it is already. Finally the social price for dealing with the problem effectively may be paid for dearly by the loss of some poorly seen freedom.

Quite aside from this, if the plutonium economy is implemented in the United States, then by symmetry it will inevitably be implemented by other major powers, and the technology would be marketed in all the small and underdeveloped countries that are struggling for stability. With reactor fuel plutonium, fission weapon capabilities are only days away. This capability makes nuclear disarmament seem remote, and is part of the responsibility of accepting the nuclear economy.

Since the Eisenhower administration the exchange of peaceful nuclear technology has been a component of our foreign policy. The peaceful atom has been internationally promoted with enough effect that access to the technology is a significant factor in obtaining signatories to the Nonproliferation Treaty. Without criticizing the Treaty or its intentions, it must be recognized that the line drawn between peaceful and nonpeaceful nuclear technology may effectively define no more than an irony.

Unless fusion reactor feasibility is demonstrated in the near future, the commitment will be made to liquid metal fast breeder reactors fueled by plutonium. Since fusion reactors are presently speculative, the decision for liquid metal fast breeder reactors should be anticipated. Considering the enormous economic inertia involved in the commitment, it is imperative that the significance of the decision be symmetrically examined prior to active promotion of the industry.

In our present society, it is doubtful that this will be done. Promotional bias and isolation of decisions will preclude it. The Atomic Energy Commission, in its posture of promoter, will be functionally unable to serve also as a critical advocate for society in general. This responsibility will be outside the restricted economic sphere of utility and vendor. In this unbalanced situation uncertainties will be unnoticed and shortcomings degraded. Public, industry and government will be effectively uninformed. Unless some new institution of assessment intercedes the consideration affecting the decision will be defective. Technology is too dominant and society too restricted for such defects to be tolerable. A flawed judgement involving plutonium, and all other decisions could be irrelevant.

issues in the radiation controversy

arthur r. tamplin

What are the real issues of the radiation controversy affecting nuclear power generation of electricity? Is there a dispute about the facts?

An illusion that there is a radiation effects controversy has caused the real issues associated with the nuclear power industry to be submerged or obscured. I would like to dispel the "effects controversy" as an obscurant and to focus attention upon what I consider to be the significant issues relative to the burgeoning nuclear power industry.

The operation of the nuclear electrical power industry will involve the release of some radioactivity to the environment and the subsequent irradiation of man. The biological consequences of such irradiation will be the induction of some number of additional cancer deaths and the production of genetic damage leading to an increase in genetic disorders in future generations. The magnitude of these effects, and hence the risk, depends upon the amount of radioactivity released. A considerable controversy has developed over how much risk of this type the public is willing to accept from nuclear generated electricity.

The proponents of the nuclear power industry are always quick to point out the obvious fact that we take risks every day. Risks, they say, are part of every day life. The most commonly employed example is the automobile. The macabre statistic of 50,000 traffic fatalities per year is cited as the kind of risk that the people of the United States are willing to accept for the benefits of the family car.

I doubt whether anyone finds this risk acceptable, including most of those who employ it as a rhetoric argument. Ralph Nader has become somewhat of a national hero by forcing manufacturers to make cars safer. But traffic fatalities are not the only hazard associated with the automobile. There is exhaust emission, asbestos particles from brakes and noise. In

Reprinted by permission of *Science and Public Affairs,* the *Bulletin of the Atomic Scientists,* September 1971, pp. 25–27. Copyright © 1971 by the Educational Foundation for Nuclear Science. The author, a biophysicist, is research associate at the Lawrence Radiation Laboratory, Livermore.

the long run the effects of these factors may pale the traffic fatalities in comparison. The automobile is an inefficient means of transportation that is rapidly depleting the world's supply of oil. To move it about, vast areas are paved.

The total adverse effect of the automobile on man and his environment is massive, and we are beginning to react to the automobile. Safety standards and exhaust emission standards are now in federal and state regulations. Expressway construction is being contested. Pressures are being exerted to apply gasoline taxes to pollution control rather than highway construction. Public transportation systems that were nearly forced out of existence by the family car are now being vigorously pursued.

We cannot, at this time, predict the ultimate fate of the automobile industry in the country. A very sizeable fraction of our economy is involved with this industry and, moreover, it is even a part of the fabric of our culture. Hence, the changes will necessarily be slow. But the processes of stunting the industry and eventually reducing its overall impact in our society have begun.

The selection of the automobile as an analogy by nuclear power advocates is a good one, but not for the reasons they propose. The automobile is an example of a good thing carried to an extreme. The care and feeding of the automobile in this country borders on a psychosis whose cure will be long and difficult.

The ever increasing demand for electrical power has all the appearances of another good thing carried to an extreme. It is this factor that forms the cornerstone for most of the opposition to nuclear power plants. It is not obvious that the benefits of more electrical power outweigh the risks. Quite the contrary, if electricity continues to be used to drive toward an ever increasing industrial growth with its attendant resource depletion and environment degradation, there may well be no benefits. The technological revolution is turning into a technological revulsion. A growth in the electrical industry driven by the same laissez-faire forces of the past is a prescription for disaster. We need to begin to solve our problems, not exacerbate them. The basic question then is one of benefit versus risk. The risks are real and apparent, and include the serious side effects of some of the imagined benefits.

On November 18, 1969, John Gofman and I presented evidence before the Senate Subcommittee on Air and Water Pollution which indicated that the biological effects of radiation were 20 times worse than was expected when the present radiation exposure guidelines were promulgated. We then suggested that the guidelines should be reduced by at least a factor of 10. The subsequent flak from the Atomic Energy Commission created the impression that we were at great odds with our scientific peers in this interpretation of the biological data.

But let us look at the record. Coincident with our testimony, the International Commission on Radiological Protection (ICRP) was circulating its latest report, "Radiosensitivity and Spatial Distribution of Dose" (Publication 14, 1969). In a previous report on "The Evolution of Risks from Radiation" (Publication 8), which was published just three years earlier in 1966, it was estimated that leukemia would be the dominant cancer induced by radiation. They estimated that the total yield of all other forms of cancer combined would be equal to that of the yield of leukemia. If 20 cases of leukemia were induced in a population, one could expect all other forms of cancer combined to yield 20 cases.

Three years later, in Publication 14, it is stated that the yield of other cancers would be expected to be five to six times the yield of leukemias. In making this estimate the ICRP failed to correct for the difference in the dosage delivered to the various organs in the study used. Had they made this correction the other cancers would have been estimated to be approximately 30 times the leukemias. Nevertheless in Appendix 4 of Publication 14, it is shown that the new evidence suggests that the radiation exposure guidelines should be reduced tenfold. There is no substantial radiation effects controversy here.

We pointed out that the biological data showed that the developing human fetus was extremely sensitive to radiation. The latest data of Alice Stewart shows a measurable increase in childhood cancer and leukemia following one x-ray examination (0.3 rad). The ICRP recognizes this much greater sensitivity. As a matter of fact the United States counterpart, the National Committee on Radiation Protection and Measurement (NCRPM) recently recommended that the occupational exposure limit for pregnant women should be reduced by a factor of 10. Although it has been a standing rule that the exposure limit of the population should be one-tenth that of the occupational limit, the NCRPM failed to make the recommendation. The rules are being changed in the middle of the game.

Once it became obvious that Gofman and I were not so out-of-tune with our scientific peers concerning the biological effects of radiation, a different approach was rigorously pursued. The argument goes like this: The guidelines are irrelevant because the nuclear industry will expose the public to only a very small fraction of the amount specified in the guidelines. We have always agreed that, in their normal day-to-day operations, it should be technically possible for the nuclear power industry to meet much more restrictive guidelines.

Thus, the "radiation effects controversy" boils down to two questions:

1. If the nuclear power industry will expose individuals to only a small fraction of the guidelines, why is the AEC so reluctant to reduce the guidelines in accordance with the latest biological data?

2. Why didn't the NCRPM also recommend that the exposure guideline for pregnant women in the general population be reduced by a factor of 10? In order to find an answer to both questions, I refer you to the 1969 Hearings before the Joint Committee on Atomic Energy, "Environmental Effects of Producing Electrical Power," where the AEC Commissioners state that these low emission rates are only design objectives, and that they are not confident that the new reactors will meet these design objectives. Moreover, they point out that the present standards may be needed to legalize radiation emissions of the fuel reprocessing plants, which are necessary to support the reactor power industry.

In June of this year, the AEC belatedly revised the design specifications for light water moderated nuclear power reactors (Title 10, Code of Federal Regulations, Part 50). These new regulations call for a hundredfold reduction in the radiation exposure limit for this type of reactor. While there is nothing iron-clad about these new regulations (e.g., they allow excursions of 4 to 8 times the specifications), the revisions are a step in the right direction. At the same time, the revisions are full of loop-holes. They apply only to light water moderated reactors. They do not apply to gas-cooled reactors, to the fast-breeder reactors or to the fuel reprocessing and waste storage and disposal facilities. Hence, the major thrust of the revisions is to indicate that the AEC itself agrees that there is a serious hazard to low level radiation.

So far as the genetic effects of radiation are concerned, it generally is felt that these are far greater than the somatic effects, such as cancer induction. Concerning the allowable genetic exposure, we quote from the ICRP "Recommendations" (Publication 9, 1966).

> *Because of the need for guidance in this regard, the Commission in its 1958 Recommendations suggested a provisional limit of 5 rems per generation for the genetic dose to the whole population, from all sources additional to natural background radiation and to medical exposures. The Commission believes that this level provides reasonable latitude for the expansion of atomic energy programs in the foreseeable future. It should be emphasized that the limit may not in fact represent a proper balance between possible harm and probable benefit, because of the uncertainty in assessing the risks and the benefits that would justify the exposure.*

The standard was established by the desire to provide a reasonable latitude for expansion of the nuclear industry. The public health principle involved seems to be the hope that the genetic effects won't be too severe.

The statement by the ICRP that the genetic limit may not be the proper balance between benefit and risk is the primary ingredient in the nuclear reactor controversy. The nuclear technologists blithely state that the benefits from nuclear power outweigh the risks, but they only imagine the benefits and minimize the risk. David Inglis brought this out quite forcefully in his article "Nuclear Energy and the Malthusian Dilemma" (*Bulletin*, February 1971).

The risks associated with nuclear power plants are not just from radioactive releases during normal day-to-day operations. They must include the possibility of a major or catastrophic accident. We don't know what the chances of such an accident are. They must include the vast amounts of radioactive wastes that are accumulating in tanks at fuel reprocessing sites. We have not devised a system for managing these wastes. And finally, the risks must certainly include the realization that we have not developed an adequate system to prevent the diversion of special nuclear material, such as plutonium and enriched uranium, into the illicit manufacture of atomic weapons.

And what about the benefits? Nuclear technologists say that nuclear plants are clean compared to coal-fired plants and that we need more electricity to improve continually our standard of living. These myths were also taken to task by Inglis. I would like to add the following in further support of his arguments.

All the nuclear critics that I know deplore fossil-fueled generating plants as much as, and even more than, nuclear plants. No one can deny the ill effects of the noxious gases that belch from their chimneys. Such plants can and should be cleaned up. If the present rash proliferation of nuclear power plants were meant to stop the drain on the world's fossil fuel resources, one might be more willing to accept some of the risk associated with these plants. But the driving force behind this proliferation is not to replace but to augment the fossil-fueled plants. Present projections indicate a tenfold increase of electrical power production by the year 2000. Only 50 percent of this is projected to be nuclear. That means a fivefold increase in fossil-fueled plants.

Consequently, focusing attention on the comparative or absolute risk of the two types of generating facilities has obscured the fundamental question associated with the electrical power industry. The fundamental question is, simply, "Why more power?" A flat and unqualified statement that power needs are doubling every eight years is not sufficient. To accept this statement without question is to accept and endorse the notion that electrical power consumption is a desirable end in itself. Today, when environmental questions are paramount, it becomes necessary to question the basis for all intrusions on the environment. I do not know that we need more power. The population of the United States increases at about one per cent per year. It is certainly not obvious that a population increase of one per cent per year demands an increased electrical power consumption of about 10 per cent a year. It is certainly not obvious that power demands are the same as power needs. How is the power to be used?

It is argued that this power is needed to increase our standard of living. Yet while we are the most industrialized nation in the world, our infant mortality and age-specific death rates are 1.5 those of a number of countries, such as Sweden, and the average life expectancy is four years less. On closer inspection we find that those in the upper 25 per cent income bracket in this country have death rates and a life expectancy comparable to Sweden's. At the same time, these biological data demonstrate that 50 per cent of the U. S. population (those below the median family income) have an infant mortality that is more than twice what it should be and have a life expectancy that is reduced by more than eight years. Moreover, 20 per cent of the U. S. population (those with the lowest family incomes) have an infant mortality that is four times what it should be and a life expectancy that is reduced by more than 16 years.

Over the last several years our energy consumption (electrical and otherwise) and our gross national product have increased. Coincident with this we have observed the strange phenomenon of a continuation of the inflationary spiral, while the ranks of the unemployed are growing. The gap between the affluent and poor appears to be growing. Where is the evidence that increasing our energy consumption will do anything but compound the problems of the poor and the environment? It would appear that our technology has become uncoupled from a large fraction of our population, and that our national machine is being driven by a smaller fraction who have enough fun money to be gluttonous consumers.

It is not unreasonable to suggest that, even in our affluent society, poverty is the number one pollutant. Our environmental neglect is just a symptom of our more fundamental neglect of people. When we compare the energy consumption in the United States with that of the rest of the world, the fact that we are facing an energy crisis is a national disgrace. I can come to no other conclusion than that the crisis is caused not by a shortage but by improper utilization. As Inglis wrote:

> *Prudence, then, would seem to require efforts to induce power-mad America to exercise a little restraint and cease to lead the revolution of rising expectations so rapidly out of sight for the world's teeming billions.*

In a world of ever decreasing resources and ever increasing demands for the resources, we are running a collision course with a nuclear war triggered by an avoidable Malthusian crisis. A terrifying question is: Do we have enough time left to bring about the drastic changes in human behavior necessary to avoid this Malthusian confrontation? A more terrifying question is: Do enough individuals who could do something about it really give a damn?

the radioactive risks of nuclear pollution

jerold lowenstein

Although precautions are taken to prevent these lethal and long-lived radioactive poisons from entering the environment, a number of storage tanks have already developed leaks, and the heat from wastes stored in salt mines could deform the walls of the mines and raise the ground temperature at the surface by several degrees. Inevitably some of these radio-isotopes will find their way into the world's waters and into the hydrobiosphere.

At a recent meeting of the United Nations Food and Agriculture Organization in Rome, it was reported that all types of pollutants in the ocean are increasing except for radioactivity. The report was widely disseminated in the news media and probably reassured millions of people who are concerned about the dangers of radioactivity in the environment. This happy situation can last only a short time. The major source of radioactive pollution of the oceans now is nuclear fallout due to atomic weapons testing in the atmosphere, which has been decreasing for the past ten years, since the U.S. and the U.S.S.R. stopped atmospheric testing. Very soon, however, this trend will be reversed because of resumed atmospheric testing of nuclear weapons by other nations, and because of the increasing numbers of nuclear power plants and nuclear ships in operation. Within a generation, we may be seeing serious radiation effects on ocean ecology and human health.

Due to fallout, that will continue for another generation from nuclear weapons already tested, the world's oceans have already been contaminated with approximately twenty million curies of strontium-90 and cesium-137, isotopes with half-lives of thirty years, which enter the metabolic cycles of all living organisms.[1] There are, at present, measurable amounts of these two radioactive isotopes in all living creatures, including man. There is

Reprinted from *Sierra Club Bulletin,* Vol. 56, July-August 1971, pp. 22–23. Copyright © 1971 *Sierra Club Bulletin.* The author is an Associate Clinical Professor of Medicine at the Radioactivity Research Center, University of California, San Francisco.

considerable scientific controversy as to the "safe" concentration of these materials, or whether there is a safe concentration. But it is important to realize that if at some point we should decide that the "safe" concentration has been exceeded, we must then wait at least 30 years for that amount to be reduced by fifty percent.

Present levels, whether safe or not, are low indeed compared with those that may be projected to the end of the century. Until now, nuclear power has been largely experimental, but by 1980 there are expected to be about 100 plants of 1000 megawatt capacity in operation. Under present U.S. regulations, the allowable release of radioactive materials into coolant water will be 2,200 curies per year. The direct discharge, however, accounts for less than one hundred millionth of the total radioactive wastes, which are either stored in tanks as corrosive liquids that will boil for more than a hundred years, or incorporated into glassy materials and stored in abandoned salt mines. By 1980, it is estimated that ten trillion curies of accumulated wastes will be stored, of which one trillion will be strontium-90.[2] Although precautions are taken to prevent these lethal and long-lived radioactive poisons from entering the environment, a number of storage tanks have already developed leaks, and the heat from wastes stored in salt mines could deform the walls of the mines and raise the ground temperature at the surface by several degrees. Inevitably some of these radioisotopes will find their way into the world's waters and into the hydrobiosphere.

What I have outlined so far takes the most optimistic view of future radioactive pollution, for it assumes that present U.S. standards will be adhered to, and that there will be no major accidents. But some other nations already have less rigorous controls of nuclear wastes, and it cannot be expected that developing nations, which are viewed as possible customers for nuclear power plants exported by the advanced nations, will adhere to waste disposal techniques which are expensive and require a high level of technology.

Nuclear shipping presents an even more direct threat to the aquatic environment. Not only does it discharge fission products into the water, especially during warmup, but a nuclear vessel carries all its radioactive power source and radioactive wastes with it, and in case of accident, the entire amount eventually may go into the ocean. One Soviet and two U.S. nuclear submarines have already been lost, with millions of curies of fission products on board. Although the reactors of these vessels are strongly contained so as to prevent accidental release, it seems likely that over many years these corrosive radioactive wastes, with half-lives of thirty, a hundred, or a thousand years, will escape into the sea. Collisions in closed harbors, where most such accidents occur, could endanger large population centers and result in closure of a harbor to commercial activities for months or years.

From these sources—continued fallout, effluents and wastes from nuclear power and nuclear shipping—we see the prospect of steadily rising radioactive pollution of the ocean for several decades. During the next ten years, there will be a ten-fold increase in the production of radioactive wastes and, as yet, there are no international agreements limiting the disposal of these wastes into the oceans.

353

So violent are the disagreements among scientists regarding the biological hazards of radioactivity, that the general public has become quite confused. Citizens' groups in the U.S. have succeeded in blocking the construction of several nuclear power plants and are fighting legal battles against several others. The power companies have counter-attacked by a massive advertising campaign to persuade the public that nuclear power is safer and cleaner than conventional power.

What are the facts?

As usual, they are complex enough to provide arguments for both sides.

Many aquatic organisms concentrate radioactive elements. Oysters, for example, have been observed to concentrate zinc-65, a common fission product, by a factor of 250,000 over its level in the surrounding water, and cobalt-60 by a factor of a million. Certain edible seaweeds concentrate iodine-131. Other typical radionuclides which may be avidly incorporated by aquatic organisms are tritium, chromium-51, iron-59, manganese-54, as well as the familiar cesium-137 and strontium-90. Some investigators point out that though the concentration factors may be high, the absolute amounts of the radionuclides in sea animals and plants are still small, and that one would have to eat very large amounts of any species in order to exceed the "allowable limit" for a particular isotope.

Other scientists insist that many of the present limits are set too high, that they are based on ignorance of the detailed or long-term effects of the radionuclides. For example, more recent studies of zinc-65 in rabbits have revealed that though the animals appeared well after small daily doses for several months, more sensitive studies showed deleterious effects on a number of proteins, on blood clotting and on immunity from disease.[3]

In humans, the allowable limits of radiation have been reduced progressively, as effects have been observed at lower and lower levels. For example, the permitted total body dose to radiation workers was set at 2500 rem/yr in 1902 (this is about three times the mean lethal dose, if given all at once); it was reduced to 100 in 1925, to 25 in 1936, to 5 in 1955; and Gofman and Tamplin believe it should be reduced now to 0.5, which is just the value that the previous downhill slope would predict for 1970![4]

Gofman and Tamplin, vocal critics of the present radiation standards, have compiled voluminous evidence that there are increased rates of cancer and leukemia at currently permitted radiation levels.[5] Other experts have denied this and supported the concept of a "threshold" radiation dose below which no ill effects occur. Against the "threshold" concept and supporting the Gofman and Tamplin view, is a recent study by Stewart and Kneale, in England, showing that children whose mothers had x-rays taken while pregnant are more likely than other children to develop cancer, and that the probability increases with the number of x-ray pictures taken.[6] The radiation dose in these cases is extremely small and, until the time of this study, was considered completely safe for humans at any age. It appears now that unborn babies and infants may be a hundred times more sensitive than adults to the carcinogenic effects of radiation.

As with DDT, the direct effects on man may prove to be less important than the indirect ecological impact due to eradication of vulnerable species. Among the disastrous effects of DDT, discovered many years after it was pronounced a safe insecticide, are the fragility it induces in some birds'

354

eggs, such as the pelican's, which in certain areas are now threatened with extinction. The Soviet biologist Polikarpov has observed that extremely low concentrations of strontium-90 cause abnormalities, especially in the spinal cords, of developing fish eggs. Almost all fish eggs float in the upper five centimeters of sea water, where they are vulnerable to fallout and industrial discharge.[1] Polikarpov predicts that one result of radioactive pollution will be to shift the ecological balance from more radiosensitive species like fish to less sensitive species like plants. Whether or not some commercial species of fish will be wiped out by radiation, as this line of research suggests, the possibility itself illustrates, in analogy with DDT, that trace amounts of pollutants can cause unexpected catastrophes by breaking a weak link of the ecological chain.

Radiation does literally break a link in the helical chain that transmits genetic information, causing abnormalities and death in descendants. These effects, while they occur at the lowest levels of radiation, may not become apparent for several generations. Therefore some of the most serious delayed consequences of radioactive pollution may not appear for ten to fifty years in affected species, which includes all species on earth. It can be argued that some mutations are useful, that improved strains of food plants have been produced by deliberate irradiation of seeds, that the process of evolution may ultimately depend on radiation-induced mutations.[7] But the ratio of harmful to useful mutations is at least a million to one, so radioactive pollution constitutes genetic experimentation on a global scale, with unpredictable consequences to all life on earth.

I am very much disturbed by the massive advertising campaign which has been launched by power companies in the United States, aimed at convincing the public that nuclear power is clean, virtually free of radiation, good for the environment, and necessary to meet the power demands which their advertising has helped to create. The parallel with the cigarette companies, which for years made unsupported health claims for their products, and have persisted in their promotional efforts despite the proved carcinogenic and other disease-inducing results of smoking, are only too striking. It seems to me grossly irresponsible to substitute the techniques of mass persuasion for the scientific investigation and careful search for answers which only many years of experience and observation will assure. In the meantime, restraint and careful planning in nuclear exploitation of the oceans, and worldwide agreements limiting radioactive pollution, are urgently needed.

1. Polikarpov, GG, *Radioecology of Aquatic Organisms,* Reinhold, 1966.
2. Mawson, CA, *Management of Radioactive Wastes,* Van Nostrand, 1965.
3. Letavet, AA and Kurlandskaya, EB, Eds., *The Toxicology of Radioactive Substances, vol. 5, Zinc-65,* Pergamon Press, 1970.
4. Schubert, J and Lapp, RE, *Global Radiation Limits,* Bull. Atomic Scientists 14–23, January 1958.
5. Gofman, JW and Tamplin, AR, *Radiation, Cancer and Environmental Health,* Hospital Practice, p. 71, October 1970.
6. Stewart, Alice and Kneale, GW, *Radiation dose effects in relation to obstetric x-rays and childhood cancers,* The Lancet 1:1185, June 6, 1970.
7. Schultz, V et al., Eds., *Radioecology,* Reinhold, 1961.

nuclear weapons: past and present

ralph e. lapp

The growth of the weapons stockpiles has been so ad astra that if one plots a semi-logarithmic curve of explosive yield (in megatons) versus calendar time, it is all too evident that physicists have split the century—and all time—in half; history is bisected into pre-atomic and atomic eras.

Man's cortical elasticity is such that he can look back at Hiroshima and refer to the atomic bomb of 1945 as a "low-yield" weapon. Yet in those days a new word, "kiloton," the explosive equivalent of a stack of 1000 tons of TNT, was minted in order to describe the destructiveness of the new weapon.

President Truman proclaimed that the first atomic bomb dropped on Japan had "the power of more than 20,000 tons of TNT," but later measurements fixed its yield at about 14 kilotons. The Hiroshima bomb was a massive device utilizing a gun tube for linear assembly of two masses of enriched uranium. In contrast, the Nagasaki bomb was a more sophisticated implosion assembly that focused on a nuclear core or "nuke" of a brand-new element, plutonium. The nuke was about the size of a baseball. Simultaneous detonation of a spherically symmetric aggregate of several tons of high explosives (shaped like prismatic lenses) served to crush the hollow plutonium core and materially raise its density so that it became super-critical. The resulting chain reaction produced a yield of 21 kilotons.

The 5-ton implosion weapon became the progenitor of a very diverse family of increasingly efficient and powerful bombs. This technology advanced at a modest rate in the early postwar years. Two weapons effects tests at Bikini Atoll in 1946 merely exercised a 1945 design; but at Eniwetok in 1948, during Operation Sandstone, three tests were made of improved and more powerful weapons with a total fission yield of about 100 kilotons.

The Yoke test in this series more than tripled the power of the Hiroshima explosion.

On August 29, 1949, the Soviets detonated their first atomic weapon, thus shattering the monopoly of the United States and setting into motion a stepped-up weapons development. The Sandstone tests proved to be milestones in nuclear history, pointing to the feasibility of low-weight weapons and to much more powerful and efficient designs which would, of course, require larger quantities of fissionable material. The Atomic Energy Commission's original two-site production plants (primarily the gaseous-diffusion plants at Oak Ridge, Tennessee, and the three nuclear reactors at Hanford, Washington) underwent a series of expansions. Five plutonium-production reactors were added at Hanford, and an equal number of heavy-water reactors were sited at the Savannah River location near Aiken, South Carolina. The Oak Ridge diffusion plants were expanded to a 1700-megawatt power level, and a 2550-megawatt diffusion complex was built near Paducah, Kentucky. Finally, a 1750-megawatt installation was constructed near Portsmouth, Ohio.

Atomic production can be assayed in terms of the electrical input into the diffusion plants, the power ratings of the production reactors, and the consumption of uranium, and it is also reflected in the financial reports of the AEC. Study of the pertinent data allows an estimate of the size of the atomic stockpile as measured in tons of fissionable material.

For example, the AEC's diffusion plants reached a 1000-megawatt power level in 1953, doubled within a year, and soared to over 6000 megawatts in 1955. A 6000-megawatt level was maintained for six years, but as atomic cutbacks were inaugurated in the early 1960s it dropped to a 2000-megawatt level in 1970.

Procurement of natural uranium escalated from an annual purchase of 2000 tons of U_3O_8 (tri-uranium octoxide) in 1948 ($35 million) to over 10,000 tons in 1956. Purchases reached a peak of 33,330 tons in 1959–60 ($700 million), dropping to 28,600 tons in 1963 and, thereafter, sliding down to 6000 tons in 1969. All in all, the United States purchased over 300,000 tons of U_3O_8 for more than $6 billion in the first quarter century of atomic production.

Production costs for nuclear material amount to $11 billion for the past two decades. The AEC's financial reports show an almost equal amount devoted to weapon development and fabrication. Production plants, processing, and test facilities involve a total capital expenditure of $5.5 billion. Making some allowance of allocation for nonweapon diversion of fissionable material, it appears that the AEC has spent about $30 billion on nuclear weapons since it began operation in 1947.

Reckoned in terms of fissionable material, the atomic stockpile amounts to approximately a thousand tons. A pound of fissionable material can yield about 4 kilotons in an efficient assembly. Thus the total explosiveness of this fissionable stockpile would be 8 million kilotons or 8 billion tons of TNT equivalent. This would figure out to be less than $4 for a ton of TNT. However, a technical development both revolutionized the economics of explosives and allowed for the fabrication of weapons of a power far beyond that considered feasible for chain-reacting nuclear assemblies.

This was the perfection of the thermonuclear weapon, known popularly as the hydrogen bomb or as the superbomb.

The decision to make a hydrogen bomb, a direct result of Soviet success in developing the atomic bomb, was made by President Truman and announced on January 31, 1950. The hydrogen bomb, as then contemplated, would have required large amounts of tritium and, consequently, great diversion of reactor production. However, this "super" was never made; instead, a light-element weapon using hydrogen and lithium isotopes was developed. Large quantities of natural lithium were isotopically refined to produce pure lithium-6. This was then incorporated in a deuteride molecule (Li^6D), an opalescent white compound. Lithium-6 serves as a source of tritium as a result of a neutron reaction. The thermonuclear reaction of deuterium (D in LiD) and tritium (T) results in the fusion of a helium nucleus and the release of a high-energy (14 Mev) neutron. The latter is sufficiently energetic to produce fast fission in U-238.

During the spring of 1951, a series of Greenhouse tests at the Eniwetok Proving Grounds provided basic data needed for a thermonuclear explosion. The first such explosion (Mike) took place on November 1, 1952, with the release of many millions of tons of TNT-equivalent energy. However this was strictly an experimental test and could not be considered a transportable bomb. It marked a new era in weaponry, symbolized by the word "megaton"—the equivalent of one million tons of TNT.

Soviet success with a thermonuclear explosion was achieved on August 21, 1953. Then, on March 1 of the following year, the United States experts detonated a deliverable bomb at Bikini Atoll. The test was conducted in strict secrecy, but a combination of events served to advertise the nature of the new weapon. A shift in the winds aloft sent the bomb cloud over inhabited islands of the Marshalls, penumbrating Rongelap and swirling radioactive coral-ash over thousands of square miles of the Pacific. The fallout of bomb debris came down on the decks of a tuna trawler, the *Lucky Dragon,* and irradiated twenty-three Japanese fishermen.

The nature of the injury to the crewmen became front-page news when they put into their home port and sought medical aid. In February of 1955, the AEC made public details of the fallout and the world learned that a new dimension had been added to the superbomb's lethality. This came hard upon the heels of the fact that the primary blast of the new weapon, fifteen megatons in yield, was one thousand times that of the Hiroshima bomb. If we take the Hiroshima fifty-percent kill-radius (i.e., distance from Ground Zero to a point where human fatality rate equals fifty percent) as 0.8 miles, then the Bikini Bravo bomb of March 1, 1954, would have an 8-mile kill-radius. This would correspond to an area of roughly 200 square miles. Thus the new superbomb possessed primary capability of obliterating life in most modern cities.

The Bikini bomb spread its radioactive lethality over an area of 7000 square miles. As was first disclosed in the pages of the *Bulletin of the Atomic Scientists,* this fallout lethality exhibits a time-persistence because of the great variety of radioactive species associated with the fission products of uranium. For example, an area exhibiting an intensity of fallout corresponding to five lethal doses in the second hour after the explosion would deliver twice this dose in the remainder of the first day. A double lethal dose would characterize the second day, another lethal dose the following day, and still another during the fourth to fifth day. The gross radioactive fallout hazard was shown to be gamma radiation capable of penetrating considerable thicknesses of building materials.

Global measurements determined that some of the Bikini radioactive debris was injected into the stratosphere and carried around the world, falling out in a slight drizzle of invisible particles. Long-lived, high-yield, radioactive species like 27-year cesium-137 and strontium-90 entered humans through food-chains. For example, the Laplanders were found to exhibit the highest body burden of any bomb product because the dietary habits of reindeer resulted in uptake of Cs-137, which, in turn, was passed on to the Lapps, who subsist on reindeer.

The internal hazard of local fallout was recently highlighted by the AEC's disclosure that Marshallese youths, exposed to fallout at the Bikini Bravo shot, subsequently developed thyroid abnormalities due to the uptake of radioiodine. In a nuclear-war situation the longer half-lived emitters such as strontium-90 would be a serious food contaminant in the post-attack period.

Summing up the Bravo experience, the new superweapon had revolutionary consequences as an instrument of war. Primary effects multiplied linear damage distances tenfold. Secondary effects, like fallout, added 1 square mile of lethality for every 2 kilotons of weapon yield, giving an awesome character to the megaton as a unit of firepower. The time-persistence and penetrating quality of the fallout, as well as the insidious nature of the long-term poison effect, scraped the bottom of the nuclear Pandora's box unlocked at Bikini.

Yet this is by no means the whole story of Bravo. The cost of the kiloton was slashed when the megaton came into being. To prove the point, we need only cite the AEC's nuclear explosive price schedule for Plowshare charges. The latter is a straight line on a semi-logarithmic chart starting at $350,000 for a 10-kiloton explosive and running to $600,000 for a 2-megaton device. The price for the first megaton added to a 1-megaton explosive is only $30,000, so that the AEC's price is $30 per kiloton or 3 cents per ton of TNT. This corresponds to more than a hundredfold price reduction when we compare fusion with fission explosives. Clearly, the main cost of a Plowshare device centers on the expensive fissionable trigger needed to initiate a thermonuclear reaction.

The Plowshare economics do not fully reveal the cheapness of nuclear weapons because peacetime devices are deliberately tailored to maximize fusion yield. In a weapon of the Bikini Bravo type the principal yield derives from a third stage of natural or even depleted (i.e., Oak Ridge diffusion plant discards) uranium. Fast-neutron capture in a layer of this uranium results in fission release on a massive scale, probably twice as great as fusion energy release. If a pound of natural uranium, fabricated at $10, releases 2 kilotons, then the unit price of a ton of TNT drops to half a penny. High-yield fission releases ("dirty" bombs) involve the ultimate in cheapness for military explosives.

Subsequent megaton experiments managed to shrink the physical size of the weapon so that a 1-megaton yield is achieved in military hardware only 24 inches in diameter. The development of compact high-yield weapons made possible such sophisticated strategic warheads as the 0.2-megaton MIRV (multiple independently targeted re-entry vehicle) for the Minuteman-III ICBM. It makes possible a triplet MRV (cluster type) where each warhead has a 0.5-megaton yield.

The mightiest thermonuclear explosion took place in late October 1962, a year in which the Soviet Union detonated more than forty weapons—and the United States twice that number. The Soviet test series featured very high-yield weapons, the most powerful being a 58-megaton air burst at an altitude of 12,000 feet. Analysis of the air-borne debris showed that the test was relatively clean, and that a jacket of lead had been substituted for uranium. Neutron absorption in the lead transformed the normal pattern of isotopic abundances in the element and minimized radioactive products. However, an energy loss was involved since fast fission did not take place; had uranium been substituted for the lead, a weapon yield in excess of 100 megatons would have been expected.

The 100-megaton weapon would qualify for air-dropping by a heavy strategic bomber, but would exceed the throw capacity of the Soviet SS-9, which is known to be capable of mounting a 20- to 25-megaton warhead. The latter is estimated by the U.S. Defense Department to be MIRVable as a triplet in which each warhead is rated as 3 to 5 megatons when configured for triangular dispersion around a tight cluster of aim points.

At the other end of the weapons spectrum are the low-yield tactical and defensive nuclear explosives, the development of which was begun on the Nevada test range in 1951. There was no doubt that the Korean war accentuated the development of these weapons. The prime object in the testing was to shrink the waistline of the hefty atomic bombs, or, in the parlance of the weapons expert, to increase the yield-to-weight ratio. Since large amounts of high explosives and tampers were required for early weapon designs, the development focused on new assembly techniques and on novel weapon geometries. Success was attained in perfecting a design for an atomic shell that could be fired from a cannon. The latter, a mammoth 85-ton gun of limited mobility, was produced in a 60-unit deployment and then declared obsolete. Ultimately, a much smaller nuclear explosive was developed to fit into the tube of a bazooka, but this Davy Crockett weapon was also abandoned after deployment.

The family of small nuclear weapons expanded to include demolition charges transportable by one or two men, land mines, and low-yield kiloton or fractional kiloton class warheads for short and intermediate range ballistic missiles. In addition, nuclear warheads were perfected for naval applications including use in torpedoes, sea mines, guns, and missiles. As the package weight of compact nuclear (fission) explosives decreased to 100 pounds, the yield became controllable in the range of 10 kilotons to 1 ton of TNT. However, the nuclear requirement for a chain-reacting assembly imposed cost limits on small weapon applications.

Development of low-yield explosives and compact, rugged warheads permitted military men to diversify the application to tactical and defensive weapons. It even aided in perfecting the somewhat higher-yield MIRV warheads for Poseidon, the submarine-launched ballistic missile. In the defensive field, the United States Army series of Nike-class missiles mounted nuclear warheads, as did the Air Force Bomarc interceptors.

The Safeguard anti-ballistic missile system currently being deployed in the continental United States consists of a one-two punch carried by a long-range Spartan ex-atmospheric missile and a short-range, atmospheric interceptor, the Sprint. The latter carries a kiloton fission warhead, whereas the Spartan will mount an uprated 4-megaton thermonuclear warhead. Spartan's kill-power consists of a burst of soft X-rays emitted by the nuclear burst *in vacuo*, i.e., in space at altitudes of 100 or more miles above sea level. Eight-tenths of the Spartan warhead's energy release is emitted in a tenth microsecond as a burst of X-radiation. Incidence of this energy on ablative surface of a re-entry vehicle can destroy the integrity of the heat shield or produce a hydrodynamic wave capable of producing disruptive effects in the re-entry vehicle's interior. The critical radius for such effects depends on how the re-entry vehicle is hardened and how the weapon is designed.

As first-generation nuclear weapons became obsolete, their nukes were reprocessed and incorporated in new assemblies. In the twenty-fifth year of nuclear manufacture, the United States weapon business is booming, as is manifest from the fact that the AEC's production, development, and fabrication budget for weapons is roughly $1.3 billion. A plant expansion is currently under way to fabricate warheads for MIRVs, ABMs, and the spectrum of defensive, tactical, and strategic weapons.

Some indication of the size of the United States weapon stockpile is given by the fact that the United States government states some 7000 nuclear weapons are deployed in Europe. In the February 20, 1970, posture statement of Defense Secretary Laird, the United States strategic forces were specified as follows:

As of September 1, 1969:	
ICBM Launchers	*1054*
SLBM Launchers	*656*
Intercont. Bombers	*646*
Total Force	
Loadings:	*4200 weapons*

This accounting would appear to understate the actual numbers of nuclear weapons the United States can commit to strategic operations. For example, the SLBM Polaris A-3 wants a minimum of three warheads (MRVs) and Minuteman-II has throw capacity to carry such a triplet MRV of higher yield. The B-52 G/H and FB-111 can carry four or more 3-megaton air-to-surface weapons, and megaton-class weapons can also be delivered by fighter-bombers and carrier-based planes. If one projects forward the MIRV capability of Minuteman-III and Poseidon, it is clear that the missile force-loadings will exceed 7000 warheads in the mid-seventies.

The foregoing material would seem to substantiate the assertion of Senator John O. Pastore that: "Today, we count our nuclear weapons in tens of thousands." It is, of course, a far cry from the meager 1950 stockpile, estimated at a few hundred atomic bombs, but it reflects the precipitous expansion of United States production and the spectacular growth of the family of nuclear weapons.

361

Had the nuclear technology of the 1940s restricted weapons experts to fission energy derivable from scarce fissionable materials, the expense of the latter would have confined the damage capability of a country like Red China. Nuclear experts in that country bypassed the forbidding and expensive fission route to weapon power by proceeding in a straight-line course to develop thermonuclear energy sources. It was simply an exercise in nuclear-weapon material economics. After testing its first atomic bomb on October 16, 1964, Mainland China proceeded to detonate a thermonuclear explosive on June 17, 1967—its sixth test.

Except for relatively modest injections of fission debris into the atmosphere by French and Chinese tests, the limited nuclear test-ban treaty of 1963 served to limit the radioactive contamination of the air. By the time the treaty went into effect, more than 500 bomb tests had been made with a total yield of half a billion tons of TNT. Since 1963, the United States and the Soviet Union have restricted their test programs to underground explosions, usually fewer than fifty tests in all per year.

Twenty-five years of weapons development cast the original 1945 vintage atomic bombs in a primitive mode. The explosive power of the Japanese bombs can be packaged in a hand-carried case. Given the package weight of the Japanese bombs, the designers today can release 30 megatons of explosive energy—more than two thousand times that of the Hiroshima weapon. The growth of the weapons stockpiles has been so *ad astra* that if one plots a semi-logarithmic curve of explosive yield (in megatons) versus calendar time, it is all too evident that physicists have split the century—and all time—in half; history is bisected into pre-atomic and atomic eras.

nuclear tyranny and the divine right of kings

gale edward christianson

How much political progress have we made since the days of the divine right of kings? The Enlightenment philosophers considered divine right to be repugnant, but they could not foresee the potential for universal destruction that would characterize the twentieth century and were thus unaware of the security in which they lived.

Before his tragic and untimely death, Senator Robert F. Kennedy put into a vivid written account the actions and events now commonly referred to as the Cuban missile crisis. He related how, beginning on October 16, 1962, and lasting for a period of 13 days, the world, already so close to the thermonuclear brink, nearly toppled into the abyss of oblivion. Many Americans and millions of Russians were unaware, at the time, of how nearly the epitaphs of their respective nations came to be written.

For some, the resolution of the Cuban missile crisis represented the quintessence of American diplomatic achievement in the 1960s. Arthur M. Schlesinger, Jr., in *A Thousand Days*, likened the United States to a great athlete who magnanimously kept itself from running up the score on an outmanned, overmatched Soviet opponent: "It was this combination of toughness and restraint, of will, nerve and wisdom, so brilliantly controlled, so matchlessly celebrated, that dazzled the world. Before the missile crisis people might have feared that we would use our power extravagantly or not use it at all. But the thirteen days gave the world—even the Soviet Union—a sense of American determination and responsibility in the use of power which, if sustained, might indeed become a turning point in the history of the relations between east and west."

It is true that the restraint, counseled by some of President Kennedy's close advisors and exercised by the President himself, contributed greatly

Reprinted by permission of *Science and Public Affairs, the Bulletin of the Atomic Scientists,* January 1971, pp. 44–46. Copyright © 1971 by the Educational Foundation for Nuclear Science. The author is a member of the department of history at Carnegie-Mellon University at Pittsburgh.

to the peaceful settlement of the issue. At the same time, however, the fact must not be overlooked that there were those, including former Secretary of State Dean Acheson and the Joint Chiefs of Staff, who advocated the use of military force to bring about a successful resolution of the problem. From the standpoint that the world passed through this supra-nationalistic confrontation without resorting to the use of armed force, it can be looked back upon as a triumph of reason and restraint. But in a larger sense—in the sense that the Cuban missile crisis even occurred—it must be viewed, along with Hiroshima, as part of one of the great moral tragedies of our time.

natural rights

The politics of nuclear tyranny truly represents the antithesis of the natural rights philosophy central to the Judeo-Christian ethic embodied in the writing of political philosophers from Cicero to Thomas Jefferson. Furthermore, it is alien to the spirit, if not the letter, of both the United States Constitution and the Declaration of Independence. In drafting these two extraordinary documents, the Founding Fathers relied heavily upon the political writings of John Locke. This was particularly true of Jefferson who was primarily responsible for drafting the Declaration of Independence.

John Locke wrote in his *Second Treatise of Civil Government* that men enter into a social contract—government—in order to protect those things which they have freely enjoyed in the state of nature: life, liberty and property. Even Thomas Hobbes, whose philosophy of authoritarian government was odious to Locke and many other democratic thinkers, contended that protection is the basic purpose for the formation of government. There is, then, no essential disagreement between Locke and Hobbes on the fundamental point that the primary function of government is to protect life. Certainly, no rational man today—regardless of his ideological convictions and viewpoints regarding natural law—would deny that without life no other considerations of a secular nature are important.

Most of the political philosophers of the eighteenth century left no doubt that they considered the theory of divine right to be a morally repugnant political philosophy. Yet they reasoned in relative, as opposed to absolute, political terms. A king might, and often did, make life miserable for his subjects: he might arbitrarily destroy some of them at will. But, theological considerations aside, these men never dreamed of a time when man's continued existence on this planet would be a question of major doubt. Even the most cruel monarch was not accorded the capacity or desire to eradicate civilization. (After all, even the feeble-minded could reason that a monarch with no subjects is not a king.) Our ancestors, unable to foresee the awesome potential for destruction to be amassed by governments in the twentieth century, were unconscious of the security in which the human species lived.

security gone

Few would advocate a return to the political systems of the seventeenth century, and I am certainly not one of them. Yet we who now inhabit the earth no longer possess the security known by our ancestors. They enjoyed the luxury of primitive military technology and its romantic associations. War was as much a game to them as an exercise in mutual inhumanity. There was even a security associated with war, in that most of those defeated in combat survived and could look forward to recuperation and even revenge. The dawn of the nuclear era and the development of the international arms race has made an anachronism of the security known in the seventeenth, eighteenth and nineteenth centuries. It has forced upon all citizens of the world, regardless of their ideology, degree of political sophistication or geographical location, a common fate should nationalistic confrontation erupt into thermonuclear war. Gone forever are the days of security in geographical isolation or the "luxury" of miscalculation by statesmen, be it honest or irresponsible. We are all bound by a common fate in the Age of Common History.

The bitter irony of the perilous contemporary situation is that it was brought about within a framework of national government, the very institutional concept that Englightenment thinkers favored as best guaranteeing protection for the individual and his rights. The destructive implements of modern warfare were created and perfected through the expenditures of national governments in the defense industry and by government subsidy of scientific research. Efforts were, and still are, directed toward the manufacture of super-weapons for the ostensible purposes of guaranteeing national concept that Enlightenment thinkers favored as best guaranteeing permanent peace have had a totally reverse effect. Never in the history of the national state has security been less assured, never before has the potential for genocidal annihilation been greater. The ultimate end for which men entered into society—the protection of life—can no longer be guaranteed by national governments. Nationalism, at least as it is presently constituted, becomes self-defeating because it nurtures the conditions which can destroy us all. Man's quest for security was cruelly perverted because he has been made less safe and secure.

conscience

Albert Einstein, the most venerable of all the atomic scientists, was one of the first to undergo the crisis of conscience attached to the past and prospective use of nuclear weapons as a means of settling major international disputes. After World War II, Einstein contended that it would be immoral for the United States to adopt permanently a code of warfare which was in direct violation of the ethical standards adhered to by this country before the beginning of the war. He was thinking, in particular, of the obliteration bombing of defenseless cities without regard for their unprotected civilian populations when he wrote in 1950: "We have emerged from a war in which we had to accept the degradingly low ethical standards of the enemy. But instead of feeling liberated from his standards, free to restore the sanctity of human life and safety of noncombatants, we are in effect making the low standards of the enemy in the last war our own. . . ." (For anyone desiring contemporary evidence testifying to the veracity of Einstein's statement he need only call to mind the fact that both the United States and the Soviet Union have hundreds of nuclear warheads pointed at each other's major cities.) J. Robert Oppenheimer shared, with Einstein, the same feeling of moral repugnancy, causing him to oppose the development of the hydrogen bomb. For his efforts, Oppenheimer was branded a "security risk" in 1954 by the Atomic Energy Commission at an inquiry whose procedural aspects bordered on those of an inquisition.

absolute power

One of the painful facts of life, and a terrifying one, is that a tiny handful of men including the President of the United States and the Chairman of the Soviet Union now possess greater destructive power than any divine right king ever dreamed of exercising. A few men, or a single individual, can literally decide, in an absolute sense, whether or not the human species will continue to survive. This absolute power is exercised on a day-to-day, hour-by-hour, minute-to-minute basis while life seemingly goes on as usual. But many of us no longer feel that life as "usual" can continue very much longer. Not, at least, until we are again guaranteed the primary right of preservation. We can be arbitrarily deprived of life at any moment of any day for reasons which could never be sufficient to justify the unleashing of nuclear power.

For this reason the Cuban missile crisis must be viewed as a tragedy rather than a triumph. Even though President Kennedy's decision not to employ physical force was a wise one, it was yet another episode in the epoch of nuclear tyranny under which we live. As long as statesmen are in a position to make such momentous decisions for all of humanity, there is no guarantee of life, and without life there is nothing. It is the height of immorality that any man or institution or nation should have the power to decide the fate of all mankind.

Ironically, the political and social philosophers of the Enlightenment attributed to science, working in conjunction with national democratic institutions, the capacity to rid mankind of the numerous vicissitudes which have stifled human development through the centuries. But science became the unwitting tool which made the political institutions of democratic nationalism obsolete. Yet when we are discussing nuclear weapons, does it really matter if the nation possessing them is Marxist or capitalist, democratic or authoritarian in ideology? As far as I know, no one has made a case that nuclear power is discriminatory. Until that power is removed from the hands of nationalists with strong vested interests to protect, no man in the world will ever again be safe.

We are living in an age where there is little trust. Where trust does not exist, there can be no compromise. Unless those on both sides of the Cold War, in positions of public responsibility, are willing to modify their rigid ethnocentric views, we shall inevitably become incinerated citizens of an incinerated planet. Governments have both the moral and political responsibility to reestablish conditions which are conducive to man's continued inhabitation of his world. The "security" in nuclear armaments as a deterrent to an enemy is no security. The manner in which the Soviets and Americans conduct their foreign affairs is the incarnation of the death wish.

The Arab-Israeli conflict threatens to engulf the world in a holocaust by enticing big-power participation, and the United States is involved in a major undeclared war uncomfortably close to the borders of Red China. As if East-West tensions were not sufficient to provoke hostilities, relations between Russia and Red China are at their modern nadir. While the latter set of circumstances may be comforting to some of those in positions of public responsibility in the West, it gives the humanitarian little cause to rejoice.

No matter where the weapons exist, there is always the danger that they will be used. Indeed, if the study of history demonstrates anything, it is that every weapon developed by man has, at one time or another, been introduced into combat. Poison gas and atomic weapons have proved no exception. Both sides employed gas in World War I, and World War II was terminated with the unfettering of nuclear fission.

Implicit in the very concept of nuclear war is a negation of the humanitarian principles which statesmen, theologians, philosophers and concerned laymen have struggled valiantly for centuries to bring into universal practice. Modern man must work as diligently to rid this planet of nuclear war, and its accompanying tyranny, as did his predecessors to destroy the theory and practice of divine right. All other social issues including civil rights, poverty and pollution pale in the light of the nuclear threat because they are based upon the promise of a better life—while the single promise of nuclear war is universal death.